Better Homes and Gardens®

OUR BEST
RECIPES

Apulian-Style Steak Sandwich
(recipe, page 69)

Better Homes and Gardens® Family Food Collection™
Des Moines, Iowa

Better Homes and Gardens® Family Food Collection™

MICHAEL L. MAINE
Director, Editorial Administration

JOY TAYLOR
Executive Editor

BRIDGET SANDQUIST
Art Director

Better Homes and Gardens®
Our Best Recipes

JULIA MARTINUSEN
Editor

CRAIG HANKEN BETHANIE ASWEGAN
Designers

Contributing Recipe Editors	SHARYL HEIKEN, ROSEMARY HUTCHINSON
Contributing Indexer	ROSEMARY HUTCHINSON
Contributing Copy Editors	GRETCHEN KAUFFMAN, DAVID WALSH

Senior Food Editors	Sandra Mosley, Lois White
Associate Art Director	Deena Zymm
Assistant Art Director	Stephanie Hunter
Administrative Assistants	Tamra McGee, Maria McLeese
Test Kitchen Director	Lynn Blanchard
Test Kitchen Product Supervisor	Jill Moberly

VICE PRESIDENT, PUBLISHING DIRECTOR
WILLIAM R. REED

Consumer Product Associate Marketing Director	Steve Swanson
Business Director	Christy Light
Business Manager	Jie Lin
Production Director	Douglas M. Johnston
Books Production Managers	Pam Kvitne, Marjorie J. Schenkelberg, Rick von Holdt

MEREDITH PUBLISHING GROUP

President	Stephen M. Lacy
President, Magazine Group	Jack Griffin
Executive Vice President, Publishing Group	Jerry Kaplan
Corporate Solutions	Michael Brownstein
Creative Services	Ellen de Lathouder
Manufacturing	Bruce Heston
Consumer Marketing	Karla Jeffries
Finance and Administration	Max Runciman

CHAIRMAN AND CHIEF EXECUTIVE OFFICER
WILLIAM T. KERR

IN MEMORIAM   E.T. MEREDITH III (1933-2003)

Better Homes and Gardens® Our Best Recipes is published by Family Food Collection™, Publishing Group of Meredith Corp., 1716 Locust St., Des Moines, IA 50309–3023.

ISBN: 0-696-21981-6

The Recipe Center at www.bhg.com/siprecipe contains more than 10,000 recipes and tips, all tested in the Better Homes and Gardens® Test Kitchen.

Pictured on the cover: Ginger Carrot Cake (recipe, page 254). Cover Photographer: Jason Wilde.
Cover Food Stylist: Charles Worthington. Cover Design/Art Director: Matt Strelecki.

1933

1941

1943

For generations, cooks have turned to *Better Homes and Gardens*® magazine for enticing family recipes they can trust. Ever since the magazine was introduced in 1922, we've been dedicated to creating recipes that are delicious, reliable, and practical for your family. Here are some of the milestones we've passed along the way.

1930s—The invention of the refrigerator and the wider availability of fruits and vegetables changed the way Americans cooked. We showed readers how to use these innovations to prepare family meals on a shoestring budget. After opening our Test Kitchen in 1928, *Better Homes and Gardens*® magazine pioneered a recipe style that offered precise ingredient amounts and more descriptive methods. This style was honed in *My Better Homes and Gardens*® *Cook Book*, first published in 1930.

1940s—Wartime Victory Gardens paved the way for pickling, preserving, and canning, and readers looked to us for the latest techniques. The now familiar red plaid design was used for the first time on the cover of the *Better Homes and Gardens*® *Cook Book*.

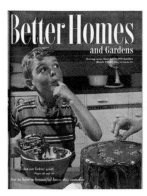

1952

1967

1975

1950s—Barbecuing, which *Better Homes and Gardens*® magazine had promoted as early as 1941, took the country by storm, and we led the way with foolproof grilling directions and sizzling recipe ideas. By 1959, we were using the *Better Homes and Gardens*® Test Kitchen seal to assure readers of our guaranteed recipe quality.

1960s—American cooks had less time to spend in the kitchen, so *Better Homes and Gardens*® publications helped them switch to simpler, speedier dishes. The growth of supermarket chains and refrigerated shipping made many ingredients, especially fruits and vegetables, available year-round. And, as more Americans traveled the world, discovering the wonders of foreign cuisines, we showed readers how to bring the exciting ethnic flavors and ingredients they found into their own kitchens.

1970s—Formal entertaining gave way to casual parties. Cooking became fun—something you could do with family and friends. Plus, with more women working, men and kids were helping more in the kitchen. We supplied our readers with ideas for new entertaining styles, recipes that families could make together, and the know-how for everything from rolling out fresh pasta to tempering chocolate.

1983

1991

2002

1980s—Nutrition was the focus during this decade. Our publications provided nutrition facts with recipes, and our editors focused on creating great-tasting calorie-trimmed, low-fat, and low-sodium recipes. Microwave ovens became a must-have cooking appliance. We showed readers how to make the best use of this revolutionary timesaver.

1990s—As the millennium drew to a close, simpler dishes made with fresh, back-to-basics ingredients were the goal. We helped readers cook with fresh herbs and artisanal cheeses. In 1991, *Better Homes and Gardens*® magazine celebrated 50 years of barbecuing. In 1997, we marked the 75th anniversary of the first issue.

2000s—Today, *Better Homes and Gardens*® magazine has gone global, creating fabulous yet practical dishes, using flavors, ingredients, and techniques from around the world. Each of our issues offers a variety of recipes, ranging from new twists on old favorites to ideas that reflect the latest cooking trends. Also, with family mealtime becoming more and more squeezed, we still provide our readers with practical ways they can gather the family for meals.

Our Best Recipes celebrates the best of our *Better Homes and Gardens* heritage. This book brings you more than 500 of the finest recipes we've ever published. To assemble this cherished collection, we spent months combing through our archives to rediscover the most delightful dishes created by our kitchen. We also rounded up our latest cooking advice and have included tips, menus, and a glossary to help you enjoy cooking more.

The recipes we selected for this book offer just the right mix of time-honored classics and new favorites, as well as homestyle ideas for every day and irresistible splurges for company. And while each recipe has been chosen to appeal to today's cooks, it still remains true to the cooking tradition of its era. You'll find ideas for everything from appetizers to desserts, many with new flavor variations or timesaving directions.

Besides offering exceptional dishes, *Our Best Recipes* gives you a glimpse into how cooking has changed over the decades. In every chapter, look for pages labeled "Yesterday" and "Today." These features showcase heirloom recipes and their modern-day counterparts. Recipe notes and tips offer another peek into our culinary history.

Our Best Recipes is one more reason to trust *Better Homes and Gardens*. We hope our recipes, kitchen expertise, and memories will inspire you to create many more unforgettable meals to experience with your family.

Favorite Family Meals

For generations, *Better Homes and Gardens®* magazine has been helping home cooks prepare delectable family-pleasing main dishes. These pages offer you a tasty sampling of the best of those entrées. They showcase everything from satisfying beef, pork, lamb, and poultry dishes to sensational fish, seafood, and meatless delights. Fix one of these family-pleasing meals tonight and you'll understand why they have stood the test of time—and taste.

Yankee Doodle Stew

Prep: 45 min. Cook: 1½ hr. + 20 min.

The definition of a terrific stew in 1941, when this recipe was first published, is pretty much the same as it is today—it's got to be hearty and satisfying. And this stew fits that description to a T.

- ¼ **cup all-purpose flour**
- 2 **lb. boneless beef chuck roast, cut into 1-inch pieces**
- 3 **Tbsp. cooking oil**
- 4 **cups water**
- ½ **cup chopped onion**
- 1 **clove garlic, minced**
- 2 **bay leaves**
- 2 **tsp. Worcestershire sauce**
- 1 **tsp. sugar**
- 1 **tsp. lemon juice**
- ½ **tsp. salt**
- ½ **tsp. pepper**
- ½ **tsp. paprika**
- **Dash ground allspice**
- 6 **tiny new potatoes, halved**
- 6 **medium carrots, quartered**
- 1 **lb. boiling onions, peeled and trimmed***
- 2 **Tbsp. cold water**
- 1 **Tbsp. all-purpose flour**
- ¼ **cup dry sherry (optional)**
- **Snipped fresh parsley (optional)**

1. Place the ¼ cup flour in a plastic bag. Add the meat pieces, a few at a time, shaking to coat. In a 4-quart Dutch oven, brown meat, *one-third* at a time, in hot oil. Drain well. Return all the meat to the Dutch oven. Add the 4 cups water, the chopped onion, garlic, and bay leaves to meat. Stir in the Worcestershire sauce, sugar, lemon juice, salt, pepper, paprika, and allspice. Bring to boiling; reduce heat. Cover and simmer for 1½ to 2 hours or until meat is nearly tender.

2. Add the potatoes, carrots, and the boiling onions to Dutch oven. Return to boiling; reduce heat. Cover and simmer for 20 to 30 minutes more or until vegetables are tender. Discard bay leaves. Transfer meat and vegetables to a serving dish. Cover and keep warm.

3. For gravy, in a small bowl, stir together the 2 tablespoons cold water and the 1 tablespoon flour. Stir into the mixture in Dutch oven. Cook and stir until thickened and bubbly. Cook and stir for 1 minute more. If desired, stir in sherry. Pour gravy over meat and vegetables. If desired, sprinkle with parsley. Makes 6 to 8 servings.

Slow-cooker directions: Coat meat with flour and brown as directed. In a 3½- to 4-quart slow cooker combine the meat, chopped onion, garlic, potatoes, carrots, and boiling onions. In a large bowl, stir together the 4 cups water, the bay leaves, Worcestershire sauce, sugar, lemon juice, salt, pepper, paprika, and allspice. Pour over the meat. Cover; cook on low-heat setting for 10 to 12 hours or on high-heat setting for 5 to 6 hours. Discard bay leaves. Transfer meat and vegetables to a serving dish; cover and keep warm. Transfer cooking liquid to a medium saucepan. Continue as directed in step 3.

*Test Kitchen Tip: To make peeling the boiling onions easier, place them in boiling water for 1 minute; drain. Trim off root ends and gently press the onions to slip the skins off.

Nutrition facts per serving: 320 cal., 8 g total fat (2 g sat. fat), 89 mg chol., 348 mg sodium, 26 g carbo., 4 g fiber, 35 g pro.

Yankee Doodle Stew

Beef Bourguignon

Prep: 30 min. Cook: 45 + 25 min.

Americans have always had a taste for the dishes they sampled on trips abroad. This stew from the early 1980s is our version of the fare found in French bistros—and it's still top-notch decades later.

1	lb. boneless beef chuck roast, cut into ¾-inch cubes
1	Tbsp. cooking oil
1½	cups chopped onion
2	cloves garlic, minced
1½	cups Pinot Noir or Burgundy wine
¾	cup beef broth
1	tsp. dried thyme, crushed
¾	tsp. dried marjoram, crushed
½	tsp. salt
¼	tsp. pepper
2	bay leaves
3	cups whole fresh mushrooms
4	medium carrots, cut into ¾-inch pieces
1	cup pearl onions, peeled, or frozen small whole onions
2	Tbsp. all-purpose flour
2	Tbsp. butter or margarine, softened
2	slices bacon, crisp-cooked, drained, and crumbled
	Hot cooked noodles or mashed potatoes

1. In a 4-quart Dutch oven, brown *half* of the meat in the hot oil; remove meat from Dutch oven. Add remaining meat, chopped onion, and garlic to Dutch oven. Cook and stir until meat is brown and onion is tender. Return all of the meat to Dutch oven.

2. Stir in wine, broth, thyme, marjoram, salt, pepper, and bay leaves. Bring to boiling; reduce heat. Cover and simmer for 45 minutes. Add mushrooms, carrots, and pearl onions. Return to boiling; reduce heat. Cover and cook for 25 to 30 minutes more or until meat and vegetables are tender. Discard bay leaves.

3. In a small bowl, stir together flour and butter until smooth; stir into meat mixture. Cook and stir until thickened and bubbly. Cook and stir for 1 minute more. Stir in bacon. Serve with noodles or mashed potatoes. Makes 6 servings.

Nutrition facts per serving: 395 cal., 14 g total fat (5 g sat. fat), 87 mg chol., 436 mg sodium, 35 g carbo., 4 g fiber, 23 g pro.

Bloody Mary Pot Roast

Bloody Mary Pot Roast

Prep: 20 min. Bake: 2 hr.

When we publish a new recipe for pot roast, it has to be something special. We like this recipe because the Bloody Mary mix spikes the flavor.

1	3-lb. boneless beef bottom round roast
3	cloves garlic, thinly sliced
2	Tbsp. cooking oil
¾	cup Bloody Mary mix or hot-style tomato juice
6	Tbsp. vodka or water
1	Tbsp. prepared horseradish
½	tsp. Worcestershire sauce
1	clove garlic, minced
4	tsp. cornstarch

1. Preheat oven to 325°F. Trim fat from roast. Cut several slits in roast, making each slit about ½ inch long and 1 inch deep. Insert a small slice of garlic into each slit.

2. In a 4-quart Dutch oven, brown roast on all sides in hot oil. Remove from heat. Drain off fat. In a small bowl, combine Bloody Mary mix or tomato juice, *4 tablespoons* of the vodka, the horseradish, Worcestershire, and minced garlic; carefully pour over roast. Bake, covered, for 2 to 2½ hours or until very tender. Transfer to a platter, reserving juices in Dutch oven; keep meat warm.

3. For gravy, measure cooking juices; skim off fat. If necessary, add enough water to juices to total 1½ cups liquid. Return juices to Dutch oven. Stir together remaining 2 tablespoons vodka and the cornstarch; stir into cooking juices. Cook and stir over medium heat until bubbly; cook and stir for 1 minute more. Slice meat thinly across the grain; serve with gravy. Makes 10 to 12 servings.

Nutrition facts per serving: 247 cal., 11 g total fat (3 g sat. fat), 87 mg chol., 145 mg sodium, 2 g carbo., 0 g fiber, 29 g pro.

Steak au Poivre

Start to finish: 30 min.

Our version of this classic recipe includes a brandy cream sauce seasoned with Dijon-style mustard.

1	Tbsp. cracked black pepper
4	beef tenderloin steaks or 2 beef top loin steaks, cut 1 inch thick (about 1 lb. total)
2	Tbsp. butter or margarine
¼	cup brandy or beef broth
¼	cup beef broth
½	cup whipping cream
2	tsp. Dijon-style mustard

1. Sprinkle pepper evenly over both sides of each steak; press in with your fingers. If using top loin steaks, cut each steak in half crosswise. In a large skillet, cook steaks in hot butter over medium heat until desired doneness, turning once. (For tenderloin steaks, allow 10 to 13 minutes for medium-rare [145°F] to medium doneness [160°F]. For top loin steaks, allow 12 to 15 minutes for medium-rare [145°F] to medium doneness [160°F].) Transfer steaks to a serving platter, reserving the drippings in the skillet. Keep warm. Remove skillet from burner; let stand for 1 minute.

2. For sauce, in a small bowl, combine brandy and beef broth (or use all beef broth); carefully stir into drippings in skillet, scraping up crusty browned bits. Stir in whipping cream and mustard. Bring to boiling. Boil gently, uncovered, over medium heat for 5 to 6 minutes or until mixture is reduced to ½ cup, stirring occasionally. Spoon sauce over steaks. Makes 4 servings.

Nutrition facts per serving: 370 cal., 25 g total fat (13 g sat. fat), 114 mg chol., 192 mg sodium, 2 g carbo., 0 g fiber, 25 g pro.

> **The *Better Homes and Gardens*® Test Kitchen opened in 1928. During the years of planning, the kitchen was rearranged and revised on paper dozens of times before the final version was approved—much like the recipes tested in it.**

Swiss Steak

Prep: 25 min. Cook: 1¼ hr.

When Swiss Steak first ran in *Better Homes and Gardens*® in 1937, round steak was seasoned only with salt and pepper and simmered with onion and mustard. In more recent versions of this dish, the beef is bathed in a flavorful sauce of tomatoes, onion, celery, and carrot.

1	lb. boneless beef round steak, cut ¾ inch thick
2	Tbsp. all-purpose flour
¼	tsp. salt
¼	tsp. pepper
1	Tbsp. cooking oil
1	14½-oz. can diced tomatoes with basil, oregano, and garlic
1	small onion, sliced and separated into rings
½	cup sliced celery
½	cup sliced carrot
	Hot cooked noodles or mashed potatoes

1. Trim fat from meat. Cut into 4 serving-size pieces. In a small bowl, combine the flour, salt, and pepper. With the notched side of a meat mallet, pound flour mixture into meat.

2. In a large skillet, brown meat on both sides in hot oil. Drain off fat. Add undrained tomatoes, the onion rings, celery, and carrot to skillet. Bring to boiling; reduce heat. Cover and simmer about 1¼ hours or until meat is tender. Skim off fat. Serve with noodles or mashed potatoes. Makes 4 servings.

Oven directions: Preheat oven to 350°F. Prepare and brown meat in skillet as directed. Transfer meat to a 2-quart square baking dish. In the same skillet, combine undrained tomatoes, onion rings, celery, and carrot. Bring to boiling, scraping up any browned bits. Pour over meat. Cover and bake about 1 hour or until tender. Serve as directed.

Nutrition facts per serving: 340 cal., 9 g total fat (2 g sat. fat), 82 mg chol., 459 mg sodium, 35 g carbo., 3 g fiber, 28 g pro.

Flank Steak Bordelaise

Flank Steak Bordelaise

Prep: 30 min. Marinate: 6 to 24 hr. Broil: 15 min.

In 1981, we used little-known flank steak in this intriguing new way. Since then, fajitas have popularized flank steak so much, you may have to place an order with your butcher to get one.

1	lb. beef flank steak
1/3	cup red wine vinegar
1/4	cup chopped onion
2	Tbsp. cooking oil
1	Tbsp. Worcestershire sauce
2	cloves garlic, minced
1/4	tsp. dry mustard
1	recipe Easy Bordelaise Sauce (right)
2½	cups coarsely shredded zucchini*
1	cup coarsely shredded carrot*
1	clove garlic, minced
1/3	cup walnuts, toasted and coarsely chopped (tip, page 102)
1	Tbsp. butter or margarine
	Salt
	Pepper
	Fresh herb sprigs (optional)

1. Score both sides of steak in a diamond pattern by making shallow diagonal cuts at 1-inch intervals. Place meat in a large resealable plastic bag set in a shallow dish. In a small bowl, combine the 1/3 cup wine vinegar, the onion, oil, Worcestershire sauce, the 2 cloves garlic, and the dry mustard; pour over meat. Seal the bag; turn to coat meat. Marinate in the refrigerator for at least 6 hours or up to 24 hours, turning the bag occasionally.

2. Drain steak; discard marinade. Pat dry. Prepare Easy Bordelaise Sauce. Place steak on unheated rack of a broiler pan. Broil 3 to 4 inches from heat 15 to 18 minutes or until medium doneness (160°F), turning once. Slice thinly across grain.

3. Meanwhile, combine zucchini, carrot, and the 1 clove garlic; place in steamer basket over boiling water. Steam about 4 minutes or just until tender. Transfer to bowl. Stir in the 1 tablespoon butter. Add the walnuts. Season to taste with salt and pepper.

4. To serve, spoon some of the Easy Bordelaise Sauce over steak; pass remaining sauce. Serve zucchini and carrot mixture with steak. If desired, garnish with fresh herb sprigs. Makes 4 servings.

Easy Bordelaise Sauce: In a medium saucepan, melt 2 tablespoons butter over medium heat. Add 1/4 cup chopped green onions; cook until tender. Stir in 1 tablespoon all-purpose flour and 1/2 teaspoon dried thyme, crushed. Stir in one 14-ounce can beef broth and 1/4 cup dry red wine or 1 tablespoon red wine vinegar. Bring to boiling, stirring occasionally; reduce heat. Boil gently, uncovered, for 15 to 20 minutes or until reduced to about 1 cup. Keep warm.

*Test Kitchen Tip: To shred the carrot or zucchini into long, thin pieces, use a shredder with medium-size holes. Leave the peel on the zucchini so it stays in even pieces and adds color to the dish.

Nutrition facts per serving: 410 cal., 27 g total fat (10 g sat. fat), 91 mg chol., 579 mg sodium, 11 g carbo., 3 g fiber, 27 g pro.

13

Yesterday

In the late 1950s when cooks wanted faster, simpler recipes, our editors created this no-fuss version of beef stroganoff. Today, we think the 15-minute total preparation and cooking time and the fabulous taste are still right on target for busy families.

15-Minute Beef Stroganoff
Start to finish: 15 min.

If you like, use exotic mushrooms such as shiitake, chanterelle, or portobello instead of buttons. Just slice the larger ones into bite-size pieces.

- 12 oz. boneless beef round steak
- 1 Tbsp. cooking oil
- 1 8-oz. pkg. fresh mushrooms, quartered, or one 2½-oz. jar sliced mushrooms, drained
- 1 8-oz. container dairy sour cream onion dip
- 2 Tbsp. all-purpose flour
- ⅔ cup milk
- ¼ tsp. pepper
  Hot cooked wide noodles or rice
  Snipped fresh parsley or chives (optional)

1. Trim fat from meat. Cut meat diagonally across grain into ¼-inch-wide strips. In a large skillet, brown meat in hot oil. Remove meat from skillet. (If necessary, add additional oil.) Add the fresh mushrooms, if using, and cook until tender.

2. Return meat to skillet. Add the canned mushrooms, if using. In a small bowl, stir together the sour cream dip and flour. Stir into mixture in skillet. Stir in milk and pepper. Cook and stir until mixture is thickened and bubbly. Cook and stir for 1 minute more. Serve over hot cooked noodles or rice. If desired, sprinkle with snipped fresh parsley or chives. Makes 5 servings.

Nutrition facts per serving: 364 cal., 18 g total fat (8 g sat. fat), 80 mg chol., 398 mg sodium, 29 g carbo., 2 g fiber, 23 g pro.

Lower-Fat 15-Minute Beef Stroganoff: Prepare as directed, except substitute light dairy sour cream dip for the dairy sour cream dip.

Nutrition facts per serving: 329 cal., 13 g total fat (5 g sat. fat), 78 mg chol., 317 mg sodium, 30 g carbo., 1 g fiber, 25 g pro.

Today

To meet the changing lifestyles of our 21st century readers, we developed this zesty recipe for two. It allows smaller families to enjoy the comfort foods of yesteryear with little effort.

Beef Stroganoff for Two

Start to finish: 30 min.

To make the ribeye steak easier to thinly slice, partially freeze it just until it is icy.

¼	cup light dairy sour cream
1	to 2 tsp. prepared horseradish
1½	cups dried wide noodles
1½	cups broccoli florets (6 oz.)
8	oz. beef ribeye steak
1	small onion, cut into ½-inch-thick slices
1	clove garlic, minced
2	tsp. cooking oil
2	tsp. all-purpose flour
¼	tsp. pepper
1	cup beef broth
2	Tbsp. tomato paste

1. In a small bowl, stir together the sour cream and horseradish. Cover and chill until serving time.

2. Cook noodles according to package directions, adding broccoli for the last 3 minutes of cooking; drain and keep warm.

3. Trim fat from beef. Cut beef into bite-size strips. In a large skillet, cook beef, onion, and garlic in hot oil until onion is tender and beef is desired doneness; remove from heat. Drain off fat. Sprinkle flour and pepper over meat. Stir to coat.

4. Add beef broth and tomato paste to skillet with beef. Cook and stir until thickened and bubbly. Cook and stir for 1 minute more. Remove from heat.

5. To serve, divide noodle-broccoli mixture between two bowls. Spoon beef mixture on top of noodle mixture. Top with sour cream mixture. Makes 2 servings.

Nutrition facts per serving: 404 cal., 14 g total fat (5 g sat. fat), 91 mg chol., 648 mg sodium, 35 g carbo., 4 g fiber, 35 g pro.

Tangy Barbecue Beef

Prep: 25 min. Cook: 10 to 12 hr. (low-heat setting)
Stand: 15 min.

Slow-simmered beef brisket makes succulent barbecue beef sandwiches. We especially like this recipe because you can leave it unattended all day in your slow cooker.

- 2 **Tbsp. chili powder**
- 1 **tsp. celery seeds**
- ½ **tsp. salt**
- ½ **tsp. pepper**
- 1 **3-lb. fresh beef brisket, trimmed of separable fat**
- 2 **onions, thinly sliced**
- 1 **cup bottled smoke-flavored barbecue sauce**
- ½ **cup beer or ginger ale**
- 8 **large sandwich buns or Portuguese rolls, split and toasted**
  Bottled hot pepper sauce (optional)
  Sliced mango

1. For rub, in a small bowl, combine the chili powder, celery seeds, salt, and pepper. Sprinkle rub evenly over all sides of the brisket; rub in with your fingers.

2. Scatter *half* of the onion slices in the bottom of a 3½-, 4-, 5-, or 6-quart slow cooker. Place the brisket on the onion slices, cutting the meat to fit the cooker, if necessary. Scatter the remaining onion slices on top of the brisket. In a small bowl, stir together the barbecue sauce and beer or ginger ale. Pour over the brisket and onions.

3. Cover and cook on low-heat setting for 10 to 12 hours or until meat is fork-tender. Transfer meat to a cutting board; let stand for 15 minutes. Halve meat crosswise. Using 2 forks, pull meat apart into shreds. Return meat to sauce mixture in slow cooker. Heat through, using the high-heat setting.

4. To serve, use a slotted spoon to transfer beef and onion mixture to the buns. If desired, season to taste with bottled hot pepper sauce. Top with sliced mango. Makes 8 servings.

Oven directions: Preheat oven to 325°F. Prepare the rub and apply to brisket as directed in step 1. Place brisket in a shallow roasting pan. Top with all of the onion slices. Combine the barbecue sauce and beer or ginger ale; pour over meat. Cover and roast about 3 hours or until meat is fork-tender. Remove meat; let stand for 15 minutes. Halve meat crosswise. Shred meat. Pour meat sauce into a large saucepan; add shredded meat. Heat through. Serve as directed above in step 4.

Nutrition facts per serving: 442 cal., 11 g total fat (3 g sat. fat), 98 mg chol., 971 mg sodium, 41 g carbo., 3 g fiber, 41 g pro.

Tangy Barbecue Beef

Minute-Minding Meats

Meat has changed a lot through the decades. Check the meat case at your supermarket and you won't find as many of the slow-cooking cuts of yesteryear. Instead, there are quick-cooking steaks and chops as well as time-saving items such as marinated meats, preshaped burgers, preassembled kabobs, and meat strips precut for stir-frying

Although the meat cuts may have changed, the need to cook them properly hasn't. Be sure to cook ground meats to 160°F and other cuts of beef or lamb to at least 145°F (medium rare). Cook pork to at least 160°F (medium).

Szechwan Beef Stir-Fry

Start to finish: 30 min.

Known for its hot, spicy dishes, Szechwan cooking is just one of the Asian cuisines the magazine has featured over the years. Here, beef and a trio of vegetables seasoned with a spunky ginger sauce give a taste of Szechwan at its best.

- 12 oz. boneless beef top round steak or sirloin steak
- 3 Tbsp. dry sherry or orange juice
- 3 Tbsp. soy sauce
- 2 Tbsp. water
- 2 Tbsp. hoisin sauce
- 1 Tbsp. grated fresh ginger
- 2 tsp. cornstarch
- 1 tsp. sugar
- 2 cloves garlic, minced
- ½ tsp. crushed red pepper (optional)
- ¼ tsp. ground black pepper
- 1 Tbsp. cooking oil
- 1 cup thinly bias-sliced carrot
- 1 14-oz. can whole baby corn, drained
- 1 red sweet pepper, cut into 1-inch pieces
  Hot cooked rice
  Lime peel strips (optional)

1. Trim fat from meat. For easier slicing, partially freeze meat. Thinly slice meat across the grain into bite-size strips. Set aside.

2. For sauce, in a small bowl, stir together sherry or orange juice, soy sauce, the water, hoisin sauce, ginger, cornstarch, sugar, garlic, crushed red pepper (if desired), and black pepper. Set aside.

3. Add oil to a wok or large skillet. Preheat over medium-high heat (add more oil if necessary during cooking). Stir-fry carrot in hot oil for 2 minutes. Add baby corn and sweet pepper. Stir-fry for 1 to 2 minutes more or until vegetables are crisp-tender. Remove from wok.

4. Add meat to wok. Stir-fry for 2 to 3 minutes or until meat is slightly pink in center. Push meat from center of wok or skillet.

5. Stir sauce. Add sauce to center of wok or skillet. Cook and stir until thickened and bubbly. Return cooked vegetables to wok or skillet. Stir all ingredients together to coat. Cook and stir for 1 to 2 minutes more or until heated through. Serve immediately with hot cooked rice. If desired, garnish with lime peel. Makes 4 servings.

Nutrition facts per serving: 387 cal., 8 g total fat (2 g sat. fat), 47 mg chol., 841 mg sodium, 48 g carbo., 3 g fiber, 26 g pro.

Szechwan Beef Stir-Fry

Zippy Beef, Mac, and Cheese
Start to finish: 30 min.

The combo of elbow macaroni, ground meat, and tomatoes often is called goulash because it's reminiscent of the paprika-flavored favorite served over noodles. We gave this version a flavor boost by adding chili powder.

    6   oz. dried elbow macaroni or corkscrew
        macaroni (about 1½ cups)
   12   oz. lean ground beef, lean ground pork,
        or uncooked ground turkey
    1   15-oz. can tomato sauce
    1   14½-oz. can stewed tomatoes or
        Mexican-style stewed tomatoes*
    4   oz. American or sharp American cheese,
        cut into small cubes
    2   to 3 tsp. chili powder*
        Finely shredded or grated Parmesan cheese

1. In a 3-quart saucepan, cook pasta according to package directions; drain and return pasta to saucepan. Meanwhile, in a large skillet, cook ground meat until brown. Drain off fat.

2. Stir ground meat, tomato sauce, undrained tomatoes, American cheese, and chili powder into cooked pasta. Cook and stir over medium heat until heated through and cheese melts. Sprinkle each serving with Parmesan cheese. Makes 4 servings.

*Test Kitchen Tip: If you're using Mexican-style stewed tomatoes, add only 2 teaspoons chili powder.

Nutrition facts per serving: 587 cal., 25 g total fat (13 g sat. fat), 93 mg chol., 1,665 mg sodium, 49 g carbo., 3 g fiber, 40 g pro.

Our Best Meat Loaf
Prep: 20 min. Bake: 1 hr. + 10 min. Stand: 10 min.

We've been publishing meat loaf recipes for more than 70 years. Our basic loaf gives options galore. You can mix and match seasonings and meats. And you can opt for a sweet ketchup topper or simply substitute ⅓ cup barbecue sauce.

    2   eggs
   ¾   cup milk
   ⅔   cup fine dry bread crumbs or
        2 cups soft bread crumbs
   ¼   cup finely chopped onion
    2   Tbsp. snipped fresh parsley
    1   tsp. salt
   ½   tsp. dried leaf sage, basil, or
        oregano, crushed
   ⅛   tsp. pepper
  1½   lb. ground beef, lamb, or pork
   ¼   cup ketchup
    2   Tbsp. packed brown sugar
    1   tsp. dry mustard

1. Preheat oven to 350°F. In a large bowl, use a fork to beat together eggs and milk; stir in bread crumbs, onion, parsley, salt, sage, and pepper. Add ground meat; mix well. Lightly pat mixture into an 8×4×2-inch loaf pan.

2. Bake for 1 to 1¼ hours or until an instant-read thermometer inserted in center registers 160°F.* Spoon off fat. In a small bowl, combine ketchup, brown sugar, and mustard; spread over meat. Bake for 10 minutes more. Let stand for 10 minutes before serving. Makes 8 servings.

*Test Kitchen Tip: The internal color of meat loaf is not a reliable doneness indicator. A beef, veal, lamb, or pork meat loaf cooked to 160°F is safe, regardless of color. To measure the doneness of a meat loaf, insert an instant-read thermometer into the center of the loaf to a depth of 2 to 3 inches.

Nutrition facts per serving: 243 cal., 13 g total fat (5 g sat. fat), 108 mg chol., 631 mg sodium, 12 g carbo., 1 g fiber, 20 g pro.

Ham Loaf: Prepare as directed, except use only soft bread crumbs. Also, substitute ½ teaspoon dry mustard for the sage, basil, or oregano and omit the salt. Substitute 12 ounces ground beef or pork and 12 ounces ground cooked ham for the 1½ pounds ground beef, lamb, or pork. Bake as directed.

Nutrition facts per serving: 236 cal., 12 g total fat (4 g sat. fat), 106 mg chol., 744 mg sodium, 13 g carbo., 0 g fiber, 19 g pro.

Hamburger Pie

Prep: 25 min. Bake: 25 min.

Long before the days of boxed hamburger fix-ups, we published this convenient prizewinning dish. In 1940, it was considered fast because it used canned green beans and condensed tomato soup.

- 1 recipe Mashed Potatoes (below)*
- 1 lb. ground beef
- ½ cup chopped onion
- ½ tsp. salt
  Dash pepper
- 2 cups loose-pack frozen green beans, thawed
- 1 10¾-oz. can condensed tomato soup
- ½ cup shredded process American cheese (2 oz.) (optional)

1. Prepare Mashed Potatoes; set aside. Preheat oven to 350°F. Grease a 1½-quart rectangular baking dish or casserole; set aside. In a large skillet, cook the ground beef and onion until meat is brown and onion is tender. Drain off fat. Add the salt and pepper. Stir in thawed beans and the soup; pour into prepared baking dish or casserole.

2. Spoon Mashed Potatoes into mounds on meat mixture or pipe on potatoes using a pastry bag and a large star tip. If desired, sprinkle potatoes with cheese. Bake, uncovered, for 25 to 30 minutes or until mixture is bubbly and potatoes are golden. Makes 4 to 6 servings.

Mashed Potatoes: Peel and quarter 1½ pounds baking potatoes. Place potatoes and ½ teaspoon salt in a medium saucepan. Add enough water to cover. Cook potatoes for 20 to 25 minutes or until tender; drain. Mash with a potato masher or beat with an electric mixer on low speed. Add 2 tablespoons butter or margarine; season to taste with additional salt and pepper. Gradually beat in enough milk (2 to 4 tablespoons) to make mixture light and fluffy.

*Test Kitchen Tip: If you wish to use packaged instant mashed potatoes, prepare 4 servings according to package directions, except reserve the milk. Season to taste with salt and pepper. Add just enough of the reserved milk so potatoes are stiff enough to mound. Spoon onto casserole (do not pipe).

Nutrition facts per serving: 455 cal., 20 g total fat (9 g sat. fat), 88 mg chol., 1,034 mg sodium, 41 g carbo., 5 g fiber, 27 g pro.

Spaghetti Pie

Prep: 30 min. Bake: 20 min.

This creative casserole, first submitted by a reader in 1974, has become one of our hallmark recipes. The cook who sent it explained when she fixed too much pasta for her meatballs, she transformed the leftovers into this pie.

- 4 oz. dried spaghetti
- 1 Tbsp. butter or margarine
- 1 egg, beaten
- ¼ cup grated Parmesan cheese (1 oz.)
- 8 oz. ground beef
- ½ cup chopped onion
- ½ cup chopped green sweet pepper
- 1 clove garlic, minced
- ½ tsp. fennel seeds, crushed
- 1 8-oz. can tomato sauce
- 1 tsp. dried oregano, crushed
  Nonstick cooking spray
- 1 cup low-fat cottage cheese, drained
- ½ cup shredded part-skim mozzarella cheese (2 oz.)

1. Preheat oven to 350°F. Cook spaghetti according to package directions. Drain. Return spaghetti to warm saucepan. Stir butter into hot pasta until melted. Stir in egg and Parmesan cheese; set aside.

2. Meanwhile, in a medium skillet, cook ground beef, onion, sweet pepper, garlic, and fennel seeds until meat is brown and onion is tender. Drain. Stir in tomato sauce and oregano; heat through.

3. Coat a 9-inch pie plate with nonstick cooking spray. Press spaghetti mixture onto bottom and up side of pie plate, forming a crust. Spread cottage cheese on the bottom and up the side of pasta crust. Spread meat mixture over cottage cheese. Sprinkle with shredded mozzarella cheese.

4. Bake for 20 to 25 minutes or until bubbly and heated through. To serve, cut into wedges. Makes 6 servings.

Nutrition facts per serving: 270 cal., 11 g total fat (6 g sat. fat), 76 mg chol., 500 mg sodium, 20 g carbo., 1 g fiber, 21 g pro.

Lasagna

Prep: 45 min. Bake: 30 min. Stand: 10 min.

Lasagna has been in our recipe files for at least a half century. Although the traditional casserole is worth the time it takes to make it, we've come up with some options for time-pressed cooks.

- 12 oz. bulk Italian or pork sausage or ground beef
- 1 cup chopped onion
- 2 cloves garlic, minced
- 1 14½-oz. can diced tomatoes, undrained
- 1 8-oz. can tomato sauce
- 1 Tbsp. dried Italian seasoning, crushed
- 1 tsp. fennel seeds, crushed (optional)
- ¼ tsp. pepper
- 6 dried lasagna noodles
- 1 egg
- 1 15-oz. container ricotta cheese or 2 cups cream-style cottage cheese, drained
- ¼ cup grated Parmesan cheese (1 oz.)
- 1½ cups shredded mozzarella cheese (6 oz.)
  Grated Parmesan cheese (optional)

1. For sauce, in a large saucepan, cook sausage, onion, and garlic until meat is brown. Drain off fat.

2. Stir undrained tomatoes, tomato sauce, Italian seasoning, fennel seeds (if desired), and pepper into meat mixture. Bring to boiling; reduce heat. Cover and simmer for 15 minutes, stirring occasionally.

3. Meanwhile, cook lasagna noodles in a large amount of boiling water for 10 to 12 minutes or until tender but still firm. Drain; rinse with cold water. Drain.

4. For filling, in a medium bowl, beat egg; stir in ricotta and the ¼ cup Parmesan cheese. Set aside.

5. Preheat oven to 375°F. Spread about ½ *cup* of the sauce over the bottom of a 2-quart rectangular baking dish. Layer *half* of the cooked noodles in the bottom of the dish, trimming or overlapping as necessary to fit. Spread with *half* of the filling. Top with *half* of the remaining meat sauce and *half* of the mozzarella cheese. Repeat layers. If desired, sprinkle additional Parmesan cheese over top.

6. Place baking dish on a baking sheet. Bake for 30 to 35 minutes or until heated through. Let stand for 10 minutes before serving. Makes 8 servings.

Make-ahead directions: Prepare as directed through step 5. Cover unbaked lasagna; chill for up to 24 hours. To serve, place baking dish on a baking sheet. Bake, covered, in a 375°F oven for 40 minutes. Uncover; bake about 20 minutes more or until heated through. Let stand for 10 minutes.

Nutrition facts per serving: 441 cal., 22 g total fat (11 g sat. fat), 97 mg chol., 658 mg sodium, 33 g carbo., 2 g fiber, 24 g pro.

Quick Lasagna: Omit the tomatoes, tomato sauce, Italian seasoning, fennel seeds, and pepper. For sauce, stir a 26-ounce jar pasta sauce into the browned meat mixture. Do not simmer. Substitute 6 no-boil lasagna noodles (one-third of a 9-ounce package) for the regular lasagna noodles and skip step 3. Continue as directed in step 4.

Nutrition facts per serving: 391 cal., 24 g total fat (11 g sat. fat), 97 chol., 1,047 mg sodium, 18 g carbo., 2 g fiber, 22 g pro.

Cider-Braised Pork Roast

Prep: 20 min. Cook: 45 + 10 + 5 min.

You'll love the subtle sweetness of apples and apricots paired with the delicate flavor of the pork in this easy-fixing, home-style dish.

- 1 1½- to 2-lb. boneless pork shoulder roast
- 2 Tbsp. cooking oil
- 1¼ cups apple juice or apple cider
- ½ cup chopped onion
- ½ tsp. salt
- 2 medium cooking apples (such as Granny Smith or Jonathan), cored and cut into wedges
- 1 6-oz. pkg. dried apricot halves
- ½ tsp. ground cardamom
- ¼ tsp. ground cinnamon

1. Trim fat from meat. In a 4-quart Dutch oven, brown meat on all sides in hot oil. Drain off fat. Add apple juice, onion, and salt to Dutch oven. Bring to boiling; reduce heat. Cover and simmer for 45 minutes.

2. Add apples, apricots, cardamom, and cinnamon. Bring to boiling; reduce heat. Cover and simmer about 10 minutes more or until meat and fruit are tender. Using a slotted spoon, transfer meat, apples, and apricots to a serving platter, reserving juices in Dutch oven. Keep meat and fruit warm.

3. For cider sauce, boil reserved juices gently for 5 to 7 minutes or until reduced to ½ cup. Spoon over meat and fruit. Makes 6 servings.

Nutrition facts per serving: 321 cal., 11 g total fat (3 g sat. fat), 73 mg chol., 292 mg sodium, 32 g carbo., 4 g fiber, 24 g pro.

Roast Pork Tangerine

Prep: 25 min. Roast: 1½ hr. + 30 min. Stand: 15 min.

First published in 1965, this mustard-rubbed roast is a scrumptious match for herbed citrus sauce.

1	**4- to 5-lb. pork loin center rib roast, backbone loosened**
1	**tsp. dry mustard**
1	**tsp. dried marjoram, crushed**
½	**tsp. salt**
2	**tsp. finely shredded tangerine peel or orange peel**
½	**cup tangerine juice or orange juice**
1	**Tbsp. packed brown sugar**
	Chicken broth or beef broth
⅔	**cup chicken broth or beef broth**
3	**Tbsp. all-purpose flour**
⅛	**tsp. dry mustard**
⅛	**tsp. dried marjoram, crushed**
	Salt
	Pepper
3	**tangerines or 2 oranges, peeled, sectioned, and seeded**

1. Preheat oven to 325°F. Place roast, rib side down, in a shallow roasting pan. In a small bowl, combine the 1 teaspoon dry mustard, the 1 teaspoon marjoram, and the ½ teaspoon salt. Sprinkle mustard mixture evenly over pork; rub in with your fingers. Insert an oven-going meat thermometer in center of meat, making sure bulb does not touch bone. Roast, uncovered, for 1½ hours.

2. In a small bowl, stir together the peel, juice, and brown sugar; spoon over the meat. Roast about 30 minutes more or until thermometer registers 155°F, spooning pan juices over meat once or twice. Transfer meat to platter. Cover and let stand for 15 minutes before slicing. (The temperature of the meat will rise about 5°F during standing.)

3. Meanwhile, strain pan juices. Skim off fat. Measure juices; add enough broth to juices to equal ¾ cup total liquid. Pour the liquid into a medium saucepan. In a screw-top jar, combine the ⅔ cup broth and the flour; shake well. Add to saucepan along with the ⅛ teaspoon dry mustard and the ⅛ teaspoon marjoram. Cook and stir until thickened and bubbly; cook and stir for 1 minute more. Season to taste with additional salt and pepper. Stir in the tangerines or oranges; heat through. Serve with pork. Makes 10 servings.

Nutrition facts per serving: 266 cal., 14 g total fat (5 g sat. fat), 87 mg chol., 246 mg sodium, 7 g carbo., 1 g fiber, 26 g pro.

Pork Chop Barbecue

3. Bake, uncovered, for 25 to 30 minutes or until meat juices run clear (160°F), turning chops once. Transfer to a serving platter. Pour sauce over all. Serves 6.

Nutrition facts per serving: 190 cal., 10 g total fat (3 g sat. fat), 44 mg chol., 475 mg sodium, 13 g carbo., 1 g fiber, 14 g pro.

Pork and Green Chiles Casserole
Prep: 25 min. Bake: 25 min. Stand: 3 min.

In September 1993, we asked readers to send us their best-loved casseroles. This zesty rice, bean, and pork medley earned a top rating. We're betting you'll give it high marks, too.

1¼	lb. lean boneless pork
1	Tbsp. cooking oil
1	15-oz. can black beans or pinto beans, rinsed and drained
1	14½-oz. can diced tomatoes, undrained
1	10¾-oz. can condensed cream of chicken soup
2	4½-oz. cans diced green chile peppers, drained
1	cup quick-cooking brown rice
¼	cup water
2	Tbsp. bottled salsa
1	tsp. ground cumin
½	cup shredded cheddar cheese (2 oz.)

1. Preheat oven to 375°F. Cut pork into thin bite-size strips. In a large skillet, stir-fry pork, half at a time, in hot oil until done; drain. Return all of the meat to the skillet. Stir in beans, undrained tomatoes, soup, chile peppers, brown rice, the water, salsa, and cumin. Heat and stir just until bubbly; pour into a 2-quart casserole.

2. Bake, uncovered, for 25 minutes. Remove from oven. Sprinkle with cheese; let stand for 3 to 4 minutes or until cheese is melted. Makes 6 servings.

Nutrition facts per serving: 350 cal., 14 g total fat (5 g sat. fat), 69 mg chol., 1,242 mg sodium, 28 g carbo., 5 g fiber, 30 g pro.

Pork Chop Barbecue
Prep: 35 min. Bake: 25 min.

These flavorful oven-baked chops prove you don't have to cook outdoors to enjoy the flavors of barbecue. The 1953 recipe has been recognized by long-time readers as one of their favorites.

½	cup water
3	Tbsp. vinegar
2	Tbsp. sugar
1	Tbsp. yellow mustard
¼	tsp. salt
¼	to ½ tsp. ground black pepper
⅛	tsp. cayenne pepper
1	slice lemon
1	medium onion, cut into thin wedges
½	cup ketchup
2	Tbsp. Worcestershire sauce
1	to 2 tsp. liquid smoke
6	pork rib chops, cut ¾ inch thick
1	to 2 Tbsp. cooking oil

1. For sauce, in a small saucepan, combine the water, vinegar, sugar, mustard, salt, black pepper, and cayenne pepper. Add lemon slice and onion wedges. Bring mixture to boiling; reduce heat. Simmer, uncovered, for 20 minutes. Stir in ketchup, Worcestershire sauce, and liquid smoke. Return to boiling. Remove from heat; discard lemon slice.

2. Meanwhile, preheat oven to 350°F. In a large skillet, brown pork chops, half at a time, in hot oil over medium-high heat. Place pork chops in a 3-quart rectangular baking dish; pour sauce over chops.

> **As early as the 1920s, *Better Homes and Gardens*® editors realized cooks appreciated precise measurements, descriptive methods, and doneness tests, so that's what we give in all of our recipes.**

Ham and Bean Soup With Vegetables

Prep: 25 min. Stand: 1 hr. Cook: 1¾ hr. + 15 min.

Ham and bean soup started out as a thrifty way to use leftover ham bones. Our editors made this old faithful taste fresher by adding parsnips, carrots, and spinach.

- 1 **cup dry navy beans**
- 1¼ **to 1½ lb. meaty smoked pork hocks or one 1- to 1½-lb. meaty ham bone**
- 1 **cup chopped onion**
- ½ **cup sliced celery**
- 1 **tsp. instant chicken bouillon granules**
- 1 **Tbsp. snipped fresh thyme or 1 tsp. dried thyme, crushed**
- ¼ **tsp. pepper**
- 2 **cups chopped peeled parsnip or rutabaga**
- 1 **cup sliced carrot**
- ½ **of a 10-oz. pkg. frozen chopped spinach, thawed and well drained**

1. Rinse beans. In a 4-quart Dutch oven, combine beans and 5 cups *cold water*. Bring to boiling; reduce heat. Simmer, uncovered, for 2 minutes. Remove from heat. Cover and let stand for 1 hour. (Or place beans in water in Dutch oven. Cover and soak beans overnight.) Drain and rinse beans.

2. In the same Dutch oven, combine 7 cups *fresh water*, beans, pork hocks or ham bone, onion, celery, bouillon granules, thyme, and pepper. Bring to boiling; reduce heat. Cover and simmer for 1¾ hours. Remove pork hocks or ham bone; set aside to cool.

Ham and Bean Soup
With Vegetables

3. Stir parsnip or rutabaga and carrot into bean mixture. Return to boiling; reduce heat. Cover and simmer about 15 minutes or until vegetables are tender.

4. Meanwhile, cut meat off bones and coarsely chop. Discard bones. Stir meat and spinach into vegetable mixture. Heat through. Makes 6 servings.

Nutrition facts per serving: 224 cal., 4 g total fat (1 g sat. fat), 16 mg chol., 572 mg sodium, 35 g carbo., 12 g fiber, 14 g pro.

Curried Split Pea Soup

Prep: 10 min. Cook: 10 to 12 hr. (low-heat setting) or 5 to 6 hr. (high-heat setting)

Our readers are experts at using their appliances to best advantage. The couple who submitted this 1998 slow cooker prizewinner were inspired by a holiday ham glazed with curried cranberries.

- 1 **lb. dry green split peas, rinsed and drained**
- 1 **lb. ham hocks**
- 1½ **cups cubed cooked ham**
- 1½ **cups chopped celery**
- 1 **cup chopped onion**
- 1 **cup chopped carrot**
- ⅓ **cup dried cranberries**
- 4 **tsp. curry powder**
- 1 **Tbsp. dried marjoram, crushed**
- 2 **bay leaves**
- ¼ **tsp. pepper**
- 6 **cups water**

1. In a 3½- or 4-quart slow cooker, combine split peas, ham hocks, ham, celery, onion, carrot, cranberries, curry powder, marjoram, bay leaves, and pepper. Stir in the water.

2. Cover and cook on low-heat setting for 10 to 12 hours or on high-heat setting for 5 to 6 hours. Discard bay leaves. Remove ham hocks. When ham hocks are cool enough to handle, remove meat from bones; discard bones. Coarsely chop meat. Return meat to soup. Makes 6 servings.

Nutrition facts per serving: 376 cal., 4 g total fat (1 g sat. fat), 25 mg chol., 626 mg sodium, 58 g carbo., 6 g fiber, 29 g pro.

Ham with Cranberry Sauce

Start to finish: 20 min.

With today's smaller families, it's hard to serve ham without gaining a refrigerator full of leftovers. We developed this fruit-sauced ham to serve just two.

- 1 **small apple, cored and chopped**
- 1 **stalk celery, sliced**
- 1 **Tbsp. butter or margarine**
- ½ **cup purchased cranberry-orange sauce**
- 2 **Tbsp. vinegar**
- ⅛ **tsp. ground allspice**
- 8 **oz. cooked ham, sliced ⅛ inch thick**

1. For sauce, in a large skillet, cook the apple and celery in hot butter until tender. Stir in the cranberry-orange sauce, vinegar, and allspice. Cook and stir until heated through. Remove from skillet; keep warm.

2. In the same skillet, cook ham over medium heat about 5 minutes or until heated through, turning once. (Overlap the slices in the skillet, if necessary.)

3. To serve, transfer ham slices to individual plates. Spoon sauce over ham. Makes 2 servings.

Nutrition facts per serving: 358 cal., 18 g total fat (7 g sat. fat), 81 mg chol., 1,587 mg sodium, 28 g carbo., 2 g fiber, 20 g pro.

Corn-Sausage Chowder

Start to finish: 30 min.

This recipe was crowned a soup classic in the February 1988 issue of *Midwest Living*® magazine, a sister publication of *Better Homes and Gardens*®.

- 1 **lb. bulk pork sausage**
- 2 **medium onions, coarsely chopped**
- 3 **cups potatoes cut into ½-inch cubes**
- 2 **cups water**
- 1 **tsp. salt**
- ½ **tsp. dried marjoram, crushed**
- ⅛ **tsp. pepper**
- 1 **15¼-oz. can whole kernel corn, drained**
- 1 **14¾-oz. can cream-style corn**
- 1 **12-oz. can (1½ cups) evaporated milk**

1. In a 4- to 5-quart Dutch oven, cook sausage and onion until sausage is brown and onion is tender. Drain well. Return sausage mixture to Dutch oven.

2. Stir potatoes, the water, salt, marjoram, and pepper into Dutch oven. Bring to boiling; reduce heat. Cover and simmer about 10 minutes or just until potato is tender.

3. Stir in the drained whole kernel corn, cream-style corn, and evaporated milk. Cook and stir until heated through. Makes 6 servings.

Nutrition facts per serving: 491 cal., 27 g total fat (12 g sat. fat), 60 mg chol., 1,135 mg sodium, 43 g carbo., 4 g fiber, 17 g pro.

Sausage Pie

Prep: 40 min. Bake: 45 min. Cool: 20 min.

We all take thin-crust pizza for granted, but pizza also comes in dozens of deep-dish forms. This is our rendition of a two-crust pizza called pizza rustica.

- 1 **16-oz. pkg. hot roll mix**
- 1 **lb. bulk sweet or hot Italian sausage**
- 4 **cups sliced fresh mushrooms**
- 1 **cup chopped onion**
- 1 **cup chopped red sweet pepper**
- 2 **cloves garlic, minced**
- 1 **8-oz. can pizza sauce**
- 2 **cups shredded smoked mozzarella or provolone cheese (8 oz.)**
- 1 **egg**
- 1 **Tbsp. water**

1. Prepare hot roll mix according to package directions through the kneading step. Cover; let dough rest for 5 to 10 minutes.

2. In a large skillet, cook sausage over medium heat until meat is brown. Drain, reserving 1 tablespoon drippings in skillet. Add mushrooms, onion, sweet pepper, and garlic to skillet. Cook over medium heat until vegetables are tender. Drain off liquid. Stir in pizza sauce. Set aside.

3. Preheat oven to 350°F. Grease the bottom and side of a 9-inch springform pan. On a lightly floured surface, roll *three-fourths* of the dough into a 15-inch circle. Fit into bottom and press up side of springform pan. Sprinkle bottom of the dough with *½ cup* of the cheese. Spoon meat mixture on top. Sprinkle remaining 1½ cups cheese over meat. Press lightly into meat filling.

4. On a lightly floured surface, roll the remaining dough into a 9-inch circle; place on top of meat-cheese mixture. Fold edge of bottom dough over top dough; pinch to seal. In a small bowl, beat together egg and the water. Brush top of pie with egg-water mixture; let dry for 5 minutes. Score the top of pie in a diamond pattern, being careful not to cut all the way through the dough.

5. Bake for 45 to 50 minutes or until golden. Cool in pan on a wire rack for 20 minutes. Loosen pie from side of pan; remove side of pan. Makes 8 servings.

Nutrition facts per serving: 482 cal., 20 g total fat (7 g sat. fat), 100 mg chol., 1,057 mg sodium, 50 g carbo., 0 g fiber, 25 g pro.

Plum-Sauced Roast Lamb

Prep: 10 min. Roast: 1¼ hr. + 45 min. Stand: 10 min.

This lamb recipe—a specialty of the Hollyhock House, a popular 1930s New England eatery—first caught our eye because it used plum jam rather than the customary mint jelly. We think it's still superb.

- 1   **5- to 6-lb. leg of lamb**
- 1   **clove garlic, halved**
- 1   **Tbsp. snipped fresh parsley**
- ½   **tsp. celery salt**
- ½   **tsp. pepper**
- ¼   **tsp. paprika**
- 3   **Tbsp. butter or margarine**
- ⅓   **cup finely chopped carrot**
- 2   **Tbsp. finely chopped onion**
- 1   **cup soft bread crumbs (1½ slices)**
- 1   **recipe Plum Jam Sauce (below)**
     Fresh plum wedges (optional)

1. Preheat oven to 325°F. Rub leg of lamb all over with cut sides of garlic. In a small bowl, combine parsley, celery salt, pepper, and paprika. Sprinkle parsley mixture evenly over lamb; rub in with your fingers. Place the lamb, fat side up, on a rack in a shallow roasting pan. Insert an oven-going meat thermometer into the center, making sure bulb does not touch bone. Roast, uncovered, for 1¼ hours.

2. Meanwhile, in a small saucepan, melt butter over medium heat. Add carrot and onion; cook 3 to 4 minutes or until vegetables are tender. Stir in bread crumbs.

3. Remove lamb from oven. Carefully pat crumb mixture over top of lamb. Continue roasting for 45 minutes to 1 hour or until desired doneness (140°F for medium-rare or 155°F for medium). Cover with foil; let stand for 10 minutes before slicing. (The temperature of the meat will rise about 5°F during standing.) Serve with warm or cooled Plum Jam Sauce. If desired, garnish with fresh plum wedges. Makes 10 to 12 servings.

Plum Jam Sauce: In a medium saucepan, whisk together ¾ cup plum jam, ¼ cup unsweetened pineapple juice, 1 tablespoon orange juice, 1 teaspoon all-purpose flour, ¼ teaspoon dry mustard, and dash ground mace. Cook and stir until thickened and bubbly. Cook and stir for 2 minutes more.

Nutrition facts per serving: 310 cal., 10 g total fat (4 g sat. fat), 110 mg chol., 218 mg sodium, 20 g carbo., 1 g fiber, 33 g pro.

Plum-Sauced Roast Lamb

Honey-Mustard Lamb Chops

Prep: 10 min. Broil: 6 + 6 min.

Team these sweet-and-tangy chops with steamed carrots and garlic mashed potatoes.

- 4   **small lamb loin chops, trimmed of separable fat (about 12 oz. total)**
- 2   **small zucchini, halved lengthwise**
- 1   **Tbsp. Dijon-style mustard**
- 1   **Tbsp. honey**
- 1½ **tsp. snipped fresh rosemary or ½ tsp. dried rosemary, crushed**

1. Preheat broiler. Arrange chops and zucchini, cut sides up, on the unheated rack of a broiler pan. In a small bowl, stir together mustard, honey, and rosemary. Spread some of the mustard mixture on top of the chops.

2. Broil chops and zucchini 3 inches from the heat for 6 minutes. Turn chops and zucchini over; spread remaining mustard mixture onto the chops and zucchini. Broil for 6 to 9 minutes more or until lamb is desired doneness and the zucchini is tender. Makes 2 servings.

Nutrition facts per serving: 182 cal., 6 g total fat (2 g sat. fat), 60 mg chol., 99 mg sodium, 12 g carbo., 1 g fiber, 21 g pro.

In the 1940s, zucchini was an unfamiliar vegetable to many cooks. The news of its versatility and fresh flavor spread from California across the country.

Sweet Potato Shepherd's Pie

Prep: 25 min. Cook: 45 + 10 + 5 min.

Thrifty cooks of yesteryear used leftovers from the Sunday meal to make this dish. In 1999, we added modern-day panache by replacing plain mashed potatoes with mashed sweet potatoes.

1¼ lb. lean boneless lamb, cut
    into ½-inch cubes
 1 Tbsp. olive oil or cooking oil
 1 cup chopped onion
 1 clove garlic, minced
1½ cups water
 ½ tsp. salt
 ½ tsp. dried savory, crushed
 ¼ tsp. ground cinnamon
 ¼ tsp. pepper
 1 cup thinly sliced carrot
 1 cup loose-pack frozen cut green beans
 2 large sweet potatoes, peeled and cubed
    (about 1 lb.)
 2 Tbsp. butter or margarine
 ¼ tsp. salt
 ⅛ tsp. ground nutmeg
    Milk (optional)
 ¼ cup cold water
 2 Tbsp. cornstarch

1. In a large skillet, brown lamb, *half* at a time, in hot oil. Return all meat to skillet. Stir in onion and garlic; cook for 1 minute. Add the 1½ cups water, the ½ teaspoon salt, the savory, cinnamon, and pepper. Bring to boiling; reduce heat. Cover; simmer about 45 minutes or until meat is nearly tender. Add carrot and beans. Cover; simmer about 10 minutes or until vegetables are tender.

2. Meanwhile, in a medium saucepan, cook sweet potatoes in a small amount of boiling water for 20 to 25 minutes or until tender. Drain. Return sweet potatoes to saucepan; add butter, the ¼ teaspoon salt, and the nutmeg. Mash cooked sweet potato mixture with a potato masher or with an electric mixer on low speed. If mixture seems dry, gradually stir in enough milk (2 to 3 tablespoons) to make potatoes fluffy. Set aside.

3. In a small bowl, combine the ¼ cup cold water and the cornstarch; add to mixture in skillet. Cook and stir until thickened and bubbly. Spoon mashed sweet potato mixture into six mounds on mixture in skillet. Simmer, uncovered, about 5 minutes more or until sweet potatoes are heated through. Makes 6 servings.

Nutrition facts per serving: 260 cal., 10 g total fat (4 g sat. fat), 70 mg chol., 407 mg sodium, 22 g carbo., 3 g fiber, 21 g pro.

Roast Chicken with Raisin Corn Bread Stuffing

Prep: 45 min. Roast: 1 hr. Stand: 10 min.

For decades, chicken for dinner was a Sunday ritual, and *Better Homes and Gardens*® published scores of ways to prepare the delicious bird. Revive the old-time tradition by serving this recipe at your house.

 ½ cup finely chopped celery
 ½ cup finely chopped onion
 ¼ cup chicken broth
 ¼ cup raisins
 ¼ tsp. dried dill weed
 ¼ tsp. salt
 2 cups coarsely crumbled corn bread*
 1 egg white, slightly beaten
    Chicken broth
 1 2½- to 3-lb. whole roasting chicken

1. Preheat oven to 375°F. In a small saucepan, combine celery, onion, and the ¼ cup chicken broth. Bring to boiling; reduce heat. Simmer, uncovered, until tender. In a medium bowl, combine undrained celery mixture, the raisins, dill weed, and salt.

2. Add corn bread and egg white; toss gently to mix. Drizzle with enough additional broth to moisten; toss.

3. Loosely spoon stuffing mixture into body cavity of chicken. Pull neck skin to back; fasten with a small skewer. Slip drumsticks under band of skin or tie the drumsticks securely to tail. Twist wing tips under the back. Place chicken, breast side up, on a rack in a shallow roasting pan. Insert an oven-going meat thermometer into center of an inside thigh muscle, not touching bone. Spoon any stuffing that won't fit in the bird into a covered casserole; chill during the first 30 minutes of the chicken's roasting time, then bake alongside the chicken for the last 30 to 45 minutes.

4. Roast, uncovered, for 1 to 1¼ hours or until thermometer registers 180°F, drumsticks move easily in their sockets, and chicken is no longer pink.

5. When chicken is done, remove it from the oven and cover with foil. Let stand for 10 minutes before carving. Serve chicken with stuffing. Makes 4 servings.

***Test Kitchen Tip:** Up to 24 hours ahead, prepare and bake the corn bread. Cover and store at room temperature.

Nutrition facts per serving: 562 cal., 31 g total fat (9 g sat. fat), 161 mg chol., 687 mg sodium, 28 g carbo., 2 g fiber, 40 g pro.

Buttermilk Fried Chicken

Prep: 30 min. Cook: 35 min.

You don't have to wait until you want to feed a crowd to fry chicken. This delectable buttermilk-dipped pan-fried recipe makes just enough for two.

- **4 chicken drumsticks and/or thighs, 2 whole chicken legs (drumstick-thigh pieces), or 1 whole chicken breast, halved lengthwise (about 1 lb. total)**
- **⅓ cup all-purpose flour**
- **½ tsp. dried basil or thyme, crushed**
- **¼ tsp. salt**
- **¼ tsp. onion powder**
- **⅛ tsp. pepper**
- **¼ cup buttermilk or sour milk***
- **2 Tbsp. cooking oil**
- **2 tsp. all-purpose flour**
- **½ tsp. instant chicken bouillon granules Dash pepper**
- **¾ cup milk**

1. If desired, skin chicken pieces. In a shallow dish, combine the ⅓ cup flour, the basil, salt, onion powder, and the ⅛ teaspoon pepper. Pour the buttermilk into another shallow dish. Coat the chicken with flour mixture, shaking off excess. Dip into buttermilk; dip again into flour mixture to coat all sides.

2. In a large skillet, cook chicken in hot oil over medium heat for 15 minutes, turning to brown evenly. Reduce heat to medium-low. Cook, uncovered, for 35 to 40 minutes or until chicken is tender and no longer pink (170°F for breast halves; 180°F for thighs, drumsticks, and legs), turning occasionally. Remove chicken from skillet; drain on paper towels. Reserve the drippings in skillet. Transfer chicken to dinner plates. Cover; keep warm.

3. For gravy, stir the 2 teaspoons flour, the bouillon granules, and the dash pepper into the reserved drippings in skillet, scraping up any crusty browned bits from bottom of skillet. Add the milk all at once. Cook and stir over medium heat until thickened and bubbly. Cook and stir for 1 minute more. Serve over chicken. Serves 2.

*Test Kitchen Tip: To make ¼ cup sour milk, place ¾ teaspoon lemon juice or vinegar in a glass measuring cup. Add enough milk to make ¼ cup total liquid; stir. Let mixture stand for 5 minutes before using.

Nutrition facts per serving: 490 cal., 28 g total fat (7 g sat. fat), 107 mg chol., 682 mg sodium, 23 g carbo., 1 g fiber, 36 g pro.

Buttermilk Fried Chicken

Maryland Fried Chicken

Prep: 20 min. Cook: 10 + 35 + 5 min.

What makes this 1968 recipe from Maryland different from other fried chicken recipes? The pieces are browned in oil, then simmered in milk, making them succulent and tender.

1   egg
3   Tbsp. milk
1   cup finely crushed saltine crackers
     (28 crackers)
1   tsp. dried thyme, crushed
½   tsp. paprika
⅛   tsp. pepper
2½   to 3 lb. meaty chicken pieces (breast
     halves, thighs, and/or drumsticks)
2   Tbsp. cooking oil
1   cup milk
1   recipe Cream Gravy (below) (optional)
     Hot mashed potatoes (optional)

1. In a small bowl, beat together egg and the 3 tablespoons milk. In a shallow bowl, combine crushed crackers, thyme, paprika, and pepper. Set aside.

2. If desired, skin chicken. Dip chicken pieces, one at a time, into egg mixture; roll in cracker mixture.

3. In a large skillet, heat oil over medium heat. Add chicken and cook, uncovered, for 10 minutes, turning occasionally to brown evenly. (Add more oil if necessary.) Drain well.

4. Add the 1 cup milk to skillet. Reduce heat to medium-low; cover tightly. Cook for 35 minutes. Uncover; cook for 5 to 10 minutes more or until chicken is tender and no longer pink (170°F for breast halves; 180°F for thighs and drumsticks).

5. Transfer chicken to a serving platter, leaving drippings in skillet. Cover chicken and keep warm. If desired, prepare Cream Gravy; serve with chicken. If desired, serve with mashed potatoes. Makes 6 servings.

Nutrition facts per serving: 327 cal., 13 g total fat (4 g sat. fat), 121 mg chol., 410 mg sodium, 19 g carbo., 0 g fiber, 31 g pro.

Cream Gravy: Skim fat from drippings in skillet. In a screw-top jar combine ¾ cup milk, 3 tablespoons all-purpose flour, ¼ teaspoon salt, and ⅛ teaspoon pepper; cover and shake until well mixed. Add to skillet. Stir in 1 cup additional milk. Cook and stir over medium heat until thickened and bubbly. Cook and stir for 1 minute more. (If desired, thin with additional milk.)

During the 1930s Great Depression, *Better Homes and Gardens®* was proud to include practical recipes to help cooks make family meals when money was tight. Offering practical recipes continues today.

Arroz con Pollo

Prep: 25 min. Cook: 10 + 20 + 20 min.

This recipe dates back to the Great Depression when chicken was a luxury. Chicken may be cheaper and more available today, but our standards for unbeatable flavor and worth-the-money results are still the same.

1   7- to 8-oz. pkg. brown-and-serve
     sausage links
3   Tbsp. all-purpose flour
½   tsp. salt
¼   tsp. pepper
6   small chicken thighs, skinned (about 2 lb.)
1   Tbsp. cooking oil
2   cups water
1   cup chopped onion
½   cup chopped celery
     Pinch thread saffron (optional)
1   cup long grain rice
1   14½-oz. can diced tomatoes
     or one 14½-oz. can diced tomatoes with
     basil, oregano, and garlic, undrained
1   cup loose-pack frozen peas
¼   cup sliced pitted ripe olives or
     pimiento-stuffed green olives

1. Cut the sausages into ½-inch pieces. In a 4-quart Dutch oven, cook sausage pieces until browned. Remove sausage pieces. Set aside.

2. In a plastic bag, combine flour, salt, and pepper. Add chicken, a few pieces at a time, and shake to coat.

3. In the Dutch oven, heat oil over medium heat. Add chicken; cook, uncovered, for 10 minutes, turning to brown evenly. Carefully drain off fat. Add the water, onion, celery, and, if desired, saffron to chicken in Dutch oven. Cover and simmer for 20 minutes. Add uncooked rice, undrained tomatoes, and sausage pieces. Simmer, covered, about 20 minutes more or until rice is tender. Add peas and olives; stir gently to combine. Cook until heated through. Makes 6 servings.

Nutrition facts per serving: 409 cal., 17 g total fat (5 g sat. fat), 92 mg chol., 748 mg sodium, 38 g carbo., 3 g fiber, 26 g pro.

Country Captain

Prep: 20 min. Cook: 35 + 2 min.

Make this blend of chicken, tomatoes, and currants as zesty as you like by adjusting the curry powder. Since brands vary, experiment with different ones until you find a favorite. For ultra authentic flavor, look for East Indian curry powder at a specialty food store.

  1 14½-oz. can stewed tomatoes, undrained
  ¼ cup dried currants or raisins
  2 to 3 tsp. curry powder
  1 tsp. instant chicken bouillon granules
  ½ tsp. ground mace or nutmeg
  ¼ tsp. sugar
  2 to 2½ lb. meaty chicken pieces (breast halves, thighs, and drumsticks), skinned
  1 Tbsp. cornstarch
  1 Tbsp. cold water
     Hot cooked rice
  2 Tbsp. snipped flat-leaf parsley (optional)
  1 Tbsp. slivered almonds, toasted (optional) (tip, page 102)

1. Cut up any large pieces of tomato. In a very large skillet, stir together undrained tomatoes, currants, curry powder, bouillon granules, mace, and sugar. Sprinkle chicken lightly with *salt* and *pepper.* Place chicken in skillet. Spoon sauce over chicken. Bring mixture to boiling; reduce heat. Cover and simmer for 35 to 45 minutes or until chicken is tender and no longer pink (170°F for breast halves; 180°F for thighs and drumsticks). Remove chicken from skillet; keep warm.

2. For sauce, skim any fat from mixture in skillet. In a small bowl, stir together cornstarch and cold water; add to skillet. Cook and stir until thickened and bubbly. Cook and stir for 2 minutes more. Serve sauce over hot rice and chicken. If desired, sprinkle with parsley and almonds. Makes 6 servings.

Nutrition facts per serving: 284 cal., 6 g total fat (1 g sat. fat), 61 mg chol., 348 mg sodium, 33 g carbo., 1 g fiber, 23 g pro.

> **The recipe for chicken Country Captain is credited by some to a British officer who brought it back from India. Over time, it's become an American standard.**

Chicken and Mushrooms

Prep: 35 min. Cook: 20 min.

Elegant, yet simple to make, this wine-simmered chicken won the thumbs up at our taste panel.

  ¼ cup all-purpose flour
  ¼ tsp. salt
  ¼ tsp. ground black pepper
  ¼ tsp. paprika
  4 chicken thighs, skinned
  4 chicken drumsticks, skinned
  2 Tbsp. cooking oil
  1 medium onion, sliced
  2 cups whole or sliced small mushrooms
  1 medium red sweet pepper, cut into 1-inch strips
  3 cloves garlic, minced
  ½ cup dry red wine or beef broth
  2 Tbsp. balsamic vinegar
  1 14½-oz. can diced tomatoes, undrained
  2 tsp. dried Italian seasoning, crushed
  ¼ cup half-and-half or light cream
  1 Tbsp. all-purpose flour
  ¼ cup snipped fresh flat-leaf parsley
     Hot cooked pasta (optional)
     Fresh flat-leaf parsley sprigs (optional)

1. In a large plastic bag, combine the ¼ cup flour, the salt, black pepper, and paprika. Add chicken, 2 or 3 pieces at a time, and shake to coat well. In a very large skillet, heat the 2 tablespoons oil over medium heat. Cook chicken in hot oil about 10 minutes or until well browned, turning to brown evenly. Remove chicken from skillet, reserving drippings in skillet.

2. Add onion, mushrooms, sweet pepper, and garlic to skillet. Cook and stir for 2 minutes. Add red wine or beef broth and balsamic vinegar. Cook and stir for 5 minutes more.

3. Add undrained tomatoes and Italian seasoning. Bring to boiling, scraping up browned bits from the bottom of the skillet. Return chicken to the skillet; reduce heat. Cover and simmer about 20 minutes or until chicken is tender and no longer pink (180°F). Remove chicken; keep warm.

4. In a small bowl, stir together half-and-half and the 1 tablespoon flour; add to skillet. Cook and stir until slightly thickened and bubbly. Cook and stir for 1 minute more. Return chicken to skillet; heat through. Sprinkle with snipped parsley. If desired, serve over hot cooked pasta and garnish with parsley sprigs. Makes 4 to 6 servings.

Nutrition facts per serving: 323 cal., 13 g total fat (3 g sat. fat), 89 mg chol., 400 mg sodium, 21 g carbo., 2 g fiber, 25 g pro.

Lombardi Chicken

Lombardi Chicken

Prep: 30 min. Bake: 20 min.

The title of this recipe, sent by a reader from Cedarburg, Wisconsin, pays homage to Green Bay Packers' legendary coach Vince Lombardi.

- 1 **lb. skinless, boneless chicken breast halves**
- 3 **to 4 Tbsp. all-purpose flour**
- 3 **Tbsp. butter or margarine**
- 1 **cup sliced fresh mushrooms**
- ½ **cup dry Marsala wine**
- ⅓ **cup chicken broth**
- ⅓ **cup shredded mozzarella or fontina cheese**
- ⅓ **cup grated Parmesan cheese**
- ¼ **cup thinly sliced green onions**

1. Preheat oven to 375°F. Cut each breast half in half lengthwise. Place each piece between two pieces of heavy plastic wrap; working from center to edges, pound with flat side of a meat mallet to ⅛-inch thickness. Remove plastic wrap. Coat chicken lightly with flour.

2. In a 12-inch skillet, melt *1 tablespoon* of the butter over medium heat; add *half* of the chicken pieces. Cook for 4 minutes, turning once. Transfer to a 2-quart rectangular baking dish. Repeat with another *1 tablespoon* of the butter and the remaining chicken pieces; transfer to the baking dish.

3. Melt the remaining 1 tablespoon butter in the skillet. Add mushrooms. Cook and stir until tender; add wine, broth, dash *salt*, and dash *pepper*. Bring to boiling; boil gently about 5 minutes or until mixture is reduced to ½ cup including mushrooms. Pour over the chicken.

4. In a small bowl, combine mozzarella cheese, Parmesan cheese, and green onions; sprinkle over the chicken. Bake, uncovered, for 20 minutes. Serves 4.

Nutrition facts per serving: 319 cal., 15 g total fat (9 g sat. fat), 102 mg chol., 474 mg sodium, 6 g carbo., 0 g fiber, 34 g pro.

It's amazing how ingredients go in and out of fashion. Fifty years ago most of our readers had never tasted salsa. Today there are very few who don't have a favorite bottled brand or make up their own to use in recipes like the one at right.

Chicken and Noodles

Prep: 40 min. Cook: 20 + 5 + 1 min.

Although old-fashioned in flavor, this comfort food is up-to-the-minute in nutrition with only 311 calories and 6 grams of fat per serving.

3	whole chicken legs (drumstick-thigh pieces) (about 2 lb. total), skinned
3	cups water
2	bay leaves
1	tsp. dried thyme, crushed
1	tsp. salt
¼	tsp. pepper
2	cups sliced carrot
1½	cups chopped onion
1	cup sliced celery
3	cups dried wide noodles (6 oz.)
1	cup loose-pack frozen peas
2	cups milk
3	Tbsp. all-purpose flour

1. In 4½-quart Dutch oven, combine chicken, water, bay leaves, thyme, ½ *teaspoon* of the salt, and the pepper. Add carrot, onion, and celery. Bring to boiling; reduce heat. Cover and simmer for 20 to 30 minutes or until chicken is tender and no longer pink (180°F). Discard bay leaves. Reserving broth mixture, remove chicken from Dutch oven; cool chicken slightly. Remove meat from bones; discard bones. Chop meat; set aside.
2. Bring broth mixture to boiling. Add noodles; cook for 5 minutes. Stir in frozen peas, *1½ cups* of the milk, and the remaining ½ teaspoon salt.
3. In a small bowl, stir together the remaining ½ cup milk and the flour; stir into noodle mixture. Cook and stir until thickened and bubbly. Stir in chopped chicken. Cook and stir for 1 to 2 minutes more or until heated through. Makes 6 servings.

Nutrition facts per serving: 311 cal., 6 g total fat (2 g sat. fat), 93 mg chol., 550 mg sodium, 39 g carbo., 5 g fiber, 25 g pro.

Cumin Chicken with Hot Citrus Salsa

Start to finish: 30 min.

Recipe contests tell us how our readers cook—the ingredients they use, the appliances they own, and the ethnic cuisines they favor. This 1993 dish told us what was hot, literally! If you like, double the recipe to serve four.

1	recipe Hot Citrus Salsa (below)
¾	tsp. ground cumin
⅛	tsp. salt
⅛	tsp. ground black pepper
2	skinless, boneless chicken breast halves (about 10 oz. total)
1	Tbsp. cooking oil
	Hot cooked rice

1. Prepare Hot Citrus Salsa; set aside. In a small bowl, combine cumin, salt, and black pepper. Sprinkle cumin mixture evenly over both sides of chicken; rub in with your fingers.
2. In a 10-inch skillet, cook chicken in hot oil over medium heat for 8 to 10 minutes or until chicken is tender and no longer pink (170°F), turning once.
3. To serve, spoon Hot Citrus Salsa over chicken. Serve with hot cooked rice. Makes 2 servings.

Hot Citrus Salsa: In a small bowl, combine 4 dried tomato halves (not oil-packed) and ½ cup boiling water. Cover; let stand for 10 minutes. Drain; chop tomatoes. Peel, section, and seed 1 medium orange over a small bowl. Chop orange sections; add to juice in bowl. Stir in chopped tomatoes; 1 tablespoon snipped fresh cilantro, basil, or parsley; 1 teaspoon grated fresh ginger; and ½ teaspoon finely chopped fresh jalapeño chile pepper.*

*Test Kitchen Tip: Because chile peppers contain volatile oils that can burn your skin and eyes, avoid direct contact with them as much as possible. When working with chile peppers, wear plastic or rubber gloves. If your bare hands do touch the peppers, wash your hands and nails well with soap and warm water.

Nutrition facts per serving: 431 cal., 12 g total fat (2 g sat. fat), 104 mg chol., 326 mg sodium, 37 g carbo., 3 g fiber, 42 g pro.

Maple-Glazed Stuffed Cornish Hens

Prep: 30 min. Roast: 1½ hr.

When you're looking for a special meal, try these pecan-and-leek-stuffed hens. Complete your menu with steamed asparagus or broccoli and dinner rolls.

- 2   slices bacon
- 1   small leek or 2 green onions, thinly sliced (¼ cup)
- 2   Tbsp. chopped pecans or walnuts
- ⅛   tsp. dried thyme or marjoram, crushed
      Dash pepper
- 1   cup dry bread cubes (1½ slices)
- 1   to 2 Tbsp. water
- 2   1¼- to 1½-lb. Cornish game hens
      Salt
      Pepper
- 1   tsp. butter or margarine, melted
- 2   Tbsp. maple-flavored syrup, pure maple syrup, or apricot syrup
- 1   Tbsp. butter or margarine, melted
- 2   tsp. Dijon-style mustard or 1 tsp. brown mustard

1. In a medium skillet, cook bacon until crisp. Remove bacon and drain on paper towels. Crumble bacon and set aside. Reserve *1 tablespoon* of the bacon drippings in skillet.

2. Cook leek and nuts in reserved bacon drippings over medium heat until leek is tender and nuts are toasted; remove from heat. Stir in bacon, thyme, and dash pepper. Stir in bread cubes. Drizzle enough of the water over bread mixture to moisten; toss lightly to mix.

3. Preheat oven to 375°F. Lightly season the cavities of the hens with salt and pepper. Lightly stuff the hens with the bread mixture. Skewer neck skin, if present, to back of each hen. Twist wing tips under backs, holding skin in place. Tie legs to tail. Place hens, breast sides up, on a rack in a shallow roasting pan. Brush with the 1 teaspoon melted butter. Cover loosely with foil. Roast for 1½ to 1¾ hours or until tender, no longer pink, and an instant-read thermometer inserted in an inside thigh muscle not touching bone registers 180°F.

4. Meanwhile, in a small bowl, stir together syrup, the 1 tablespoon butter, and the mustard. Uncover hens and brush the syrup mixture on them frequently during the last 15 minutes of roasting. Makes 4 servings.

Nutrition facts per serving: 511 cal., 35 g total fat (11 g sat. fat), 191 mg chol., 385 mg sodium, 16 g carbo., 1 g fiber, 32 g pro.

Chicken Kiev à la Pecan

Prep: 25 min. Chill: 30 min. to 24 hr. Bake: 15 min.

Here's a nutty version of the legendary chicken Kiev. Slice into one of the rolls and you'll uncover a gentle ooze of melted Havarti, chopped pecans, and green onions in place of the usual herbed butter.

- 2   skinless, boneless chicken breast halves (about 10 oz. total)
      Salt
      Pepper
- 2   2-inch-long sticks Havarti or provolone cheese (1 oz. total)
- 1   green onion, thinly sliced
- 1   Tbsp. finely chopped pecans, walnuts, or almonds
- 1   egg
- 1   Tbsp. water
- 2   Tbsp. all-purpose flour
- ¼   cup ground pecans, walnuts, or almonds
- 1   Tbsp. butter

1. Place each chicken breast half between two pieces of heavy plastic wrap. Working from center to edges, pound lightly with the flat side of a meat mallet to ⅛-inch thickness. Remove plastic wrap. Season lightly with salt and pepper.

2. To assemble, place 1 piece of the cheese in the center of each chicken piece. Sprinkle each piece with half of the green onion and half of the finely chopped nuts. Fold in the sides of each piece; roll up into a spiral, pressing the edges to seal.

3. In a shallow dish, beat together egg and the water. Place flour in another shallow dish; place ground nuts in a third shallow dish. Coat each chicken roll with flour, dip into egg mixture, and finally roll in nuts to coat. Transfer to a 9-inch pie plate. Cover and chill for at least 30 minutes or up to 24 hours.

4. Preheat oven to 400°F. In a medium skillet, cook the chicken rolls in hot butter over medium heat about 5 minutes or until golden, turning to brown all sides. Return to pie plate. Bake for 15 to 18 minutes or until no longer pink in the center and an instant-read thermometer inserted into the center registers 170°F. Transfer to serving plates. Makes 2 servings.

Nutrition facts per serving: 440 cal., 28 g total fat (6 g sat. fat), 214 mg chol., 304 mg sodium, 9 g carbo., 2 g fiber, 38 g pro.

Deep-Dish Chicken Pie

Prep: 50 min. Bake: 30 min. Stand: 20 min.

Chicken potpie made its first appearance in our *New Cook Book* in 1968. Since then, we've updated this perennial pleaser by adding leeks and mushrooms.

1	recipe Pastry Topper (right)
3	medium leeks or 1 large onion, chopped
1	cup sliced fresh mushrooms
¾	cup sliced celery
½	cup chopped red sweet pepper
2	Tbsp. butter or margarine
⅓	cup all-purpose flour
1	tsp. poultry seasoning
¼	tsp. salt
¼	tsp. ground black pepper
1½	cups chicken broth
1	cup half-and-half, light cream, or milk
2½	cups chopped, cooked chicken (about 13 oz.)
1	cup loose-pack frozen peas
1	egg, beaten

1. Prepare Pastry Topper; set aside. Preheat oven to 400°F. In a large saucepan, cook leeks, mushrooms, celery, and sweet pepper in hot butter over medium heat for 4 to 5 minutes or until tender. Stir in the flour, poultry seasoning, salt, and black pepper. Add broth and half-and-half. Cook and stir until thickened and bubbly. Stir in chicken and frozen peas. Pour into an ungreased 2-quart rectangular baking dish.

2. Place Pastry Topper over hot mixture. Turn under edges of pastry; flute to dish edges. Brush with egg. If desired, place pastry shapes on top. Brush again with egg. Bake, uncovered, for 30 to 35 minutes or until crust is golden. Let stand for 20 minutes. Makes 6 servings.

Pastry Topper: In a medium bowl, stir together 1¼ cups all-purpose flour and ¼ teaspoon salt. Using a pastry blender, cut in ⅓ cup shortening until pieces are pea-size. Sprinkle 1 tablespoon cold water over part of the mixture; gently toss with a fork. Push moistened dough to side of bowl. Sprinkle additional cold water over remaining flour mixture, 1 tablespoon at a time, tossing with a fork until all dough is moistened (use 4 to 5 tablespoons cold water total). Form into a ball. On a lightly floured surface, roll dough into a 13×9-inch rectangle. Using a knife, cut slits in pastry to allow steam to escape. If desired, cut shapes from pastry; reserve.

Nutrition facts per serving: 471 cal., 26 g total fat (10 g sat. fat), 113 mg chol., 543 mg sodium, 33 g carbo., 3 g fiber, 26 g pro.

Brunswick Stew

Prep: 30 min. Cook: 35 + 10 + 1 min.

Originally a concoction of squirrel meat and onions, this stew originated in Brunswick County, Virginia, and was served at Southern barbecues. Through the years, the ingredients have changed—this recent chicken version makes a great family meal.

2   lb. meaty chicken pieces (breast halves, thighs, and/or drumsticks), skinned*
2   smoked pork hocks (1½ to 2 lb. total)
3   medium onions, cut into thin wedges
1   14½-oz. can diced tomatoes, undrained
½   cup chicken broth
4   cloves garlic, minced
1   Tbsp. Worcestershire sauce
1   tsp. dry mustard
1   tsp. dried thyme, crushed
¼   tsp. pepper
¼   tsp. bottled hot pepper sauce
2   cups loose-pack frozen cut okra
1   cup loose-pack frozen baby lima beans
1   cup loose-pack frozen whole kernel corn
¼   cup cold water
2   Tbsp. all-purpose flour

1. In a large Dutch oven, combine the chicken, pork hocks, onions, undrained tomatoes, chicken broth, garlic, Worcestershire sauce, mustard, thyme, pepper, and hot pepper sauce. Bring to boiling; reduce heat. Cover and simmer for 35 to 45 minutes or until chicken is tender and no longer pink (170°F for breast halves; 180°F for thighs and drumsticks). Remove pork hocks (and chicken, if desired); cool slightly.

2. Cut meat from hocks; discard bones. Chop meat; set aside. (If desired, cut chicken meat into bite-size pieces; discard bones.) Add okra, lima beans, and corn to mixture in Dutch oven. Return to boiling; reduce heat. Cover and simmer for 10 to 15 minutes more or just until vegetables are tender.

3. In a small bowl, stir together cold water and flour. Stir into stew. Cook and stir until thickened and bubbly; cook and stir 1 minute more. Stir in pork (and chicken, if cut up). Makes 4 or 5 servings.

*Test Kitchen Tip: If you like, brown the chicken before cooking. Heat 2 tablespoons cooking oil in the Dutch oven. Add chicken and cook over medium heat about 15 minutes or until browned, turning to brown the chicken evenly. Drain off fat. Continue as directed.

Nutrition facts per serving: 454 cal., 10 g total fat (3 g sat. fat), 109 mg chol., 794 mg sodium, 44 g carbo., 5 g fiber, 48 g pro.

Spicy Stir-Fried Chicken With Cashews

Start to finish: 25 min.

This 30-Minute Dinner winner from October 1997 seasons chicken, chile peppers, and cashews with a gutsy combination of oyster and fish sauces.

2   Tbsp. oyster-flavored sauce
1   Tbsp. fish sauce or soy sauce
1   Tbsp. packed brown sugar
2   tsp. cornstarch
⅓   cup cold water
2   Tbsp. cooking oil
1   cup red and/or yellow sweet pepper cut into bite-size strips
1   medium onion, sliced
2   to 4 fresh red chile peppers, seeded and cut into thin strips (tip, page 32)
1   clove garlic, minced
12   oz. skinless, boneless chicken breast halves, cut into bite-size strips
½   cup roasted cashews
    Hot cooked rice
    Roasted cashews (optional)

1. For sauce, in a small bowl, stir together oyster-flavored sauce, fish sauce or soy sauce, brown sugar, and cornstarch. Stir in the cold water.

2. Pour oil into a wok or large skillet. Preheat over medium-high heat. Add sweet pepper and onion; stir-fry for 1 minute. Add chile peppers and garlic; stir-fry for 1 to 2 minutes more or until sweet pepper and onion are crisp-tender. Remove with slotted spoon; set aside.

3. Add chicken to wok or skillet. Stir-fry for 3 to 4 minutes or until no longer pink. Push chicken from center of wok or skillet. Stir sauce; add to wok or skillet. Cook and stir until thickened and bubbly. Return onion, chile peppers, and garlic to skillet. Cook for 1 minute more, stirring to coat all ingredients. Stir in the ½ cup cashews. Serve over hot cooked rice. If desired, sprinkle with additional cashews. Makes 4 servings.

Nutrition facts per serving: 398 cal., 16 g total fat (3 g sat. fat), 49 mg chol., 705 mg sodium, 38 g carbo., 2 g fiber, 26 g pro.

Chicken on Call

In generations past, if a recipe called for cooked poultry, cooks had to use leftovers or pull out the stew pot. Today, you can stop at your supermarket's deli counter and pick up a roasted chicken. One chicken will give you about 2 cups of cooked meat.

Busy-Day El Rancho Chicken

Prep: 20 min. Bake: 45 + 3 min. Stand: 10 min.

This family-pleasing casserole was shared with us as a prime example of the best in South Texas Tex-Mex cooking. When we tasted it, we agreed.

- 1 10¾-oz. can reduced-fat and reduced-sodium condensed cream of mushroom soup
- 1 10¾-oz. can reduced-fat and reduced-sodium condensed cream of chicken soup
- 1 10-oz. can chopped tomatoes and green chile peppers, undrained
- 1 medium green sweet pepper, chopped
- 1 medium onion, chopped
- 1½ tsp. chili powder
- ¼ tsp. ground black pepper
- 12 6- or 7-inch corn tortillas, cut into thin bite-size strips
- 3 cups cubed cooked chicken (about 1 lb.)
- 2 cups shredded cheddar cheese (8 oz.)

1. Preheat oven to 350°F. In a large bowl, combine soups, undrained tomatoes with chiles, sweet pepper, chopped onion, chili powder, and black pepper. Set aside.

2. To assemble, sprinkle about *one-third* of the tortilla strips over bottom of an ungreased 3-quart rectangular baking dish. Layer *half* of the chicken over tortilla strips; spoon *half* of the soup mixture on top. Sprinkle *half* of the cheese and *another one-third* of the tortilla strips over the soup mixture. Layer with remaining chicken, soup mixture, and tortilla strips.

3. Bake, covered, about 45 minutes or until bubbly around edges and hot in center. Uncover; sprinkle with remaining cheese. Bake for 3 to 4 minutes more or until cheese is melted. Let stand for 10 minutes. Serves 8.

Nutrition facts per serving: 376 cal., 16 g total fat (7 g sat. fat), 81 mg chol., 691 mg sodium, 32 g carbo., 2 g fiber, 26 g pro.

California Club Sandwich

Start to finish: 25 min.

The club sandwich that appeared in the 1953 edition of the *Better Homes and Gardens® New Cook Book* was a simple stacking of toast, chicken, and bacon. Since then, the layered combo has undergone numerous transformations. This lively version from 2001 is a delicious case in point.

- 1 8-oz. tub cream cheese
- 2 Tbsp. honey mustard
- 1 6½-oz. jar marinated artichoke hearts, drained and chopped
- ¼ cup chopped pitted ripe olives, pitted green olives, or Greek black olives
- 1 16-oz. loaf crusty French bread
- 2 cups loosely packed fresh spinach, stems removed
- 2 cups sliced fresh mushrooms
- 1 small red onion, thinly sliced
- 8 oz. thinly sliced cooked turkey breast
- 4 slices bacon, crisp-cooked, drained, and crumbled
- ¼ cup roasted and salted sunflower seeds

1. In a small bowl, stir together cream cheese and honey mustard. Gently stir in chopped artichokes and olives; set aside.

2. Cut bread loaf in half lengthwise. Hollow out bottom half of bread loaf, leaving a ½-inch-thick shell (reserve cutout bread for another use). Spread bread shell with ⅔ *cup* of the cream cheese mixture. Layer spinach, mushrooms, red onion, and turkey into bottom half of loaf. Sprinkle with bacon and sunflower seeds.

3. Spread *another* ⅔ *cup* of the cream cheese mixture onto cut side of top half of bread. (Reserve any remaining cream cheese mixture for another use.) Place top half of bread, cream cheese mixture side down, onto sandwich. Cut into 4 serving-size pieces. Makes 4 servings.

Make-ahead directions: Prepare as directed. Wrap sandwich in plastic wrap. Chill for up to 4 hours.

Nutrition facts per serving: 665 cal., 34 g total fat (16 g sat. fat), 85 mg chol., 1,941 mg sodium, 62 g carbo., 5 g fiber, 31 g pro.

Turkey Enchiladas

Turkey Enchiladas
Prep: 40 min. Bake: 40 + 5 min.

In 1992, a reader sent her recipe for creamy turkey-filled tortilla rolls for a nutrition makeover. We revamped the recipe with spectacular results—and only 11 grams of fat per enchilada.

½   **cup chopped onion**
½   **of an 8-oz. pkg. reduced-fat cream cheese (Neufchâtel), softened**
1   **Tbsp. water**
1   **tsp. ground cumin**
¼   **tsp. ground black pepper**
⅛   **tsp. salt**
4   **cups chopped cooked turkey or chicken breast (about 1¼ lb.)**
¼   **cup chopped pecans, toasted (tip, page102)**
12   **7- to 8-inch flour tortillas**
   Nonstick cooking spray
1   **10¾-oz. can reduced-fat and reduced-sodium condensed cream of chicken soup**
1   **8-oz. carton light dairy sour cream**
1   **cup fat-free milk**
2   **to 4 Tbsp. finely chopped, pickled jalapeño chile peppers (tip, page 32)**
½   **cup shredded reduced-fat sharp cheddar cheese (2 oz.)**
   Chopped tomatoes (optional)
   Chopped green sweet pepper (optional)
   Snipped fresh cilantro or parsley (optional)

1. Preheat oven to 350°F. For filling, in a covered small saucepan, cook onion in a small amount boiling water until tender; drain. In medium bowl, combine cream cheese, the 1 tablespoon water, the cumin, black pepper, and salt. Stir in cooked onion, turkey, and pecans.

2. Wrap the tortillas in foil. Heat in the oven about 10 minutes or until softened. (Or wrap tortillas in microwave-safe paper towels. Microwave tortillas on 100% power [high] about 30 seconds or until warmed.)

3. Meanwhile, coat a 3-quart rectangular baking dish with nonstick cooking spray. For each enchilada, spoon *about ¼ cup* of the filling onto a tortilla; roll up. Place tortilla, seam side down, in the prepared baking dish. Repeat with the remaining filling and tortillas.

4. For sauce, in a medium bowl, stir together the soup, sour cream, milk, and jalapeño peppers. Pour sauce over enchiladas.

5. Cover and bake about 40 minutes or until heated through. Sprinkle with cheddar cheese. Bake, uncovered, about 5 minutes more or until cheese is melted. If desired, top with tomatoes, sweet pepper, and cilantro. Makes 12 enchiladas.

Make-ahead directions: Prepare as directed through step 4. Cover and chill for at least 4 hours or up to 24 hours. Bake, covered, in a 350°F oven about 1 hour or until heated through. Continue as directed.

Nutrition facts per enchilada: 273 cal., 11 g total fat (4 g sat. fat), 55 mg chol., 417 mg sodium, 21 g carbo., 1 g fiber, 21 g pro.

> **Turkey recipes to help with Thanksgiving dinner are an annual tradition on the November pages of *Better Homes and Gardens*® magazine. Many a cook has turned to our Turkey Roasting Guide to help prepare the family feast.**

Turkey Frame Soup

Prep: 30 min. Cook: 1½ hr. + 10 + 8 min.

Great cooks don't let anything go to waste. This old-style recipe shows why. It turns the leftover meat and bones from a roasted or grilled turkey into an incredible soup.

1   meaty turkey frame
8   cups water
2   large onions, quartered
2   stalks celery, sliced
1   Tbsp. instant chicken bouillon granules
3   cloves garlic, minced
    Chopped cooked turkey
1   14½-oz. can diced tomatoes, undrained
1½ tsp. dried oregano, basil, marjoram, or thyme, crushed
¼   tsp. pepper
3   cups (any combination) sliced celery, carrot, parsnips, or mushrooms; chopped onion or rutabagas; or broccoli or cauliflower florets
1½ cups dried medium noodles

1. Break turkey frame or cut in half with kitchen shears. Place in an 8- to 10-quart kettle or Dutch oven. Add the water, quartered onions, 2 stalks celery, bouillon granules, and garlic. Bring to boiling; reduce heat. Cover and simmer for 1½ hours.

2. Remove turkey frame. When cool enough to handle, remove meat from bones. Discard bones. Coarsely chop meat. If necessary, add enough cooked turkey to equal 2 cups total meat; set turkey aside.

3. Strain broth, discarding solids. Skim fat from broth. Return broth to kettle. Stir in undrained tomatoes, crushed herb, and pepper. Stir in desired vegetables. Return to boiling; reduce heat. Cover; simmer 10 minutes. Stir in noodles. Simmer for 8 to 10 minutes more or until noodles are tender but still firm and vegetables are tender. Stir in turkey; heat through. Makes 6 servings.

Nutrition facts per serving: 182 cal., 4 g total fat (1 g sat. fat), 52 mg chol., 608 mg sodium, 17 g carbo., 2 g fiber, 20 g pro.

Creamy Turkey Pie

Prep: 25 min. Bake: 30 min. Stand: 5 min.

This winner of our October 1993 Meat Pie Prize Tested Recipes® contest sports an easy biscuit crust, a creamy turkey sausage and mushroom filling, and a rich cottage cheese topper.

1   lb. bulk uncooked turkey sausage or uncooked ground turkey*
1   medium onion, chopped
1   3-oz. pkg. cream cheese, cubed
1   4½-oz. jar sliced mushrooms, drained
1   7½-oz. pkg. (10) refrigerated biscuits
1   egg
1   cup cream-style cottage cheese
1   Tbsp. all-purpose flour
    Chopped tomato (optional)
    Snipped fresh chives (optional)

1. Preheat oven to 350°F. In a large skillet, cook turkey sausage or ground turkey and onion until meat is brown. Drain off fat. Stir in cream cheese until melted; stir in mushrooms. Cover and keep warm.

2. For crust, lightly grease a 9-inch deep-dish pie plate. Arrange biscuits in pie plate, pressing together onto the bottom and up side to form an even crust. Spoon turkey mixture into crust, spreading evenly.

3. In a blender or food processor, combine egg, cottage cheese, and flour. Cover and blend or process until smooth. Spread evenly over turkey mixture.

4. Bake, uncovered, about 30 minutes or until edge is browned and top is set. Let stand for 5 to 10 minutes before serving. If desired, garnish with chopped tomato and snipped chives. Makes 6 servings.

***Test Kitchen Tip:** If you're using ground turkey, add: ¼ teaspoon salt; ¼ teaspoon dried sage, crushed; and ¼ teaspoon pepper to the meat mixture.

Nutrition facts per serving: 420 cal., 24 g total fat (10 g sat. fat), 85 mg chol., 1,406 mg sodium, 26 g carbo., 2 g fiber, 26 g pro.

Caesar Salmon Pizzas

Prep: 15 min. Bake: 8 min.

Our first pizza recipes often were take-offs on the red-sauced variety with a from-scratch crust. But over the years, we've looked for easier ways to make crusts and often use innovative toppers, such as this salmon-and-spinach combo.

2   6-inch Italian bread shells (Boboli)
¼   cup bottled creamy Caesar salad dressing
2   cups torn fresh spinach
2   oz. smoked salmon, flaked and skin and
     bones removed
¼   cup walnut pieces, toasted (tip, page102)
¼   cup finely shredded Parmesan cheese (1 oz.)
2   Tbsp. thinly bias-sliced green onion
1   tsp. drained capers (optional)

1. Preheat oven to 400°F. Lightly spread bread shells with some of the Caesar dressing. Place the bread shells on a baking sheet.

2. Top the bread shells with spinach, salmon, walnuts, *half* of the Parmesan cheese, the green onion, and, if desired, capers.

3. Bake, uncovered, for 8 to 10 minutes or just until heated through. Drizzle with the remaining Caesar dressing; sprinkle with the remaining Parmesan cheese. Makes 2 servings.

Nutrition facts per serving: 652 cal., 39 g total fat (6 g sat. fat), 19 mg chol., 1,480 mg sodium, 54 g carbo., 4 g fiber, 26 g pro.

Yesterday

Basic Tuna-Noodle Casserole has remained a favorite for decades. Our 1930s version featured tuna, mushrooms, and noodles in a cheese sauce. We liked it so well that this version from the current *New Cook Book* has only minimal updates.

Tuna-Noodle Casserole
(recipe, page 42)

Today

In 2001, we gave a new spin to tuna-noodle casserole by replacing the cheese sauce with Alfredo pasta sauce, switching noodles to rigatoni, and adding a dash of tomato pesto and Parmesan cheese. This isn't your grandmother's tuna delight!

Tuna Alfredo Casserole
(recipe, page 42)

41

Yesterday
Tuna-Noodle Casserole

Prep: 25 min. Bake: 20 min.

Almost any small pasta works in this casserole. Cavatelli or medium shells are intriguing options to the noodles or elbow macaroni. (Photo on page 40.)

3 cups dried medium noodles (4 oz.) or 1 cup dried elbow macaroni (3½ oz.)
½ cup soft bread crumbs
1 Tbsp. butter or margarine, melted
1 cup chopped celery
¼ cup chopped onion
¼ cup butter or margarine
¼ cup all-purpose flour
½ tsp. salt
½ tsp. dry mustard
¼ tsp. ground black pepper
2 cups milk
1 9- or 9¼-oz. can tuna, drained and broken into chunks, or two 6-oz. cans skinless, boneless salmon, drained
1 cup cheddar cheese cubes (4 oz.)
¼ cup chopped roasted red sweet pepper or pimiento

1. Preheat oven to 375°F. Cook noodles or macaroni according to package directions. Drain and set aside. Meanwhile, in a small bowl, combine bread crumbs and the 1 tablespoon melted butter; set aside.

2. For sauce, in a medium saucepan, cook celery and onion in the hot ¼ cup butter until tender. Stir in flour, salt, dry mustard, and black pepper. Add milk all at once; cook and stir until slightly thickened and bubbly.

3. In a large bowl, stir together sauce, tuna or salmon, cheese cubes, roasted pepper or pimiento, and cooked noodles. Transfer to a 1½-quart casserole. Sprinkle with crumb mixture.

4. Bake, uncovered, for 20 to 25 minutes or until bubbly and topping is golden. Makes 4 servings.

Nutrition facts per serving: 588 cal., 34 g total fat (18 g sat. fat), 127 mg chol., 986 mg sodium, 37 g carbo., 2 g fiber, 34 g pro.

Vegetable Tuna-Noodle Casserole: Prepare as directed, except add 1 cup loose-pack frozen vegetables, thawed, with the tuna or salmon. Transfer tuna or salmon mixture to a 2-quart casserole.

Nutrition facts per serving: 615 cal., 34 g total fat (18 g sat. fat), 127 mg chol., 986 mg sodium, 43 g carbo., 4 g fiber, 35 g pro.

Test Kitchen Tip: For a faster version, substitute a 10¾-ounce can condensed cream of mushroom soup mixed with ¾ cup milk for the sauce.

Today
Tuna Alfredo Casserole

Prep: 20 min. Bake: 10 min.

Serve this Italian-accented dish with a tossed salad, steamed carrots, and crusty Italian bread. (Photo on page 41.)

3 cups dried rigatoni or penne pasta*
1 cup fresh pea pods
1 10-oz. container refrigerated Alfredo pasta sauce or four-cheese pasta sauce or 1¼ cups bottled Alfredo pasta sauce or four-cheese pasta sauce
3 Tbsp. milk
2 Tbsp. purchased dried tomato pesto
1 12-oz. can water-pack solid white tuna, drained and broken into chunks
¼ cup finely shredded Parmesan cheese (1 oz.)

1. Preheat oven to 425°F. In a Dutch oven, cook pasta according to package directions, adding the pea pods during the last minute of cooking. Drain well; return to Dutch oven.

2. Meanwhile, in a medium bowl, combine Alfredo sauce, milk, and pesto. Add to pasta, stirring gently to coat. Gently fold in tuna. Transfer pasta mixture to an ungreased 2-quart oval baking dish. Sprinkle with Parmesan cheese.

3. Bake for 10 to 15 minutes or until heated through and cheese is just melted. Makes 6 servings.

*Test Kitchen Tip: You'll need 7 to 8 ounces of rigatoni or 9 ounces of penne to make 3 cups.

Nutrition facts per serving: 414 cal., 20 g total fat (2 g sat. fat), 51 mg chol., 516 mg sodium, 33 g carbo., 1 g fiber, 23 g pro.

As a recipe goes through the *Better Homes and Gardens®* Test Kitchen, we analyze every aspect —flavor, texture, appearance, pan sizes, cooking temperatures, timings, and much more. Why? So when you make one of them, it will taste delicious and work without a hitch.

Pecan Salmon with Sweet Pepper Mayo

Prep: 25 min. Chill: 30 min. Cook: 6 min.

When we went Fishing for Favorites in our September 1999 Prize Tested Recipes® contest, one catch of the month was this stellar salmon topped with an enticing topping of mango chutney, mayonnaise, and roasted red peppers.

- 1½   lb. fresh or frozen skinless salmon fillet
- ¾   cup finely chopped pecans
- ½   cup fine dry bread crumbs
- ½   to 1 tsp. ground black pepper
- ½   tsp. salt
- 1   egg
- 2   Tbsp. water
- ⅓   cup all-purpose flour
- 1   recipe Sweet Pepper Mayo (below)
- 2   Tbsp. cooking oil

1. Thaw fish, if frozen. Rinse fish; pat dry with paper towels. Slice fish in half horizontally so it is of even thickness (about ½ inch thick). Cut fish into 6 equal portions.

2. In a shallow dish, combine pecans, bread crumbs, black pepper, and salt. In another shallow dish, beat together egg and water; place flour in a third shallow dish. Coat each fish portion with flour, dip into egg mixture, and finally into pecan mixture. Place portions on a large plate; cover and chill for up to 30 minutes while preparing Sweet Pepper Mayo.

3. In a 12-inch nonstick skillet, heat oil over medium-high heat. Add fish; cook for 6 to 7 minutes or until fish flakes easily when tested with a fork, turning once. (Reduce heat as necessary during cooking to prevent overbrowning.) Serve with Sweet Pepper Mayo. Makes 6 servings.

Sweet Pepper Mayo: Drain ½ of a 7-ounce jar roasted red sweet peppers (about ½ cup); pat dry with paper towels. Coarsely chop. In a small serving bowl, stir together the chopped sweet peppers, ¼ cup mayonnaise or salad dressing, 1 tablespoon finely chopped mango chutney, 1 tablespoon lemon juice, ¼ teaspoon garlic salt, and ⅛ teaspoon cayenne pepper.

Nutrition facts per serving: 379 cal., 26 g total fat (4 g sat. fat), 61 mg chol., 457 mg sodium, 17 g carbo., 2 g fiber, 20 g pro.

A Rainbow of Salmon

In the 1930s and 1940s when cooks talked about salmon, it usually meant the canned variety. After World War II, however, salmon became more available. Depending on where you live and the time of year, you can find all types of salmon. Atlantic salmon, which is higher in oil than other types, varies in color from pink to red to orange. Chinook or king salmon is the most expensive variety and can be pinkish orange to white. Coho or silver salmon is firm-textured and pink to red-orange. And, sockeye or red salmon is the type most used for canned salmon.

Salmon Patties

Start to finish: 30 min.

Cooks of the 1930s served canned salmon every which way, including shaping it into croquettes. This modern-day salmon patty is a tasty descendant of that old-fashioned dish.

- 1   egg
- ¼   cup milk
- ¼   cup chopped green onion
- 1   Tbsp. snipped fresh dill or 1 tsp. dried dill weed
- ¼   tsp. pepper
- 1   14¾-oz. can salmon, drained, flaked, and skin and bones removed
- ¼   cup fine dry bread crumbs
- 1   Tbsp. cooking oil
- 1   recipe Honey Mustard Sauce (below) (optional)

1. In a medium bowl, beat egg; stir in milk, green onion, dill, and pepper. Add salmon and bread crumbs; mix well. Form mixture into eight ½-inch-thick patties. In a large skillet, cook patties in hot oil over medium-low heat about 6 minutes or until golden, turning once. If desired, serve with Honey Mustard Sauce. Serves 4.

Honey Mustard Sauce: In a small bowl, stir together ¼ cup mayonnaise or salad dressing and 1 tablespoon honey mustard. Cover and chill until serving time.

Nutrition facts per serving: 231 cal., 12 g total fat (3 g sat. fat), 112 mg chol., 656 mg sodium, 6 g carbo., 0 g fiber, 24 g pro.

Catfish with a Crunch

Catfish with a Crunch

Start to finish: 25 min.

A pretzel coating adds a a new twist to traditional fried catfish. Serve it with coleslaw on the side.

- 4 **4-oz. fresh or frozen catfish fillets, about ½ inch thick**
- 1 **egg**
- 3 **Tbsp. Dijon-style mustard**
- 1 **Tbsp. milk**
- ¼ **tsp. pepper**
- ¼ **cup all-purpose flour**
- 1 **cup coarsely crushed pretzels**
- 2 **Tbsp. cooking oil**
  Cooked red onion (optional)
  Lemon slices (optional)

1. Thaw fish, if frozen. Rinse fish; pat dry with paper towels. In a shallow dish, combine the egg, Dijon-style mustard, milk, and pepper, beating with a whisk or fork until smooth. Place flour in another shallow dish. Place coarsely crushed pretzels in a third shallow dish.

2. Coat each fish fillet with flour. Dip into the mustard mixture, then into the crushed pretzels. In a large skillet, cook fish in hot oil over medium heat for 6 to 8 minutes or until golden and fish flakes easily when tested with a fork. (Reduce heat as necessary during cooking to prevent overbrowning.) If desired, serve with red onion and lemon slices. Makes 4 servings.

Nutrition facts per serving: 362 cal., 18 g total fat (4 g sat. fat), 107 mg chol., 537 mg sodium, 25 g carbo., 1 g fiber, 23 g pro.

Red Pepper and Snapper Soup

Prep: 25 min. Cook: 20 + 5 min.

When the weather turns chilly, ladle up bowls of this sassy 1999 Fishing for Favorites prizewinning soup.

- 1¼ **lb. fresh or frozen skinless red snapper, orange roughy, or other firm-fleshed fish fillets**
- 3 **medium red sweet peppers, coarsely chopped (2¼ cups)**
- 1 **cup chopped shallots or onions**
- 2 **Tbsp. olive oil**
- 3 **14-oz. cans reduced-sodium chicken broth (5¼ cups total)**
- ¼ **tsp. salt**
- ¼ **tsp. ground black pepper**
- ⅛ **tsp. cayenne pepper**
- ½ **cup snipped fresh flat-leaf parsley**

1. Thaw fish, if frozen. Rinse fish; pat dry with paper towels. Cut fish into 1-inch pieces; set aside. In a large saucepan or Dutch oven, cook sweet peppers and shallots in hot oil for 5 minutes. Carefully add *1 can* of the broth. Bring to boiling; reduce heat. Cover and simmer about 20 minutes or until sweet peppers are very tender. Remove from heat; cool slightly.

2. Pour *half* of the sweet pepper mixture into a blender. Cover and blend until nearly smooth. Pour into a medium bowl. Repeat with remaining sweet pepper mixture. Return all to saucepan or Dutch oven. Add remaining broth, the salt, black pepper, and cayenne pepper. Bring to boiling; reduce heat.

3. Add fish to broth mixture. Cover; simmer about 5 minutes or until fish flakes easily when tested with a fork; stir once or twice. Stir in parsley. Makes 5 servings.

Nutrition facts per serving: 223 cal., 8 g total fat (1 g sat. fat), 42 mg chol., 859 mg sodium, 10 g carbo., 0 g fiber, 27 g pro.

Sesame-Teriyaki Sea Bass

Start to finish: 20 min.

This teriyaki-glazed fish recipe delivers big—a quick recipe that's nutritious and low in fat with lots of knock-your-socks-off flavor!

- 4 **4-oz. fresh or frozen sea bass fillets, ½ to 1 inch thick**
- ¼ **tsp. pepper**
- 3 **Tbsp. soy sauce**
- 3 **Tbsp. sweet rice wine (mirin)**
- 2 **Tbsp. dry white wine**
- 1½ **tsp. sugar**
- 1½ **tsp. honey**
- 2 **tsp. cooking oil**
- 1 **Tbsp. sesame seeds or black sesame seeds**

1. Thaw fish, if frozen. Rinse; pat dry with paper towels. Cut into 8 pieces. Sprinkle with pepper; set aside.

2. For glaze, in a small saucepan, combine soy sauce, rice wine, white wine, sugar, and honey. Bring to boiling; reduce heat. Simmer, uncovered, about 10 minutes or until glaze is reduced to ¼ cup; set aside.

3. Meanwhile, in a large nonstick skillet, heat the oil over medium heat. Add fish fillets. Cook fish until it is golden and flakes easily when tested with a fork, turning once. (Allow 6 to 8 minutes for ½-inch-thick fillets or 10 to 12 minutes for 1-inch-thick fillets.) Drain on paper towels. To serve, transfer fish to a serving platter. Drizzle glaze over fillets. Sprinkle with sesame seeds. Serves 4.

Nutrition facts per serving: 185 cal., 6 g total fat (1 g sat. fat), 47 mg chol., 851 mg sodium, 6 g carbo., 0 g fiber, 22 g pro.

What-a-Catch Citrus Scallops

Steamed Fish with Vegetables

Start to finish: 20 min.

As readers requested simpler, healthier recipes made with fresh ingredients, we responded. This dish for two is made with only 5 ingredients—all fresh—and has only 2 grams of fat per serving.

- 2   6-oz. fresh or frozen orange roughy or other fish fillets
  Whole fresh basil leaves
- 2   tsp. shredded fresh ginger
- 1   cup thinly sliced green or red sweet peppers
- 8   oz. fresh asparagus spears

1. Thaw fish, if frozen. Rinse fish; pat dry with paper towels. Using a sharp knife, make bias cuts about ¾ inch apart into the fish fillets. (Do not cut completely through fish.) Tuck *1 or 2* basil leaves into *each* cut. Rub fillets with ginger.

2. Place the sweet peppers and asparagus in a steamer basket. Place fish on top of vegetables. Place basket into a large, deep saucepan or wok over 1 inch of boiling water. Cover and steam for 6 to 8 minutes or until fish flakes easily when tested with a fork. Makes 2 servings.

Nutrition facts per serving: 254 cal., 2 g total fat (0 g sat. fat), 37 mg chol., 61 mg sodium, 36 g carbo., 3 g fiber, 21 g pro.

What-a-Catch Citrus Scallops

Start to finish: 35 min.

Every once in a while we like to try something a little exotic, such as sea scallops with haricots vert, blood oranges, and fresh tarragon—all served with Israeli couscous.

- 1   lb. fresh or frozen jumbo sea scallops
- 2   Tbsp. all-purpose flour
- ¼   tsp. salt
- ¼   tsp. pepper
- 1   cup Israeli couscous* (about 5 oz.) or couscous
- 2   Tbsp. cooking oil
- 2   cups chicken broth
- 8   oz. fresh haricots vert (long, thin green beans) or thin green beans
- 2   Tbsp. butter or margarine
- 1½ cups orange-tangerine juice or orange juice
- 1   Tbsp. snipped fresh tarragon or ¾ tsp. dried tarragon, crushed
- 2   small blood oranges, clementines, or other oranges, peeled and sliced
  Fresh tarragon sprigs (optional)
  Orange wedges (optional)

1. Thaw scallops, if frozen. Rinse scallops; pat dry with paper towels. In a plastic bag, combine flour, ⅛ *teaspoon* of the salt, and ⅛ *teaspoon* of the pepper. Add scallops and toss to coat; set aside.

2. In a medium saucepan, cook and stir Israeli couscous, if using, in hot oil over medium heat for 3 to 4 minutes or until couscous is slightly golden brown. Carefully add chicken broth. Bring to boiling; reduce heat. Cover and simmer for 8 to 10 minutes or until Israeli couscous is tender. (If using regular couscous, prepare according to package directions using the amount of chicken broth specified.)

3. Meanwhile, in a covered medium saucepan, cook haricots vert or green beans in a small amount of boiling water for 10 to 15 minutes or until crisp-tender. Drain; keep warm.

4. In a large skillet, cook scallops in hot butter over medium-high heat about 4 minutes or until golden brown and opaque in center, turning once. (Reduce heat as necessary during cooking to prevent overbrowning.) Remove scallops from skillet and transfer to a baking sheet, reserving drippings. Place scallops in a warm oven.

5. Add juice and snipped or dried tarragon to skillet. Bring to boiling, stirring browned bits from bottom of skillet. Reduce heat. Cook, uncovered, about 7 minutes or until sauce is reduced by half (¾ cup) and slightly thickened. Season with remaining ⅛ teaspoon salt and remaining ⅛ teaspoon pepper. Cool slightly. Place sauce in four individual glasses or cups.

6. Divide cooked couscous, haricots vert, and orange slices among four dinner plates. Place the scallops next to couscous mixture. Serve with sauce. If desired, garnish sauce with tarragon sprigs and orange wedges. Makes 4 servings.

*Test Kitchen Tip: Israeli couscous, sometimes called pearl pasta, looks like tiny round pearls. You'll find it at specialty food stores and larger supermarkets.

Nutrition facts per serving: 512 cal., 19 g total fat (5 g sat. fat), 52 mg chol., 1,204 mg sodium, 60 g carbo., 5 g fiber, 28 g pro.

Pasta with Shrimp

Start to finish: 25 min.

Pasta was everywhere in the 1990s, including on our pages. This favorite from the late 1990s tosses together asparagus, shrimp, and angel hair pasta with a splash of wine and a whisper of garlic.

- 8   oz. fresh or frozen shrimp in shells
- 8   thin stalks fresh asparagus
- ½   of a 9-oz. pkg. refrigerated angel hair pasta
- 2   cloves garlic, minced
- 1   tsp. olive oil
- 3   medium plum tomatoes, seeded and coarsely chopped
- 2   Tbsp. dry white wine
- ⅛   tsp. salt
- ⅛   tsp. pepper
- 2   tsp. butter or margarine
- 2   Tbsp. finely shredded fresh basil

1. Thaw shrimp, if frozen. Peel and devein shrimp, leaving tails intact if desired. Rinse shrimp; pat dry with paper towels. Set aside.

2. Trim woody ends off asparagus. Remove tips and set aside. Bias-slice the stalks into 1- to 1½-inch pieces. Set aside. Cook pasta according to package directions; drain. Return pasta to saucepan; cover and keep warm.

3. Meanwhile, in a medium skillet, cook and stir garlic in hot oil over medium heat for 15 seconds. Add tomatoes; cook and stir for 2 minutes.

4. Add the asparagus stalks, wine, salt, and pepper. Cook, uncovered, for 3 minutes. Stir in shrimp and asparagus tips. Cook, uncovered, for 2 to 3 minutes more or until shrimp turn opaque. Stir in butter until melted.

5. To serve, add the shrimp mixture and basil to pasta; toss gently to coat. Makes 2 servings.

Nutrition facts per serving: 379 cal., 10 g total fat (4 g sat. fat), 208 mg chol., 361 mg sodium, 41 g carbo., 3 g fiber, 28 g pro.

Pasta with Shrimp

Shrimp Creole

Prep: 25 min. Cook: 15 + 2 min.

Shrimp Creole has a long history with us. In the 1937 edition of the *Better Homes and Gardens® Cook Book*, it called for canned shrimp, heavy cream, and tomato sauce. This recipe from the current edition uses fresh shrimp and vegetables for a fresher flavor.

    1 lb. fresh or frozen medium shrimp in
       shells
    1 medium onion, chopped
    ½ cup chopped celery
    ½ cup chopped green sweet pepper
    2 cloves garlic, minced
    2 Tbsp. butter or margarine
    1 14½-oz. can diced tomatoes, undrained
    2 Tbsp. snipped fresh parsley
    ½ tsp. salt
    ½ tsp. paprika
    ⅛ to ¼ tsp. cayenne pepper
    1 bay leaf
    ⅓ cup cold water
    2 tsp. cornstarch
       Hot cooked rice

1. Thaw shrimp, if frozen. Peel and devein shrimp. Rinse shrimp; pat dry with paper towels. Set aside.

2. In a large skillet, cook onion, celery, sweet pepper, and garlic in hot butter over medium heat about 5 minutes or until tender. Stir in undrained tomatoes, parsley, salt, paprika, cayenne pepper, and bay leaf. Bring to boiling; reduce heat. Cover; simmer for 15 minutes.

3. Discard bay leaf. In a small bowl, stir together cold water and cornstarch. Stir cornstarch mixture and shrimp into tomato mixture. Cook and stir until thickened and bubbly; cook and stir about 2 minutes more or until shrimp turn opaque. Serve over rice. Makes 4 servings.

Nutrition facts per serving: 275 cal., 7 g total fat (4 g sat. fat), 53 mg chol., 575 mg sodium, 33 g carbo., 2 g fiber, 18 g pro.

Fish Creole: Prepare as directed, except substitute 12 ounces fresh or frozen fish fillets for the shrimp. Thaw fish, if frozen. Rinse fish and cut into 1-inch pieces. Add fish to the tomato mixture after the mixture is thickened and bubbly. Cook and stir about 3 minutes more or until fish flakes easily when tested with a fork.

Nutrition facts per serving: 261 cal., 7 g total fat (4 g sat. fat), 136 mg chol., 659 mg sodium, 32 g carbo., 2 g fiber, 17 g pro.

> We don't give a second thought to the supply of shrimp and other fresh seafood at today's fish counters. However, in the 1940s, it was plentiful only on the coasts. So it took until the 1950s, when seafood became readily available everywhere, for it to capture the imagination of heartland cooks.

Thai Shrimp and Noodles

Start to finish: 40 min.

Americans seek out all types of Asian dishes, enjoying them in restaurants and at home. This 1995 Prize Tested Recipes® winner is a hit because of its ease and exotic ginger-sesame flavor.

    2 lb. fresh or frozen shrimp in shells
    8 oz. dried spaghetti, broken
    5 cups broccoli florets (about 12 oz. florets)
    ⅓ cup creamy peanut butter
    ¼ cup soy sauce
    3 Tbsp. rice vinegar
    2 Tbsp. toasted sesame oil
    1 Tbsp. chile oil*
    1 Tbsp. grated fresh ginger
    3 cloves garlic, minced
    4 green onions, chopped
    ⅓ cup chopped cashews or almonds

1. Thaw shrimp, if frozen. Peel and devein the shrimp, leaving tails intact if desired. Rinse shrimp.

2. In a Dutch oven, bring a large amount of water to boiling. Add spaghetti; cook for 4 minutes. Add broccoli; cook for 2 minutes. Add shrimp; cook for 2 to 3 minutes more or until shrimp turn opaque and spaghetti is done.

3. Meanwhile, in a small bowl, stir together peanut butter and soy sauce. Stir in vinegar, sesame oil, chile oil, ginger, and garlic. Drain spaghetti mixture; return to Dutch oven. Add peanut butter mixture, green onion, and nuts. Toss gently to coat. Makes 6 servings.

*Test Kitchen Tip: If you can't find chile oil at your supermarket or local Asian food store, substitute 1 tablespoon cooking oil plus a dash of bottled hot pepper sauce for the 1 tablespoon chile oil.

Nutrition facts per serving: 495 cal., 21 g total fat (4 g sat. fat), 186 mg chol., 959 mg sodium, 41 g carbo., 5 g fiber, 38 g pro.

Macaroni-Cheese Puff

Prep: 30 min. Bake: 25 min.

For a change of pace, make this easy meatless dish with Swiss cheese instead of American cheese.

- ½ cup dried elbow macaroni
- 1½ cups milk
- 6 oz. process American cheese slices, torn
- 3 Tbsp. butter or margarine
- 3 egg yolks
- 1 cup soft bread crumbs (about 1½ slices)
- ¼ cup diced pimiento, well drained
- 1 Tbsp. snipped fresh parsley
- 1 Tbsp. finely chopped onion
- 3 egg whites
- ¼ tsp. cream of tartar

1. Preheat oven to 325°F. In a medium saucepan, cook macaroni according to package directions; drain. Set aside.

2. Meanwhile, in a large saucepan, combine the milk, cheese, and butter. Cook and stir over low heat until cheese is melted. Remove from heat.

3. In a small mixing bowl, beat the egg yolks with a rotary beater. Stir about *½ cup* of the hot cheese mixture into the egg yolks. Pour egg yolk mixture into remaining cheese mixture in saucepan, stirring to combine. Add the drained macaroni, bread crumbs, pimiento, parsley, and onion. Set aside.

4. In a medium mixing bowl, beat egg whites and cream of tartar with an electric mixer on medium to high speed until stiff peaks form (tips stand straight). Gently fold beaten egg whites into macaroni mixture. Pour mixture into six ungreased 1-cup soufflé dishes or an ungreased 2-quart soufflé dish. Bake for 25 to 30 minutes for 1-cup soufflé dishes or about 45 minutes for 2-quart soufflé dish or until puffed and browned. Serve immediately. Makes 6 servings.

Nutrition facts per serving: 284 cal., 19 g total fat (11 g sat. fat), 154 mg chol., 565 mg sodium, 15 g carbo., 1 g fiber, 13 g pro.

Yesterday

If your family thinks the only way to make macaroni and cheese is from a box, introduce everyone to this golden oldie from 1968. Its feather-light, soufflélike quality sets it apart from other baked versions.

Company-Special Macaroni And Cheese

Prep: 25 min. Bake: 25 min. Stand: 10 min.

Port du Salut, a French cheese, is mild and smooth with a pale yellow color and an orange rind.

12 oz. dried tricolor bow tie pasta, penne, rigatoni, and/or other short tubular pasta (4 cups)
2 cloves garlic, minced
1 Tbsp. butter or margarine
2 Tbsp. all-purpose flour
2 cups milk
8 oz. Port du Salut or other semisoft cheese, shredded (2 cups)
1 cup shredded American cheese (4 oz.)
2 Tbsp. snipped fresh oregano or 1 teaspoon dried oregano, crushed
½ cup soft light rye or wheat bread crumbs

1. Preheat oven to 350°F. Cook pasta according to package directions. Drain. Meanwhile, in a large saucepan, cook garlic in hot butter over medium heat for 30 seconds. Stir in flour. Add milk. Cook and stir until thickened and bubbly; reduce heat. Add shredded Port du Salut and American cheeses. Stir until melted. Remove from heat. Stir in cooked pasta and oregano. Spoon mixture into an ungreased 1½- to 2-quart casserole. Top with bread crumbs.

2. Bake, uncovered, for 25 minutes. Let stand for 10 minutes before serving. Makes 6 servings.

Nutrition facts per serving: 508 cal., 22 g total fat (13 g sat. fat), 80 mg chol., 613 mg sodium, 51 g carbo., 2 g fiber, 25 g pro.

Today

You might not think of serving old-fashioned macaroni and cheese for a dinner party, but we spiffed up the ultimate comfort food with bow tie pasta and Port du Salut cheese for a fabulous casual dinner for six.

Choose-a-Cheese Soufflé

Prep: 40 min. Stand: 30 min. Bake: 40 min.

In the 1930s, *Better Homes and Gardens®* routinely featured recipes from famous personalities. One of our earliest soufflés was a cheese version favored by then Vice President Henry A. Wallace. In the years since, soufflé recipes have come and gone, but we especially like this 1990s recipe.

4	eggs
2	cups shredded aged goat cheese, Havarti, or montasio cheese
2	tsp. snipped fresh thyme or ½ tsp. dried thyme, crushed
¼	cup butter or margarine
¼	cup all-purpose flour
⅛	tsp. cayenne pepper
1	cup milk
1	recipe Honey-Cider Pears (below)

1. Separate eggs into two bowls; cover both bowls with plastic wrap. Let stand at room temperature for 30 minutes. In another small bowl, toss shredded cheese with thyme; cover and set aside.

2. Preheat oven to 350°F. In a medium saucepan, melt the ¼ cup butter; stir in flour and cayenne pepper. Add milk all at once. Cook and stir over medium heat just until thickened and bubbly. Remove from heat. Add cheese mixture, a little at a time, stirring just until melted.

3. In a bowl, beat egg yolks with a fork until smooth. Gradually stir cheese sauce into yolks. Cool 5 minutes.

4. In a large bowl, beat egg whites with an electric mixer on medium to high speed until stiff peaks form (tips stand straight). Gently fold *about half* of the beaten egg whites into the cheese mixture; gently fold that mixture into remaining egg whites in the bowl. Pour into an ungreased 1½-quart soufflé dish. Bake about 40 minutes or until a knife inserted near center comes out clean.

5. Meanwhile, Prepare Honey-Cider Pears. Serve soufflé immediately with Honey-Cider Pears. Makes 6 servings.

Honey-Cider Pears: In a medium skillet, melt 1 tablespoon butter over medium heat. Add 2 medium ripe (yet firm) pears, cored and thinly sliced, and 2 large shallots, very thinly sliced (¼ cup). Cook, uncovered, for 4 to 5 minutes or until shallots are tender, stirring often. Add 1 tablespoon cider vinegar, ½ teaspoon honey, and dash salt; cook and stir for 2 minutes more.

Nutrition facts per serving: 377 cal., 29 g total fat (8 g sat. fat), 219 mg chol., 376 mg sodium, 16 g carbo., 2 g fiber, 15 g pro.

Herbed Egg and Cheese Casserole

Prep: 20 min. Bake: 25 min.

Hard-cooked egg casseroles are less popular now than in the 1930s and 1940s. But what may seem old-fashioned deserves a second look. This 1999 brunch dish does great-grandma's casserole one better by adding herbs, sharp cheddar, and bacon.

¼	cup butter or margarine
¼	cup all-purpose flour
¼	tsp. dried thyme, crushed
¼	tsp. dried basil, crushed
¼	tsp. dried marjoram, crushed
1	12-oz. can (1½ cups) evaporated milk or 1⅓ cups half-and-half or light cream
⅔	cup milk
2	cups shredded sharp cheddar cheese (8 oz.)
18	eggs, hard-cooked and thinly sliced
8	oz. bacon, crisp-cooked, drained, and crumbled
¼	cup finely snipped fresh parsley
1	cup fine dry bread crumbs
¼	cup butter or margarine, melted

1. Preheat oven to 350°F. In a medium saucepan, melt ¼ cup butter. Stir in flour, thyme, basil, and marjoram. Stir in evaporated milk and milk all at once. Cook and stir over medium heat until thickened and bubbly. Remove from heat. Gradually add cheese to sauce, stirring after each addition until cheese is melted.

2. Lightly grease a 3-quart rectangular baking dish. Layer *half* of the sliced eggs, *half* of the bacon, and *half* of the parsley in dish. Pour *half* of the sauce over all. Repeat layers, ending with sauce.

3. In a small bowl, stir together bread crumbs and ¼ cup melted butter; sprinkle onto casserole. Bake for 25 to 30 minutes or until heated through. Makes 12 servings.

Nutrition facts per serving: 372 cal., 27 g total fat (13 g sat. fat), 374 mg chol., 472 mg sodium, 13 g carbo., 0 g fiber, 20 g pro.

Herbed Egg and
Cheese Casserole

Our Favorite Quiche Lorraine
Prep: 30 min. Bake: 50 min. Stand: 10 min.

Quiche was the darling of the 1970s, appearing in restaurants and on magazine pages in a variety of flavors. Our Test Kitchen chose this as our best.

- 1 **recipe Pastry for Single-Crust Pie (below)**
- 8 **slices bacon**
- 1 **medium onion, thinly sliced**
- 4 **eggs, beaten**
- 1 **cup half-and-half or light cream**
- 1 **cup milk**
- ¼ **tsp. salt**
  Dash ground nutmeg
- 1½ **cups shredded Swiss cheese (6 oz.)**
- 1 **Tbsp. all-purpose flour**
  Tomato wedges (optional)
  Fresh parsley (optional)

1. Preheat oven to 450°F. Prepare Pastry for a Single-Crust Pie. Line the unpricked pastry shell with a double thickness of heavy-duty foil. Bake for 8 minutes. Remove foil. Bake for 4 to 5 minutes more or until pastry is set and dry. Remove from oven. Reduce oven temperature to 325°F. (Pie shell should still be hot when filling is added; do not partially bake pastry shell ahead of time.)

2. Meanwhile, in a large skillet, cook bacon until crisp. Drain, reserving *2 tablespoons* of the drippings in skillet. Crumble bacon finely; set aside. Cook sliced onion in reserved drippings over medium heat until tender; drain.

3. In a medium bowl, stir together the eggs, half-and-half, milk, salt, and nutmeg. Stir in the crumbled bacon and cooked onion. In a medium bowl, toss together shredded cheese and flour. Add cheese mixture to egg mixture; mix well.

4. Pour egg mixture into the hot, baked pastry shell. Bake for 50 to 60 minutes or until a knife inserted near the center comes out clean. If necessary, cover edge of crust with foil to prevent overbrowning. Let stand for 10 minutes before serving. If desired, garnish with tomato wedges and parsley. Makes 6 servings.

Pastry for a Single-Crust Pie: In a medium bowl, stir together 1¼ cups all-purpose flour and ¼ teaspoon salt. Using a pastry blender, cut in ⅓ cup shortening until pieces are pea-size. Sprinkle 1 tablespoon cold water over part of the flour mixture; gently toss with a fork. Push moistened dough to the side of the bowl. Add additional cold water, 1 tablespoon at a time, until all is moistened (use 4 or 5 tablespoons cold water total). Form dough into a ball.

On a lightly floured surface, use your hands to slightly flatten dough. Roll dough from center to edge into a circle about 12 inches in diameter. To transfer pastry, wrap it around the rolling pin. Unroll pastry onto a 9-inch pie plate; ease pastry into pie plate, being careful not to stretch pastry. Trim pastry to ½ inch beyond edge of pie plate. Fold under extra pastry. Crimp edge as desired. Do not prick pastry.

Nutrition facts per serving: 523 cal., 37 g total fat (16 g sat. fat), 199 mg chol., 517 mg sodium, 25 g carbo., 1 g fiber, 21 g pro.

Cheese Frittata with Mushrooms and Dill
Prep: 30 min. Stand: 5 min.

This no-fuss frittata makes a delicious meatless headliner for breakfast or supper.

- 6 **eggs**
- ⅓ **cup shredded Gruyère or Swiss cheese**
- ¼ **cup water**
- ¼ **tsp. salt**
- ⅛ **tsp. pepper**
- 2 **Tbsp. butter or margarine**
- 1½ **cups thinly sliced fresh mushrooms (such as shiitake, chanterelle, brown, or button)**
- ¼ **cup sliced green onions**
- 1 **Tbsp. snipped fresh flat-leaf parsley**
- 1 **Tbsp. snipped fresh dill**

1. In a medium mixing bowl, whisk together eggs, cheese, the water, salt, and pepper; set aside.

2. In a 10-inch nonstick skillet, melt butter over medium heat. Add mushrooms; cook and stir for 4 to 5 minutes or until tender. Stir in the green onions, parsley, and dill.

3. Pour the egg mixture into skillet over mushroom mixture. Cook, uncovered, over medium heat. As the egg mixture begins to set, run a spatula around edge of skillet, lifting egg mixture so the uncooked portion flows underneath. Continue cooking and lifting edge until the egg mixture is almost set, about 3 minutes (surface will be moist). Remove from heat.

4. Cover and let stand about 5 minutes or until top is set. Cut into wedges. Makes 4 servings.

Nutrition facts per serving: 222 cal., 18 g total fat (8 g sat. fat), 347 mg chol., 341 mg sodium, 3 g carbo., 0 g fiber, 14 g pro.

Spinach and Cheese Omelet

Start to finish: 20 min.

The *Better Homes and Gardens*® omelet recipes from the 1930s simply listed a sketchy technique followed by suggestions for fillings. These days, we give you a little more to go on.

Spinach and Cheese Omelet

- 1 **recipe Red Pepper Relish (below)**
- 4 **eggs or 1 cup refrigerated or frozen egg product, thawed**
  Dash salt
  Dash cayenne pepper
  Nonstick cooking spray
- ¼ **cup shredded sharp cheddar cheese (1 oz.)**
- 1 **Tbsp. snipped fresh chives, flat-leaf parsley, or chervil**
- 1 **cup small fresh spinach leaves**

1. Prepare Red Pepper Relish; set aside. In a large mixing bowl, combine eggs, salt, and cayenne pepper. Using a rotary beater or wire whisk, beat the egg mixture until frothy.

2. Coat an unheated 8-inch nonstick skillet with flared sides with nonstick cooking spray. Heat skillet over medium heat.

3. Pour egg mixture into hot skillet. Reduce heat to medium. Immediately begin stirring egg mixture gently but continuously with a wooden spoon or plastic spatula until mixture resembles small pieces of cooked egg surrounded by liquid egg. Stop stirring. Cook for 30 to 60 seconds more or until egg mixture is set but shiny.

4. Sprinkle with cheese and chives. Top with *¾ cup* of the spinach and *2 tablespoons* of the Red Pepper Relish. Fold one side of omelet partially over filling. Top with the remaining ¼ cup spinach and 1 tablespoon of the relish. (Cover and chill the remaining relish for up to 3 days. Serve with grilled or broiled burgers or fish.) Cut the omelet in half. Makes 2 servings.

Red Pepper Relish: In a small bowl, combine ⅔ cup chopped red sweet pepper, 2 tablespoons finely chopped onion, 1 tablespoon cider vinegar, and ¼ teaspoon ground black pepper.

Nutrition facts per serving: 214 cal., 15 g total fat (6 g sat. fat), 440 mg chol., 303 mg sodium, 3 g carbo., 2 g fiber, 17 g pro.

Easy-Does-It Eggs

Eggs have had their ups and downs. Throughout the 1930s, 1940s, and 1950s, our cost-conscious readers used them to create nutritious, economical meals for their families. Later, some folks shied away from eggs because of health concerns over their cholesterol content. Today, health experts are reevaluating eggs, and time-strapped cooks see them as a great way to create quick meals.

Egg-Salad Sandwiches

Start to finish: 15 min.

Some basics never go out of style. Take egg salad—it tastes just as good today as it did 60 years ago. This up-to-the-minute version has a bonus—Greek-style and California-style options.

    4   hard-cooked eggs, chopped
    2   Tbsp. finely chopped green onion
    1   Tbsp. diced pimiento
    2   Tbsp. mayonnaise or salad dressing
    2   tsp. yellow mustard
        Salt
        Pepper
    4   slices bread, 2 small pita bread rounds
        (halved crosswise), or 2 bagels (split)
        Lettuce leaves

1. In a medium bowl, combine chopped eggs, green onion, and pimiento. Stir in mayonnaise and mustard. Add salt and pepper to taste. Spread egg mixture onto 2 slices of the bread, in pita halves, or onto bagel bottoms. Top with lettuce and, if not using pitas, remaining bread slices or bagel tops. Makes 2 servings.

Nutrition facts per serving: 396 cal., 24 g total fat (5 g sat. fat), 433 mg chol., 675 mg sodium, 28 g carbo., 2 g fiber, 17 g pro.

Greek-Style Egg-Salad Sandwiches: Prepare as directed, except omit the pimiento and mustard. Stir ½ cup crumbled feta cheese (2 ounces), ¼ cup finely chopped seeded tomato, and 2 tablespoons sliced pitted ripe olives into egg mixture. Use 6 slices of bread, 3 pitas, or 3 bagels. Makes 3 servings.

Nutrition facts per serving: 381 cal., 22 g total fat (7 g sat. fat), 311 mg chol., 829 mg sodium, 28 g carbo., 2 g fiber, 17 g pro.

California-Style Egg-Salad Sandwiches: Prepare as directed, except omit pimiento. Substitute avocado slices and thin slices of Monterey Jack cheese for lettuce. Makes 2 servings.

Nutrition facts per serving: 573 cal., 39 g total fat (12 g sat. fat), 458 mg chol., 829 mg sodium, 31 g carbo., 4 g fiber, 25 g pro.

> Over the years, the number of recipes perfected in the *Better Homes and Gardens*® Test Kitchen has steadily risen. Currently it's in the thousands—totaling more than 60,000 recipes published over 75 years.

Egg Salad with Fresh Veggies

Prep: 25 min. Chill: 4 to 24 hr.

To satisfy our readers' desire for something different, yet familiar, our editors keep giving old standbys new twists. This salad starts with basic egg salad and dolls it up with zucchini, creamy Italian salad dressing, and Dijon-style mustard.

    8   hard-cooked eggs, chopped
    1   small zucchini, quartered lengthwise
        and sliced (1 cup)
    ½   cup chopped celery
    ½   cup shredded carrot
    2   Tbsp. finely chopped green onion
    2   Tbsp. diced pimiento
    ⅓   cup mayonnaise or salad dressing
    2   Tbsp. bottled creamy Italian or creamy
        cucumber salad dressing
    1   Tbsp. snipped fresh dill or 1 tsp.
        dried dill weed
    1   tsp. Dijon-style mustard
    ⅛   tsp. salt
        Boston or Bibb lettuce leaves
    1   to 2 Tbsp. milk (optional)

1. In a large bowl, combine chopped eggs, the zucchini, celery, carrot, green onion, and pimiento. Stir in mayonnaise, Italian or cucumber salad dressing, dill, mustard, and salt. Cover and chill for at least 4 hours or up to 24 hours.

2. To serve, line four dinner plates with lettuce leaves. Stir egg mixture gently. If necessary, stir in enough of the milk to moisten. Divide the egg mixture among the lettuce-lined plates. Makes 4 servings.

Nutrition facts per serving: 330 cal., 28 g total fat (6 g sat. fat), 431 mg chol., 405 mg sodium, 5 g carbo., 1 g fiber, 14 g pro.

Eggs Sonoma

Start to finish: 25 min.

This Mexican-inspired breakfast dish did its skillet proud in a 1974 story about the benefits of nonstick, even-cooking cookware. It also was ahead of the times. Decades before breakfast burritos hit fast food restaurant menus, it spiced up our mornings.

⅓   cup seeded, chopped tomato
1   4-oz. can diced green chile peppers, drained*
2   Tbsp. finely chopped celery
1   Tbsp. finely chopped onion
1   tsp. white wine vinegar
½   tsp. sugar
⅛   tsp. dried rosemary, crushed
6   eggs
¼   tsp. salt
     Dash ground black pepper
1   Tbsp. butter or margarine
4   6- to 7-inch corn or flour tortillas
     Shredded cheddar or Monterey Jack cheese (optional)
     Edible flowers (optional)

1. In a small bowl, combine the tomato, chile peppers, celery, onion, vinegar, sugar, and rosemary; set aside. In a medium mixing bowl, combine eggs, salt, and black pepper; beat with a whisk or rotary beater until well mixed. Add tomato mixture to egg mixture.

2. In a large skillet, melt butter over medium heat; pour in egg mixture. Cook over medium heat, without stirring, until mixture begins to set on bottom and around edge. With a spatula or large spoon, lift and fold the partially cooked egg mixture so the uncooked portion flows underneath. Continue cooking over medium heat for 2 to 3 minutes or until egg mixture is cooked through but is still glossy and moist. Remove from heat immediately.

3. Meanwhile, heat tortillas according to package directions. To serve, top each tortilla with some of the egg mixture. If desired, sprinkle with cheese. If desired, garnish with edible flowers. Makes 4 servings.

*Test Kitchen Tip: If you like especially fiery food, substitute ⅓ cup chopped jalapeño chile peppers (tip, page 32) for the chopped green chile peppers.

Nutrition facts per serving: 210 cal., 11 g total fat (4 g sat. fat), 327 mg chol., 430 mg sodium, 16 g carbo., 2 g fiber, 11 g pro.

Eggs Sonoma

Tortilla and Black Bean Casserole

Prep: 25 min. Bake: 30 min. Stand: 10 min.

This colorful casserole won $1,000 in the Go-Along category of our 1992 Great American Barbecue Contest. Although it originally was a side dish for 10, we think it makes a standout entrée for six.

 2   large onions, chopped
1½   cups chopped green sweet pepper
 1   14½-oz. can diced tomatoes or whole tomatoes, undrained, cut up
 ¾   cup bottled picante sauce
 2   cloves garlic, minced
 2   tsp. ground cumin
 2   15-oz. cans black beans or red kidney beans, rinsed and drained
12   6-inch corn tortillas
 2   cups shredded reduced-fat Monterey Jack or cheddar cheese (8 oz.)
 2   cups shredded lettuce (optional)
 2   medium tomatoes, chopped (optional)
     Sliced green onions (optional)
     Sliced pitted ripe olives (optional)
 ½   cup dairy sour cream or plain yogurt (optional)

1. In a large skillet, combine onions, sweet pepper, undrained canned tomatoes, picante sauce, garlic, and cumin. Bring to boiling; reduce heat. Simmer, uncovered, for 10 minutes. Stir in beans.

2. Preheat oven to 350°F. Spread *one-third* of the bean mixture onto bottom of an ungreased 3-quart rectangular baking dish. Top with *half* of the tortillas, overlapping as necessary; sprinkle with *half* of the cheese. Add *another one-third* of the bean mixture, the remaining tortillas, and remaining bean mixture. Cover and bake for 30 to 35 minutes or until heated through. Sprinkle with remaining cheese. Let stand for 10 minutes before serving.

3. If desired, top with lettuce, chopped tomatoes, green onions, and ripe olives. Cut into squares to serve. If desired, serve with sour cream or yogurt. Makes 6 servings.

Nutrition facts per serving: 295 cal., 8 g total fat (4 g sat. fat), 20 mg chol., 689 mg sodium, 46 g carbo., 8 g fiber, 18 g pro.

Spinach-Stuffed Pasta Shells

Prep: 35 min. Bake: 40 min.

If you like lasagna but don't want to feed a crowd, try this mouthwatering alternative. These giant shells are chock-full of a cheesy spinach filling.

 1   recipe Two-Tomato Sauce (below)
 2   eggs
12   dried jumbo shell macaroni or 8 dried manicotti
 1   10-oz. pkg. frozen chopped spinach, thawed
 1   8-oz. pkg. shredded Italian cheese blend (2 cups)
 1   cup ricotta cheese

1. Prepare Tomato Sauce; set aside. Preheat oven to 350°F. Cook pasta according to package directions; drain. Rinse with cold water; drain again.

2. Meanwhile, drain thawed spinach well, pressing out excess liquid.

3. For filling, in a medium bowl, beat eggs; stir in spinach, eggs, *1½ cups* of the Italian cheese blend, and the ricotta cheese. Spoon *about 3 tablespoons* of the filling into *each* jumbo shell or *about ⅓ cup* of the filling into *each* manicotti shell.

4. Place 3 jumbo shells or 2 manicotti shells into each of four individual au gratin dishes. Top with the Tomato Sauce.

5. Cover and bake about 40 minutes or until heated through. Sprinkle with remaining ½ cup Italian cheese blend before serving. Makes 4 servings.

Two-Tomato Sauce: In a medium saucepan melt 1 tablespoon butter or margarine over medium heat. Add ⅓ cup chopped onion; cook until onion is tender. Carefully stir in one 14½-ounce can diced tomatoes with basil, oregano, and garlic, undrained; ¼ cup tomato paste; ¼ teaspoon sugar; dash salt; and dash pepper. Bring to boiling; reduce heat. Simmer, uncovered, about 10 minutes or until desired consistency, stirring often.

Make-ahead directions: Prepare as directed through step 4. Cover casseroles with plastic wrap, then foil. Chill for up to 24 hours or seal, label, and freeze up to 3 months. To serve, remove plastic wrap; cover with foil. Bake chilled shells in a 375°F oven about 45 minutes or until heated through; bake frozen shells in a 375°F oven about 55 minutes or until hot.

Nutrition facts per serving: 509 cal., 28 g total fat (16 g sat. fat), 186 mg chol., 1265 mg sodium, 34 g carbo., 4 g fiber, 31 g pro.

Roasted Vegetable Pizza

Prep: 30 min. Rise: 45 min. Roast: 30 + 10 min.
Bake: 15 min.

This sophisticated version of pizza was a
September 1998 Prize Tested Recipes® contest
winner. If you're in a hurry, skip making the pizza
crusts and substitute small Italian bread shells.

1⅓	cups bread flour or all-purpose flour
1	pkg. active dry yeast
1	tsp. sugar
1	tsp. salt
1¼	cups warm water (120°F to 130°F)
2	tsp. olive oil
1⅓	cups semolina pasta flour
	Bread flour or all-purpose flour
2	medium zucchini, cut into ½-inch cubes
1	medium sweet potato, cut into ½-inch cubes
2	whole tiny new red potatoes, cut into ½-inch cubes
1	cup chopped onion
2	cloves garlic, minced
⅛	tsp. salt (optional)
⅛	tsp. pepper (optional)
1	Tbsp. olive oil
¼	cup snipped fresh basil
1	Tbsp. snipped fresh sage
1	cup purchased chunky pasta sauce
1	cup finely shredded Parmesan cheese (4 oz.)

1. For crust, in a medium bowl, combine the 1⅓ cups
bread or all-purpose flour, the yeast, sugar, and salt. Add
the warm water and the 2 teaspoons olive oil. Beat with
an electric mixer on low speed for 30 seconds, scraping
side of bowl constantly. Beat on high speed for 3 minutes.
Stir in semolina flour. Turn out dough onto a lightly floured
surface. Knead in additional bread flour or all-purpose
flour, if necessary, to make a moderately stiff dough that is
smooth and elastic (6 to 8 minutes total). Shape dough
into a ball. Place in a lightly greased bowl; turn once to
grease the surface. Cover; let rise in a warm place until
double in size (45 to 60 minutes).

2. Meanwhile, preheat oven to 325°F. Grease a
13×9×2-inch baking pan. In the prepared baking pan,
combine vegetable cubes, onion, and garlic. If desired,
sprinkle with salt and pepper. Drizzle the 1 tablespoon
oil over vegetables; toss to coat. Roast, covered, for
30 minutes; stir once. Increase oven temperature to
425°F. Roast, uncovered, for 10 to 15 minutes more or
until tender; stir occasionally. Stir in basil and sage.

3. Grease 2 large baking sheets; set aside. Punch
down dough; divide into 4 portions. Cover and let rest
for 10 minutes. On lightly floured surface, roll each
portion into a 6- to 8-inch round. Build up edges slightly.
Transfer dough rounds to prepared baking sheets.
Spread pasta sauce on crusts. Top sauce with vegetables.
Sprinkle pizzas with Parmesan cheese. Bake for 15 to
20 minutes or until crusts are golden. Makes 4 pizzas.

Nutrition facts per serving: 626 cal., 15 g total fat (1 g sat. fat),
20 mg chol., 934 mg sodium, 98 g carbo., 5 g fiber, 27 g pro.

Fresh Tomato Pizza with Pesto

Start to finish: 15 min.

1	16-oz. Italian bread shell (Boboli)
½	cup purchased pesto
3	medium tomatoes, thinly sliced
1	2¼-oz can sliced, pitted ripe olives, drained (about ⅔ cup)
2	cups shredded Monterey Jack or mozzarella cheese (8 oz.)

1. Preheat oven to 425°F. Place bread shell on a large
pizza pan or baking sheet. Spread pesto onto bread shell.
Arrange tomato slices on top. Sprinkle with olives and
cheese. Bake for 10 to 15 minutes or until cheese melts.
Cut into wedges. Makes 6 servings.

Nutrition facts per serving: 467 cal., 27 g total fat (10 g sat. fat),
42 mg chol., 830 mg sodium, 38 g carbo., 2 g fiber, 22 g pro.

Historians say pizza, an Italian
creation dating back to the 16th
century, may have evolved from
an Egyptian flatbread. It became
popular in the United States
when soldiers returning from
World War II brought home a
taste for the dish. We first
published pizza recipes in the
1950s, but we've been tweaking
and reinventing our take on
pizza ever since.

Chiles Rellenos Casserole

Prep: 20 min. Bake: 15 min. Stand: 5 min.

Although chiles rellenos is a traditional south-of-the-border classic, we gave this version a modern slant by turning it into an easy-fixing casserole.

- 2 **large fresh poblano chile peppers, Anaheim chile peppers, or green sweet peppers**
- 1 **cup shredded Monterey Jack cheese with jalapeño peppers or Mexican-blend cheese (4 oz.)**
- 3 **eggs**
- ¼ **cup milk**
- ⅓ **cup all-purpose flour**
- ½ **tsp. baking powder**
- ¼ **tsp. cayenne pepper**
- ⅛ **tsp. salt**
- ½ **cup shredded Monterey Jack cheese with jalapeño peppers or Mexican-blend cheese (2 oz.)**
  Bottled picante sauce (optional)
  Dairy sour cream (optional)

1. Preheat oven to 450°F. Well grease a 2-quart square baking dish; set aside. Quarter the chile peppers (tip, page 32) or sweet peppers; remove seeds, stems, and veins. Immerse peppers into boiling water for 3 minutes; drain. Invert peppers on paper towels to drain. Place peppers in the prepared baking dish. Top with the 1 cup cheese.

3. In a medium mixing bowl, combine eggs and milk; beat with a rotary beater until well mixed. Add flour, baking powder, cayenne pepper, and salt; beat until smooth. Pour egg mixture over peppers and cheese.

4. Bake, uncovered, about 15 minutes or until a knife inserted into the egg mixture comes out clean. Sprinkle with the ½ cup cheese. Let stand about 5 minutes or until cheese melts. If desired, serve with picante sauce and sour cream. Makes 4 servings.

Nutrition facts per serving: 286 cal., 18 g total fat (10 g sat. fat), 206 mg chol., 466 mg sodium, 14 g carbo., 0 g fiber, 18 g pro.

Lower-Fat Chiles Rellenos Casserole: Prepare as directed, except use reduced-fat Monterey Jack cheese with jalapeño peppers (or reduced-fat plain Monterey jack cheese plus 2 teaspoons chopped fresh jalapeño chile peppers [tip, page 32]) or reduced-fat Mexican-blend cheese. Substitute ¾ cup refrigerated or frozen egg product (thawed) for the eggs and fat-free milk for the milk.

Nutrition facts per serving: 207 cal., 9 g total fat (6 g sat. fat), 30 mg chol., 569 mg sodium, 15 g carbo., 1 g fiber, 18 g pro.

Eggplant Panini

Start to finish: 25 min.

When artisan breads found their way into bakeries everywhere, we added them to our recipes. Here's a sandwich that showcases focaccia (Italian flatbread).

- 1 **cup torn arugula**
- 2 **tsp. red wine vinegar**
- 1 **tsp. olive oil**
- ⅓ **cup seasoned fine dry bread crumbs**
- 2 **Tbsp. grated Pecorino Romano or Parmesan cheese**
- 1 **egg**
- 1 **Tbsp. milk**
- 2 **Tbsp. all-purpose flour**
- ½ **tsp. salt**
- 1 **medium eggplant, cut crosswise into ½-inch-thick slices**
- 1 **Tbsp. olive oil**
- 3 **oz. fresh mozzarella cheese, thinly sliced**
- 1 **12-inch plain or seasoned Italian flatbread (focaccia),* halved horizontally**
- 1 **large tomato, thinly sliced**

Say Cheese During the 1990s, Americans rediscovered cheese. The decade saw a growing variety of domestic and imported cheeses—as well as some terrific locally produced artisan cheeses—pop up at speciality food shops everywhere. Take advantage of this wide selection by serving cheese as part of an appetizer buffet or for dessert. For best results, serve cheese at room temperature. Colder temperatures mute the flavor and aroma and also can affect texture. For example, a creamy cheese like Brie or Camembert will seem tough and rubbery if you serve it cold.

1. In a small bowl, toss together the arugula, vinegar, and the 1 teaspoon oil; set aside. In a shallow dish, stir together the bread crumbs and Pecorino Romano cheese. In another shallow dish, beat together the egg and milk. In a third shallow dish, stir together the flour and salt. Coat each eggplant slice with flour mixture, dip into egg mixture, and finally coat both sides with crumb mixture.

2. In a 12-inch nonstick skillet, heat the 1 tablespoon oil over medium heat. Add eggplant slices; cook for 6 to 8 minutes or until lightly browned, turning once. (Add more oil as necessary during cooking.) Top the eggplant with mozzarella cheese; reduce heat to low. Cover and cook just until cheese begins to melt.

3. To serve, place the eggplant slices, cheese sides up, on bottom half of bread. Top with the arugula mixture, tomato slices, and top half of bread. Cut into wedges. Makes 6 servings.

*Test Kitchen Tip: For easier slicing, purchase focaccia at least 2½ inches thick.

Nutrition facts per serving: 318 cal., 10 g total fat (4 g sat. fat), 48 mg chol., 447 mg sodium, 45 g carbo., 5 g fiber, 13 g pro.

Starting in the 1970s, our staff, along with many home cooks, became fascinated with the possibilities of meatless cooking. Since then, we've combined fresh ingredients in new ways, creating satisfying meatless dishes that our readers can fit into menus for family meals or dinner parties.

Vegetable Reuben Sandwich

Start to finish: 20 min.

The Reuben—corned beef, sauerkraut, and Swiss cheese piled on pumpernickel and drizzled with Thousand Island dressing—has been a longtime sandwich standout. We captured all that flavor in a meatless version by replacing the beef with zucchini.

- 2 **Tbsp. bottled Thousand Island or Russian salad dressing**
- 4 **slices dark or light rye, pumpernickel, or marbled bread**
- 8 **thin slices zucchini or cucumber**
- 4 **thin slices tomato**
- 6 **thin green or red sweet pepper rings**
- 2 **very thin slices red onion, separated into rings**
- ½ **cup sauerkraut, rinsed and well drained**
- 4 **slices Swiss, Monterey Jack, or cheddar cheese**

1. Preheat broiler. Spread the salad dressing onto *one side of half* of the bread slices. Place bread slices, dressing sides up, on the unheated rack of a broiler pan.

2. Layer the zucchini, tomato, sweet pepper, and red onion on bread; top with sauerkraut. Place the cheese on the remaining bread slices.

3. Place bread, vegetable or cheese sides up, on rack. Broil about 4 inches from the heat about 1 minute or until cheese is melted. Invert the cheese-topped bread slices over the vegetables. Broil about 1 minute more or until bread is lightly toasted; turn once. Makes 2 servings.

Nutrition facts per serving: 464 cal., 23 g total fat (11 g sat. fat), 55 mg chol., 892 mg sodium, 42 g carbo., 6 g fiber, 22 g pro.

Minestrone

Prep: 45 min. Cook: 10 + 15 min.

In the 1930s, we called this soup Minestrone à la Genovese and made it with navy beans, fine noodles, and canned vegetables. Today it's just Minestrone and it's brimming with white kidney beans, linguine, and fresh vegetables.

- 6 **cups water**
- 1 **28-oz. can tomatoes, undrained, cut up**
- 1 **8-oz. can tomato sauce**
- 1 **large onion, chopped**
- 1 **cup chopped cabbage**
- 1 **medium carrot, chopped**
- 1 **stalk celery, chopped**
- 1 **Tbsp. instant beef bouillon granules**
- 1 **Tbsp. dried Italian seasoning, crushed**
- 1 **tsp. salt**
- 2 **cloves garlic, minced**
- ¼ **tsp. pepper**
- 1 **15-oz. can white kidney beans (cannellini beans) or Great Northern beans**
- 1 **10-oz. pkg. frozen lima beans or one 9-oz. pkg. frozen Italian-style green beans**
- 4 **oz. dried linguine or spaghetti, broken**
- 1 **small zucchini, halved lengthwise and sliced**
- 2 **to 3 Tbsp. purchased pesto (optional) Grated Parmesan cheese (optional)**

1. In a 5- to 6-quart Dutch oven, combine the water, undrained tomatoes, tomato sauce, onion, cabbage, carrot, celery, bouillon granules, Italian seasoning, salt, garlic, and pepper. Bring to boiling; reduce heat. Cover and simmer for 10 minutes. Stir in undrained white kidney beans, lima beans, linguine, and zucchini. Return to boiling; reduce heat. Simmer, uncovered, for 15 minutes.

2. To serve, ladle into soup bowls. If desired, top *each* serving with *about 1 teaspoon* of the pesto and pass Parmesan cheese. Makes 8 servings.

Make-ahead directions: Cool soup. Ladle soup into freezer containers. Seal, label, and freeze for up to 3 months. To serve, in a saucepan, heat soup over low heat until heated through, stirring frequently.

Nutrition facts per serving: 176 cal., 1 g total fat (0 g sat. fat), 0 mg chol., 1,011 mg sodium, 37 g carbo., 7 g fiber, 10 g pro.

Vegetarian Chili

Prep: 40 min. Cook: 1½ hr. + 30 min.

We picked this as one of our best recipes from the first 75 years of *Better Homes and Gardens*® because the beans and veggies simmer into an aromatic, satisfying stew. The nuts add just the right crunch.

2	Tbsp. olive oil or cooking oil
1½	cups chopped celery
1½	cups chopped green sweet pepper
1	cup chopped onion
3	cloves garlic, minced
2	28-oz. cans tomatoes, undrained, cut up
3	15- to 16-oz. cans beans (such as kidney, black, Great Northern, and/or pinto) and/or chickpeas (garbanzo beans), rinsed and drained
½	cup raisins
¼	cup red wine vinegar
3	to 4 tsp. chili powder
1½	tsp. dried basil, crushed
1½	tsp. dried oregano, crushed
1½	tsp. ground cumin
1	tsp. sugar
1	tsp. ground allspice
½	tsp. salt
¼	tsp. ground black pepper
¼	tsp. bottled hot pepper sauce
1	bay leaf
1	12-oz. can beer or nonalcoholic beer
¾	cup cashews
1	cup shredded Monterey Jack, mozzarella, or cheddar cheese (4 oz.)

1. In a 4- or 6-quart Dutch oven, heat oil over medium heat. Add celery, sweet pepper, onion, and garlic. Cook, covered, about 10 minutes or until vegetables are tender, stirring occasionally.

2. Stir in undrained tomatoes, drained beans and/or chickpeas, raisins, vinegar, chili powder, basil, oregano, cumin, sugar, allspice, salt, black pepper, hot pepper sauce, and bay leaf. Bring to boiling; reduce heat. Cover and simmer for 1½ hours.

3. Stir in the beer. Return to boiling; reduce heat. Simmer, uncovered, about 30 minutes more or until desired consistency. Discard bay leaf. Stir in cashews. Sprinkle cheese over each serving. Makes 8 servings.

Test Kitchen Tip: If you're concerned about sodium, use low-sodium whole tomatoes, reduced-sodium canned beans, and unsalted cashews.

Nutrition facts per serving: 404 cal., 15 g total fat (4 g sat. fat), 12 mg chol., 1,177 mg sodium, 53 g carbo., 15 g fiber, 17 g pro.

Vegetarian Chili

America's infatuation with backyard barbecuing reached a fever

pitch as early as the 1950s and has remained strong ever since.

Better Homes and Gardens® magazine has been there all along,

providing our readers with outdoor cooking

Hot
Off the
Grill

ideas for all sorts of occasions. Here you

will find a top-notch selection of grilling recipes published

throughout the decades, including ideas for roasts, steaks, chops,

burgers, poultry, fish and seafood, vegetables, and side dishes.

92

68

86

82

91

74

Spicy Grilled Brisket

Prep: 25 min. Soak: 1 hr. Grill: 3 hr. Stand: 10 min.

Beef brisket slowly smoked until fork-tender is a down-home grilling tradition. Throughout the years, we've published numerous versions of this favorite. This mesquite-smoked brisket is one of the best.

- 4   to 6 cups mesquite wood chips
- 1   4- to 5-lb. fresh beef brisket
- 1   Tbsp. cooking oil
- 2   Tbsp. paprika
- 1   Tbsp. coarse salt or coarse kosher salt
- 1   Tbsp. ground black pepper
- 1   tsp. cayenne pepper
- 1   tsp. dried thyme, crushed
- 1   recipe Sweet and Hot Barbecue Sauce (below) or 3 cups bottled barbecue sauce

1. At least 1 hour before grilling, soak wood chips in enough water to cover.

2. Meanwhile, trim fat from brisket. Brush brisket with oil. For rub, in a small bowl, stir together paprika, salt, black pepper, cayenne pepper, and thyme. Sprinkle rub evenly onto both sides of meat; rub in with your fingers.

3. Drain wood chips. In a grill with a cover, arrange medium-low coals around a drip pan. Test for low heat above pan. Sprinkle some of the drained wood chips over the coals. Place brisket on grill rack over pan. Cover and grill for 3 to 3¾ hours or until meat is tender, adding more coals and remaining wood chips as needed.

4. Meanwhile, prepare Sweet and Hot Barbecue Sauce or warm the bottled barbecue sauce in a saucepan over low heat. Let meat stand for 10 minutes before thinly slicing across the grain. Serve with barbecue sauce. Makes 15 servings.

Sweet and Hot Barbecue Sauce: In a large saucepan cook ½ cup chopped onion; 6 fresh jalapeño chile peppers, seeded and chopped (tip, page 32); and 2 cloves garlic, minced, in 1 tablespoon hot cooking oil until onion is tender. Stir in 2 cups ketchup, ¼ cup packed brown sugar, ¼ cup white wine vinegar, ¼ cup orange juice, 3 tablespoons Worcestershire sauce, and 1 teaspoon dry mustard. Bring to boiling; reduce heat. Simmer, uncovered, for 10 to 15 minutes or until sauce is desired consistency.

Nutrition facts per serving: 253 cal., 9 g total fat (2 g sat. fat), 71 mg chol., 956 mg sodium, 15 g carbo., 1 g fiber, 27 g pro.

Garlic Steaks with Nectarine-Onion Relish

Prep: 15 min. Stand: 20 min. Grill: 11 min.

Minty fruit and garlic-studded steak team up to tantalize the taste buds.

- 4   boneless beef top loin steaks, cut 1 inch thick (1½ to 2 lb. total)
- 6   cloves garlic, thinly sliced
    Salt
    Pepper
- 2   medium onions, coarsely chopped
- 1   tsp. olive oil
- 2   Tbsp. cider vinegar
- 1   Tbsp. honey
- 1   medium nectarine, chopped
- 2   tsp. snipped fresh applemint, pineapplemint, or spearmint
    Fresh mint sprigs (optional)

1. Trim fat from steaks. With a paring knife, make small slits in steaks. Insert *half* of the garlic into slits. Wrap steaks in plastic wrap; let stand at room temperature for up to 20 minutes. (For more flavor, refrigerate up to 8 hours.) Sprinkle with salt and pepper.

2. Meanwhile, for relish, in a large nonstick skillet, cook onions and remaining garlic in hot oil over medium heat about 10 minutes or until onions are golden, stirring occasionally. Stir in vinegar and honey. Stir in nectarine and the snipped mint; heat through.

3. Grill steaks on the rack of an uncovered grill directly over medium coals to desired doneness, turning once. (Allow 11 to 15 minutes for medium-rare doneness [145°F] or 14 to 18 minutes for medium doneness [160°F].) Serve the relish with steaks. If desired, garnish with mint sprigs. Makes 4 servings.

Nutrition facts per serving: 272 cal., 9 g total fat (3 g sat. fat), 97 mg chol., 108 mg sodium, 13 g carbo., 1 g fiber, 34 g pro.

Garlic Steaks with Nectarine-Onion Relish

Lemony London Broil

Prep: 15 min. Marinate: 2 to 24 hr. Grill: 17 min.

Scoring the steak in a diagonal pattern gives more surface area for the marinade to penetrate.

- 1   1½-lb. beef flank steak
- 1   tsp. finely shredded lemon peel
- ½   cup lemon juice
- 2   Tbsp. sugar
- 2   Tbsp. soy sauce
- 2   tsp. snipped fresh oregano
     or ½ tsp. dried oregano, crushed
- ⅛   tsp. pepper
     Grilled lemon wedges (optional)
     Shredded lemon peel (optional)

1. Trim fat from steak. Score both sides of steak in a diamond pattern by making shallow diagonal cuts at 1-inch intervals. Place steak in a resealable plastic bag set in a shallow dish.

2. For marinade, in a small bowl, combine the 1 teaspoon lemon peel, the lemon juice, sugar, soy sauce, oregano, and pepper. Pour marinade over steak. Seal bag; turn to coat steak. Marinate in refrigerator for at least 2 hours or up to 24 hours; turn bag occasionally.

3. Drain steak, reserving marinade. Grill steak on the rack of an uncovered grill directly over medium coals for 17 to 21 minutes or until medium doneness (160°F), turning and brushing once with reserved marinade halfway through grilling. Discard remaining marinade.

4. To serve, slice steak across the grain. If desired, serve with grilled lemon wedges and garnish with additional lemon peel. Makes 6 servings.

Nutrition facts per serving: 191 cal., 7 g total fat (3 g sat. fat), 43 mg chol., 364 mg sodium, 6 g carbo., 0 g fiber, 24 g pro.

Yesterday

In the early days of barbecue at *Better Homes and Gardens.*, our stories taught readers the fundamentals of grilling. For the most part, the recipes were simple and straightforward, as in the case of this marinated flank steak.

Apulian-Style Steak Sandwich

Prep: 45 min. Grill: 17 min.

If you like, toast the rolls by brushing them with olive oil and grilling them, cut sides down, for 1 to 2 minutes.

- 1 **small eggplant**
- ½ **tsp. salt**
- 1½ **tsp. olive oil**
- 1 **recipe Chile Pepper Spread (below)**
- 12 **oz. beef flank steak or boneless beef sirloin steak, cut about 1 inch thick**
-   **Salt (optional)**
-   **Ground black pepper (optional)**
- 2 **tsp. dried Italian seasoning, crushed**
- 4 **6-inch Italian sourdough rolls, split horizontally**
-   **Salad greens or romaine leaves**
- 2 **oz. shaved Parmesan cheese (optional)**

1. Trim off and discard ends of eggplant. Cut lengthwise into ¼-inch-thick slices; discard outside "peel" slices. Arrange in single layer on a baking sheet. Sprinkle with salt; cover and set aside for 30 minutes. Rinse eggplant; pat dry. Rub eggplant with olive oil; set aside.

2. Meanwhile, prepare Chile Pepper Spread.

3. Score both sides of steak in a diamond pattern by making shallow diagonal cuts at 1-inch intervals. If desired, sprinkle steak with additional salt and black pepper. Sprinkle Italian seasoning evenly onto both sides of steak; rub in with your fingers.

4. Grill steak on rack of uncovered grill directly over medium coals for 17 to 21 minutes or until medium doneness (160°F), turning once. Halfway through grilling, place eggplant slices alongside steak; grill eggplant for 6 to 8 minutes or until cooked through, turning once.

5. To assemble, spread about *1 tablespoon* of the Chile Pepper Spread on bottom half of *each* Italian roll. Top with greens and eggplant slices. Slice steak across grain into very thin strips. Arrange sliced steak on eggplant slices. If desired, add Parmesan. Lightly spread top halves of Italian rolls with remaining pepper spread. Makes 4 servings.

Nutrition facts per serving: 616 cal., 18 g total fat (7 g sat. fat), 47 mg chol., 1,300 mg sodium, 75 g carbo., 7 g fiber, 37 g pro.

Today

Over the years, our focus has shifted from teaching the basics to giving our readers innovative seasonings for popular meat cuts. This flank steak sandwich, for example, boasts the fresh ingredients and flavors of the Apulia region of Italy.

Chile Pepper Spread: Remove stems from 8 ounces fresh mild red cherry chile peppers or mild banana chile peppers; halve and seed peppers (tip, page 32). In a large skillet, heat 1½ teaspoons olive oil over medium heat. Cook ½ cup chopped onion and 4 cloves garlic, minced, in hot oil about 5 minutes or until onion turns golden, stirring often. Add cherry or banana peppers, 2 tablespoons balsamic vinegar, and ¼ teaspoon salt; cook and stir for 2 minutes. Reduce heat to low. Cover and cook about 10 minutes more or until mixture is soft, stirring occasionally. Remove chile pepper mixture from heat. Let cool. Spoon chile pepper mixture into a food processor or blender; cover and process or blend until nearly smooth. Set aside.

Steak with Blue Cheese Butter

Prep: 10 min. Grill: 11 min.

- ¼ **cup butter or margarine, softened**
- ¼ **cup crumbled blue cheese (1 oz.)**
- 1 **Tbsp. snipped fresh parsley**
- 2 **tsp. snipped fresh basil or ½ tsp. dried basil, crushed**
- 1 **clove garlic, minced**
- 6 **beef T-bone or porterhouse steaks, cut 1 inch thick**

1. For butter mixture, stir together the butter, blue cheese, parsley, basil, and garlic. Set aside.

2. Trim fat from steaks. If desired, sprinkle steaks with *pepper*. Grill steaks on rack of an uncovered grill directly over medium coals to desired doneness, turning once. (Allow 11 to 14 minutes for medium-rare doneness [145°F] or 13 to 16 minutes for medium doneness [160°F].) To serve, top *each* steak with *about 1 tablespoon* of the butter mixture. Serves 6.

Steak for Two: Prepare butter mixture as directed. Divide butter mixture into thirds. Refrigerate or freeze two of the portions to use to season vegetables or for steak another time. Grill 2 beef T-bone or porterhouse steaks, cut 1 inch thick, as directed. Serve with remaining portion of butter as directed.

Nutrition facts per serving: 493 cal., 27 g total fat (13 g sat. fat), 153 mg chol., 285 mg sodium, 0 g carbo., 0 g fiber, 59 g pro.

The Heat's On the secret

of great grilling has always been getting the temperature right, whether you're cooking with charcoal or gas. Hold your hand over the heat at the level the food will cook and count, "one thousand one, one thousand two, …" If you can only hold your hand there for 2 seconds, the fire is hot; 3 seconds, it is medium-hot; 4 seconds, it is medium; and 5 seconds, it is low. For indirect grilling, hot coals provide medium-hot heat, medium-hot coals give medium heat, medium coals give medium-low heat, and medium-low coals provide low heat.

Tropical Fiesta Steak

Prep: 25 min. Marinate: 12 to 24 hr. Grill: 14 min.

This timeless steak—seasoned with an orange marinade and topped with a fresh fruit relish—was a prizewinner in *Better Homes and Gardens*® 1992 Great American Barbecue contest.

- ⅓ **cup orange juice concentrate, thawed**
- 3 **Tbsp. cooking oil**
- 3 **Tbsp. honey**
- 1 **Tbsp. sliced green onion**
- 2 **tsp. spicy brown or Dijon-style mustard**
- 1 **tsp. snipped fresh mint or ¼ tsp. dried mint, crushed**
    Few drops bottled hot pepper sauce
- 1 **1½-lb. boneless beef sirloin steak, cut 1 inch thick**
- ½ **cup chopped red sweet pepper**
- ½ **cup chopped red apple**
- ½ **cup chopped pear**
- ½ **cup chopped peeled peach**
- ¼ **cup chopped celery**
- 2 **Tbsp. sliced green onion**
- 2 **tsp. lemon juice**

1. For marinade, in a small bowl, stir together orange juice concentrate, oil, honey, the 1 tablespoon green onion, the mustard, mint, and hot pepper sauce. Remove ¼ *cup* of the mixture for relish; cover and refrigerate until needed.

2. Place steak in a resealable plastic bag set in a shallow bowl. Pour remaining marinade over steak. Seal bag; turn to coat steak. Marinate in the refrigerator for at least 12 hours or up to 24 hours, turning bag occasionally.

3. For fruit relish, in a medium bowl, combine the reserved ¼ cup honey mixture, the sweet pepper, apple, pear, peach, celery, the 2 tablespoons green onion, and the lemon juice. Cover and refrigerate up to 24 hours.

4. Drain steak, reserving marinade. Grill steak on rack of an uncovered grill directly over medium coals to desired doneness, turning once halfway through grilling and brushing occasionally with reserved marinade during the first 8 minutes of grilling. (Allow 14 to 18 minutes for medium-rare doneness [145°F] or 18 to 22 minutes for medium doneness [160°F].) Discard any remaining marinade.

5. To serve, thinly slice steak. Serve with fruit relish. Makes 6 servings.

Nutrition facts per serving: 227 cal., 8 g total fat (2 g sat. fat), 53 mg chol., 101 mg sodium, 14 g carbo., 1 g fiber, 25 g pro.

Zesty Steak Carbonade

Prep: 20 min. Marinate: 1 to 24 hr. Grill: 11 min.

The cook who entered this winning recipe in our June 1994 Prize Tested Recipes® contest said she adapted a Flemish dish made with beef, beer, and onion.

- ½ **cup beer**
- ½ **cup chopped onion**
- ⅓ **cup ketchup**
- 1 **Tbsp. sugar**
- 1 **Tbsp. lemon juice**
- 1 **Tbsp. Worcestershire sauce**
- ½ **tsp. chili powder**
- ¼ **to ½ tsp. crushed red pepper**
- 6 **beef top loin steaks, cut 1 inch thick (about 3 lb. total)**

1. For marinade, in a small saucepan, combine beer, onion, ketchup, sugar, lemon juice, Worcestershire sauce, chili powder, and crushed red pepper. Bring to boiling; reduce heat. Simmer, uncovered, for 5 minutes. Cool.

2. Score both sides of steaks in a diamond pattern by making shallow diagonal cuts at 1-inch intervals. Place steaks in a large resealable plastic bag set in a deep bowl. Add marinade. Seal bag; turn to coat steaks. Marinate in refrigerator for at least 1 hour or up to 24 hours; turning bag occasionally.

Colossal Stuffed Burger

3. Drain steaks; reserve marinade. Grill steaks on the rack of an uncovered grill directly over medium coals to desired doneness, turning once. (Allow 11 to 15 minutes for medium-rare doneness [145°F] or 14 to 18 minutes for medium doneness [160°F].) Place the reserved marinade in saucepan; bring to boiling. Boil gently, uncovered, for 2 minutes. Serve with steaks. Serves 6.

Nutrition facts per serving: 368 cal., 13 g total fat (5 g sat. fat), 133 mg chol., 305 mg sodium, 8 g carbo., 0 g fiber, 49 g pro.

Colossal Stuffed Burger

Prep: 20 min. Grill: 35 min.

Grilled burgers take on a whole new dimension when you make one giant burger for the entire family.

- 2 **lb. lean ground beef or lamb**
- ¼ **cup grated Parmesan cheese (1 oz.)**
- 2 **tsp. dried oregano, crushed**
- 1 **tsp. lemon juice**
- 1 **tsp. bottled teriyaki sauce**
- ½ **tsp. garlic salt**
- ¼ **cup tomato paste**
- 1 **4-oz. can mushroom stems and pieces, drained and chopped**
- ¼ **cup shredded mozzarella cheese (1 oz.)**
- 1 **8-inch pita bread round, halved horizontally**
  Torn mixed greens

1. In a large bowl, combine ground meat, Parmesan cheese, oregano, lemon juice, teriyaki sauce, and garlic salt. Divide meat mixture in half. Shape each half into a ball; pat each ball onto waxed paper to form a flat patty 8 inches in diameter. Spread tomato paste in the center of *one circle* of the meat. Top tomato paste with mushrooms and mozzarella cheese. Top with the second circle of meat. Press to seal edge.

2. In a grill with a cover, arrange medium-hot coals around a drip pan. Test for medium heat above pan. Place burger on grill rack over pan. Cover and grill about 35 minutes or until meat is done (160°F).* Cut into wedges. To serve, place burger on bottom half of pita; top burger with mixed greens. Cut into six wedges. Makes 6 servings.

*Test Kitchen Tip: The internal color of a burger is not a reliable indication of doneness. A patty containing beef or lamb cooked to 160°F is safe, regardless of color. To measure the doneness of a patty, insert an instant-read thermometer through the side of the patty to a depth of 2 to 3 inches.

Nutrition facts per serving: 318 cal., 16 g total fat (7 g sat. fat), 101 mg chol., 393 mg sodium, 10 g carbo., 2 g fiber, 32 g pro.

Yesterday

In the early days of backyard grilling, burgers weren't fancy. They were made with basic ground beef. This recipe from 1956 is proof positive that a great recipe will delight generation after generation

Mushroom-Stuffed Cheeseburgers

Prep: 30 min. Grill: 14 min.

When grilling burgers, resist pressing down on them with a spatula as they cook. This squeezes out the juices and makes them dry and tough.

- 2 eggs
- ¾ cup soft bread crumbs
- ¼ cup finely chopped onion
- ¼ cup ketchup
- ½ tsp. salt
- 1½ lb. ground beef
- 1 4-oz. can mushroom stems and pieces, drained and coarsely chopped
- 6 slices process American cheese food (¾ oz. each)
- 6 hamburger buns, split and toasted
- 6 slices tomato
- 6 slices red onion
   Condiments (such as ketchup, mustard, pickle slices, sliced radishes, and/or prepared horseradish) (optional)

1. In a large bowl, beat eggs with a fork. Stir in bread crumbs, onion, the ¼ cup ketchup, and the salt. Add beef; mix well. Form into twelve ¼-inch-thick patties.

2. Divide mushrooms among centers of *half* of the patties, leaving a border of meat. Top with remaining patties; seal edges.

3. Grill burgers on the rack of an uncovered grill directly over medium coals for 14 to 18 minutes or until meat is done (160°F) (tip, page 71), turning once. Top burgers with cheese; grill just until melted.

4. Serve burgers on buns with tomato and onion. If desired, serve with condiments. Makes 6 servings.

Nutrition facts per serving: 538 cal., 27 g total fat (12 g sat. fat), 186 mg chol., 1,070 mg sodium, 31 g carbo., 2 g fiber, 41 g pro.

Over the years, our burgers have evolved—using a wide range of ingredients in new and interesting ways. This pork-and-chicken combo topped with Brie is a novel twist on the cheeseburger.

Bistro Burgers

Prep: 20 min. Chill: 30 min. Grill: 11 min.

Grilling burgers over medium coals may take a little longer, but it lets the patties cook through without getting too brown on the surface.

2	Tbsp. dry white wine or water
¼	tsp. salt
¼	tsp. ground black pepper
12	oz. ground pork
12	oz. uncooked ground chicken breast or turkey breast
2	Tbsp. creamy Dijon-style mustard blend
1	Tbsp. snipped fresh chives
1	to 2 cloves garlic, minced
1	4½-oz. round Brie cheese, rind removed and cut into 12 slices
12	slices French bread or bagel halves, toasted
	Radicchio or leaf lettuce
	Cracked black pepper (optional)
8	slices red and/or yellow tomato (optional)

1. In a medium bowl, combine the wine or water, salt, and ground black pepper. Add the ground pork and chicken; mix well. Shape meat mixture into six ½-inch-thick patties. Cover and chill for 30 minutes.

2. Meanwhile, in a small bowl, stir together the mustard blend, chives, and garlic. Set aside.

3. Grill burgers on the rack of an uncovered grill directly over medium coals for 11 to 14 minutes or until done (165°F),* turning once. Top each burger with 2 slices of the cheese. Grill about 3 minutes more or until cheese begins to melt. To serve, spread sauce on *one side* of *half* of the toasted bread slices. Add radicchio or leaf lettuce. Top with meat patties. If desired, sprinkle with cracked black pepper. If desired, add tomato slices. Top with remaining bread slices. Serves 6.

*Test Kitchen Tip: The internal color of a burger is not a reliable indication of doneness. A patty containing chicken or turkey cooked to 165°F is safe, regardless of color. To measure the doneness of a patty, insert an instant-read thermometer through the side of the patty to a depth of 2 to 3 inches.

Nutrition facts per serving: 349 cal., 12 g total fat (6 g sat. fat), 81 mg chol., 658 mg sodium, 28 g carbo., 2 g fiber, 29 g pro.

Mushroom-Stuffed Pork Chops

Prep: 25 min. Grill: 35 min.

For the novice, plain grilled pork chops are just fine.
But before long, grill aficionados usually want to
branch out. Here's just the ticket—a chop with a
ginger glaze and a mushroom and spinach stuffing.

½	**cup coarsely chopped fresh mushrooms (such as button, chanterelle, or shiitake)**
¼	**cup chopped onion**
1	**Tbsp. butter or margarine**
1	**tsp. grated fresh ginger**
¼	**tsp. salt**
¼	**tsp. pepper**
1	**cup coarsely chopped fresh spinach leaves**
¼	**cup soft sourdough or white bread crumbs**
4	**pork loin chops or pork rib chops, cut 1¼ inches thick (about 3 lb. total)**
	Salt
	Pepper
¼	**cup ginger jelly or preserves or orange marmalade**
12	**green onions**
2	**tsp. olive oil**

1. In a small bowl, soak 8 wooden picks in water
for 10 minutes. Meanwhile, for stuffing, in a saucepan,
cook mushrooms and onion in hot butter until onion
is tender. Remove from heat. Stir in grated ginger, the
¼ teaspoon salt, and the ¼ teaspoon pepper. Add
spinach and bread crumbs, tossing gently to combine.

2. Make a pocket in each chop by cutting horizontally
from the outside edge almost to the bone. Divide stuffing
evenly among pockets in chops. Secure openings with
soaked wooden picks. Sprinkle with salt and pepper.

3. In a grill with a cover, arrange medium-hot coals
around a drip pan. Test for medium heat above pan.
Place chops on grill rack over pan. Cover and grill for
35 to 40 minutes or until juices run clear (160°F), turning
once and brushing occasionally with ginger jelly during
the last 5 minutes of grilling. Remove wooden picks.

4. Meanwhile, trim roots and tops of the green
onions. In a medium skillet, cook green onions in hot
oil for 1 to 3 minutes or until slightly softened. Serve
green onions with chops. Makes 4 servings.

Nutrition facts per serving: 442 cal., 17 g total fat (6 g sat. fat),
140 mg chol., 355 mg sodium, 19 g carbo., 2 g fiber, 50 g pro.

Pesto-Packed Pork Chops

Prep: 20 min. Grill: 30 min.

In 1997, these triple-seasoned loin chops won top prize in the Barbecued Ribs and Chops category of our Prize Tested Recipes® contest. What makes them so remarkable are a rub, a pesto stuffing, and a jalapeño jelly glaze.

- 3   **Tbsp. crumbled feta cheese**
- 4   **to 5 Tbsp. refrigerated basil pesto**
- 1   **Tbsp. pine nuts, toasted (tip, page 102)**
- 2   **Tbsp. jalapeño chile pepper jelly**
- 1   **Tbsp. balsamic vinegar**
- 4   **pork loin chops or boneless pork top loin chops, cut 1¼ inches thick**
- 2   **cloves garlic, minced**
- 1   **tsp. ground black pepper**
- ½   **tsp. cayenne pepper**
- ½   **tsp. celery seeds, crushed**
- ½   **tsp. fennel seeds, crushed**
- ¼   **tsp. dried thyme, crushed**
- ¼   **tsp. ground cumin**

1. In a small bowl, soak 8 wooden picks in water for 10 minutes. Meanwhile, for filling, in a small bowl, stir together feta cheese, *2 tablespoons* of the pesto, and the pine nuts. Set aside.

2. For glaze, in a small saucepan, melt jelly over low heat. Stir in the remaining 2 to 3 tablespoons pesto and the balsamic vinegar; heat through. Set aside.

3. Trim fat from chops. Make a pocket in each chop by cutting horizontally from the fatty side almost to the bone or the opposite side. Divide filling among pockets in chops. Secure openings with soaked wooden picks.

4. For rub, in a small bowl, combine garlic, black pepper, cayenne pepper, celery seeds, fennel seeds, thyme, and cumin. Sprinkle mixture evenly over both sides of each chop; rub in with your fingers.

5. In a grill with a cover, arrange medium-hot coals around a drip pan. Test for medium heat above pan. Place chops on grill rack over pan. Cover and grill for 30 to 40 minutes or until juices run clear (160°F), turning once and brushing occasionally with glaze during the last 10 minutes of grilling. Makes 4 servings.

Nutrition facts per serving: 477 cal., 30 g total fat (7 g sat. fat), 121 mg chol., 336 mg sodium, 12 g carbo., 0 g fiber, 39 g pro.

> **Because our barbecue recipes usually run in the summer, we often test six months ahead (when the cold wind blows in Iowa). Our Test Kitchen staff have become real pros at grilling in their winter coats.**

Marvelous Mustard Ribs

Prep: 20 min. Chill: 2 to 6 hr. Grill: 1½ hr.

Our editors raved about this recipe when it won our July 1992 Prize Tested Recipes® contest for barbecued ribs. Today, we're still thrilled with its spicy-sweet flavor.

- ⅓   **cup granulated sugar**
- 2   **tsp. paprika**
- 1   **tsp. pepper**
- 1   **tsp. curry powder**
- ½   **tsp. salt**
- 3½   **to 4 lb. pork country-style ribs**
- 1   **cup packed brown sugar**
- ½   **cup white vinegar or cider vinegar**
- ½   **cup chopped onion**
- ⅓   **cup spicy brown mustard or Dijon-style mustard**
- 2   **cloves garlic, minced**
- 2   **Tbsp. honey**
- 2   **tsp. liquid smoke**
- ¼   **tsp. celery seeds**

1. In a small bowl, combine granulated sugar, paprika, pepper, curry powder, and salt. Sprinkle onto ribs; rub in. Place ribs in a shallow pan. Cover and chill for at least 2 hours or up to 6 hours.

2. In a grill with a cover, arrange medium-hot coals around a drip pan. Test for medium heat above pan. Place ribs, bone sides down, on grill rack over pan. Cover and grill for 1½ to 2 hours or until tender, turning once and adding more coals as needed.

3. Meanwhile, for sauce, in a medium saucepan, combine the brown sugar, vinegar, onion, mustard, garlic, honey, liquid smoke, and celery seeds. Bring to boiling; reduce heat. Cook, uncovered, for 25 to 30 minutes or until slightly thickened, stirring occasionally.

4. Brush sauce onto ribs occasionally during the last 10 to 15 minutes of grilling. Reheat any remaining sauce until bubbly; pass with ribs. Makes 8 servings.

Nutrition facts per serving: 352 cal., 9 g total fat (3 g sat. fat), 70 mg chol., 371 mg sodium, 44 g carbo., 1 g fiber, 22 g pro.

Southwestern Ribs with a Rub

Prep: 20 min. Soak: 1 hr.
Cook: 25 min. Grill: 1½ hr.

When it comes to grilling, our readers can't be outdone. One of them won $200 for this recipe. For extra kick, the ribs are smeared with a peppery rub and slathered with a zippy sauce.

4	cups mesquite wood chips
1	cup ketchup
½	cup light-colored corn syrup
¼	cup white vinegar
¼	cup packed brown sugar
¼	cup finely chopped onion
2	Tbsp. yellow mustard
1½	tsp. Worcestershire sauce
2	cloves garlic, minced
½	tsp. ground black pepper
½	tsp. bottled hot pepper sauce
¼	tsp. ground cumin or chili powder
⅛	tsp. cayenne pepper
4	lb. pork loin back ribs
1	recipe Rib Rub (below)

1. At least 1 hour before grilling, soak wood chips in enough water to cover.

2. For sauce, in a 1½-quart saucepan, combine ketchup, corn syrup, white vinegar, brown sugar, onion, mustard, Worcestershire sauce, garlic, black pepper, hot pepper sauce, cumin or chili powder, and cayenne pepper. Bring to boiling; reduce heat. Simmer, uncovered, for 25 to 30 minutes or until thickened, stirring occasionally.

3. Cut the ribs into serving-size pieces. Sprinkle Rib Rub evenly over all sides of ribs; rub in with your fingers.

4. Drain wood chips. In a grill with a cover, arrange medium-hot coals around a drip pan. Test for medium heat above pan. Put some of the drained mesquite chips onto coals. Place ribs, bone sides down, on grill rack over pan. Cover and grill for 1½ to 1¾ hours or until ribs are tender, adding more coals and remaining mesquite chips as needed. Brush ribs with some of the sauce during the last 10 minutes of grilling. Pass remaining sauce. Makes 6 servings.

Rib Rub: In a blender or small food processor, combine 2 teaspoons dried rosemary, 2 teaspoons dried thyme, 2 teaspoons dried minced onion, 2 teaspoons dried minced garlic, 1 teaspoon coarse salt, and ¾ teaspoon ground black pepper. Blend or process until coarsely ground.

Nutrition facts per serving: 477 cal., 14 g total fat (5 g sat. fat), 90 mg chol., 970 mg sodium, 44 g carbo., 2 g fiber, 43 g pro.

Warren's Barbecued Ribs

Prep: 15 min. Grill: 1½ hr.

This recipe was the specialty of Warren, the husband of Myrna Johnston, a *Better Homes and Gardens*® food editor for more than 30 years. He typically brushed the sauce onto ribs, but it's also terrific on burgers, steaks, chops, and chicken.

1	cup water
1	cup ketchup
3	Tbsp. vinegar
1	Tbsp. sugar
1	Tbsp. Worcestershire sauce
1	tsp. celery seeds
¼	tsp. bottled hot pepper sauce
4	lb. pork loin back ribs or meaty spareribs
	Salt
	Pepper

1. For sauce, in a medium saucepan, combine the water, ketchup, vinegar, sugar, Worcestershire sauce, celery seeds, and hot pepper sauce. Bring to boiling; reduce heat. Simmer, uncovered, for 30 minutes, stirring occasionally. Remove sauce from heat; set aside.

2. Meanwhile, sprinkle ribs with salt and pepper. In a grill with a cover, arrange medium-hot coals around a drip pan. Test for medium heat above pan. Place ribs on the grill rack over pan. Cover and grill for 1½ to 1¾ hours or until ribs are tender, brushing with some of the sauce during the last 15 minutes of grilling. Pass remaining sauce. Makes 6 servings.

Nutrition facts per serving: 405 cal., 14 g total fat (5 g sat. fat), 129 mg chol., 612 mg sodium, 14 g carbo., 1 g fiber, 52 g pro.

During our travels over the years, we've learned how grilled foods differ from region to region. Whether it's tangy vinegar-based pulled pork from the South, sweet and spicy sauces from the Midwest, chile pepper-laced brisket from the Southwest, or Asian-influenced ribs from the West Coast, we have fun bringing our readers the best of American barbecue.

Hickory-Smoked Pork Loin

Prep: 10 min. Chill: 2 to 4 hr. Soak: 1 hr.
Grill: 1½ hr. Stand: 15 min.

A brown sugar-and-orange rub gives this lean, boneless roast a glossy coating and loads of flavor.

 1 **3-lb. boneless pork top loin roast (double loin, tied)**
 3 **Tbsp. packed brown sugar**
 1½ **tsp. finely shredded orange peel**
 1½ **tsp. ground coriander**
 1½ **tsp. paprika**
 ¾ **tsp. salt**
 ¾ **tsp. ground ginger**
 ¼ **tsp. pepper**
 3 **cups hickory or oak wood chips**

1. Trim fat from meat. Place meat in a shallow dish. For rub, in a small bowl, stir together brown sugar, orange peel, coriander, paprika, salt, ginger, and pepper. Sprinkle rub evenly onto all sides of meat; rub in with your fingers. Cover and chill in the refrigerator for at least 2 hours or up to 4 hours.

2. Meanwhile, at least 1 hour before grilling, soak wood chips in enough water to cover.

3. Drain wood chips. In a grill with a cover, arrange medium-hot coals around a drip pan. Test for medium heat above pan. Insert an oven-going meat thermometer into center of roast. Sprinkle some of the drained wood chips over the coals. Place roast on grill rack over pan. Cover and grill for 1½ to 2 hours or until thermometer registers 155°F. Add more coals and remaining wood chips as needed.

4. Remove meat from grill; cover with foil and let stand for 15 minutes before slicing. (The temperature of the meat will rise about 5°F during standing.) Makes 8 to 10 servings.

Nutrition facts per serving: 260 cal., 8 g total fat (3 g sat. fat), 93 mg chol., 282 mg sodium, 6 g carbo., 0 g fiber, 37 g pro.

Yesterday

When our readers were buying their first grills in the 1950s, we shared all we knew. For roasts, we suggested adding flavor by rubbing the meat with spices and grilling over aromatic wood chips.

Jalapeño-Honey Pork Tenderloin

Prep: 20 min. Marinate: 12 to 24 hr. Grill: 40 min.
Stand: 10 min.

When the weather turns blustery, roast these
marinated pork tenderloins in your oven instead
of on your grill. They're just as tasty either way.

- **2   12-oz. pork tenderloins**
- **⅓   cup honey**
- **3   Tbsp. light soy sauce**
- **1   Tbsp. toasted sesame oil**
- **2   fresh jalapeño chile peppers, seeded
  and finely chopped (tip, page 32)**
- **1   Tbsp. grated fresh ginger**
- **¼   to ½ tsp. crushed red pepper**
  Hot cooked rice (optional)
  Fresh cilantro sprigs (optional)
  Fresh whole chile peppers (optional)

1. Trim fat from meat. Place meat in a resealable plastic
bag set in a shallow dish. For marinade, in a small
bowl, combine honey, soy sauce, sesame oil, the chopped
jalapeño peppers, the ginger, and crushed red pepper.
Pour marinade over meat. Seal bag; turn to coat meat.
Marinate in the refrigerator for at least 12 hours or up
to 24 hours, turning bag occasionally.

2. Drain meat, reserving marinade. In a grill with
a cover, arrange hot coals around a drip pan. Test
for medium-high heat above pan. Place meat on grill
rack over pan. Cover and grill for 40 to 50 minutes
or until juices run clear (160°F), brushing once with
reserved marinade after 15 minutes of grilling. Discard
any remaining marinade.

3. Remove meat from grill cover with foil and let
stand for 10 minutes before slicing. If desired, serve
with hot cooked rice and garnish with cilantro sprigs
and whole chile peppers. Makes 6 servings.

Oven directions: Prepare recipe as directed in
step 1. Drain meat, reserving marinade. Place meat on
a rack in a roasting pan. Roast in a 425°F oven for
25 to 35 minutes or until juices run clear (160°F),
brushing once with reserved marinade after 10 minutes
of roasting. Discard any remaining marinade. Remove
from oven; cover with foil. Let stand for 10 minutes
before slicing.

Nutrition facts per serving: 205 cal., 5 g total fat (1 g sat. fat),
67 mg chol., 330 mg sodium, 16 g carbo., 0 g fiber, 23 g pro.

Today

This present-day grilled roast has
more fiery seasonings than recipes
of years past because today's cooks
crave more intense flavors. It's
marinated in a sesame oil and soy
sauce mixture that gets its heat from
jalapeño chile peppers and crushed
red pepper.

Grilled Italian Sausage
With Sweet and Sour Peppers

Grilled Italian Sausage with Sweet and Sour Peppers

Prep: 20 min. Grill: 10 +10 min.

For your next backyard cookout, try these colorful Italian sausage links. They boast a serve-along of grilled sweet peppers tossed in a tangy almond-and-raisin dressing.

3   Tbsp. slivered almonds
¼   cup raisins
3   Tbsp. red wine vinegar
2   Tbsp. sugar
¼   tsp. salt
⅛   tsp. ground black pepper
1   Tbsp. olive oil
2   green sweet peppers, cut into
    1-inch-wide strips
2   red sweet peppers, cut into
    1-inch-wide strips
1   medium red onion, thickly sliced
6   4- to 6-oz. uncooked sweet Italian
    sausage links
    Toasted slivered almonds (optional)
    (tip, page 102)

1. In a small nonstick skillet, cook and stir the 3 tablespoons almonds for 1 to 2 minutes or until golden. Stir in raisins. Remove skillet from heat. Cool for 1 minute. Carefully stir in vinegar, sugar, salt, and black pepper. Cook and stir just until sugar dissolves.

2. Drizzle oil onto sweet pepper strips and onion slices. Prick sausages several times with a fork. In a grill with a cover, arrange medium-hot coals around a drip pan. Test for medium heat above pan. Place sausages on grill rack over pan. Cover and grill for 10 minutes.

3. Turn sausages. Place vegetables on rack alongside sausages. Cover and grill for 10 to 20 minutes more or until sausages are cooked through (160°F)* and vegetables are tender, turning vegetables once. Remove vegetables when done.

4. In a large bowl, toss vegetables with the almond mixture; spoon onto a serving platter. Serve sausages with vegetable mixture. If desired, sprinkle with additional toasted slivered almonds. Makes 6 servings.

*Test Kitchen Tip: The internal color of a fresh sausage link is not a reliable indication of doneness. A fresh pork sausage link cooked to 160°F is safe, regardless of color. To measure doneness of a link, insert an instant-read thermometer from one end into center.

Nutrition facts per serving: 433 cal., 30 g total fat (11 g sat. fat), 77 mg chol., 722 mg sodium, 16 g carbo., 2 g fiber, 18 g pro.

Mustard-Rosemary Grilled Lamb

Prep: 20 min. Chill: 2 to 3 hr. Grill: 12 min.

In judging our Grilled Chops and Steaks Prize Tested Recipes® contest in August 2002, we rated these wine-and-honey marinated chops as outstanding.

8   lamb rib or loin chops, cut 1 inch thick
    (about 2 lb. total)
¼   cup stone ground mustard
2   green onions, thinly sliced
2   Tbsp. dry white wine
1   Tbsp. balsamic vinegar or rice vinegar
3   cloves garlic, minced
1   tsp. snipped fresh rosemary
1   tsp. honey
½   tsp. salt
½   tsp. pepper

1. Trim fat from chops. In a small bowl, stir together mustard, green onions, wine, vinegar, garlic, rosemary, honey, salt, and pepper. Spread mixture evenly onto both sides of each chop. Place chops on a large plate; cover loosely with plastic wrap. Chill in the refrigerator for at least 2 hours or up to 3 hours.

2. Grill chops on the rack of an uncovered grill directly over medium coals to desired doneness, turning once. (Allow 12 to 14 minutes for medium-rare doneness [145°F] or 15 to 17 minutes for medium doneness [160°F].) Makes 4 servings.

Nutrition facts per serving: 194 cal., 9 g total fat (3 g sat. fat), 64 mg chol., 557 mg sodium, 4 g carbo., 0 g fiber, 21 g pro.

Lemon-Rosemary Lamb Kabobs

Prep: 15 min. Marinate: 2 to 6 hr. Grill: 8 min.

It's hard to resist the classic combination of lamb and rosemary. In this dinner on a stick, the dynamite duo gets a flavor boost from garlic, lemon peel, and cumin.

- 1   lb. lean boneless leg of lamb
- ¼   cup olive oil
- 1   tsp. finely shredded lemon peel
- 3   Tbsp. lemon juice
- 1   Tbsp. snipped fresh rosemary
- ½   tsp. ground cumin
- ½   tsp. pepper
- ¼   tsp. salt
- 2   cloves garlic, minced
- 2   small red onions, each cut into 8 wedges
      Hot cooked couscous (optional)

1. Trim fat from meat. Cut meat into 1½-inch pieces. Place meat in a resealable plastic bag set in a shallow dish. For marinade, in a small bowl, combine oil, lemon peel, lemon juice, rosemary, cumin, pepper, salt, and garlic. Pour marinade over meat. Seal bag; turn to coat meat. Marinate in the refrigerator for at least 2 hours or up to 6 hours, turning bag occasionally.

2. In a covered medium saucepan, cook onions in a small amount of boiling water for 3 minutes; drain. Drain meat, reserving marinade. On 8 long metal skewers, alternately thread meat and onion wedges, leaving about ¼ inch of space between pieces. Brush onion wedges with some of the reserved marinade.

3. Grill kabobs on the rack of an uncovered grill directly over medium coals for 8 to 12 minutes or until medium-rare doneness (145°F), turning once and brushing once with reserved marinade halfway through grilling. Discard any remaining marinade. If desired, serve with hot cooked couscous. Makes 4 servings.

Nutrition facts per serving: 277 cal., 18 g total fat (4 g sat. fat), 72 mg chol., 200 mg sodium, 4 g carbo., 1 g fiber, 24 g pro.

Feta-Stuffed Pita Burgers

Prep: 15 min. Grill: 14 min.

These Greek-inspired burgers are flavored with cayenne pepper, lemon pepper, cumin, and oregano. What's more, they hide a pocket of feta cheese.

- 2   Tbsp. milk
- 2   Tbsp. cornmeal
- 1   Tbsp. finely chopped onion
- 1   clove garlic, minced
- ¼   tsp. salt
- ¼   tsp. dried oregano, crushed
- ¼   tsp. ground cumin
- ⅛   tsp. cayenne pepper
- ⅛   tsp. lemon-pepper seasoning
- 8   oz. lean ground lamb
- 8   oz. lean ground beef
- ¼   cup finely crumbled feta cheese (1 oz.)
- 2   large pita bread rounds, split
- 1½ cups shredded fresh spinach

1. In a medium bowl, combine milk, cornmeal, onion, garlic, salt, oregano, cumin, cayenne pepper, and lemon-pepper seasoning. Add meats; mix well. Shape into 8 oval patties, each about ¼ inch thick. Place *1 tablespoon* of the feta in center of *each of 4* of the ovals. Top with remaining ovals; press edges to seal. Reshape patties as necessary.

2. Grill patties on the rack of an uncovered grill directly over medium coals for 14 to 18 minutes or until done (160°F) (tip, page 71). Serve patties in pitas with shredded spinach. Makes 4 servings.

Nutrition facts per serving: 345 cal., 17 g total fat (7 g sat. fat), 80 mg chol., 493 mg sodium, 22 g carbo., 1 g fiber, 25 g pro.

In the 1970s, American cooks set their sights abroad, taking an avid interest in foreign cooking. Responding to the trend, we featured more international flavors in our recipes, including those cooked over a hot fire. The recipes for sauces, rubs, and fillings became (and are) perfect ways for our readers to try unfamiliar ingredients and new flavor combinations.

Yesterday

Finger-lickin' barbecued chicken has been a cookout headliner for decades. Our tried-and-true version with a honey and molasses sauce is a knockout. Be sure to supply plenty of napkins to wipe what you can't lick off your fingers.

Sticky Sloppy Barbecue
Chicken (recipe, page 84)

82

Peanut-Ginger Chicken with
California Salsa (recipe, page 84)

Today

In looking for a new take on old-fashioned barbecued chicken,
we chose these peanut butter-marinated chicken thighs topped
with a fresh fruit-and-cilantro salsa. The recipe is an intriguing
blend of Asian and Tex-Mex cooking.

Sticky Sloppy Barbecue Chicken

Prep: 20 min. Marinate: 2 to 4 hr. Grill: 50 min.

Honey and molasses combine with two kinds of pepper for a sweet, yet sassy, chicken brush-on. (Photo on page 82.)

      3   to 4 lb. meaty chicken pieces
          (breast halves, thighs, and drumsticks)
   1 ½   cups dry sherry
      1   cup finely chopped onion
      ¼   cup lemon juice
      6   cloves garlic, minced
      2   bay leaves
      1   15-oz. can tomato puree
      ¼   cup honey
      3   Tbsp. molasses
      1   tsp. salt
      ½   tsp. dried thyme, crushed
      ¼   to ½ tsp. cayenne pepper
      ¼   tsp. ground black pepper
      2   Tbsp. white vinegar

1. Place chicken in a resealable plastic bag set in a shallow dish. For marinade, in a medium bowl, stir together sherry, onion, lemon juice, garlic, and bay leaves. Pour marinade over chicken. Seal bag; turn to coat chicken. Marinate in the refrigerator for at least 2 hours or up to 4 hours, turning bag occasionally.

2. Drain chicken, reserving marinade. In a grill with a cover, arrange medium-hot coals around a drip pan. Test for medium heat above pan. Place chicken pieces, bone sides down, on grill rack over drip pan. Cover and grill for 50 to 60 minutes or until tender and no longer pink (170°F for breast halves; 180°F for thighs and drumsticks), brushing with some of the sauce during the last 15 minutes of grilling.

3. Meanwhile, for sauce, in a large saucepan, combine the reserved marinade, the tomato puree, honey, molasses, salt, thyme, cayenne pepper, and black pepper. Bring to boiling; reduce heat. Simmer, uncovered, about 30 minutes or until reduced to 2 cups. Remove from heat. Discard bay leaves. Stir in vinegar.

4. To serve, reheat remaining sauce until bubbly; serve with chicken. Makes 6 servings.

Nutrition facts per serving: 454 cal., 13 g total fat (4 g sat. fat), 104 mg chol., 504 mg sodium, 32 g carbo., 1 g fiber, 35 g pro.

Peanut-Ginger Chicken With California Salsa

Prep: 35 min. Marinate: 12 to 24 hr. Grill: 50 min.

For a snazzy tropical presentation, line dinner plates with ti leaves. (Photo on page 83.)

     12   chicken thighs (about 3 lb.), skinned
      ½   cup boiling water
      ½   cup creamy peanut butter
      ¼   cup bottled chili sauce
      3   Tbsp. soy sauce
      2   Tbsp. cooking oil
      2   Tbsp. vinegar
      4   cloves garlic, minced
      1   Tbsp. grated fresh ginger
          or ¾ tsp. ground ginger
      ¼   tsp. cayenne pepper
      1   recipe California Salsa (below)
          Hot cooked rice (optional)
          Green onions, slivered (optional)

1. Place chicken in a large resealable plastic bag set in a shallow bowl. For marinade, in a medium bowl, gradually stir boiling water into peanut butter (mixture will stiffen at first.) Stir in chili sauce, soy sauce, oil, vinegar, garlic, ginger, and cayenne pepper; pour over chicken. Seal; turn to coat. Marinate in refrigerator for at least 12 hours or up to 24 hours, turning occasionally.

2. Drain chicken, discarding marinade. Prepare California Salsa. In a grill with a cover, arrange medium-hot coals around drip pan. Test for medium heat above pan. Place chicken on grill rack over drip pan. Cover and grill for 50 to 60 minutes or until chicken is tender and no longer pink (180°F), turning once. Serve with California Salsa. If desired, serve with rice and garnish with green onions. Makes 6 servings.

California Salsa: In a medium bowl, combine 1 ½ cups chopped fresh fruit (such as peeled peaches, nectarines, plums, or pears), ½ cup chopped seeded cucumber, 2 tablespoons thinly sliced green onion, 2 tablespoons snipped fresh parsley or cilantro, 1 tablespoon sugar, 1 tablespoon cooking oil, and 1 tablespoon lime juice or vinegar. Cover and chill in the refrigerator for at least 1 hour or up to 2 hours.

Nutrition facts per serving: 290 cal., 15 g total fat (3 g sat. fat), 91 mg chol., 426 mg sodium, 13 g carbo., 2 g fiber, 27 g pro.

Test Kitchen Tip: If you're using ti leaves, be sure they have not been sprayed or treated in a way that would make them unsafe for contact with food. Wash them well before using. Although ti leaves aren't toxic, they should not be eaten.

Honey-Dijon Barbecued Chicken

Prep: 15 min. Marinate: 2 to 4 hr. Grill: 50 min.

We snagged this recipe for great-tasting chicken from a member of the Kansas City Barbecue Society, a group with a passion for barbecue and lots of experience in grilling competitions.

1	3-lb. broiler-fryer chicken, quartered
¼	cup olive oil
¼	cup white Zinfandel wine
2	Tbsp. honey
2	Tbsp. Dijon-style mustard
1	clove garlic, minced
½	tsp. pepper
¼	tsp. salt

1. Place chicken in a resealable plastic bag set in a large bowl. For marinade, in a small bowl, mix oil, wine, honey, mustard, garlic, pepper, and salt. Pour over chicken. Seal bag; turn to coat chicken. Marinate in refrigerator for at least 2 hours or up to 4 hours, turning bag occasionally.

2. Drain chicken, reserving marinade. In a grill with a cover, arrange medium-hot coals around a drip pan. Test for medium heat above the pan. Place chicken, bone sides up, on grill rack over drip pan. Cover and grill for 50 to 60 minutes or until chicken is tender and no longer pink (170°F for breast portions; 180°F for thigh-drumstick portions), brushing once with reserved marinade after 30 minutes of grilling. Discard any remaining marinade. Makes 4 servings.

Nutrition facts per serving: 380 cal., 23 g total fat (6 g sat. fat), 118 mg chol., 171 mg sodium, 3 g carbo., 0 g fiber, 37 g pro.

Honey-Dijon
Barbecued Chicken

Spice-Grilled Chicken

Prep: 20 min. Grill: 1 hr. for whole bird;
50 min. for drumsticks Stand: 10 min.

This recipe allows you to choose between grilling a whole bird or drumsticks for dinner. The cinnamon and allspice rub and the jasmine rice and fruit pilaf give the grilled poultry exotic flair.

2	tsp. packed brown sugar
1½	tsp. ground cinnamon
1	tsp. smoked paprika or paprika
½	tsp. salt
½	tsp. pepper
½	tsp. ground allspice
1	3-lb. whole roasting chicken or 12 chicken drumsticks
4	tsp. cooking oil
2	cups chicken broth
1	cup jasmine or long grain rice
¼	cup snipped dried apricots
¼	cup golden raisins
2	Tbsp. chopped peanuts

1. In a small bowl, combine brown sugar, cinnamon, paprika, salt, pepper, and allspice. Set aside *1½ teaspoons* of the mixture. For whole chicken, skewer chicken neck skin to back and twist wing tips under back. Brush whole chicken or drumsticks with oil. Sprinkle remaining cinnamon mixture evenly onto chicken; rub in with your fingers. For whole chicken, tie legs to tail.

2. In a grill with a cover, arrange medium-hot coals around a drip pan. Test for medium heat above pan. Place whole chicken, breast side up, on the grill rack over drip pan. Cover and grill for 1 to 1¼ hours or until an instant-read thermometer inserted in center of an inside thigh muscle registers 180°F. Add more coals as needed. (Or grill drumsticks on grill rack over drip pan for 50 to 60 minutes or until chicken is tender and no longer pink [180°F].)

3. Meanwhile, in a medium saucepan, combine the 1½ teaspoons reserved cinnamon mixture, the broth, and uncooked rice. Bring to boiling; reduce heat. Cover and simmer for 15 minutes. Remove from heat. Stir in dried apricots and raisins. Cover and let stand for 5 minutes before serving.

4. Remove chicken from grill. Cover with foil; let stand for 10 minutes. Using kitchen shears, cut whole chicken into 4 to 6 pieces. Spoon rice onto platter; top with chicken. Sprinkle with peanuts. Serves 6.

Nutrition facts per serving: 534 cal., 28 g total fat (7 g sat. fat), 115 mg chol., 631 mg sodium, 37 g carbo., 2 g fiber, 33 g pro.

Lemon-Herb Chicken
And Vegetable Kabobs

Prep: 30 min. Marinate: 2 hr. Grill: 5 + 5 min.

Try a different combination of herbs each time
you grill these eye-catching potato, squash, and
marinated chicken kabobs.

- 8 **tiny new potatoes, halved**
- 1 **medium yellow summer squash, cut into
  1-inch pieces**
- 2 **skinless, boneless chicken breast halves
  (about 10 oz. total), cut into 1-inch pieces**
- ⅓ **cup lemon juice or lime juice**
- 2 **Tbsp. olive oil or cooking oil**
- 2 **Tbsp. water**
- 3 **cloves garlic, minced**
- 4 **tsp. snipped fresh basil or oregano
  or 1 tsp. dried basil or oregano, crushed**
- 2 **tsp. snipped fresh thyme or rosemary or
  ½ tsp. dried thyme or rosemary, crushed**
- ½ **tsp. salt**
- ¼ **tsp. ground black pepper**
- 1 **large red sweet pepper, cut into
  1-inch pieces**

1. In a covered medium saucepan, cook potatoes
in a small amount of boiling water for 12 minutes. Add
squash; cook, covered, for 1 to 2 minutes more or until
vegetables are nearly tender. Drain and cool.

2. Place chicken in a resealable plastic bag set in a
medium bowl. For marinade, in a small bowl, combine
lemon juice, oil, the water, garlic, basil or oregano, thyme
or rosemary, salt, and black pepper. Add potatoes,
squash, and sweet pepper to chicken in plastic bag.
Pour marinade over chicken and vegetables. Seal bag;
turn to coat chicken and vegetables. Marinate in the
refrigerator for 2 hours, turning bag occasionally.

3. Meanwhile, soak wooden skewers in enough water
to cover for 30 minutes; drain. Drain the chicken and
vegetables, reserving the marinade. On the soaked
skewers, alternately thread the chicken, potato, squash,
and sweet pepper pieces, leaving about ¼ inch of space
between pieces.

4. Place kabobs on the rack of uncovered gill directly
over medium-hot coals. Grill for 5 minutes, brushing
frequently with reserved marinade. Discard any remaining
marinade. Turn; grill for 5 to 7 minutes more or until
chicken is tender and no longer pink. Makes 4 servings.

Broiling directions: Prepare as directed through
step 3. Preheat broiler. Place kabobs on the unheated
rack of a broiler pan. Broil 4 to 5 inches from heat for
5 minutes, brushing frequently with reserved marinade.
Discard any remaining marinade. Turn and broil for
5 to 7 minutes more or until chicken is tender and no
longer pink.

Nutrition facts per serving: 194 cal., 5 g total fat (1 g sat. fat),
41 mg chol., 187 mg sodium, 19 g carbo., 3 g fiber, 19 g pro.

Jambalaya on a Stick

Prep: 35 min. Marinate: 1 to 2 hr. Grill: 12 min.

This grill-side adaptation of a Cajun favorite served on skewers won top honors in our Short-Order Kabobs Prize Tested Recipes® contest in July 2000.

18	fresh or frozen large shrimp in shells (about 12 oz.)
12	oz. cooked smoked sausage links, cut into 12 pieces
8	oz. skinless, boneless chicken breast halves, cut into 1-inch pieces
1	medium green sweet pepper, cut into 1-inch pieces
1	medium onion, cut into 1-inch wedges
⅓	cup white wine vinegar
⅓	cup tomato sauce
2	Tbsp. olive oil
2	tsp. dried thyme, crushed
2	tsp. bottled hot pepper sauce
¾	tsp. dried minced garlic
3	cups hot cooked rice
2	Tbsp. snipped fresh parsley
6	cherry tomatoes

1. Thaw shrimp, if frozen. Peel and devein shrimp. Rinse shrimp; pat dry with paper towels. Place shrimp, sausage, chicken, sweet pepper, and onion in a resealable plastic bag set in a large bowl.

2. For marinade, in a small bowl, combine vinegar, tomato sauce, oil, thyme, hot pepper sauce, and garlic. Pour *half* of the tomato sauce mixture over meat and vegetables. Seal bag; turn to coat pieces. Marinate in refrigerator at least 1 hour or up to 2 hours, turning bag occasionally. Cover and chill remaining marinade.

3. Meanwhile, soak wooden skewers in enough water to cover for 30 minutes; drain. Drain meat and vegetables, discarding marinade. On soaked skewers, alternately thread meat and vegetables, leaving about ¼ inch of space between pieces.

4. Grill kabobs on rack of an uncovered grill directly over medium coals for 12 to 14 minutes or until shrimp turn opaque and chicken is no longer pink, turning occasionally.

5. Meanwhile, in a small saucepan, heat chilled tomato sauce mixture until bubbly. Combine cooked rice and the parsley. Serve rice mixture and cherry tomatoes with kabobs. Pass warmed tomato sauce mixture. Makes 6 servings.

Nutrition facts per serving: 451 cal., 23 g total fat (9 g sat. fat), 112 mg chol., 632 mg sodium, 30 g carbo., 2 g fiber, 27 g pro.

Indoor Grilling

With the introduction of tabletop indoor grills in the 1990s, Americans took to indoor grilling in a big way. In 2000, we jumped on the bandwagon and published *Better Homes and Gardens® Indoor Grilling* cookbook. Indoor grills are available both covered and uncovered and in many styles and sizes. Some are even designed for indoor or outdoor use. Although recipes are tested specifically for the indoor grill, many of your favorite outdoor grilling recipes may work indoors on these units too. When adapting a recipe for the indoor grill, keep these pointers in mind:

• Look for a similar recipe in the owner's manual or cookbook that came with your unit and be sure to follow the manufacturer's directions and timings.

• For best results, use your indoor grill for direct grilling items no more than 1 inch thick. Burgers, steaks, chops, skinless, boneless chicken breasts, fish fillets or steaks, and hot dogs or other cooked sausages work best.

• For covered grills, opt for boneless cuts because the bone-in steaks and chops may prevent the lid from closing.

• Choose recipes that add a sauce or glaze only during the last few minutes of grilling; otherwise, the brush-on may burn and give an unpleasant flavor.

Turkey Tenderloin And Vegetables

Prep: 20 min. Grill: 20 + 10 min.

Grilling turkey tenderloin pieces is an easy way to put dinner on the table in a hurry. In this editors' favorite recipe, vegetable juice—with a few added ingredients—doubles as a basting sauce.

⅓ cup vegetable juice
⅓ cup mayonnaise or salad dressing
2 tsp. snipped fresh thyme
    or ½ tsp. dried thyme, crushed
2 cloves garlic, minced
2 Tbsp. olive oil
¼ tsp. salt
¼ tsp. pepper
1 lb. turkey breast tenderloins
2 small zucchini, bias-cut into
    ½-inch-thick slices
2 large plum tomatoes, halved
    or quartered lengthwise
    Fresh chives with blossoms (optional)

1. For sauce, in a small bowl, gradually stir vegetable juice into mayonnaise; stir in *half* of the thyme and the garlic. Cover and chill until needed.

2. In another small bowl, stir together olive oil, salt, pepper, and remaining thyme. Brush *some* of the oil mixture over turkey.

3. In a grill with a cover, arrange medium-hot coals around a drip pan. Test for medium heat above pan. Place turkey on grill rack over pan. Cover and grill for 20 minutes. Add zucchini and tomatoes, cut sides down, to outside edge of grill rack over coals. Brush with remaining oil mixture. Grill about 10 minutes more or until zucchini and tomatoes are tender and turkey is no longer pink (170°F), turning vegetables once. (If the zucchini and tomatoes are done before the turkey, remove them from the grill and keep them warm.) Serve with sauce. If desired, garnish with chives. Makes 4 servings.

Nutrition facts per serving: 343 cal., 23 g total fat (4 g sat. fat), 79 mg chol., 362 mg sodium, 6 g carbo., 1 g fiber, 28 g pro.

Turkey Tenderloin and Vegetables

Glazed Turkey Burgers

Prep: 20 min.   Grill: 14 min.

These best-loved burgers get a delightful fruit flavor from preserves slathered on just at the end of grilling.

- 1   **Tbsp. yellow mustard**
- 1   **Tbsp. cherry, apricot, peach, or pineapple preserves**
- 1   **egg**
- ¼   **cup quick-cooking rolled oats**
- ¼   **cup finely chopped celery**
- 3   **Tbsp. snipped dried tart cherries or dried apricots (optional)**
- ¼   **tsp. salt**
- ⅛   **tsp. pepper**
- 1   **lb. uncooked ground turkey or chicken**
- 4   **kaiser rolls or hamburger buns, split and toasted**
  Mayonnaise or salad dressing, lettuce leaves, and/or tomato slices (optional)

1. For glaze, in a small bowl, stir together mustard and preserves; set aside. In a medium bowl, beat egg with a fork. Stir in rolled oats, celery, dried cherries or apricots (if desired), salt, and pepper. Add the ground turkey; mix well. Shape the turkey mixture into four ¾-inch-thick patties.

2. Grill patties on the rack of an uncovered grill directly over medium coals for 14 to 18 minutes or until no longer pink (165°F) (tip, page 73), turning once halfway through grilling and brushing with glaze during the last minute of grilling.

3. Brush any remaining glaze onto patties. Serve patties on buns. If desired, serve burgers with mayonnaise, lettuce, and/or tomato. Makes 4 servings.

Nutrition facts per serving: 397 cal., 14 g total fat (3 g sat. fat), 143 mg chol., 599 mg sodium, 38 g carbo., 2 g fiber, 28 g pro.

> **Chicken and turkey pieces weren't commonly available in supermarkets until the 1940s. Before that, cooks had to cut apart whole birds themselves or ask a butcher do it.**

Rosemary-Orange Turkey

Prep: 20 min.   Soak: 1 hr. (optional)   Grill: 2½ hr.

Turkey isn't just for Thanksgiving any more. In fact, it's ideal for summer barbecues and family reunions. This hickory-smoked version will be a surefire hit at your next backyard party.

- 4   **cups hickory wood chips (optional)**
- 2   **Tbsp. butter or margarine, softened**
- 2   **Tbsp. snipped fresh rosemary**
- 2   **Tbsp. finely shredded orange peel**
- ¼   **tsp. salt**
- 1   **8- to 10-lb. turkey**
- 2   **Tbsp. cooking oil**

1. If using wood chips, at least 1 hour before grilling, soak wood chips in enough water to cover. In a small bowl, combine butter, rosemary, orange peel, and salt; set aside.

2. Remove the neck and giblets from turkey; save for another use or discard. Rinse the inside of the turkey; pat dry with paper towels. Slip your fingers between the skin and meat to loosen turkey skin over breast area. Lift turkey skin and carefully spread butter mixture directly over turkey meat. Skewer the neck skin to the back. Twist wing tips under back. Tuck drumsticks under the band of skin across the tail or tie legs to tail with 100%-cotton kitchen string. Insert an oven-going meat thermometer into the center of an inside thigh muscle, making sure bulb does not touch bone. Brush turkey with oil.

3. Drain wood chips, if using. In a grill with a cover, arrange medium-hot coals around a drip pan. Test for medium heat above pan. If using wood chips, sprinkle some of them over the coals. Place turkey on grill rack over pan. Cover; grill for 2½ to 3 hours or until meat thermometer registers 180°F. Add coals and remaining wood chips as needed. Makes 10 to 12 servings.

Nutrition facts per serving: 406 cal., 16 g total fat (5 g sat. fat), 226 mg chol., 201 mg sodium, 0 g carbo., 0 g fiber, 61 g pro.

When we first published grilled fish recipes half a century ago, many areas of the country were limited in the types available. Salmon, however, was one of the few fish most cooks could get. Here's a great grilled salmon recipe from our archives.

Dilly Salmon Fillets

Prep: 15 min. Marinate: 10 min. Grill: 5 + 2 min.

If you think your salmon may fall apart on the grill, cook it on foil. Cut slits in a double layer of heavy foil and lightly grease the foil. Place the fish on the foil and place it on the grill rack; turn the fish with a wide spatula.

   4   5- to 6-oz. fresh or frozen skinless
       salmon fillets, ½ to ¾ inch thick
   3   Tbsp. lemon juice
   2   Tbsp. snipped fresh dill
   2   Tbsp. mayonnaise or salad dressing
   2   tsp. Dijon-style mustard
       Dash pepper
       Lemon slices (optional)
       Fresh dill sprigs (optional)

1. Thaw fish, if frozen. Rinse fish; pat dry with paper towels. Place fish in a shallow dish. In a small bowl, combine the lemon juice and *1 tablespoon* of the snipped dill; pour over fish. Turn fish to coat. Marinate at room temperature for 10 minutes. Meanwhile, in a small bowl, stir together the remaining 1 tablespoon snipped dill, the mayonnaise, mustard, and pepper; set aside.

2. In a grill with a cover, arrange medium-hot coals around a drip pan. Drain fish, discarding marinade. Test for medium heat above pan. Place the fish on the lightly greased grill rack over the drip pan. Cover and grill for 5 minutes.

3. Turn fish; spoon the mayonnaise mixture onto fish. Cover and grill for 2 to 8 minutes more or just until fish flakes easily when tested with a fork. If desired, garnish with lemon slices and dill sprigs. Makes 4 servings.

Nutrition facts per serving: 211 cal., 11 g total fat (2 g sat. fat), 35 mg chol., 204 mg sodium, 1 g carbo., 0 g fiber, 25 g pro.

Grilled Bass with Star Fruit Salsa

Prep: 25 min.   Grill: 14 min.

Enjoy this refreshing salsa-topped sea bass for dinner when the weather's hot and sultry.

4	fresh or frozen sea bass or red snapper fillets, about 1 inch thick (1 lb. total)
½	to 1 tsp. cumin seeds
3	large star fruit (carambola)
1	small lime
2	Tbsp. snipped fresh cilantro
½	of a small fresh poblano chile pepper, seeded and finely chopped (tip, page 32)
½	tsp. salt
¼	tsp. cayenne pepper
	Hot cooked couscous (optional)
	Lime wedges (optional)
	Snipped fresh cilantro (optional)

1. Thaw fish, if frozen. Rinse fish; pat dry with paper towels. Set aside.

2. For salsa, in a dry skillet, cook cumin seeds, uncovered, over medium-high heat for 1 to 2 minutes or until toasted, shaking the skillet frequently. Set cumin seeds aside. Slice a star fruit; cover and chill. Chop remaining star fruit; set aside. Finely shred peel of the small lime; set aside. Complete removing lime peel; seed and chop small lime. In a small bowl, combine toasted cumin seeds, chopped star fruit, chopped lime, the 2 tablespoons cilantro, the poblano pepper, and *⅛ teaspoon* of the salt; cover and chill.

3. Sprinkle fish with shredded lime peel, remaining salt, and the cayenne pepper. In a grill with a cover, arrange medium-hot coals around a drip pan. Test for medium heat above pan. Place fish fillets on grill rack over drip pan. Cover and grill for 14 to 18 minutes or just until fish flakes easily when tested with a fork. If desired, serve fish with hot cooked couscous. Serve with star fruit salsa; garnish with the sliced star fruit. If desired, serve with lime wedges and sprinkle with additional snipped cilantro. Makes 4 servings.

Nutrition facts per serving: 143 cal., 3 g total fat (1 g sat. fat), 47 mg chol., 280 mg sodium, 8 g carbo., 1 g fiber, 22 g pro.

Ginger Tuna Kabobs

Prep: 25 min. Stand: 20 min. Grill: 8 min.

These eye-catching, prizewinning tuna and pineapple kabobs appeared in the July 2000 issue of the *Better Homes and Gardens®* magazine.

12	oz. fresh or frozen skinless tuna steaks
3	Tbsp. reduced-sodium soy sauce
3	Tbsp. water
1	Tbsp. snipped green onion tops or snipped fresh chives
2	tsp. grated fresh ginger
½	of a medium pineapple, peeled, cored, and cut into 1-inch cubes
1	medium red or green sweet pepper, cubed
6	green onions, cut into 2-inch pieces
¼	cup honey

1. Thaw fish, if frozen. Rinse fish; pat dry with paper towels. Cut fish into 1-inch cubes. Place in a resealable plastic bag. For marinade, in a small bowl, combine soy sauce, the water, snipped green onion tops or chives, and ginger. Pour marinade over fish. Seal bag; turn gently to coat fish. Let stand at room temperature for 20 minutes.

2. Drain, reserving marinade. On 8 long metal skewers, alternately thread fish, pineapple, sweet pepper, and green onion pieces, leaving about ¼ inch of space between pieces. Grill kabobs directly over medium coals for 8 to 12 minutes or just until fish flakes easily when tested with a fork, turning once.

3. Meanwhile, bring reserved marinade to boiling; strain. Discard any solids. Stir honey into hot marinade. Brush fish, fruit, and vegetables generously with honey-soy mixture just before serving. Makes 4 servings.

Nutrition facts per serving: 251 cal., 5 g total fat (1 g sat. fat), 32 mg chol., 446 mg sodium, 32 g carbo., 2 g fiber, 22 g pro.

Grilling became so popular that in the 1953 edition of the *Better Homes and Gardens® New Cook Book,* we added an Outdoor Cooking section. It focused on tips and recipes that made barbecuing fun for the whole family.

Fiesta Shrimp Skewers

Fiesta Shrimp Skewers

Prep: 30 min. Marinate: 30 min. to 1 hr. Grill: 5 min.

Fire up the grill for your next party and serve these sassy ale-marinated shrimp. Tame the heat from the marinade with plenty of creamy cilantro dip.

1	lb. fresh or frozen medium shrimp in shells
½	cup amber ale or other desired ale
½	tsp. finely shredded lime peel
¼	cup lime juice
2	Tbsp. snipped fresh cilantro
1	small fresh jalapeño chile pepper, seeded and finely chopped (tip, page 32)
1	clove garlic, minced
¼	tsp. ground cumin
⅛	tsp. cayenne pepper
2	fresh poblano chile peppers, seeded and cut into 1-inch pieces (tip, page 32)
2	limes, cut up
1	recipe Cool Cilantro Dip (top right)

1. Thaw shrimp, if frozen. Peel and devein shrimp, leaving tails intact. Rinse shrimp; pat dry with paper towels. Place shrimp in a resealable plastic bag set in a shallow dish. For marinade, in a small bowl, combine ale, lime peel, lime juice, cilantro, jalapeño pepper, garlic, cumin, and cayenne pepper. Pour marinade over shrimp. Seal bag; turn to coat shrimp. Marinate in the refrigerator for 30 minutes to 1 hour, turning bag occasionally.

2. Meanwhile, soak wooden skewers in enough water to cover for 30 minutes; drain. Drain shrimp, reserving marinade. On soaked skewers, alternately thread shrimp, poblano peppers, and lime pieces, leaving about ¼ inch of space between pieces. Brush with reserved marinade. Discard any remaining marinade.

3. Grill skewers on the rack of an uncovered grill directly over medium coals for 5 to 8 minutes or until shrimp turn opaque, turning once. Serve with Cool Cilantro Dip. Makes 10 to 12 appetizer servings.

Cool Cilantro Dip: In a small bowl, stir together one 8-ounce carton light dairy sour cream, 2 tablespoons snipped fresh cilantro, 1 tablespoon bottled salsa, ½ teaspoon finely shredded lime peel, and 1 clove garlic, minced. Cover and chill until serving time.

Nutrition facts per serving: 81 cal., 3 g total fat (1 g sat. fat), 59 mg chol., 71 mg sodium, 5 g carbo., 1 g fiber, 9 g pro.

Sizzling Vegetable Sandwiches
Prep: 30 min. Grill: 12 min.

Professional and home cooks alike enjoy tinkering with new ingredient and flavor combinations. Our staff is no exception. Here's one of our 1990s creations—a grilled summer vegetable sandwich spruced up with a cumin-flavored mayonnaise.

1	**small eggplant, cut lengthwise into ½-inch-thick slices**
1	**medium zucchini, cut lengthwise into ¼-inch-thick slices**
1	**medium yellow summer squash, cut lengthwise into ¼-inch-thick slices**
1	**medium red sweet pepper, seeded and quartered**
⅓	**cup olive oil**
1	**small onion, cut into ½-inch-thick slices**
	Salt
	Ground black pepper
4	**kaiser rolls, French rolls, or other sandwich rolls, split**
1	**recipe Cumin Mayo (top right)**

1. Brush eggplant, zucchini, yellow squash, and sweet pepper with some of the olive oil. Using a long metal skewer, skewer onion slices through sides to secure; brush with some of the olive oil. Lightly sprinkle the vegetables with salt and black pepper.

2. Grill vegetables on the rack of an uncovered grill directly over medium coals for 12 to 15 minutes or until the vegetables are tender, turning once. (If some vegetables cook more quickly than others, remove and keep warm.) Cut up vegetables.

3. Meanwhile, brush the cut sides of the rolls with remaining olive oil. Grill rolls, cut sides down, about 1 minute or until toasted.

4. Spread tops and bottoms of rolls with Cumin Mayo. Layer grilled vegetables on the bottom halves of the rolls. Cover sandwiches with roll tops. Makes 4 servings.

Cumin Mayo: In a small bowl, stir together ½ cup mayonnaise or salad dressing; 1 tablespoon lime juice; 1 clove garlic, minced; and ½ teaspoon cumin seeds, crushed, or ¼ teaspoon ground cumin.

Broiling directions: Brush vegetables with some of the olive oil. Place half of the vegetables on unheated rack of a broiler pan. Broil 3 to 4 inches from the heat for 12 to 15 minutes or until vegetables are tender, turning once. Remove and cover to keep warm. Repeat with remaining vegetables. Cut up vegetables. Toast rolls under broiler about 1 minute. Serve as directed.

Nutrition facts per serving: 572 cal., 43 g total fat (6 g sat. fat), 10 mg chol., 611 mg sodium, 41 g carbo., 5 g fiber, 8 g pro.

Sizzling Vegetable Sandwiches

Hobo Potatoes

Hobo Potatoes

Prep: 15 min. Grill: 20 min.

Cooking vegetables in a foil packet dates back to our earliest coverage of grilling. Our 1995 version dresses up the old standby potatoes with bacon, sweet pepper, onion, and cheddar cheese.

    Nonstick cooking spray
3   **slices bacon, coarsely chopped**
4   **cups ¼-inch-thick sliced potatoes**
½   **cup chopped green sweet pepper**
½   **cup chopped onion**
1   **cup shredded cheddar cheese (4 oz.)**
¼   **tsp. seasoned salt**
¼   **tsp. ground black pepper**

1. Fold a 36×18-inch piece of heavy foil in half to make an 18-inch square. Lightly coat one side of the foil square with nonstick cooking spray. On coated surface, arrange *half* of the bacon in the center of the foil. Top with *half* of the potatoes, *half* of the sweet pepper, *half* of the onion, and *half* of the cheese. Top with remaining potatoes, remaining sweet pepper, and remaining onion. Sprinkle with seasoned salt and black pepper. Top with remaining cheese and remaining bacon.

2. Lightly coat one side of another 18-inch square piece of double thickness heavy foil with nonstick cooking spray; place foil, coated side down, on top of potato stack. Seal all edges with a double fold, leaving space for steam to build. Grill vegetable packet on the grill rack of an uncovered grill directly over medium coals for 20 to 25 minutes or until potatoes are tender, turning the packet once. Makes 8 servings.

Nutrition facts per serving: 284 cal., 20 g total fat (11 g sat. fat), 47 mg chol., 377 mg sodium, 14 g carbo., 2 g fiber, 12 g pro.

Tomato Melts

Prep: 15 min. Grill: 12 min.

Enjoy summer's fresh tomatoes with this easy fix-up that won our July 1999 Summertime Starters Prize Tested Recipes® category. Serve it either as an appetizer or a side dish.

3   **large tomatoes and/or a variety of smaller tomatoes (about 1½ lb. total)**
1   **cup shredded Monterey Jack cheese with jalapeño peppers or Monterey Jack cheese**
1   **small green, yellow, purple, or red sweet pepper, finely chopped**
¼   **cup sliced almonds, toasted (tip, page 102)**

1. Cut each tomato into 4 slices, each about ½ inch thick. (If using smaller tomatoes, halve each one.) In a disposable foil pan, arrange tomato slices in 4 rows (3 slices per row), overlapping slices slightly. (Or if using smaller tomatoes, arrange in a single layer in a shallow disposable foil pan.) Sprinkle tomatoes with cheese, sweet pepper, and toasted almonds.

2. In a grill with a cover, arrange medium-hot coals around the edge of the grill; test for medium heat above the center of the grill (not over coals). Place the foil pan with the tomatoes in the center of the grill rack (not over coals). Cover and grill for 12 to 15 minutes or until cheese is bubbly. Makes 4 servings.

Nutrition facts per serving: 203 cal., 14 g total fat (6 g sat. fat), 25 mg chol., 172 mg sodium, 13 g carbo., 2 g fiber, 10 g pro.

Portobello Flats

Prep: 15 min. Grill: 6 min.

In the 1990s, Americans fell in love with portobello mushrooms, and we found a host of ways to use them. This sandwich makes the most of the mushroom's meaty texture and rich flavor. Serve it with a hearty soup or salad.

⅔   **cup chopped tomato**
2   **tsp. snipped fresh basil, thyme, and/or oregano**
⅛   **tsp. salt**
2   **medium fresh portobello mushrooms (about 4 inches in diameter)**
1   **tsp. balsamic vinegar or red wine vinegar**
½   **tsp. olive oil**
½   **of a 12-inch Italian flatbread (focaccia), quartered, or ½ of a 12-inch thin-crust Italian bread shell (Boboli)**

1. In a small bowl, stir together tomato, desired herb, and salt; set aside. Cut the mushroom stems even with the caps; discard stems. Rinse mushroom caps; gently pat dry with paper towels.

2. In a small bowl, stir together vinegar and oil. Gently brush vinegar-oil mixture onto the mushrooms. Grill mushrooms on the rack of an uncovered grill directly over medium coals for 6 to 8 minutes or just until tender, turning once. Thinly slice mushrooms.

3. Place the bread on the grill rack during the last 2 to 3 minutes of grilling to heat through. To serve, top bread with mushrooms and tomato mixture. Serves 4.

Nutrition facts per serving: 157 cal., 3 g total fat (1 g sat. fat), 0 mg chol., 80 mg sodium, 28 g carbo., 4 g fiber, 7 g pro.

Vegetable Packet Deluxe

Prep: 20 min. Grill: 15 min.

Packet cooking continues to be a favorite with our editors for three reasons: It seals in wonderful flavor, it allows you to cook vegetables almost unattended, and it eliminates messy cleanup.

¼	**cup butter or margarine, melted**
2	**tsp. snipped fresh basil, thyme, or rosemary, or ½ tsp. dried basil, thyme, or rosemary, crushed**
8	**oz. fresh asparagus spears, trimmed and cut into 1-inch pieces**
1	**medium red sweet pepper, cut into ½-inch-thick strips**
1	**small zucchini, cut into ½-inch-thick slices**
1	**small yellow summer squash, bias-sliced into ½-inch-thick slices**
	Salt
	Ground black pepper
	Fresh herb sprigs (optional)

Vegetable Packet Deluxe

1. In a small bowl, stir together melted butter and desired herb; set aside. In a large bowl, toss together asparagus, sweet pepper, zucchini, and yellow summer squash.

2. Fold a 36×18-inch piece of heavy foil in half to make an 18-inch square. Place vegetables in center of the foil. Drizzle butter mixture over vegetables. Sprinkle with salt and black pepper. Bring up opposite edges of foil; seal with a double fold. Fold remaining edges together to completely enclose vegetables, leaving space for steam to build.

3. Grill vegetable packet on rack of an uncovered grill directly over medium coals for 15 to 20 minutes or until vegetables are tender. Serve immediately. If desired, garnish with fresh herb sprigs. Makes 4 to 6 side-dish servings.

Nutrition facts per serving: 124 cal., 12 g total fat (7 g sat. fat), 31 mg chol., 203 mg sodium, 5 g carbo., 2 g fiber, 2 g pro.

Grilled Banana Split

Prep: 20 min. Soak: 30 min. Grill: 5 min.

Grilling toppers for sundaes has a long history at *Better Homes and Gardens*®. Take this updated banana split for example.

3	**medium bananas, cut into 1-inch chunks**
1½	**cups large strawberries, halved**
1½	**cups fresh pineapple chunks**
1	**pint vanilla ice cream**
½	**cup caramel and/or chocolate ice cream topping**
	Chopped nuts (optional)
	Whipped cream (optional)
	Maraschino cherries (optional)

1. Soak eight 6- or 8-inch wooden skewers in enough water to cover for 30 minutes; drain. Alternately thread bananas, strawberries, and pineapple onto skewers, leaving a ¼-inch of space between pieces.

2. Grill fruit skewers on the rack of an uncovered grill directly over medium coals about 5 minutes or until fruits are warm and bananas are lightly browned, turning occasionally. Remove from grill.

3. Place a scoop of ice cream and 2 fruit skewers in each serving dish. Drizzle with caramel and/or chocolate ice cream topping. If desired, sprinkle with nuts and garnish with whipped cream and maraschino cherries. Makes 4 servings.

Nutrition facts per serving: 434 cal., 13 g total fat (8 g sat. fat), 45 mg chol., 153 mg sodium, 79 g carbo., 5 g fiber, 4 g pro.

Potluck Pleasers

Reunions, church suppers, block parties—no matter what the occasion, potluck meals are a time-honored way to share food and fun with family and friends. Throughout the years, our readers and food editors have exchanged numerous mouthwatering ideas for totable dishes. You'll find the best here in this chapter. So the next time you're looking for a new dish to take along, choose one of these scrumptious main dishes, salads, side dishes, or desserts.

Eight-Layer Casserole

Prep: 30 min. Bake: 45 + 10 min. Stand: 10 min.

One of our readers submitted this homespun ground beef-and-noodle "hot dish" to us in 1991, saying it was her favorite to take to church suppers.

- 6 **oz. dried medium noodles**
- 1 **lb. ground beef**
- 2 **8-oz. cans tomato sauce**
- 1 **tsp. dried basil, crushed**
- ½ **tsp. sugar**
- ½ **tsp. garlic powder**
- ¼ **tsp. salt**
- ¼ **tsp. pepper**
- 1 **8-oz. carton dairy sour cream**
- 1 **8-oz. pkg. cream cheese, softened**
- ½ **cup milk**
- 1 **small onion, chopped**
- 1 **10-oz. pkg. frozen chopped spinach, cooked and well drained**
- 1 **cup shredded cheddar cheese (4 oz.)**

1. Preheat oven to 350°F. Grease a 2-quart casserole or a 2-quart square baking dish; set aside. Cook noodles according to package directions; drain and set aside.

2. Meanwhile, in a large skillet, cook beef until brown. Drain off fat. Stir tomato sauce, basil, sugar, garlic powder, salt, and pepper into beef in skillet. Bring to boiling; reduce heat. Simmer, uncovered, for 5 minutes.

3. In a medium mixing bowl, combine sour cream and cream cheese; beat with an electric mixer on medium speed until smooth. Stir in milk and onion.

4. In prepared casserole or baking dish, layer *half* of the noodles (about 2 cups), *half* of the meat mixture (about 1½ cups), *half* of the cream cheese mixture (about 1 cup), and all of the spinach. Top with the remaining meat mixture and noodles. Cover and chill remaining cream cheese mixture until needed.

5. Cover casserole or baking dish with lightly greased foil. Bake about 45 minutes. or until heated through.

6. Uncover; spread with remaining cream cheese mixture. Sprinkle with the cheddar cheese. Bake, uncovered, about 10 minutes more or until cheese is melted. Let stand for 10 minutes before serving. Makes 8 servings.

Make-ahead directions: Prepare as directed through step 4. Cover with lightly greased foil and chill in the refrigerator for up to 24 hours. Preheat oven to 350°F. Bake for 60 to 70 minutes or until heated through. Uncover; spread with remaining cream-cheese mixture. Sprinkle with the cheddar cheese. Bake, uncovered, about 10 minutes more or until cheese is melted. Let stand for 10 minutes before serving.

Nutrition facts per main-dish serving: 472 cal., 30 g total fat (17 g sat. fat), 127 mg chol., 683 mg sodium, 25 g carbo., 3 g fiber, 27 g pro.

Upside-Down Pizza Casserole

Prep: 20 min. Bake: 15 min.

Adjust this recipe as you would pizza. Substitute Italian sausage for the beef. Add sliced mushrooms or olives to the meat mixture. Or use Monterey Jack cheese in place of the mozzarella.

- 1½ **lb. lean ground beef**
- 1 **15-oz. can Italian-style tomato sauce**
- 1½ **cups shredded mozzarella cheese (6 oz.)**
- 1 **10-oz. pkg. refrigerated biscuits (10 biscuits)**

1. Preheat oven to 400°F. In a large skillet, cook beef until brown. Drain off fat. Stir in tomato sauce; heat through. Transfer to an ungreased 2-quart rectangular baking dish. Sprinkle with cheese.

2. Flatten each biscuit with hands; arrange the biscuits on top of cheese. Bake about 15 minutes or until biscuits are golden. Makes 10 servings.

Nutrition facts main-dish serving: 321 cal., 20 g total fat (8 g sat. fat), 58 mg chol., 551 mg sodium, 15 g carbo., 1 g fiber, 17 g pro.

The years after the end of World War II ushered in the era of the car. It seemed everybody had one. To go along with the new mobility, tailgating and picnics became novel ways to enjoy a meal with friends and family. Our food and entertaining editors were only too happy to create recipe after recipe to inspire our readers.

Upside-Down Pizza Casserole

Beef-and-Bean Medley

Prep: 25 min. Cook: 4 to 6 hr. (low-heat setting) or
2 to 3 hr. (high-heat setting)

This tempting recipe originally came from a 4-H
cookbook—a tried-and-true favorite of young cooks.

- 1 **lb. ground beef**
- 1 **cup chopped onion**
- 6 **slices bacon, crisp-cooked, drained,
  and crumbled**
- 2 **16-oz. cans baked beans**
- 1 **15-oz. can butter beans, rinsed and drained**
- 1 **15-oz. can red kidney beans,
  rinsed and drained**
- 1 **cup ketchup**
- ½ **cup water**
- 3 **Tbsp. vinegar**
- 2 **Tbsp. packed brown sugar**
- ⅛ **tsp. pepper**
  Corn chips or tortilla chips (optional)
  Shredded cheddar cheese (optional)
  Sliced green onions (optional)

1. In a large skillet, cook ground beef and onion until
beef is brown. Drain off fat. Transfer beef mixture to a
3½- or 4-quart slow cooker. Add crumbled bacon, baked
beans, butter beans, and kidney beans.

2. In a small bowl, combine ketchup, the water,
vinegar, brown sugar, and pepper. Add ketchup mixture
to slow cooker. Stir to combine. Cover and cook on low-
heat setting for 4 to 6 hours or on high-heat setting for
2 to 3 hours. If desired, serve over corn or tortilla chips
and sprinkle with cheddar cheese and green onions.
Makes 8 to 10 servings.

Oven directions: Preheat oven to 350°F. Coat a
2½-quart casserole with nonstick cooking spray; set
aside. In a large saucepan, cook ground beef and onion
until beef is brown. Drain off fat. Stir in crumbled bacon,
baked beans, butter beans, and kidney beans. In a small
bowl, combine ketchup, the water, vinegar, brown sugar,
and pepper. Add ketchup mixture to saucepan. Stir to
combine. Transfer mixture to prepared casserole. Cover
and bake about 45 minutes or until heated through.
If desired, serve over corn or tortilla chips and sprinkle
with cheddar cheese and green onions.

Nutrition facts per main-dish serving: 420 cal., 12 g total fat (4 g sat. fat),
43 mg chol., 1,113 mg sodium, 57 g carbo., 11 g fiber, 26 g pro.

Cajun Chicken Lasagna

Prep: 45 min. Bake: 1 hr. Stand: 15 min.

This white lasagna won top honors in the Pasta Bakes category of our Prize Tested Recipes® contest in September 2001. Andouille sausage and Cajun seasoning give the casserole a Louisiana kick.

 16   dried lasagna noodles
  1   lb. andouille sausage or smoked pork sausage, quartered lengthwise and sliced
  1   lb. skinless, boneless chicken breast halves, cut into ¾-inch cubes
  2   to 3 tsp. Cajun seasoning
  1   tsp. dried sage, crushed
  ½   cup chopped onion
  ½   cup chopped celery
  ¼   cup chopped green sweet pepper
  6   cloves garlic, minced
  2   10-oz. containers refrigerated light Alfredo sauce
  ½   cup grated Parmesan cheese (2 oz.)
      Nonstick cooking spray
 1½ cups shredded mozzarella cheese (6 oz.)

1. Preheat oven to 325°F. Cook noodles according to package directions. Drain; rinse. In a large bowl, combine sausage, chicken, Cajun seasoning, and sage.

2. In a large skillet, cook meat mixture about 8 minutes or until chicken is no longer pink. Using a slotted spoon, remove from skillet, reserving drippings in skillet. Set meat mixture aside; keep warm. In drippings in skillet, cook onion, celery, sweet pepper, and garlic until vegetables are tender. Stir in meat mixture, *1 container* of the Alfredo sauce, and the grated Parmesan cheese.

3. Lightly coat a 3-quart rectangular baking dish with nonstick cooking spray. Arrange *4* of the noodles in bottom of the baking dish. Spread with *2 cups* of the meat-vegetable mixture. Sprinkle with *½ cup* of the mozzarella. Repeat layers twice. Top with remaining noodles. Carefully spread remaining Alfredo sauce over the top (if sauce is too thick, heat slightly).

4. Cover; bake about 1 hour or until heated through. Let stand for 15 to 20 minutes before carefully cutting. Makes 12 servings.

Make-ahead directions: Prepare as directed through step 3. Cover and chill in the refrigerator for up to 24 hours. Preheat oven to 325°F. Bake, covered, for 1½ to 1¾ hours or until heated through. Let stand for 15 to 20 minutes before carefully cutting.

Nutrition facts per main-dish serving: 469 cal., 24 g total fat (11 g sat. fat), 79 mg chol., 1,187 mg sodium, 34 g carbo., 1 g fiber, 29 g pro.

Teacher's Casserole

Prep: 25 min. Bake: 30 + 5 min.

The cook who sent us this recipe boasted that it's so popular, the men at her church prepared it for a mother-daughter banquet.

- 1 6-oz. pkg. long grain and wild rice mix
- 3 cups bite-size pieces cooked chicken
- 1 14½-oz. can French-cut green beans, drained
- 1 10¾-oz. can condensed cream of celery soup
- 1 8-oz. can sliced water chestnuts, drained
- 1 medium onion, chopped
- ½ cup mayonnaise or salad dressing
- 3 Tbsp. sliced almonds
- 1 2-oz. jar sliced pimiento, drained
- 1 tsp. lemon juice
- 1 cup shredded cheddar cheese (4 oz.)

1. Preheat oven to 350°F. Prepare rice mix according to package directions. Meanwhile, in a very large bowl, combine the chicken, green beans, celery soup, water chestnuts, onion, mayonnaise, almonds, pimiento, and lemon juice. Stir in cooked rice mixture. Spoon into an ungreased 3-quart rectangular baking dish.

2. Bake, covered, for 30 minutes. Uncover. Sprinkle with cheese; bake, uncovered, about 5 minutes or until heated through and cheese is melted. Serves 8 to 10.

Make-ahead directions: Prepare as directed in step 1. Cover unbaked casserole; seal cheese in plastic bag. Chill both in the refrigerator for up to 24 hours. Preheat oven to 350°F. Bake casserole, covered, for 45 minutes. Uncover. Sprinkle with cheese; bake, uncovered, about 5 minutes more or until heated through and cheese is melted.

Nutrition facts per main-dish serving: 434 cal., 25 g total fat (6 g sat. fat), 75 mg chol., 971 mg sodium, 30 g carbo., 2 g fiber, 24 g pro.

The casseroles so popular in the 1950s spawned a new type of party—the covered-dish supper. These occasions were a chance for friends and neighbors to share their favorite one-dish meal or "hot dish."

Triple-Cheese Pasta Casserole

Prep: 25 min. Bake: 25 min.

This crowd-size version of macaroni and cheese pleases adults and youngsters alike with corkscrew macaroni, sweet peppers, Gouda cheese, and herbs.

- 12 oz. dried tricolored corkscrew macaroni (rotini)
- 1 16-oz. pkg. frozen yellow, green, and red sweet peppers and onion stir-fry vegetables
- 3 Tbsp. all-purpose flour
- 2 Tbsp. snipped fresh oregano or basil or 1 tsp. dried oregano or basil, crushed
- ¼ tsp. salt
- ¼ tsp. ground black pepper
- ¼ tsp. ground nutmeg
- 3½ cups milk
- 8 oz. smoked Gouda cheese, shredded (2 cups)
- ½ of an 8-oz. pkg. cream cheese, cut up
- ⅓ cup finely shredded Parmesan cheese

1. Preheat oven to 350°F. Lightly grease a 3-quart rectangular baking dish. In a Dutch oven, cook corkscrew macaroni in lightly salted boiling water for 7 minutes. Add the frozen vegetables; return to boiling. Cook about 2 minutes more or until pasta is tender. Drain well.

2. In a screw-top jar, combine flour, dried herb (if using), salt, black pepper, and nutmeg. Add *1 cup* of the milk; shake well to mix. Pour into a large saucepan; add remaining 2½ cups milk. Cook and stir over medium-high heat until slightly thickened and bubbly. Gradually add cheeses, stirring until melted. Stir in cooked pasta and vegetables and the fresh herb (if using). Transfer to prepared baking dish.

3. Bake, covered, about 25 minutes or until heated through. Makes 8 servings.

Make-ahead directions: Prepare as directed through step 2. Cover unbaked casserole. Chill in the refrigerator for up to 4 hours. Preheat oven to 350°F. Bake for 35 to 40 minutes or until heated through.

Nutrition facts per main-dish serving: 390 cal., 16 g total fat (10 g sat. fat), 49 mg chol., 688 mg sodium, 45 g carbo., 2 g fiber, 17 g pro.

Curried Fruit and Nut Salad

Start to finish: 30 min.

In 1980, *Better Homes and Gardens*® sponsored a Busy People's Recipe Contest. This colorful tossed side-dish salad won second prize.

- 1 **head red leaf lettuce or romaine, torn (about 7 cups)**
- 2 **cups torn fresh spinach**
- 1 **11-oz. can mandarin orange sections, chilled and drained**
- 1 **cup seedless grapes, halved**
- ½ **cup slivered almonds, toasted (below)**
- ¼ **cup salad oil**
- ¼ **cup white wine vinegar**
- 2 **Tbsp. packed brown sugar**
- 2 **Tbsp. snipped fresh chives**
- 1 **clove garlic, minced**
- 1½ **to 2 tsp. curry powder**
- 1 **tsp. soy sauce**
- 1 **avocado, peeled, pitted, and sliced (optional)**

1. In a large salad bowl, toss together the lettuce, spinach, orange sections, grapes, and almonds.

2. For the dressing, in a screw-top jar, combine salad oil, vinegar, brown sugar, chives, garlic, curry powder, and soy sauce. Cover; shake well. Just before serving, toss some of the dressing with the salad. If desired, garnish with avocado slices. Pass remaining dressing. Serves 12.

Nutrition facts per side-dish serving: 117 cal., 8 g total fat (1 g sat. fat), 0 mg chol., 36 mg sodium, 12 g carbo., 2 g fiber, 2 g pro.

Chicken Curried Fruit and Nut Salad: Prepare as directed, except add 3 cups cubed cooked chicken to lettuce mixture.

Nutrition facts per main-dish serving: 175 cal., 9 g total fat (1 g sat. fat), 30 mg chol., 62 mg sodium, 12 g carbo., 2 g fiber, 13 g pro.

Toasting 'Em
Over 75 years of recipe testing, we've learned a few nifty tricks of the trade. Here's one: To give nuts and coconut a fuller flavor, toast them. Just spread the pieces in a single layer in a shallow baking pan. Bake in a 350°F oven for 5 to 10 minutes or until light brown; stir occasionally.

Peanut Potato Salad

Peanut Potato Salad

Prep: 30 min. Cook: 20 min. Chill: 4 to 24 hr.

Looking for an alternative to the usual potato salad to take to the next picnic or block party? We recommend this nutty number that boasts a tangy peanut butter-and-mayo dressing.

- 3 **lb. red potatoes**
- 12 **slices bacon, crisp-cooked, drained, and crumbled (optional)**
- ¾ **cup mayonnaise or salad dressing**
- ½ **cup chunky peanut butter**
- 1 **medium red sweet pepper, chopped**
- ½ **cup salted Spanish peanuts**
- 2 **stalks celery, chopped**
- 4 **green onions, chopped**
- ¼ **cup snipped fresh cilantro**
- ¼ **cup snipped fresh parsley**
- 3 **to 4 Tbsp. cider vinegar**

1. In a large saucepan, cook potatoes in large amount of boiling water for 20 to 25 minutes or just until tender; drain well and let cool. Cut potatoes into 1-inch cubes.

2. In a very large bowl, combine bacon (if using), mayonnaise, peanut butter, sweet pepper, peanuts, celery, green onions, cilantro, parsley, and vinegar. Add potato cubes. Toss lightly to mix. Cover and chill for at least 4 hours or up to 24 hours. Makes 12 servings.

Nutrition facts per side-dish serving: 311 cal., 20 g total fat (3 g sat. fat), 8 mg chol.,175 mg sodium, 30 g carbo., 2 g fiber, 7 g pro.

Lower-Fat Peanut Potato Salad: Prepare as directed, except omit bacon and use fat-free mayonnaise dressing and reduced-fat chunky peanut butter. (The salad will be slightly sweeter. If desired, add 1 to 2 tablespoons more vinegar.)

Nutrition facts per side-dish serving: 225 cal., 7 g total fat (1 g sat. fat), 0 mg chol., 281 mg sodium, 35 g carbo., 2 g fiber, and 7 g pro.

Spinach-German Potato Salad

Prep: 20 min. Cook: 8 to 10 hr. (low-heat setting) or
4 to 5 hr. (high-heat setting)

Our wilted spinach salad dates back to the 1941
edition of the *New Cook Book*, and German-style
potato salad earned a spot in the 1968 version.
In 2003, we combined the old timers into a new
slow-cooker recipe that's ideal for toting to potlucks.

2	lb. potatoes, peeled and cut into ¼-inch-thick slices (about 6 cups)
1	cup chopped onion
1	cup chopped celery
¾	cup water
⅔	cup cider vinegar
¼	cup sugar
1	tsp. salt
¾	tsp. celery seeds
¼	tsp. pepper
6	slices bacon, crisp-cooked, drained, and crumbled
1	10-oz. bag prewashed spinach
	Snipped fresh dill (optional)

1. In a 3½- or 4-quart slow cooker, combine potatoes, onion, and celery. In a medium bowl, combine the water, vinegar, sugar, salt, celery seeds, and pepper. Pour over potatoes.

2. Cover; cook on low-heat setting for 8 to 10 hours or on high-heat setting for 4 to 5 hours. Stir in bacon. Spoon over fresh spinach leaves. If desired, garnish with snipped dill. Makes 8 servings.

Nutrition facts per side-dish serving: 135 cal., 3 g total fat (1 g sat. fat), 4 mg chol., 415 mg sodium, 25 g carbo., 3 g fiber, 5 g pro.

Oven directions: Preheat oven to 350°F. Coat a 2½- to 3-quart casserole with nonstick cooking spray; set aside. Thinly slice peeled potatoes. In a large saucepan, cook onion and celery in 1 tablespoon cooking oil until tender. Add potatoes and the water to saucepan. Bring to boiling; reduce heat. Cover and simmer for 8 minutes. Drain, reserving ¼ cup cooking liquid. Transfer vegetables to the prepared casserole. In a medium bowl, combine the reserved cooking liquid, ½ cup vinegar, the sugar, salt, celery seeds, and pepper; stir to dissolve sugar. Pour mixture over vegetables. Cover and bake about 50 minutes or until potatoes are tender. Serve as directed.

Nutrition facts per side-dish serving: 149 cal., 4 g total fat (1 g sat. fat), 4 mg chol., 415 mg sodium, 25 g carbo., 3 g fiber, 5 g pro.

Spinach-German Potato Salad

Yesterday

In 1981, when this recipe was first published, layered salads that could be assembled and chilled up to 24 hours ahead were favorites because they eliminated the last-minute gathering of ingredients. Today, our super-busy readers appreciate them even more.

24-Hour Vegetable Salad
Prep: 30 min. Chill: 2 to 24 hr.

To make this easy salad even faster, substitute a prepackaged torn lettuce mixture for the iceberg.

4   cups torn iceberg lettuce, romaine, leaf lettuce, Bibb or Boston lettuce, and/or fresh spinach
    Salt (optional)
    Pepper (optional)
2   cups sliced fresh mushrooms, small broccoli florets, and/or frozen peas
1   cup shredded carrots
2   hard-cooked eggs, sliced
6   slices bacon, crisp-cooked, drained, and crumbled
¾   cup shredded American, cheddar, or Swiss cheese (3 oz.)
¼   cup thinly sliced green onions
¾   cup mayonnaise or salad dressing
1   Tbsp. lemon juice
1½ tsp. snipped fresh dill or ½ tsp. dried dill weed
    Thinly sliced green onions (optional)

1. Place lettuce in a 2- to 2½-quart salad bowl. If desired, sprinkle with salt and pepper. Layer ingredients on top of lettuce in the following order: mushrooms, broccoli, and/or peas; carrots; eggs; bacon; ½ *cup* of the cheese; and the ¼ cup green onions.

2. For dressing, in small bowl, combine mayonnaise, lemon juice, and dill. Spread dressing on top of salad. If desired, seal to edge of bowl. Sprinkle with the remaining ¼ cup cheese. If desired, garnish with additional green onions. Tightly cover salad with plastic wrap. Chill in the refrigerator for at least 2 hours or up to 24 hours. Just before serving, toss to coat vegetables. Makes 6 to 8 servings.

Nutrition facts per side-dish serving: 349 cal., 33 g total fat (8 g sat. fat), 101 mg chol., 514 mg sodium, 5 g carbo., 1 g fiber, 9 g pro.

24-Hour Salad with Orange Mayonnaise Dressing

Prep: 25 min. Chill: 2 to 24 hr.

Orange slices, feta cheese, and kalamata olives give this contemporary fix-and-forget salad a novel Mediterranean flavor.

- 5 cups torn mixed salad greens
- 1 medium carrot
- 1 cup sliced fresh mushrooms
- ½ cup crumbled feta cheese (2 oz.)
- ½ cup coarsely chopped pitted kalamata olives
- 1 medium cucumber, halved, seeded, and cut into ¼-inch-thick slices (1¾ cups)
- ¼ cup bias-sliced green onions
- 1 recipe Orange Dressing (below)
- 1 medium orange, peeled, sliced, and seeded
- ¼ cup coarsely chopped walnuts
  Orange peel strips (optional)

1. Place salad greens in a 2½- to 3-quart clear straight-sided bowl or soufflé dish. Using a vegetable peeler, peel carrot, then carefully cut carrot into long, paper-thin ribbons; set aside. Layer ingredients on top of salad greens in the following order: mushrooms, ¼ cup of the cheese, the olives, cucumber, carrot ribbons, and green onion.

2. Prepare Orange Dressing; spread over the top of salad, sealing to edge of bowl. Sprinkle with the remaining ¼ cup cheese. Tightly cover salad with plastic wrap. Chill in the refrigerator for at least 2 hours or up to 24 hours.

3. Top with orange slices, walnuts, and, if desired, orange peel strips. Just before serving, toss to coat vegetables. Makes 6 to 8 servings.

Orange Dressing: In a small bowl, combine ½ cup mayonnaise or salad dressing, ¼ cup cup plain low-fat yogurt, 1 teaspoon finely shredded orange peel, ½ to ¾ teaspoon crushed red pepper, and ⅛ to ¼ teaspoon ground black pepper.

Nutrition facts per side-dish serving: 236 cal., 23 g total fat (5 g sat. fat), 16 mg chol., 268 mg sodium, 8 g carbo., 2 g fiber, 4 g pro.

Today

A colorful layered make-ahead salad is just as eye-catching and convenient today as it was in the 1980s, so our Test Kitchen tinkered with ingredients and came up with this refreshing new version.

Two-Bean and Rice Salad

Start to finish: 35 min.

When it's going to be a jam-packed day but a potluck is on the calendar, remember this recipe.

 1 **recipe Garlic Dressing (below) or ¾ cup bottled Italian salad dressing**
 3 **cups chilled cooked rice**
 1 **15-oz. can pinto beans, rinsed and drained**
 1 **15-oz. can black beans, rinsed and drained**
 1 **10-oz. pkg. frozen peas, thawed**
 1 **cup sliced celery**
 ½ **cup chopped red onion**
 2 **4½-oz. cans diced green chile peppers, drained**
 ¼ **cup snipped fresh cilantro or fresh parsley**

 1. If using, prepare Garlic Dressing. In a large bowl, combine rice, pinto beans, black beans, peas, celery, onion, chile peppers, and cilantro. Pour Garlic Dressing or Italian salad dressing over rice mixture; toss. Serves 16.

 Garlic Dressing: In a screw-top jar, combine ⅓ cup white wine vinegar, ¼ cup olive oil, 2 tablespoons water, ½ teaspoon salt, ½ teaspoon garlic powder, and ½ teaspoon ground black pepper. Cover and shake well.

 Make-ahead directions: Prepare as directed. Cover and chill for up to 24 hours.
 Nutrition facts per side-dish serving: 131 cal., 4 g total fat (1 g sat. fat), 0 mg chol., 309 mg sodium, 20 g carbo., 4 g fiber, 5 g pro.

The Long and Short of It

Before the 1990s, when cooks shopped for rice, their choices were few: white or brown; long grain or short grain; regular or quick-cooking. But as the 90s wore on, aromatic rices with nutty flavors invaded the supermarket shelves. Today there are a myriad of choices: basmati rice from India, jasmine from Thailand, wild pecan from Louisiana, and more.

Orange Sherbet Salad

Prep: 20 min. Chill: 4 to 6 hr.

When flavored gelatin hit the cooking scene in the early 1900s, innovative American cooks quickly embraced it and gelatin salad was born.

 1 **6-oz. pkg. orange-flavored gelatin**
 1 **pint orange sherbet**
 1 **11-oz. can mandarin orange sections, drained**
 1 **20-oz. can crushed pineapple (juice pack), drained**

 1. In a large bowl, stir together gelatin and 2 cups *boiling water* until gelatin is dissolved. Add sherbet; stir until melted. Stir in oranges and pineapple. Pour into a 2-quart square baking dish or 2-quart mold. Cover and chill for 4 to 6 hours or until set. Makes 12 servings.
 Nutrition facts per side-dish serving: 143 cal., 1 g total fat (0 g sat. fat), 2 mg chol., 54 mg sodium, 34 g carbo., 1 g fiber, 2 g pro.

Trifle Fruit Salad

Prep: 30 min. Chill: 2 to 8 hr.

This dazzling combination is the culinary cousin of salads from decades past, such as the Waldorf, the 5-cup, and the ambrosia.

 2 **cups 1-inch chunks fresh pineapple or one 20-oz. can pineapple chunks (juice pack), drained**
 2 **cups halved fresh strawberries**
 2 **cups fresh or frozen blueberries, thawed**
 2 **cups seedless green grapes**
 1 **4-serving-size pkg. instant banana cream pudding mix**
 1¼ **cups milk**
 ½ **cup dairy sour cream**
 1 **8-oz. can crushed pineapple**
   Pineapple leaves (optional)

 1. In a 2-quart clear glass bowl, layer pineapple chunks, strawberries, blueberries, and grapes; set aside.
 2. In a medium bowl, whisk together dry pudding mix, the milk, and sour cream. Stir in undrained crushed pineapple. Pour over the layered fruit. Cover and chill for at least 2 hours or up to 8 hours. If desired, garnish each serving with pineapple leaves. Makes 10 to 12 servings.
 Nutrition facts per side-dish serving: 159 cal., 3 g total fat (2 g sat. fat), 7 mg chol., 172 mg sodium, 33 g carbo., 3 g fiber, 2 g pro.

Truck-Stop Potatoes

Prep: 30 min. Bake: 30 min. Stand: 10 min.

Just like the hash browns that are standard fare at many roadside cafés, these cheesy spuds are stick-to-the-ribs good. They'll be king of the road at just about any type of gathering.

- 2 to 2¼ lb. small red potatoes, coarsely chopped (about 6 cups)
- 1 large onion, chopped
- 1 8-oz. carton dairy sour cream
- 1 cup shredded Monterey Jack cheese (4 oz.)
- 1 cup shredded sharp cheddar cheese (4 oz.)
- ½ tsp. salt
- ¼ to ½ tsp. cayenne pepper
- 1 14½-oz. can diced tomatoes, drained

1. Preheat oven to 350°F. In a large covered saucepan, cook potatoes and chopped onion in a large amount of boiling water about 20 minutes or until tender; drain and return to saucepan.

2. Stir in the 8 ounces sour cream, the Monterey Jack cheese, cheddar cheese, salt, and cayenne pepper. Stir in diced tomatoes. Spoon into an ungreased 2-quart rectangular baking dish.

3. Bake, uncovered, about 30 minutes or until heated through. Cover; let stand for 10 minutes. Serves 10.

Nutrition facts per side-dish serving: 220 cal., 12 g total fat (8 g sat. fat), 32 mg chol., 333 mg sodium, 20 g carbo., 2 g fiber, 9 g pro.

Truck-Stop Potatoes

Lower-Fat Truck-Stop Potatoes: Prepare as directed, except use light dairy sour cream, reduced-fat Monterey Jack cheese, and reduced-fat cheddar cheese.

Nutrition facts per serving: 181 cal., 7 g total fat (4 g sat. fat), 23 mg chol., 397 mg sodium, 20 g carbo., 2 g fiber, 9 g pro.

Baked Bean Quintet

Prep: 10 min. Bake: 1 hr.

From bean pots, simmered all day by pioneers, to the latest slow-cooker versions, baked beans have a hallowed place on our nation's tables. This rendition has appeared in the last four editions of our *New Cook Book*. So you know it's great.

- 1 cup chopped onion
- 6 slices bacon, cut up
- 1 clove garlic, minced
- 1 16-oz. can lima beans, drained
- 1 16-oz. can pork and beans in tomato sauce
- 1 15½-oz. can red kidney beans, rinsed and drained
- 1 15-oz. can butter beans, rinsed and drained
- 1 15-oz. can chickpeas (garbanzo beans), rinsed and drained
- ¾ cup ketchup
- ½ cup molasses
- ¼ cup packed brown sugar
- 1 Tbsp. yellow mustard
- 1 Tbsp. Worcestershire sauce

1. Preheat oven to 375°F. In a large skillet, cook onion, bacon, and garlic until bacon is crisp and onion is tender. Drain off fat.

2. In a large bowl, combine onion mixture, lima beans, pork and beans, red kidney beans, butter beans, chickpeas, ketchup, molasses, brown sugar, mustard, and Worcestershire sauce.

3. Transfer bean mixture to an ungreased 3-quart casserole. Bake, covered, for 1 hour. Makes 12 to 16 servings.

Slow-cooker directions: Prepare bean mixture as directed in step 1. Transfer to a 3½- or 4-quart slow cooker. Cover and cook on low-heat setting for 10 to 12 hours or on high-heat setting for 4 to 5 hours.

Nutrition facts per serving: 245 cal., 3 g total fat (1 g sat. fat), 5 mg chol., 882 mg sodium, 47 g carbo., 9 g fiber, 10 g pro.

Apple-Spiced Sweet Potatoes

Prep: 20 min. Cook: 6 to 8 hr. (low-heat setting) or
3 to 4 hr. (high-heat setting)

Americans have enjoyed candied sweet potatoes
since Colonial times. So it's no surprise the golden
taters appeared in the 1930 edition of our cookbook.
This nutty version is ideal for a potluck because you
can keep it warm in a slow cooker.

>   **Nonstick cooking spray**
> 3½ **to 4 lb. sweet potatoes, peeled and cut**
>   **into 2-inch chunks**
> 1   **20-oz. can apple pie filling**
> ⅔   **cup golden raisins**
> 3   **Tbsp. butter or margarine, cut up**
> 1½ **tsp. apple pie spice**
> 1   **recipe Candied Pecans (right)**

1. Lightly coat the liner of a 3½- or 4-quart slow
cooker with nonstick cooking spray. Add sweet potato
chunks, apple pie filling, raisins, butter, and the apple pie
spice; mix well.

2. Cover; cook on low-heat setting for 6 to 8 hours or
on high-heat setting for 3 to 4 hours.

3. Meanwhile, prepared Candied Pecans. To serve,
top each serving of potatoes with some of the pecans.
Makes 10 servings.

Candied Pecans: In a heavy, large skillet combine
1 cup coarsely chopped pecans, ⅓ cup sugar, and
2 tablespoons butter. Cook and stir over medium heat
for 8 to 10 minutes or until sugar mixture clinging to nuts
turns golden and starts to melt. Pour nut mixture onto a
large piece of foil; cool completely. When nut mixture is
cool, coarsely crush.

Nutrition facts per side-dish serving: 413 cal., 14 g total fat (5 g sat. fat),
16 mg chol., 109 mg sodium, 70 g carbo., 7 g fiber, 4 g pro.

Herbed Dressing Casserole

Prep: 30 min. Cook: 3½ hr. (low-heat setting)

When our Test Kitchen staff prepared this toothsome totable side dish in the slow cooker, they loved leaving the oven free for other dishes. Add cooked chicken or turkey, and turn it into a main dish for six.

4½	**cups sliced fresh mushrooms (12 oz.)**
1	**cup sliced celery**
1	**cup chopped onion**
6	**Tbsp. butter or margarine**
⅓	**cup snipped fresh basil or 1 Tbsp. dried basil, crushed**
½	**tsp. pepper**
12	**cups dry bread cubes***
1	**14-oz. can chicken broth**
¾	**cup chopped pecans, toasted (tip, page 102)**

1. In a very large skillet, cook mushrooms, celery, and onion in butter over medium heat about 5 minutes or until tender. Remove from heat; stir in basil and pepper.

2. In a very large bowl, combine mushroom mixture and bread cubes. Add the chicken broth, tossing gently to moisten.

3. Spoon dressing mixture into a 3½- or 4-quart slow cooker. Cover; cook on low-heat setting for 3½ to 4 hours. To serve, gently stir in nuts. Makes 12 servings.

*Test Kitchen Tip: To make 12 cups dry bread cubes, preheat oven to 300°F. Cut 20 to 21 slices bread into ½-inch cubes. (You should have about 14 cups cubed bread.) Spread cubes in a single layer in a large, shallow roasting pan. Bake, uncovered, for 10 to 15 minutes or until dry, stirring twice. Cool. (Bread will continue to dry and crisp as it cools.) Or let bread stand, loosely covered without baking, at room temperature 8 to 12 hours.

Nutrition facts per side-dish serving: 234 cal., 13 g total fat (5 g sat. fat), 17 mg chol., 399 mg sodium, 24 g carbo., 2 g fiber, 6 g pro.

Herbed Chicken and Dressing Casserole: Prepare as directed in step 1, except stir in 3 cups coarsely chopped cooked chicken or turkey with the bread cubes. Continue as directed. Makes 6 servings.

Nutrition facts per main-dish serving: 600 cal., 32 g total fat (11 g sat. fat), 96 mg chol., 858 mg sodium, 48 g carbo., 5 g dietary fiber, 33 g pro.

At *Better Homes and Gardens*® we keep readers up to date on the latest in tabletop appliances. From the 1930s electric mixer to the slow cooker of the 1960s to the 1990s indoor grill, we go deliciously beyond the instruction book.

Creamed Corn Deluxe

Prep: 10 min. Cook: 8 to 10 hr. (low-heat setting) or 4 to 5 hr. (high-heat setting)

For generations, whenever the clan gathered for a meal, there was a good chance creamed or scalloped corn would be served. Extended families get together less often these days, but the classic veggie is still a winner for potluck meals.

2	**16-oz. pkg. frozen whole kernel corn**
2	**cups coarsely chopped red or green sweet pepper**
1	**cup chopped onion**
¼	**tsp. ground black pepper**
1	**10¾-oz. can condensed cream of celery soup**
1	**8-oz. tub cream cheese with chive and onion or cream cheese with garden vegetables**
¼	**cup milk**

1. In a 3½- or 4-quart slow cooker, combine frozen corn, sweet pepper, onion, and black pepper. In a medium bowl, combine soup, cream cheese, and milk. Whisk to combine. Add to slow cooker; stir to combine.

2. Cover; cook on low-heat setting for 8 to 10 hours or on high-heat setting for 4 to 5 hours. Serves 12.

Nutrition facts per side-dish serving: 171 cal., 8 g total fat (5 g sat. fat), 19 mg chol., 278 mg sodium, 22 g carbo., 3 g fiber, 4 g pro.

Oven directions: Preheat oven to 375°F. Lightly coat a 2-quart casserole with nonstick cooking spray; set aside. Place corn in a colander and thaw by running under cool water; drain. In a large saucepan, cook sweet pepper and onion in 1 tablespoon hot butter or margarine until tender. Stir in corn and black pepper. In a medium bowl, combine soup, cream cheese, and milk; whisk to combine. Stir into corn mixture. Transfer to prepared casserole. Cover and bake for 50 to 55 minutes or until heated through, stirring once.

Nutrition facts per side-dish serving: 180 cal., 9 g total fat (6 g sat. fat), 22 mg chol., 289 mg sodium, 22 g carbo., 3 g dietary fiber, 4 g pro.

Green Beans in Cheese-Bacon Sauce

Prep: 10 min. Cook: 5 to 6 hr. (low-heat setting) or 2½ to 3 hr. (high-heat setting)

It only takes 10 minutes to assemble this slow-simmering, people-pleasing side dish.

 2 16-oz. pkg. frozen cut green beans
 ½ cup finely chopped onion
 1 4-oz. jar sliced pimiento, drained
 1 4-oz. can sliced mushrooms, drained
 1 10¾-oz. can condensed cream of mushroom soup
 1½ cups shredded cheddar cheese (6 oz.)
 ¼ tsp. pepper
 6 slices bacon, crisp-cooked, drained, and crumbled

1. In a 3½- or 4-quart slow cooker, combine frozen green beans, the onion, pimiento, and mushrooms. Stir in soup, cheese, and pepper. Sprinkle with bacon.

2. Cover; cook on low-heat setting for 5 to 6 hours or on high-heat setting for 2½ to 3 hours. Stir before serving. Makes 8 to 10 servings.

Nutrition facts per side-dish serving: 199 cal., 13 g total fat (6 g sat. fat), 27 mg chol., 536 mg sodium, 14 g carbo., 4 g fiber, 10 g pro.

Holiday Cauliflower

Prep: 25 min. Bake: 15 min.

Dotted with green sweet pepper and pimiento, this Swiss cheese-sauced cauliflower has the perfect colors for holiday get-togethers, yet it's tasty enough to serve all year long.

 6 cups water
 6 cups cauliflower florets (1 large head cauliflower)
 1 4-oz. can sliced mushrooms, drained
 ¼ cup chopped green sweet pepper
 ¼ cup butter or margarine
 ⅓ cup all-purpose flour
 ¼ tsp. salt
 2 cups milk
 1 cup shredded Swiss cheese (4 oz.)
 2 Tbsp. diced pimiento

1. Preheat oven to 325°F. In large saucepan, bring the water to boiling. Add cauliflower; cook 4 to 6 minutes or until crisp-tender. Drain cauliflower; set aside.

2. For sauce, in a medium saucepan, cook mushrooms and sweet pepper in hot butter until pepper is tender. Stir in flour and salt. Add the milk all at once. Cook and stir until thickened and bubbly. Remove from heat. Stir in Swiss cheese and pimiento until cheese is melted.

3. In an ungreased 1½-quart casserole, layer *half* of the cauliflower and *half* of the sauce. Top with remaining cauliflower and sauce. Bake, uncovered, for 15 minutes. Serve warm. Makes 8 servings.

Nutrition facts per side-dish serving: 177 cal., 11 g total fat (7 g sat. fat), 34 mg chol., 297 mg sodium, 11 g carbo., 3 g fiber, 9 g pro.

Take Potluck

In the 1950s as potlucks became popular, we advised our readers to keep hot foods hot and cold foods cold when toting a dish away from home. That advice still holds true.

• To transport a heated dish, plan to take the food from the oven just before leaving. (Or for foods in a slow cooker, plan your departure time for the end of the cooking range.) Cover the dish or cooker tightly and wrap it in layers of newspaper or a heavy towel. Or for casserole dishes, use an insulated casserole carrier.

• For a refrigerated recipe, make sure the dish is thoroughly chilled before packing. Also chill an insulated cooler by filling it with ice and letting it stand for at least 30 minutes. Place the dish in the cooler just before leaving, surrounding it with ice. (You'll need at least 10 pounds of ice to fill a 54-quart cooler.) In hot weather, carry the cooler in the air-conditioned interior of your car, not in the trunk.

Italian Cream Cake

Prep: 40 min. Bake: 25 min.

Scan community cookbooks and you'll often see recipes for this luscious cake. When we asked our readers for their potluck recipes in 1992, we weren't surprised to find it among the entries.

    2   cups all-purpose flour
    1   tsp. baking soda
    ½   cup butter, softened
    ½   cup shortening
    2   cups granulated sugar
    5   egg yolks
    1   tsp. vanilla
    1   cup buttermilk or sour milk
        (tip, page 116)
    1   cup flaked coconut
    ½   cup finely chopped pecans, toasted
        (tip, page 102)
    5   egg whites
    1   recipe Pecan-Cream Cheese Frosting (below)

1. Preheat oven to 350°F. Grease and flour three 8×1½-inch or 9×½-inch baking pans. Combine the flour and baking soda.

2. In a very large mixing bowl, beat butter and shortening with electric mixer 30 seconds. Add sugar; beat until fluffy. Add yolks and vanilla; beat on medium speed until combined. Add flour mixture and buttermilk alternately to yolk mixture, beating on low speed after each addition just until mixed. Fold in coconut and nuts.

3. Thoroughly wash and dry beaters. In a medium mixing bowl, beat egg whites until stiff peaks form (tips stand straight). Fold about *one-third* of the egg whites into cake batter to lighten. Fold in remaining whites. Spread cake batter evenly into prepared pans.

4. Bake for 25 to 30 minutes or until a wooden toothpick inserted near cake centers comes out clean. Cool layers in pans on wire racks for 10 minutes; remove from pans. Cool completely on wire racks. Prepare Pecan-Cream Cheese Frosting; fill and frost cake layers. Store cake, covered, in refrigerator until serving time or up to 2 days. Makes 16 servings.

Pecan-Cream Cheese Frosting: In large bowl, combine: one 8-ounce package cream cheese, softened; ½ cup butter, softened; and 1 teaspoon vanilla. Beat with an electric mixer on medium speed until smooth. Gradually add 4 cups sifted powdered sugar; beat until smooth. Stir in ½ cup chopped pecans.

Nutrition facts per serving: 573 cal., 32 g total fat (16 g sat. fat), 115 mg chol., 303 mg sodium, 66 g carbo., 2 g fiber, 6 g pro.

Upside-Down Chip Cake

Prep: 20 min. Bake: 40 min. Stand: 30 min.

Looking for a recipe to boost your reputation as a terrific cook? Try this prizewinner from our April 2000 Prize Tested Recipes® contest.

    3   Tbsp. butter
    ½   cup packed brown sugar
    4   tsp. water
    ½   cup coconut
    ½   cup coarsely chopped pecans
    1   cup all-purpose flour
    ⅔   cup granulated sugar
    ½   cup unsweetened cocoa powder
    ¼   cup packed brown sugar
    2   tsp. baking powder
    ½   cup milk
    ¼   cup butter, softened
    2   eggs
    1   tsp. vanilla
    ¾   cup miniature semisweet chocolate
        pieces

1. Preheat oven to 350°F. Melt the 3 tablespoons butter in a 9×1½-inch round baking pan. Stir in the ½ cup brown sugar and the water. Sprinkle coconut and pecans into pan. Set pan aside.

2. In a medium mixing bowl, stir together flour, granulated sugar, cocoa powder, the ¼ cup brown sugar, and the baking powder. Add milk, the ¼ cup butter, the eggs, and vanilla. Beat with an electric mixer on low speed until combined. Beat on medium speed for 1 minute. By hand, stir in ½ *cup* of the chocolate pieces. Spread batter into prepared pan.

3. Bake for 40 to 45 minutes or until cake feels firm when lightly touched. Cool on a wire rack 5 minutes. Loosen side; invert onto a serving plate. Immediately sprinkle with remaining ¼ cup chocolate pieces; let stand for 30 minutes before slicing. Serve warm. Serves 8.

Nutrition facts per serving: 456 cal., 24 g total fat (11 g sat. fat), 83 mg chol., 239 mg sodium, 52 g carbo., 3 g fiber, 6 g pro.

Upside-Down Chip Cake

Floribbean Pound Cake

Prep: 35 min. Bake: 55 min.

Originally pound cakes used a pound of each of the major ingredients. When we started publishing recipes in the 1920s, we adjusted the proportions, adding baking powder for a lighter cake. This 1997 version is a true descendant of our early loaves.

- 3 **cups all-purpose flour**
- 1½ **tsp. baking powder**
- 1½ **cups butter, softened**
- 1½ **cups sugar**
- 6 **eggs**
- 4 **to 5 tsp. finely shredded lime peel (about 3 limes)**
- ⅓ **cup canned unsweetened coconut milk or regular milk**
- ½ **cup sugar**
- ⅓ **cup lime juice**
- ½ **to 1 cup coconut, toasted (tip, page102) Whipped cream (optional) Assorted tropical fruits (such as mango and kiwifruit slices)**

1. Preheat oven to 325°F. Grease and flour a 10-inch fluted tube pan; set aside. In a medium bowl, stir together the flour and baking powder; set aside.

2. In a large mixing bowl, beat butter with an electric mixer on medium to high speed for 30 seconds. Gradually add the 1½ cups sugar, *2 tablespoons* at a time, beating on medium-high speed about 6 minutes total or until very light and fluffy. Add eggs, *one* at a time, beating 1 minute after each addition, scraping side of bowl often. Beat in lime peel.

3. Gradually add flour mixture to butter mixture, beating on medium-low speed just until combined. Beat in coconut milk or regular milk. Spread batter evenly into prepared fluted tube pan. Bake for 55 to 60 minutes or until a wooden toothpick inserted near center comes out clean.

4. Meanwhile, for syrup, in a small saucepan, combine the ½ cup sugar and the lime juice; cook and stir over medium heat until sugar is dissolved.

5. Cool cake in the pan on a wire rack for 10 minutes. Invert cake onto another wire rack (place a sheet of waxed paper under the rack); remove pan. Prick top and side of cake with a toothpick; brush with the syrup. Immediately sprinkle with coconut. Cool. Serve slices of cake with whipped cream (if desired), any remaining coconut, and fresh fruit. Makes 18 servings.

Test Kitchen Tip: To transport to a potluck, slice cake and arrange on a platter; cover with plastic wrap. Pack whipped cream (if desired) and fresh fruit in airtight containers and place on ice in an insulated cooler.

Nutrition facts per serving: 335 cal., 19 g total fat (11 g sat. fat), 112 mg chol., 212 mg sodium, 39 g carbo., 1 g fiber, 4 g pro.

Yesterday

This crowd-size version of apple pie, sometimes called slab pie, has been a *Better Homes and Gardens*® favorite for 30-plus years and is as popular as ever. Take it to your next neighborhood gathering and you'll be deluged with requests for the recipe.

Danish Pastry Apple Bars

Prep: 30 min. Bake: 50 min.

For a special treat, top the flaky pastry and spiced apples with scoops of vanilla ice cream.

2½ cups all-purpose flour
1 tsp. salt
1 cup shortening
1 egg yolk
   Milk
1 cup cornflakes
8 to 10 tart baking apples (such as Cortland, Rome Beauty, or Granny Smith), peeled, cored, and sliced (8 cups)
½ cup granulated sugar
1 tsp. ground cinnamon
1 egg white
1 Tbsp. water
   Sifted powdered sugar (optional)

1. Preheat oven to 375°F. For pastry dough, in a large bowl, stir together the flour and salt. Using a pastry blender, cut in shortening until mixture resembles coarse crumbs. Lightly beat egg yolk in a glass measuring cup. Add enough milk to egg yolk to make ⅔ cup total liquid; mix well. Stir egg yolk mixture into flour mixture; mix well. Divide dough in half.

2. On a lightly floured surface, roll *half* of the dough to an 18×12-inch rectangle. To transfer pastry, wrap it around the rolling pin; unroll into an ungreased 15×10×1-inch baking pan (pastry will hang over edges of pan). Sprinkle pastry in pan with cornflakes; top with apples. In a small bowl, combine granulated sugar and cinnamon; sprinkle over apples. Roll remaining dough to a 16×12-inch rectangle; place over apples. Seal edges; cut slits in top for steam to escape. In a small bowl, beat egg white and the water; brush onto pastry.

3. Bake about 50 minutes or until golden brown. Cool in pan on a wire rack. Serve warm or cool. If desired, sprinkle with powdered sugar. Makes 30 bars.

Nutrition facts per bar: 141 cal., 7 g total fat (2 g sat. fat), 7 mg chol., 88 mg sodium, 18 g carbo., 1 g fiber, 2 g pro.

114

We liked the apple version of slab pie so much that in 2002, we came up with this sweet and sassy apricot and cherry rendition. It makes the ideal easy-to-fix take-along.

Apricot-Cherry Slab Pie

Prep: 30 min. Bake: 40 min.

Because this pie uses canned fruit, you can keep the ingredients on hand and enjoy it anytime.

3¼   cups all-purpose flour
1   tsp. salt
1   cup shortening
1   egg yolk
     Milk
3   15¼-oz. cans apricot halves, drained
½   cup sugar
3   Tbsp. cornstarch
1   16-oz. can pitted tart red cherries, drained
1   recipe Vanilla Glaze (right)

1. Preheat oven to 375°F. For dough, in a large bowl, stir together flour and salt. Using a pastry blender, cut in shortening until mixture resembles coarse crumbs.

2. Lightly beat egg yolk in a glass measuring cup. Add enough milk to egg yolk to make ¾ cup total liquid; mix well. Stir egg yolk mixture into flour mixture; mix well.

3. On a lightly floured surface, roll *two-thirds* of the dough into an 18×12-inch rectangle. To transfer pastry, wrap it around rolling pin; unroll into an ungreased 15×10×1-inch baking pan (pastry will hang over edges of pan).

4. Cut up apricots. In a large bowl, combine sugar and cornstarch. Stir in apricots and cherries. Spoon into prepared crust.

5. Roll the remaining pastry dough into a 16×11-inch rectangle; place over fruit. Bring bottom pastry up and over top pastry. Seal edges with the tines of a fork. Prick top pastry over entire surface with the tines of a fork.

6. Bake about 40 minutes or until golden brown. Cool in pan on a wire rack. Serve warm or cool. Prepare Vanilla Glaze; drizzle over top pastry. Cut into bars. Makes 24 bars.

Vanilla Glaze: In a small bowl, combine 1¼ cups sifted powdered sugar, ½ teaspoon vanilla, and enough milk (5 to 6 teaspoons) to make of drizzling consistency.

Nutrition facts per bar: 223 cal., 9 g total fat (2 g sat. fat), 10 mg chol., 106 mg sodium, 34 g carbo., 1 g fiber, 3 g pro.

Chocolate Revel Bars

Prep: 30 min. Bake: 25 min.

These rich chocolate-filled oatmeal bars have become a *Better Homes and Gardens*® classic. Our Test Kitchen first perfected them for *Successful Farming*® magazine, a sister publication, in the 1960s.

1	**cup butter, softened**
2	**cups packed brown sugar**
1	**tsp. baking soda**
2	**eggs**
2	**tsp. vanilla**
2½	**cups all-purpose flour**
3	**cups quick-cooking rolled oats**
1½	**cups semisweet chocolate pieces***
1	**14-oz. can (1¼ cups) regular or low-fat sweetened condensed milk**
½	**cup chopped walnuts or pecans**
2	**tsp. vanilla**

1. Preheat oven to 350°F. Set aside *2 tablespoons* of the butter. In a large mixing bowl, beat the remaining butter with an electric mixer on medium to high speed for 30 seconds. Add the brown sugar and baking soda. Beat until combined, scraping side of bowl occasionally. Beat in eggs and 2 teaspoons vanilla until combined. Beat in as much of the flour as you can with the mixer. Stir in any remaining flour. Stir in the rolled oats.

2. For filling, in a medium saucepan, combine the reserved 2 tablespoons butter, the chocolate pieces, and sweetened condensed milk. Cook over low heat until chocolate is melted, stirring occasionally. Remove from heat. Stir in the nuts and 2 teaspoons vanilla.

3. Press *two-thirds* of the oat mixture (about 3⅓ cups) onto the bottom of an ungreased 15×10×1-inch baking pan. Spread filling evenly over the oat mixture. Dot remaining oat mixture onto filling.

4. Bake about 25 minutes or until top is lightly browned (chocolate filling will still look moist). Cool in pan on a wire rack. Cut into bars. Makes 60 bars.

*Test Kitchen Tip: Be sure to use real semisweet chocolate pieces. Do not substitute products labeled imitation chocolate pieces or chocolate-flavored pieces.

Nutrition facts per bar: 146 cal., 6 g total fat (3 g sat. fat), 18 mg chol., 68 mg sodium, 21 g carbo., 1 g fiber, 2 g pro.

Peanut Butter-Chocolate Revel Bars: Prepare as directed, except substitute ½ cup peanut butter for the 2 tablespoons butter when making the chocolate filling and substitute peanuts for the walnuts or pecans.

Nutrition facts per bar: 156 cal., 7 g total fat (3 g sat. fat), 17 mg chol., 74 mg sodium, 21 g carbo., 1 g fiber, 3 g pro.

Whole Wheat-Chocolate Revel Bars: Prepare as directed, except reduce the all-purpose flour to 1½ cups and add 1 cup whole wheat flour.

Nutrition facts per bar: 145 cal., 6 g total fat (3 g sat. fat), 18 mg chol., 68 mg sodium, 21 g carbo., 1 g fiber, 2 g pro.

Buttermilk Brownies

Prep: 30 min. Bake: 25 min.

One of our current editors, who hails from the Lone Star State, remembers these rich cakelike brownies from her childhood. Down home, they called the recipe Texas sheet cake.

2	**cups all-purpose flour**
2	**cups granulated sugar**
1	**tsp. baking soda**
¼	**tsp. salt**
1	**cup butter**
1	**cup water**
⅓	**cup unsweetened cocoa powder**
2	**eggs**
½	**cup buttermilk or sour milk (see tip, page 255)**
1½	**tsp. vanilla**
1	**recipe Chocolate-Buttermilk Frosting (opposite)**

1. Preheat oven to 350°F. Grease a 15×10×1-inch or a 13×9×2-inch baking pan; set aside. In a medium mixing bowl, stir together flour, granulated sugar, baking soda, and salt; set aside.

Buttermilk Brownies

2. In a medium saucepan, combine butter, the water, and cocoa powder. Bring mixture just to boiling, stirring constantly. Remove from heat. Add the cocoa mixture to the flour mixture; beat with an electric mixer on medium speed until combined. Add the eggs, buttermilk, and vanilla. Beat for 1 minute (batter will be thin). Pour batter into prepared pan.

3. Bake about 25 minutes for the 15×10×1-inch pan, about 35 minutes for the 13×9×2-inch pan, or until a wooden toothpick inserted in the center comes out clean.

4. Prepare Chocolate-Buttermilk Frosting; pour warm frosting onto the warm brownies, spreading evenly. Cool in pan on a wire rack. Cut into bars. Makes 24 brownies.

Chocolate-Buttermilk Frosting: In a medium saucepan, combine ¼ cup butter, 3 tablespoons unsweetened cocoa powder, and 3 tablespoons buttermilk or sour milk. Bring mixture to boiling. Remove from heat. Add 2¼ cups sifted powdered sugar and ½ teaspoon vanilla. Beat until smooth. If desired, stir in ¾ cup coarsely chopped pecans.

Make-ahead directions: Prepare, bake, and frost brownies as directed. Cover and chill for up to 3 days. (Or place frosted brownies in a single layer in a freezer container; cover. Freeze for up to 3 months. Thaw at room temperature.)

Nutrition facts per brownie: 237 cal., 10 g total fat (6 g sat. fat), 44 mg chol., 185 mg sodium, 35 g carbo., 0 g fiber, 2 g pro.

Paul's Pumpkin Bars

Prep: 30 min. Bake: 25 min.

In the 1970s, *Better Homes and Gardens*® ran a column called "He Cooks," which showcased recipes from men. The recipe for these moist bars was submitted in 1976 by an accountant named Paul.

- 2 **cups all-purpose flour**
- 2 **tsp. baking powder**
- 2 **tsp. ground cinnamon**
- 1 **tsp. baking soda**
- ¼ **tsp. salt**
- 4 **eggs**
- 1 **15-oz. can pumpkin**
- 1⅔ **cups sugar**
- 1 **cup cooking oil**
- ¾ **cup chopped pecans, toasted (optional) (tip, page 102)**
- 1 **recipe Cream Cheese Frosting (right) Pecan halves, toasted (optional) (tip, page 102)**

Paul's Pumpkin Bars

1. Preheat oven to 350°F. In a medium bowl, stir together flour, baking powder, cinnamon, baking soda, and salt; set aside.

2. In a large mixing bowl, beat together eggs, pumpkin, sugar, and oil. Add flour mixture to egg mixture; beat with an electric mixer on medium speed until mixed. If desired, stir in chopped pecans.

3. Spread batter in an ungreased 15×10×1-inch baking pan. Bake for 25 to 30 minutes or until a wooden toothpick inserted in center comes out clean. Cool in pan on wire rack.

4. Prepare Cream Cheese Frosting; frost baked layer. If desired, top with pecan halves. Cut into bars. Store in refrigerator. Makes 24 bars.

Cream Cheese Frosting: In a medium mixing bowl, combine two 3-ounce packages cream cheese, softened; ½ cup butter, softened; and 2 teaspoons vanilla. Beat with an electric mixer on medium speed until fluffy. Gradually add 4 cups sifted powdered sugar, beating until smooth.

Nutrition facts per bar: 315 cal., 17 g total fat (6 g sat. fat), 54 mg chol., 184 mg sodium, 40 g carbo., 1 g fiber, 3 g pro.

Holiday Cooking

At holiday time, generations gather together to share good times, fond memories, and, of course, cherished foods. For our *Better Homes and Gardens®* publications, we work up to a year in advance to develop, test, and perfect recipes for families to enjoy during seasonal celebrations. This festive assortment is a repertoire of our greatest holiday dishes ever. It includes main dishes, side dishes, desserts, cookies, and candies to let you feast in style.

138

124

123

130

141

145

Classic Roast Turkey with Fruit-Chestnut Stuffing

Prep: 1¼ hr. Roast: 2½ hr. + 45 min. Stand: 15 min.

This 2002 recipe, which features a new version of chestnut stuffing, is our way of helping 21st-century cooks with holiday turkey roasting.

 1 **lb. fresh chestnuts in shells
     or one 10-oz. can whole peeled
     chestnuts, rinsed and drained**
 ½ **cup chopped celery**
 ½ **cup chopped onion**
 ⅓ **cup butter**
 1 **cup coarsely chopped red cooking apple**
 ½ **cup golden raisins**
 1 **Tbsp. snipped fresh thyme
     or 1 tsp. dried thyme, crushed**
 ½ **tsp. salt**
 ¼ **tsp. pepper**
 8 **cups dry 1-inch sourdough bread
     cubes (10 oz.)**
 ¾ **to 1 cup apple juice or chicken broth**
 1 **10- to 12-lb. turkey**
 2 **Tbsp. olive oil**
    Salt
    Pepper
    Small red cooking apples (optional)
    Fresh herb sprigs (optional)

1. To roast fresh chestnuts, preheat oven to 400°F. Cut an X on the flat side of each chestnut. Place chestnuts in a large shallow baking pan. Roast for 15 minutes, stirring occasionally. Peel chestnuts while still warm. (You should have 2 cups fresh shelled chestnuts.) In a medium saucepan, cook peeled chestnuts in boiling water about 15 minutes or just until tender. Drain and cool slightly. Coarsely chop fresh or canned chestnuts. Place chestnuts in a very large bowl; set aside.

2. Preheat oven to 325°F. In a medium saucepan, cook celery and onion in hot butter over medium heat for 3 minutes. Add the chopped apple; cook for 2 minutes more. Remove from heat. Stir in raisins, thyme, the ½ teaspoon salt, and the ¼ teaspoon pepper. Add apple-raisin mixture to the bowl with the chestnuts. Add bread cubes; toss to mix. Add enough of the apple juice or broth to moisten; toss lightly to mix.

3. Remove neck and giblets from the turkey. Rinse the inside of the turkey; pat dry with paper towels. Spoon some of the stuffing loosely into the neck cavity of the turkey. Pull the neck skin to the back; fasten with a skewer. Lightly spoon more stuffing into the body cavity. (Place any remaining stuffing into an ungreased casserole; cover and chill. If desired, for a moister stuffing, drizzle with additional apple juice or broth. Bake stuffing in casserole alongside turkey about 45 minutes or until heated through.) Tie legs to tail with 100%-cotton kitchen string or tuck the ends of the drumsticks under the band of skin across the tail. Twist the wing tips under the back.

4. Place the turkey, breast side up, on a rack in a shallow roasting pan. Brush with oil; season with additional salt and pepper. Insert an oven-going meat thermometer into the center of one of the inside thigh muscles, making sure the bulb does not touch bone. Cover turkey loosely with foil. Roast turkey for 2½ hours.

5. Cut the string or band of skin between the drumsticks so the thighs will cook evenly. Uncover; roast for 45 minutes to 1¼ hours more or until meat thermometer registers 180°F and an instant-read thermometer inserted in stuffing registers at least 165°F. Remove turkey from oven. Cover; let stand for 15 minutes before carving. If desired, serve on a platter garnished with small apples and herb sprigs. Makes 12 to 14 servings.

Nutrition facts per serving: 528 cal., 15 g total fat (6 g sat. fat), 179 mg chol., 478 mg sodium, 36 g carbo., 2 g fiber, 59 g pro.

> **Helping cooks prepare moist, flavorful turkeys for holiday meals is an ongoing custom that goes way back with *Better Homes and Gardens®* magazine. In fact, directions for roasting have run in the November issue for decades.**

Classic Roast Turkey with Fruit-Chestnut Stuffing

Crimson Cherry-Glazed Holiday Hens

Prep: 30 min. Roast: 40 min.

If you're looking for a special entrée, these cherry-glazed game hens are fabulous. Roast whole hens for those with hearty appetites or half hens for others.

- 4   1¼- to 1½-lb. Cornish game hens*
- 6   cloves elephant garlic, peeled and halved
- 3   Tbsp. butter, melted
- ½   tsp. salt
- ¼   tsp. pepper
- 2   Tbsp. butter
- ⅓   cup sliced or chopped shallots
- 1   cup red cherry preserves (with whole cherries)
- ¼   cup red wine vinegar
- ½   tsp. ground allspice
- ¼   tsp. ground cloves

1. Preheat oven to 425°F. Rub the skin of hens with cut sides of garlic cloves; reserve garlic. Tie drumsticks to tails. Brush hens with the 3 tablespoons melted butter; sprinkle with salt and pepper. Place hens on a rack in a shallow roasting pan; twist wing tips under backs. Place halved garlic cloves around the hens.

2. Roast for 40 to 45 minutes or until an instant-read meat thermometer inserted into the thigh of each hen registers 180°F. (The thermometer should not touch bone.) (The garlic may turn green during roasting.)

3. Meanwhile, in a small saucepan, melt the 2 tablespoons butter over medium heat. Add shallots and cook about 3 minutes or until tender, stirring often. Stir in preserves, vinegar, allspice, and cloves. Bring to boiling; reduce heat. Boil gently, uncovered, about 20 minutes or until desired glazing consistency. Remove *one* garlic piece from the roasting pan; cool slightly. Finely chop slightly cooled garlic; stir into sauce.

4. To serve, transfer hens and remaining garlic to a serving platter. Spoon glaze over hens. Makes 4 whole hens or 8 half hens.

*Test Kitchen Tip: For smaller portions, split hens in half lengthwise. Ask the butcher to cut the hens in half for you and remove the backbone. (Or use a long heavy knife or kitchen shears to split the hens lengthwise. Cut through the breast bone, just off-center, and cut through the backbone; discard the backbone.) Place hen halves, skin sides up, on a rack in a shallow roasting pan. Add the garlic to the pan and roast as directed.

Nutrition facts per whole hen: 956 cal., 52 g total fat (18 g sat. fat), 240 mg chol., 624 mg sodium, 60 g carbo., 2 g fiber, 62 g pro.

Yesterday

Our earliest recipes for roast turkey simply told cooks to fill the bird with a favorite stuffing. Cooks then could choose from the likes of bread, celery, mushrooms, chestnuts, sausage, or apples for their dressings. This recipe blends the best of those early bread and celery stuffings.

Old-Fashioned Bread Stuffing
Prep: 15 min. Bake: 30 min.

Poultry seasoning is a blend of thyme, sage, pepper, marjoram, and sometimes rosemary. Use the blend if you don't want to go heavy on the sage.

- 1½   cups sliced celery
- 1   cup chopped onion
- ½   cup butter
- 1   Tbsp. snipped fresh sage or 1 tsp. poultry seasoning or ground sage
- ¼   tsp. pepper
- 12   cups dry bread cubes*
- 1   to 1¼ cups chicken broth

1. Preheat oven to 325°F. In a large skillet, cook celery and onion in hot butter until tender. Remove from heat. Stir in sage or poultry seasoning and pepper. Place dry bread cubes in a large bowl; add onion mixture. Drizzle with enough of the chicken broth to moisten; toss lightly to combine.

2. Place stuffing in an ungreased 2½-quart casserole. Bake, covered, for 30 to 45 minutes or until heated through. (Or to use to stuff one 10- to 12-pound turkey, prepare as above, except use ¾ cup to 1 cup chicken broth instead of 1 to 1¼ cups broth. At end of roasting, internal temperature of stuffing should register 165°F on an instant-read thermometer.) Makes 12 to 14 servings.

Make-ahead directions: Prepare as directed through step 1. Place stuffing in a 2½-quart casserole. Cover and chill up to 24 hours. Preheat oven to 325°F. Bake casserole, covered, for 50 to 60 minutes or until heated through. (For safety reasons, do not make stuffing ahead if planning to use for stuffing a turkey.)

*Test Kitchen Tip: To make 12 cups dry bread cubes, preheat oven to 300°F. Cut 20 to 21 slices bread into ½-inch cubes. (You should have about 14 cups cubed bread.) Spread cubes in a single layer in a large, shallow roasting pan. Bake, uncovered, for 10 to 15 minutes or until dry, stirring twice. Cool. Bread will continue to dry and crisp as it cools. (Or let bread stand, loosely covered, at room temperature for 8 to 12 hours.)

Nutrition facts per serving: 181 cal., 10 g total fat (5 g sat. fat), 22 mg chol., 342 mg sodium, 20 g carbo., 1 g fiber, 4 g pro.

Carrot-Mushroom Stuffing

Prep: 25 min. Bake: 50 min.

If you enjoy a moist stuffing, be sure to use all of the water suggested.

- ¼ **cup butter**
- 6 **cups sliced fresh shiitake and/or button mushrooms**
- ¼ **cup sliced green onions**
- 1 **Tbsp. soy sauce**
- 1½ **tsp. snipped fresh rosemary or ½ tsp. dried rosemary, crushed**
- ¼ **tsp. pepper**
- 6 **cups herb-seasoned stuffing croutons (about 12 oz.)**
- 3 **cups coarsely shredded carrots (6 medium)**
- 1¼ **to 1½ cups water**

1. Preheat oven to 325°F. In a large skillet, melt the butter over medium heat. Add mushrooms. Cook about 5 minutes or just until tender, stirring occasionally. Add green onions for the last 1 minute of cooking. Remove from heat. Stir in soy sauce, rosemary, and pepper.

2. In a very large bowl, combine mushroom mixture, herb-seasoned stuffing croutons, and carrots. Drizzle with enough of the water to moisten, tossing to combine.

3. Place stuffing in an ungreased 2½-quart casserole. Bake, covered, for 50 to 60 minutes or until heated through. (Or to use to stuff a 10- to 12-pound turkey, prepare as above, except use 1 to 1¼ cups water instead of 1¼ to 1½ cups water. At end of roasting, internal temperature of stuffing should register 165°F on an instant-read thermometer.) Makes 12 servings.

Make-ahead directions: Prepare as directed through step 2. Place in a 2½-quart casserole. Cover and chill up to 24 hours. Preheat oven to 325°F. Bake casserole, covered, for 60 to 70 minutes or until heated through. (For safety reasons, do not make stuffing ahead if planning to use for stuffing a turkey.)

Nutrition facts per serving: 151 cal., 8 g total fat (4 g sat. fat), 12 mg chol., 387 mg sodium, 17 g carbo., 2 g fiber, 4 g pro.

Today

This 2000 recipe contest winner impressed our staff because it adds shiitake mushrooms and soy sauce to convenient herb-seasoned stuffing mix for a fresh Asian spin on classic stuffing.

Walnut-Encrusted Pork Roast

Prep: 15 min. Roast: 1¼ hr. Stand: 15 min.

In December 1999, we asked our readers for their dazzling beef and pork dishes as part of our Prize Tested Recipes® contest. This pork top loin roast served with lingonberries, a tiny cousin of the cranberry, won top prize.

- 1   2- to 2¼-lb. boneless pork top loin roast (single loin)
- ⅓   cup finely chopped walnuts
- 1   Tbsp. snipped fresh rosemary
      Salt
      Pepper
- ½   cup Merlot or dry red wine
- 1   cup canned lingonberries* (about ⅔ of a 14½-oz. jar) or whole cranberry sauce (about ½ of a 16-oz. can)
- 1   Tbsp. lemon juice
- 1   sprig fresh rosemary (about 6 inches)

1. Preheat oven to 325°F. Place roast on a rack in a shallow roasting pan. In a small bowl, combine walnuts and snipped rosemary; press onto top and sides of roast. Sprinkle with salt and pepper. Insert an oven-going meat thermometer into center of roast. Roast for 1¼ to 1½ hours or until thermometer registers 155°F. Remove roast from oven. Cover with foil; let stand for 15 minutes before carving. (The temperature of the meat will rise about 5°F during standing.)

2. Meanwhile, for sauce, in a small saucepan, combine wine, lingonberries or cranberry sauce, lemon juice, and rosemary sprig. Bring to boiling; reduce heat. Boil gently, uncovered, about 15 minutes or until sauce is reduced to 1 cup. Remove sauce from heat; let stand for 15 minutes. Discard rosemary sprig. (Sauce thickens slightly as it cools.)

3. To serve, slice roast; spoon sauce over pork. Pass remaining sauce. Makes 8 servings.

*Test Kitchen Tip: Look for canned lingonberries in the gourmet section of your supermarket or with the other canned fruits.

Nutrition facts per serving: 265 cal., 11 g total fat (3 g sat. fat), 57 mg chol., 92 mg sodium, 19 g carbo., 1 g fiber, 19 g pro.

Pork Pinwheels with Roasted-Garlic Mayonnaise

Prep: 30 min. Roast: 45 min. Stand: 30 min.
Chill: 3 to 8 hr.

Whether you need an appetizer or a main dish for holiday entertaining, these versatile swirls of pork, Parmesan cheese, and walnuts make a company-pleasing choice.*

1	recipe Roasted Garlic Mayonnaise (right)
3	leeks, thinly sliced (1 cup)
1	Tbsp. olive oil
1	cup snipped fresh parsley
2	Tbsp. snipped fresh thyme or 1 tsp. dried thyme, crushed
¼	cup grated Parmesan cheese or Romano cheese (1 oz.)
¼	tsp. salt
¼	tsp. pepper
3	Tbsp. olive oil or cooking oil
¼	cup chopped walnuts
2	12-oz. pork tenderloins
	Salt
	Pepper

1. Prepare Roasted Garlic Mayonnaise. Preheat oven to 325°F. In a medium skillet, cook leeks in the 1 tablespoon hot oil until tender; remove from heat.

2. In a blender or food processor, combine parsley, thyme, Parmesan cheese, the ¼ teaspoon salt, and the ¼ teaspoon pepper. Cover and blend or process with several on-off turns until finely chopped. With the machine running, gradually add the 3 tablespoons oil; blend or process until the consistency of soft butter. Add leeks and nuts; blend or process with several on-off turns until nuts are coarsely chopped. Set aside.

3. Remove fat and paper-thin membrane from surface of tenderloins. Use a sharp knife to cut each tenderloin lengthwise to, but not through, opposite side. Cover *one tenderloin* with plastic wrap. Using the flat side of a meat mallet and working from center to edges, pound the tenderloin to a 12×8-inch rectangle. Remove plastic wrap; repeat with the remaining tenderloin.

4. Sprinkle tenderloins lightly with additional salt and pepper. Spread *half* of the parsley mixture evenly onto *each* tenderloin to within 1 inch of edges. Starting from a short side, roll up each tenderloin into a spiral. If necessary, tie rolls with 100%-cotton kitchen string. Insert an oven-going meat thermometer into center of one tenderloin. Place tenderloins, seam sides down, on a rack in a shallow roasting pan.

5. Roast, uncovered, for 45 to 60 minutes or until thermometer registers 160°F. Let stand at room temperature for 30 minutes. Remove string; cut into slices about ½ inch thick. Cover and chill for at least 3 hours or up to 8 hours.

6. Serve pork slices with Roasted Garlic Mayonnaise. Makes about 32 slices.

Roasted Garlic Mayonnaise: Preheat oven to 325°F. Peel away outer skin from 1 medium garlic head. Cut off the pointed top portion with a knife, leaving the bulb intact but exposing the individual cloves. Place in a small baking dish; drizzle with 2 teaspoons olive oil. Cover and bake for 45 to 60 minutes or until cloves are very soft. Cool slightly. Press to remove garlic "paste" from individual cloves. Mash garlic with tines of a fork. Stir together mashed garlic and ½ cup light mayonnaise dressing or salad dressing. If necessary, thin mixture with a little milk. Cover and chill for at least 3 hours or up to 8 hours.

*****Test Kitchen Tip:** For an appetizer, serve one pinwheel slice with a teaspoon of the garlic mayonnaise. For an entrée, serve three or four slices with about a tablespoon of the garlic mayonnaise.

Nutrition facts per slice with 1 teaspoon mayonnaise: 79 cal., 5 g total fat (1 g sat. fat), 16 mg chol., 82 mg sodium, 2 g carbo., 0 g fiber, 5 g pro.

Thanks to Julia Child, American cooks became fascinated by "gourmet" cooking and haute cuisine in the 1960s. That interest grew in the 1970s and 1980s and continues to thrive today. Our staff has been only too happy to help our readers navigate the world of caramelizing, pureeing, and deglazing. But we make it a point to take some of the mystery out of classic techniques by writing clear, concise directions and making steps quicker and easier.

Berry-Burgundy Glazed Ham
Prep: 10 min. Bake: 2¼ hr.

The burgundy and mustard add a sophisticated tang to this festive cranberry sauce.

- 1 10- to 14-lb. bone-in cooked ham
  Whole cloves
- 1 16-oz. can whole cranberry sauce
- ½ cup packed brown sugar
- ½ cup Burgundy or other dry red wine
- 1 Tbsp. yellow mustard

1. Preheat oven to 325°F. Score ham in a diamond pattern by making diagonal cuts at 1-inch intervals; stud with whole cloves. Place the ham, fat side up, on a rack in a shallow roasting pan. Insert an oven-going meat thermometer into center of ham, making sure the bulb does not touch bone. Bake for 2¼ to 2¾ hours or until thermometer registers 140°F.

2. Meanwhile, in a medium saucepan, stir together cranberry sauce, brown sugar, wine, and mustard. Bring to boiling; reduce heat. Simmer, uncovered, for 5 minutes. During the last 20 minutes of roasting, spoon *half* of the sauce over ham. Reheat remaining sauce and pass with ham. Makes 32 to 40 servings.

Nutrition facts per serving: 187 cal., 5 g total fat (2 g sat. fat), 54 mg chol., 1,306 mg sodium, 8 g carbo., 0 g fiber, 24 g pro.

Yesterday

Baked ham is a traditional star on holiday dinner tables, and we've published numerous adaptations of the classic. In 1969, a California cook won top prize in our Prize Tested Recipes® contest with this berry-glazed version. More than three decades later, it's still a special way to dress up the holiday ham.

Ham with Five Great Glazes

Prep: 15 min. Bake: 1½ hr.

- 1   **5- to 6-lb. bone-in cooked ham (rump half or shank portion)**
- 1   **recipe Raspberry-Chipotle Glaze (pictured right), Chutney Glaze, Cranberry Glaze, Maple-Pecan Glaze, or Honey-Orange Glaze (below)**

1. Preheat oven to 325°F. Score ham in a diamond pattern by making diagonal cuts at 1-inch intervals. Place on rack in a shallow roasting pan. Insert a meat thermometer into center, making sure bulb does not touch bone. Bake for 1½ to 2¼ hours or until 140°F. During the last 20 minutes of roasting, brush ham often with desired glaze. Reheat any remaining glaze and pass with ham. Makes 16 to 20 servings.

Raspberry-Chipotle Glaze: In a medium saucepan, combine: 1½ cups seedless raspberry preserves; 2 tablespoons vinegar; 2 or 3 canned chipotle chile peppers in adobo sauce, drained and chopped (tip, page 32); and 3 cloves garlic, minced. Cook and stir just until boiling; reduce heat. Simmer, uncovered, for 5 minutes more. Makes 1½ cups.

Nutrition facts per serving: 320 cal., 9 g total fat (3 g sat. fat), 109 mg chol., 97 mg sodium, 21 g carbo., 0 g fiber, 35 g pro.

Chutney Glaze: In a food processor or blender, combine one 12-ounce jar chutney, 1 teaspoon finely shredded orange peel, 2 tablespoons orange juice, and 1 tablespoon stone-ground mustard. Process or blend until almost smooth. Makes 1½ cups.

Nutrition facts per serving: 269 cal., 9 g total fat (3 g sat. fat), 109 mg chol., 137 mg sodium, 9 g carbo., 1 g fiber, 36 g pro.

Cranberry Glaze: In a saucepan, mix one 12-ounce frozen can cranberry juice concentrate, thawed; 3 tablespoons Dijon-style mustard; 2 tablespoons packed brown sugar; 2 tablespoons lemon juice; 4 teaspoons cornstarch; and ¼ teaspoon ground cloves. Cook and stir until thickened and bubbly. Cook and stir 2 minutes more. Makes 1⅔ cups.

Nutrition facts per serving: 290 cal., 9 g total fat (3 g sat. fat), 109 mg chol., 92 mg sodium, 14 g carbo., 0 g fiber, 35 g pro.

Maple-Pecan Glaze: In a medium saucepan, combine 1 cup pure maple syrup and 1 cup orange marmalade. Heat and stir until bubbly. Stir in 1 tablespoon butter. Stir in ½ cup chopped pecans, toasted (tip, page 102). Makes 2½ cups.

Nutrition facts per serving: 366 cal., 12 g total fat (4 g sat. fat), 111 mg chol., 95 mg sodium, 27 g carbo., 0 g fiber, 36 g pro.

Today

Through the years, we've teamed baked ham with a variety of glazes. Gradually the flavors have become bolder and the ingredients more varied. Here's a five-pack of our delicious brush-ons.

Honey-Orange Glaze: In a medium saucepan, combine 1 cup packed brown sugar, ½ cup honey, ¼ cup orange juice, ¼ cup bourbon or orange juice, and 2 tablespoons Dijon-style mustard. Cook and stir over medium heat until brown sugar is dissolved. Makes 1½ cups.

Nutrition facts per serving: 331 cal., 9 g total fat (3 g sat. fat), 109 mg chol., 90 mg sodium, 23 g carbo., 0 g fiber, 35 g pro.

Celebration Roast

Prep: 25 min. Roast: 1¾ hr. Stand: 15 min.

Looking for a new way to serve roast beef for the holidays? If so, we suggest this boneless ribeye roast rubbed with horseradish, garlic, and pepper. You serve it with a horseradish cream sauce.

2	Tbsp. cream-style prepared horseradish
4	cloves garlic, minced
4	to 5 tsp. pink and black peppercorns, cracked, or cracked black pepper
½	tsp. salt
1	4- to 6-lb. boneless beef ribeye roast
8	medium onions
6	small red and/or white onions (optional)
1	Tbsp. olive oil
1	recipe Horseradish-Peppercorn Cream (optional) (below)

1. Preheat oven to 350°F. In a small bowl, stir together cream-style horseradish, garlic, *3 teaspoons* of the cracked peppercorns, and the salt. Rub horseradish mixture onto beef roast. Place beef roast, fat side up, on a rack in a shallow roasting pan. Insert an oven-going meat thermometer into center of roast. Roast, uncovered, until desired doneness. (For medium-rare doneness, allow 1¾ to 2 hours or until thermometer registers 135°F; for medium doneness, allow 2 to 2½ hours or until thermometer registers 150°F.) Remove roast from oven. Cover with foil; let stand for 15 minutes. (The temperature of the meat will rise about 10°F during standing.)

2. Meanwhile, slice root ends off the medium and, if using, small onions (so onions will stand upright). Brush onions with olive oil. Sprinkle with remaining 1 to 2 teaspoons cracked peppercorns. For the last 1¼ hours of roasting time, arrange onions upright around roast.

3. If desired, prepare Horseradish-Peppercorn Cream. Serve with roast and roasted onions. Serves 12 to 16.

Nutrition facts per serving: 294 cal., 16 g total fat (7 g sat. fat), 89 mg chol., 199 mg sodium, 5 g carbo., 1 g fiber, 31 g pro.

Horseradish-Peppercorn Cream: In a medium mixing bowl, beat ½ cup whipping cream with an electric mixer on medium speed just until soft peaks form (tips curl). Fold in 2 tablespoons cream-style prepared horseradish and 1 teaspoon Dijon-style mustard. If not using immediately, cover and store horseradish mixture in the refrigerator for up to 6 hours. To serve, sprinkle with 1 to 2 tablespoons pink and black peppercorns, cracked. Makes about 1 cup.

Nutrition facts per 1-tablespoon serving: 28 cal., 3 g total fat (2 g sat. fat), 10 mg chol., 31 mg sodium, 1 g carbo., 0 g fiber, 0 g pro.

Wellington-Style Beef Tenderloin

Prep: 25 min. Stand: 30 min. Bake: 18 min.

Showcase these elegant pastry-wrapped steaks at an intimate holiday dinner for four. Team them with steamed asparagus spears.

½	of a 17.3-oz. pkg. frozen puff pastry (1 sheet)
4	4- to 5-oz. beef tenderloin steaks, cut ¾ inch thick
1	Tbsp. cooking oil
2	Tbsp. butter or margarine
2	cups fresh mushrooms, finely chopped (1½ cups)
8	green onions, thinly sliced
2	Tbsp. Marsala or dry white wine (optional)
1	Tbsp. horseradish mustard
2	tsp. snipped fresh thyme or ½ tsp. dried thyme, crushed
¼	tsp. salt
¼	tsp. pepper
1	Tbsp. butter or margarine, melted

1. To thaw puff pastry, let stand at room temperature for 30 minutes. (Or thaw overnight in the refrigerator.)

2. Preheat oven to 425°F. Season steaks with *salt* and *pepper*. In a large skillet, heat oil over medium-high heat. Add steaks; cook for 2 minutes, turning once. Drain on paper towels. Set aside.

3. In the same skillet, melt the 2 tablespoons butter over medium heat. Add mushrooms, green onions, and, if desired, wine; cook over medium heat for 5 to 6 minutes or until vegetables are tender and liquid has evaporated. Remove skillet from heat. Stir in horseradish mustard, thyme, the ¼ teaspoon salt, and the ¼ teaspoon pepper.

4. Unfold puff pastry and place on a lightly floured surface. Roll into an 11-inch square. Cut into four 5½-inch squares. Brush pastry edges with water. Place some of the mushroom mixture in the center of each square. Place a steak on top. For each, fold 2 opposite sides of pastry over meat, pressing seams and ends to seal. If necessary, trim excess pastry. Reserve pastry trimmings. Turn over bundles. If desired, cut small shapes from trimmings; moisten with water and place on top of bundles. Brush bundles with melted butter. Place bundles, seam sides down, on a rack in a shallow baking pan. Bake, uncovered, about 18 minutes or until meat is medium-rare doneness (145°F). Serves 4.

Nutrition facts per serving: 574 cal., 40 g total fat (9 g sat. fat), 81 mg chol., 633 mg sodium, 26 g carbo., 1 g fiber, 29 g pro.

Rack of Lamb

Prep: 45 min. Marinate: 8 to 24 hr. Roast: 25 min.

In 1983, when we featured holiday recipes from country inns, this festive wine-marinated lamb recipe came from a hotel nestled in the Napa Valley.

- 2 **1-lb. French-style lamb rib roasts (each rack about 8×4×1½ inches and 8 ribs)**
- 2 **cups dry white wine**
- ½ **cup chopped onion**
- 4 **shallots or green onions, chopped**
- 1 **tsp. olive oil or cooking oil**
- ½ **tsp. cracked black pepper**
- ½ **tsp. dried basil, crushed**
- ¼ **tsp. dried rosemary, crushed**
- 1 **bay leaf**
- 1 **recipe Rich Brown Sauce (right)**
- 2 **Tbsp. brandy**
- ¼ **tsp. dried thyme or basil, crushed**

1. Place meat in a large resealable plastic bag set in a deep large bowl. For marinade, in a medium bowl, combine the wine, onion, shallots or green onions, oil, pepper, the ½ teaspoon basil, the rosemary, and bay leaf. Pour marinade over meat. Seal bag; turn to coat meat. Marinate in refrigerator for at least 8 hours or up to 24 hours, turning bag occasionally.

2. Drain meat, reserving marinade. In a saucepan, bring marinade to boiling. Boil gently, uncovered, about 35 minutes or until reduced to about ¾ cup. Strain, discarding solids (should have about ¼ cup liquid).

3. Meanwhile, preheat oven to 450°F. Pat meat dry with paper towels. Place the meat, rib sides down, in a shallow roasting pan. Roast for 25 to 30 minutes or until medium-rare doneness (140°F). To prevent overbrowning, cover loosely with foil during the last 5 minutes of roasting. (If roast is thicker than specified dimensions, increase roasting time by 10 to 15 minutes and cover with foil during the last 10 minutes of roasting.) Transfer meat to a platter, reserving drippings in pan; cover meat and keep warm. (The temperature of the meat will rise about 5°F during standing.)

4. For sauce, in a small saucepan, combine *1 tablespoon* of the reserved pan drippings and the reduced marinade. Add the Rich Brown Sauce, brandy, and the ¼ teaspoon thyme or basil. Bring to boiling; reduce heat. Simmer, uncovered, for 10 minutes. Serve sauce with meat. Makes 8 servings.

Rich Brown Sauce: In a medium saucepan, melt 2 tablespoons butter or margarine over medium heat. Add ½ cup chopped onion and ½ cup sliced carrot; cook about 5 minutes or until tender. Stir in 2 teaspoons sugar. Cook and stir for 5 minutes. Stir in 4 teaspoons all-purpose flour. Cook and stir for 2 minutes. Add: 1½ cups beef broth; 2 tablespoons tomato paste; ½ teaspoon dried thyme, crushed; 1 bay leaf; and ⅛ teaspoon ground black pepper. Bring to boiling; reduce heat. Simmer, uncovered, for 10 to 15 minutes or until reduced to 1½ cups. Strain, discarding solids.

Nutrition facts per serving: 197 cal., 8 g total fat (4 g sat. fat), 40 mg chol., 225 mg sodium, 8 g carbo., 1 g fiber, 11 g pro.

Yesterday

Along with the recipes for its Thanksgiving partners, roast turkey and bread stuffing, the recipe for glazed sweet potatoes dates back to the first edition of the *New Cook Book*. Since then, we've given the recipe a few tweaks—such as a sprinkling of marshmallows or nuts or the option of using canned sweet potatoes. But it's still the same recipe with the same great old-fashioned taste.

Candied Sweet Potatoes

Prep: 25 min. Bake: 30 + 5 min.

If you like, top these taters with both marshmallows and nuts. Pecans, almonds, or walnuts are crunchy choices.

- 4 **medium sweet potatoes or yams (about 2 lb.) or two 18-oz. cans sweet potatoes, drained**
- ¼ **cup packed brown sugar**
- 3 **Tbsp. butter or margarine, melted**
- ½ **cup tiny marshmallows or chopped nuts**

1. Preheat oven to 375°F. Peel fresh sweet potatoes; cut into 1½-inch chunks. In a covered large saucepan, cook fresh sweet potatoes in enough boiling water to cover for 10 to 12 minutes or just until tender; drain. (Or cut up canned sweet potatoes.)

2. Transfer potatoes to an ungreased 2-quart baking dish. Add the brown sugar and melted butter; stir gently to combine.

3. Bake for 30 to 35 minutes or until potatoes are glazed, gently stirring twice. Sprinkle with the marshmallows; bake for 5 minutes more. Serves 6.

Make-ahead directions: Prepare as directed through step 2. Cover and chill in the refrigerator for up to 24 hours. Uncover and bake as directed.

Nutrition facts per serving: 218 cal., 6 g total fat (4 g sat. fat), 16 mg chol., 81 mg sodium, 39 g carbo., 3 g fiber, 2 g pro.

Today

Each year, our editors and Test Kitchen take on the challenge of creating innovative recipes for Thanksgiving that are somehow reminiscent of the time-honored favorites. Here's a spirited rendition of timeless candied sweet potatoes.

Candied Mashed Sweet Potatoes

Prep: 25 min. Bake: 1¼ hr. + 30 min.

- **5 lb. sweet potatoes**
- **½ cup chopped pecans**
- **¼ cup granulated sugar**
- **1 Tbsp. butter or margarine**
- **¼ cup Irish cream liqueur, orange liqueur, praline liqueur, or milk**
- **2 Tbsp. butter or margarine**
- **2 Tbsp. packed brown sugar**
- **¾ tsp. pumpkin pie spice**
- **½ tsp. salt**

1. Preheat oven to 350°F. Grease 2 baking sheets; set aside. Wash sweet potatoes; pierce with a fork. Bake on 1 baking sheet about 1¼ hours or until tender.

2. Meanwhile, in a heavy, small skillet, cook and stir pecans, granulated sugar, and the 1 tablespoon butter over medium heat for 6 to 8 minutes or until sugar melts and turns golden brown. (Don't overcook.)

3. Immediately remove from heat; spread nut mixture onto second prepared baking sheet; separate into clusters. Cool completely.

4. Lightly grease a 2-quart square or rectangular baking dish. Scoop sweet potato pulp into a large mixing bowl; discard peel. Beat with an electric mixer on medium speed until smooth. Stir in liqueur, the 2 tablespoons butter, the brown sugar, spice, and salt. Beat until fluffy. Spread in prepared baking dish.

5. Chop nut mixture into small pieces;l sprinkle onto sweet potatoes. Bake, uncovered, about 30 minutes or until heated through. Makes 12 servings.

Make-ahead directions: Prepare as directed through step 3. Wrap nut mixture in plastic wrap. Cover unbaked casserole with foil. Store separately in refrigerator for up to 3 days. Preheat oven to 350°F. Bake casserole, covered with foil, for 20 minutes. Uncover; sprinkle with nut mixture Continue as directed.

Nutrition facts per serving: 243 cal., 6 g total fat (4 g sat. fat), 23 mg chol., 138 mg sodium, 44 g carbo., 6 g fiber, 3 g pro.

Holiday Scalloped Potatoes

Prep: 40 min. Bake: 40 + 30 min.

Red-skinned round potatoes and golden sweet potatoes seasoned with fresh thyme give this classic comfort food a festive flair.

1½ **lb. round red potatoes or Yukon Gold potatoes**
12 **oz. sweet potatoes**
1 **medium onion, chopped**
¼ **cup butter or margarine**
3 **Tbsp. all-purpose flour**
2¼ **cups milk**
½ **cup grated Parmesan cheese**
1 **Tbsp. snipped fresh tarragon or ½ tsp. dried tarragon, crushed**
½ **tsp. salt**
½ **tsp. pepper**
   Fresh tarragon (optional)

1. Preheat oven to 350°F. Thinly slice the red or Yukon Gold potatoes (do not peel). Peel and thinly slice the sweet potatoes. Grease a 2-quart square or rectangular baking dish.

2. For sauce, in a medium saucepan, cook onion in hot butter about 5 minutes or until tender. Stir in flour; cook and stir for 1 minute. Add milk all at once. Cook and stir until thickened and bubbly. Stir in Parmesan cheese, tarragon, salt, and pepper.

3. Arrange *half* of the red or Yukon Gold potatoes and *half* of the sweet potatoes into prepared baking dish, alternating in rows if desired. Spoon *half* of the sauce over the potatoes. Arrange remaining red or Yukon gold potatoes and sweet potatoes over sauce. Top with remaining sauce.

4. Cover and bake for 40 minutes. Uncover; bake about 30 minutes more or until potatoes are tender and sauce is golden. If desired, garnish with fresh tarragon. Makes 8 servings.

Nutrition facts per serving: 237 cal., 10 g total fat (6 g sat. fat), 26 mg chol., 366 mg sodium, 30 g carbo., 3 g fiber, 8 g pro.

Duchess Potatoes

Prep: 25 min. Cook: 20 min. Bake: 10 min.

Homey mashed potatoes take an elegant twirl when you turn them into these golden mounds for the holidays.

1¼ **lb. baking potatoes (about 4 medium), peeled and quartered**
½ **tsp. salt**
2 **Tbsp. butter or margarine**
   Salt
   Pepper
1 **to 2 Tbsp. milk**
1 **egg**
2 **Tbsp. butter or margarine, melted**

1. In a covered medium saucepan, cook potatoes and ½ teaspoon salt in enough boiling water to cover for 20 to 25 minutes or until tender; drain.

2. In a medium mixing bowl, mash potatoes with a potato masher or beat with an electric mixer on low speed. Add 2 tablespoons butter. Season to taste with salt and pepper. Gradually beat in enough of the milk to make the mixture light and fluffy. Cool slightly. With an electric mixer on low speed, beat in egg.

3. Preheat oven to 450°F. Grease a 15×10×1-inch baking pan. Using a pastry bag with a large star tip, pipe potatoes into 4 mounds on prepared baking pan. (Or spoon 4 mounds onto the baking pan.)

4. Drizzle mounds with 2 tablespoons melted butter. Bake for 10 to 12 minutes or until lightly browned. Makes 4 servings.

Make-ahead directions: Prepare as directed through step 3. Cover with plastic wrap. Chill in the refrigerator for up to 4 hours. Drizzle with butter and bake as directed.

Nutrition facts per serving: 218 cal., 14 g total fat (8 g sat. fat), 86 mg chol., 366 mg sodium, 21 g carbo., 2 g fiber, 4 g pro.

In the 1940s when cooks made mashed potatoes, they made them from the white baking potatoes. Today's cooks have a rainbow of choices. Yellow-, purple-, blue-, and red-fleshed varieties can turn mashed potatoes from ordinary to holiday special.

Crave Cranberries?

Cranberries go back a long way in American cooking. They grew wild during Colonial times and cooks were quick to use them every autumn in sauces, relishes, and desserts. Still as popular as ever, cranberries no longer have to be relegated to the fall. Tuck a supply in your freezer so your family can enjoy favorite cranberry dishes all year long. Simply freeze them right in their sealed bag and substitute the frozen berries for fresh whenever you like.

Cranberry-Pear Relish

Start to finish: 20 min.

Cranberries, sometimes called bounceberries because they bounce when they're ripe, get a flavor assist from pears and rosemary in this tangy relish.

    1   12-oz. pkg. fresh cranberries (3 cups)
    ¾   cup apple juice or apple cider
    ½   cup sugar
    1   Tbsp. lemon juice
    1   tsp. dried minced onion
    ½   tsp. dried rosemary, crushed
    2   medium pears, cored and chopped
        (2 cups)

1. In a medium saucepan, combine cranberries, apple juice, sugar, lemon juice, onion, and rosemary. Cook, uncovered, over medium heat about 5 minutes or until cranberries pop. Stir in pears and cook, uncovered, about 2 minutes more or just until the pears are tender. Serve warm or chilled. Makes 3 cups.

Make-ahead directions: Prepare as directed. Cover and chill in the refrigerator for up to 24 hours.

Nutrition facts per ¼-cup serving: 69 cal., 0 g total fat, 0 mg chol., 1 mg sodium, 18 g carbo., 2 g fiber, 0 g pro.

Layered Cranberry-Apple Mold

Prep: 30 min. Chill: 30 + 30 min. + 6 hr.

Deck out your holiday buffet table with this shimmering winter fruit mold. It was a featured Prize Tested Recipe® in 1979.

    1   6-oz. pkg. lemon-flavored gelatin
    ½   cup sugar
    1   cup boiling water
    1½   cups cranberry-apple drink
    1   16-oz. can whole cranberry sauce
    1   1.3-oz. envelope dessert topping mix
    1   large apple, finely chopped (about 1¼ cups)
    ¼   cup mayonnaise or salad dressing
         Sugared cranberries (optional)*
         Fresh mint (optional)

1. In a medium bowl, combine gelatin and sugar; stir in the boiling water, stirring until gelatin and sugar dissolve. Stir in cranberry-apple drink. Transfer 1¾ *cups* of the mixture to a small bowl; cover and chill about 30 minutes or until partially set (the consistency of unbeaten egg whites). Let remaining gelatin-drink mixture stand at room temperature.

2. Fold cranberry sauce into partially set gelatin-drink mixture; pour into an 8-cup ring mold or a 2-quart square dish. Cover and chill about 30 minutes or until almost firm. Chill remaining gelatin-drink mixture about 30 minutes or until partially set (the consistency of unbeaten egg whites).

3. Meanwhile, prepare topping mix according to package directions. Fold prepared topping, unpeeled apple, and mayonnaise into partially set gelatin-drink mixture. Spoon over chilled cranberry sauce-gelatin layer in mold or dish.

4. Cover and chill about 6 hours or until firm. Unmold gelatin onto platter. (For easier unmolding, set mold in a sink filled with warm water for several seconds or until gelatin separates from the mold.) If desired, garnish with sugared cranberries and fresh mint. Makes 12 servings.

*Test Kitchen Tip: For sugared cranberries, freeze cranberries; roll in sugar until coated.

Nutrition facts per serving: 222 cal., 5 g total fat (2 g sat. fat), 2 mg chol., 95 mg sodium, 44 g carbo., 1 g fiber, 2 g pro.

Coconut Eggnog

Prep: 20 min. Chill: 3 to 24 hr.

Eggnog was part of our holiday tradition almost from the very beginning. In those days, nog was a simple custard with puffs of stiffly beaten egg whites. Over the years, our recipes became richer, often calling for a touch of spirits.

- 3 cups milk
- 6 egg yolks, beaten
- 1 15- to 16-oz. can cream of coconut
- ½ cup rum
- 2 tsp. vanilla
- ½ cup whipping cream (optional)
- 1 Tbsp. sugar (optional)
  Shaved or shredded coconut, toasted (optional) (tip, page 102)

1. In a medium saucepan, combine milk and egg yolks. Cook and stir just until boiling; remove from heat. Immediately stir in cream of coconut, rum, and vanilla. Transfer to a large bowl or large pitcher. Cover and chill for at least 3 hours or up to 24 hours.

2. To serve, If desired, in a chilled medium mixing bowl, combine whipping cream and sugar. Beat with chilled beaters of an electric mixer on medium speed until soft peaks form (tips curl). Spoon whipped cream onto eggnog in punch bowl or individual glasses. If desired, sprinkle with coconut. Makes 10 (4-ounce) servings.

Nutrition facts per serving: 207 cal., 14 g total fat (11 g sat. fat), 133 mg chol., 69 mg sodium, 8 g carbo., 1 g fiber, 6 g pro.

Braided Cranberry Bread with a Twist

Prep: 30 min. Rise: 1 hr. + 30 min. Bake: 25 min.

In 1997 when we asked our readers for their favorite holiday breads, this brimming-with-berries-and-nuts brunch loaf was given to us by a cook in Washington state.

- 2¾ to 3 cups all-purpose flour
- 1 pkg. active dry yeast
- ½ cup milk
- ¼ cup water
- 2 Tbsp. granulated sugar
- 2 Tbsp. butter or margarine
- ½ tsp. salt
- 1 egg
- ½ cup finely chopped fresh cranberries
- ¼ cup packed brown sugar
- 2 Tbsp. finely chopped pecans
- 1½ tsp. finely shredded orange peel
- ¼ tsp. ground cinnamon
- ¼ tsp. ground nutmeg
- ⅛ tsp. ground cloves
- 1½ tsp. butter or margarine, melted
- 1 recipe Orange Icing (below)

1. In a large mixing bowl, combine *1 cup* of the flour and the yeast; set aside. In a medium saucepan, heat and stir milk, the water, granulated sugar, the 2 tablespoons butter, and the salt until warm (120°F to 130°F) and butter almost melts. Add milk mixture to flour mixture; add egg. Beat with an electric mixer on low to medium speed for 30 seconds, scraping side of bowl constantly. Beat on high speed for 3 minutes. Using a wooden spoon, stir in as much of the remaining flour as you can.

2. Turn out dough onto a floured surface. Knead in enough of the remaining flour to make a soft dough that is smooth and elastic (3 to 5 minutes total). Shape into a ball. Place in a lightly greased bowl; turn once. Cover and let rise in a warm place until double (1 to 1½ hours).

3. Meanwhile, for filling, in a small bowl, stir together the cranberries, brown sugar, pecans, orange peel, cinnamon, nutmeg, and cloves; set aside.

4. Punch down dough. Turn out onto a lightly floured surface. Cover and let rest for 10 minutes.

5. Meanwhile, grease a baking sheet. Roll dough into a 14×10-inch rectangle. Brush with the melted butter. Spread filling over dough. Starting from a long side, roll up dough. Seal seam. Cut roll in half lengthwise. Turn cut sides up. Loosely twist halves together, keeping the cut sides up. Pinch ends to seal. Place loaf on the prepared baking sheet. Cover; let rise in a warm place until nearly double (about 30 minutes).

6. Preheat oven to 375°F. Bake about 25 minutes or until golden brown. Remove from baking sheet. Cool on a wire rack. Drizzle with Orange Icing. Makes 18 servings.

Orange Icing: In a small bowl, combine ½ cup sifted powdered sugar and enough orange juice (1 to 3 teaspoons) to make an icing of drizzling consistency.

Nutrition facts per serving: 67 cal., 2 g total fat (1 g sat. fat), 10 mg chol., 47 mg sodium, 12 g carbo., 1 g fiber, 2 g pro.

Festive Fruit-and-Nut Panettone

Prep: 45 min. Rise: 1½ hr. + 45 min. Bake: 20 + 30 min.

In many Italian and Italian-American homes, the holidays just aren't complete without butter-slathered slices of this sweet yeast bread. The rich raisin, citron, and pine nut loaf traditionally is baked in a cylindrical mold. In our 1999 variation, we swapped dried tart cherries for the citron.

   1   **cup milk**
   2   **pkg. active dry yeast**
 4½   **to 5 cups bread flour**
   2   **eggs**
   ½   **cup butter, cut up**
   ½   **cup granulated sugar**
   1   **Tbsp. finely shredded lemon peel**
   1   **tsp. anise seeds**
   ½   **tsp. salt**
   1   **cup dried tart cherries**
   ¾   **cup pine nuts, toasted (tip, page 102)**
   ½   **cup golden raisins**
       Nonstick cooking spray
   1   **egg**
   1   **Tbsp. water**
   1   **recipe Powdered Sugar Icing (optional)**
       (below right)
       Thin strips lemon peel (optional)

1. In a small saucepan, heat milk just until lukewarm (105°F to 115°F). Pour milk into a a large mixing bowl. Sprinkle the yeast over the milk and stir to dissolve. Let stand for 5 minutes.

2. Add *1½ cups* of the flour, the 2 eggs, the butter, sugar, lemon peel, the anise seeds, and salt. Beat with an electric mixer on low to medium speed for 30 seconds, scraping side of bowl constantly. Beat on high speed for 3 minutes. Using a wooden spoon, stir in cherries, pine nuts, and raisins. Stir in as much of the remaining flour as you can. Dough should be just stiff enough to knead.

3. Turn out dough onto a floured surface; knead in enough of the remaining flour to make a moderately soft dough that is smooth and elastic (3 to 5 minutes total). Cover; let rise in warm place until double in size (about 1½ hours). Punch down dough.

4. Cover; let rest 10 minutes. Coat a 12-cup panettone mold or a 10-inch fluted tube pan with cooking spray. Set aside. Shape dough into a ball; form a hole in center of the ball. Transfer dough to prepared pan and flatten slightly to cover bottom of pan. Cover; let rise until almost double in size (45 to 60 minutes).

5. Preheat oven to 375°F. In a small bowl, slightly beat egg and water; brush onto top of loaf.

Festive Fruit-and-Nut Panettone

6. Bake for 20 minutes. Cover top of bread with foil; bake about 30 minutes more or until an instant-read thermometer inserted in center of bread registers 195°F to 200°F. Cool in pan on a wire rack for 10 minutes. Remove from pan. Cool completely on wire rack.

7. If desired, prepare Powdered Sugar Icing. Drizzle over bread and garnish with lemon peel strips. Makes 12 to 16 servings.

Bread machine directions: Add milk, eggs, butter, 4½ cups bread flour, the granulated sugar, lemon peel, the anise seeds, salt, and yeast to the pan of a 2-pound loaf bread machine according to manufacturer's directions. Select dough cycle. About 20 minutes into the cycle of the machine (or when the machine signals), add the dried cherries and pine nuts. When bread-machine dough cycle is complete, remove dough. Punch down dough. On a lightly floured surface, gently knead in the raisins. Continue as directed in steps 4 through 7.

Powdered Sugar Icing: In a small bowl, combine 1 cup sifted powdered sugar, 1 tablespoon milk, and ¼ teaspoon vanilla. Stir in additional milk, 1 teaspoon at a time, until icing reaches drizzling consistency.

Nutrition facts per serving: 426 cal., 16 g total fat (7 g sat. fat), 77 mg chol., 208 mg sodium, 62 g carbo., 2 g fiber, 12 g pro.

Chocolate-Hazelnut Yule Log

Stand: 30 min. Prep: 40 min. Bake: 12 min. Cool: 1 hr.

A tradition that originated in France, the Yule log is a favorite recipe for magazine holiday food pages. This version gets incredible hazelnut flavor from both the nuts and the liqueur.

5	egg whites
1	cup all-purpose flour
¼	cup unsweetened cocoa powder
¼	tsp. salt
5	egg yolks
2	Tbsp. hazelnut liqueur or milk
1	cup granulated sugar
¼	tsp. cream of tartar
	Sifted powdered sugar
1	recipe Hazelnut-Cream Filling (right)
1	recipe Rich Chocolate Frosting (right)

1. Allow egg whites to stand at room temperature for 30 minutes. Meanwhile, preheat oven to 375°F. Grease and lightly flour a 15×10×1-inch jelly-roll pan; set aside. In a medium bowl, sift together flour, cocoa powder, and salt; set side. In a large mixing bowl, beat egg yolks and liqueur or milk with an electric mixer on high speed about 5 minutes or until thick and lemon-colored. Gradually add ½ *cup* of the granulated sugar, beating until sugar is almost dissolved.

2. Thoroughly wash beaters. In a very large mixing bowl, beat egg whites and cream of tartar on medium to high speed until soft peaks form (tips curl). Gradually add the remaining ½ cup granulated sugar, *2 tablespoons* at a time, beating on medium to high speed until stiff peaks form (tips stand straight). Fold *1 cup* of the egg white mixture into egg yolk mixture. Fold egg yolk mixture into remaining egg white mixture. Fold in flour mixture; spread batter in prepared pan.

3. Bake for 12 to 15 minutes or until top springs back when lightly touched. Immediately loosen edges of cake from pan. Turn out cake onto a towel sprinkled with powdered sugar. Roll up towel and warm cake into a spiral, starting from one of the cake's short sides. Cool on a wire rack about 1 hour or until completely cooled.

4. Prepare Hazelnut-Cream Filling and Rich Chocolate Frosting. Gently unroll cake. Spread filling onto cake to within 1 inch of the edges. Roll up cake without towel. Spread cake with frosting. Transfer frosted cake to a serving platter. Use the tines of a fork to score the cake lengthwise to resemble tree bark. If desired, cover cake and chill for up to 4 hours. Cover and store any leftovers in refrigerator. Serves 10.

Hazelnut-Cream Filling: In a chilled medium mixing bowl, combine 1 cup whipping cream, ¼ cup sifted powdered sugar, and 1 tablespoon hazelnut liqueur. Beat with chilled beaters of an electric mixer on medium speed until soft peaks form (tips curl). Fold in ½ cup chopped hazelnuts (filberts), toasted (tip, page 102).

Rich Chocolate Frosting: In a medium saucepan, heat and stir 3 ounces unsweetened chocolate and 3 tablespoons butter until chocolate is melted. Remove from heat. Stir in 1½ cups sifted powdered sugar, 3 tablespoons milk, and 1 tablespoon hazelnut liqueur or milk. Stir in an additional 1½ cups sifted powdered sugar and enough additional milk (1 to 2 tablespoons) to make of spreading consistency.

Nutrition facts per serving: 524 cal., 24 g total fat (12 g sat. fat), 150 mg chol., 141 mg sodium, 71 g carbo., 2 g fiber, 8 g pro.

To the Peak

Before electric mixers and rotary beaters found their way into many kitchens, whisking egg whites was a test of arm strength and endurance. With the help of a mixer or beater, the job is almost child's play. To get egg whites to the right consistency, start by placing the whites in a clean glass or metal bowl (do not use plastic). Let stand for 30 minutes. Beat with an electric mixer on medium speed or a rotary beater.

• For *soft peaks*, beat until the tips curl when the beaters are lifted out.

• For *stiff peaks*, increase the speed of the mixer to high or beat vigorously with a rotary beater and continue beating the soft peaks until the tips of the peaks are stiff and stand straight.

Keep in mind any speck of fat, oil, or egg yolk in the whites will prevent them from beating to full volume.

Pumpkin Cake Roll

Stand: 30 min. Prep: 45 min. Bake: 15 min.
Cool: 1 hr. Chill: 2 to 48 hr.

Pumpkin takes center stage on the food pages of magazines in November—just in time for Thanksgiving baking. This pumpkin jelly roll is one of our prizewinning Pumpkin Desserts.

    3   eggs
    ¾   cup all-purpose flour
    2   tsp. ground cinnamon
    1   tsp. baking powder
    1   tsp. ground ginger
    ½   tsp. salt
    ½   tsp. ground nutmeg
    1   cup granulated sugar
    ⅔   cup canned pumpkin
    1   tsp. lemon juice
    1   cup finely chopped walnuts
        Sifted powdered sugar
    1   recipe Cream Cheese Filling (below)

1. Allow eggs to stand at room temperature for 30 minutes. Preheat oven to 375°F. Meanwhile, grease a 15×10×1-inch baking pan. Line bottom of pan with waxed paper or parchment paper; grease paper. Set pan aside. In a small bowl, stir together the flour, cinnamon, baking powder, ginger, salt, and nutmeg; set aside.

2. In a large mixing bowl, beat eggs with an electric mixer on high speed for 5 minutes. Gradually beat in the granulated sugar. Stir in pumpkin and lemon juice. Fold in flour mixture. Spread batter evenly in prepared pan. Top with walnuts.

3. Bake about 15 minutes or until top springs back when lightly touched. Immediately loosen edges of cake from pan. Turn out cake onto a towel sprinkled with powdered sugar. Remove waxed paper or parchment paper. Roll up towel and warm cake into a spiral, starting from one of the cake's short sides. Cool on a wire rack about 1 hour or until completely cooled.

4. Prepare Cream Cheese Filling. Gently unroll cake. Spread filling onto cake to within 1 inch of edges. Roll up cake without towel. Trim ends. Cover and chill for at least 2 hours or up to 48 hours. Makes 8 servings.

Cream Cheese Filling: In a medium bowl, beat: two 3-ounce packages cream cheese, softened; ¼ cup butter, softened; and ½ teaspoon vanilla with an electric mixer on medium speed until smooth. Gradually beat in 1 cup sifted powdered sugar until smooth.

Nutrition facts per serving: 456 cal., 25 g total fat (10 g sat. fat), 120 mg chol., 346 mg sodium, 52 g carbo., 2 g fiber, 8 g pro.

Pumpkin Tiramisu

Prep: 40 min. Chill: 6 to 24 hr.

In the 1990s, the Italian classic tiramisu was a popular dessert on restaurant menus. Cooks began improvising the rich layered creation at home, and when we asked our readers for their best pumpkin recipes, we were delighted to find the recipe for this innovative version in the mail.

    ⅔   cup hot brewed coffee
    2   Tbsp. packed brown sugar
    ½   cup brewed coffee, cooled
    1   envelope unflavored gelatin
    1   15-oz. can pumpkin
    1   8-oz. carton mascarpone cheese
    ½   cup granulated sugar
    2   tsp. ground cinnamon
    ¼   tsp. ground nutmeg
    1   cup whipping cream
    2   3-oz. pkg. ladyfingers, split (24 total)
    ½   cup whipping cream
        Ground cinnamon

1. In a small bowl, combine the ⅔ cup hot coffee and the brown sugar, stirring to dissolve sugar. Set aside. In a small saucepan, stir together the ½ cup cooled coffee and the gelatin. Let stand for 5 minutes. Cook and stir over medium heat until the gelatin is dissolved. Set aside.

2. In a large mixing bowl, combine pumpkin, mascarpone cheese, granulated sugar, the 2 teaspoons cinnamon, and the nutmeg; beat with an electric mixer on medium speed until smooth. While continuing to beat, gradually drizzle in gelatin mixture.

3. Thoroughly wash the beaters. Run under cold water to chill; dry beaters. In a chilled medium mixing bowl, beat the 1 cup whipping cream with electric mixer on medium speed until soft peaks form (tips curl); fold into pumpkin mixture.

4. Arrange *one-third* of the ladyfinger halves in the bottom of a 2-quart square dish. Drizzle with *one-third* of the brown sugar mixture. Spoon *one-third* of the pumpkin mixture over ladyfingers. Repeat layers twice. Cover and chill for at least 6 hours or up to 24 hours.

5. To serve, in a chilled small mixing bowl, beat the ½ cup whipping cream with the chilled beaters of an electric mixer on medium speed until soft peaks form (tips curl). Spread over pumpkin layer. Sprinkle with additional ground cinnamon. Makes 9 servings.

Nutrition facts per serving: 391 cal., 28 g total fat (17 g sat. fat), 56 mg chol., 63 mg sodium, 32 g carbo., 2 g fiber, 9 g pro.

Festive Cranberry-Apricot Pie

Festive Cranberry-Apricot Pie

Prep: 30 min. Bake: 35 + 15 min.

Dried cranberries and canned apricots costar in this dazzling holiday pie. The sweet-tart treat received the best-loved designation in the 2002 edition of our *New Cook Book*.

- 1 recipe Pastry for a Double-Crust Pie (below)
- ½ cup sugar
- 3 Tbsp. cornstarch
- 1½ tsp. pumpkin pie spice
- ¼ tsp. salt
- 3 15¼-oz. cans apricot halves, drained and cut into quarters
- ½ cup dried cranberries, snipped
- 1 egg white
- 1 Tbsp. milk
- 1 Tbsp. sugar
- ¼ tsp. pumpkin pie spice

1. Preheat oven to 375°F. Prepare Pastry for a Double-Crust Pie. Line a 9-inch pie plate with *half* of the pastry; trim pastry to ½ inch beyond edge of pie plate. Fold under extra pastry edge. Crimp edge.

2. For fruit filling, in a large bowl, combine the ½ cup sugar, the cornstarch, the 1½ teaspoons pumpkin pie spice, and the salt. Stir in apricots and cranberries. Spoon fruit filling into pastry-lined pie plate.

3. Roll remaining dough into a circle about 12 inches in diameter. Using a 1- to 1½-inch leaf-shape cutter or other cutter, cut 36 to 40 shapes from the dough.

4. In a small bowl, stir together egg white and milk; brush onto pastry shapes. Reserve remaining egg white mixture. In a small bowl, stir together the 1 tablespoon sugar and the ¼ teaspoon pumpkin pie spice; sprinkle onto *half* of the pastry shapes. Arrange 10 to 12 of the shapes, alternating brushed and sprinkled shapes, in a circle in center of the fruit-filled pie. Brush edge of crust with remaining egg white mixture. Evenly distribute the remaining pastry shapes around edge of fruit-filled pie. To prevent overbrowning, cover edge of pie lightly with foil.

5. Bake for 35 minutes. Remove foil. Bake for 15 minutes more. Cool on a wire rack. Serves 8.

Pastry for a Double-Crust Pie: In a medium bowl, stir together 2¼ cups all-purpose flour and ¾ teaspoon salt. Using a pastry blender, cut in ⅔ cup shortening until pieces are pea-size. Sprinkle 1 tablespoon cold water over part of the flour mixture; gently toss with a fork. Push moistened dough to the side of the bowl. Add additional cold water, 1 tablespoon at a time, until all is moistened (use 8 or 10 tablespoons cold water total). Divide dough in half; form each half into a ball. On a lightly floured surface, use your hands to slightly flatten *one* of the dough balls. Roll dough from center to edge into a circle about 12 inches in diameter. To transfer pastry, wrap it around the rolling pin. Unroll pastry into a 9-inch pie plate. Ease pastry into pie plate, being careful not to stretch pastry. Trim pastry as directed. Add filling and roll out remaining dough as directed.

Nutrition facts per serving: 437 cal., 18 g total fat (4 g sat. fat), 0 mg chol., 308 mg sodium, 67 g carbo., 4 g fiber, 5 g pro.

Toasted Pecan Pie

Prep: 30 min. Bake: 25 + 20 min.

For many of our readers, a slice of pecan pie is the ultimate holiday indulgence.

- 1½ cups pecan halves, toasted (tip, page 102)
- 1 recipe Pastry for a Single-Crust Pie (page 54)
- 4 eggs
- 1 cup sugar
- ⅔ cup light-colored corn syrup
- ⅓ cup maple-flavored syrup
- ¼ cup butter, melted
- 1 tsp. vanilla
- ⅛ tsp. salt
- 3 Tbsp. sugar
- 3 Tbsp. maple-flavored syrup
- 1 Tbsp. butter

1. Preheat oven to 350°F. Chop *half* of the pecans. Set aside. Prepare Pastry for a Single-Crust Pie.

2. For filling, in a medium bowl, beat eggs with a fork; stir in the 1 cup sugar, the corn syrup, the ⅓ cup maple-flavored syrup, the ¼ cup melted butter, the vanilla, and salt. Mix well. Stir in chopped pecans. Pour the filling into pastry shell.

3. Cover edge of pie with foil. Bake for 25 minutes. Remove foil; bake for 20 to 30 minutes more or until a knife inserted off-center comes out clean.

4. For topping, in a small saucepan, combine the pecan halves, the 3 tablespoons sugar, the 3 tablespoons maple-flavored syrup, and the 1 tablespoon butter. Cook and stir over low heat until sugar and butter are melted. [Or combine mixture in a microwave-safe bowl. Microwave on 100% power (high) for 1½ minutes; stir.] Spoon topping over the warm baked pie. Cool on a wire rack. Makes 12 servings.

Nutrition facts per serving: 453 cal., 25 g total fat (7 g sat. fat), 85 mg chol., 214 mg sodium, 56 g carbo., 2 g fiber, 5 g pro.

Yesterday

When this dessert appeared in our April 1961 issue, it drew high praise from Myrna Johnston, then food editor of the magazine. She declared the creamy concoction, "Rich, luscious, magnificent!" More than 40 years later, it's every bit as tantalizing.

Best-Ever Cheesecake

Prep: 30 min. Bake: 40 min. Cool: 2 hr. Chill: 4 to 24 hr.

1¾	cups finely crushed gingersnaps or graham crackers
¼	cup finely chopped walnuts
½	tsp. ground cinnamon
½	cup butter, melted
3	8-oz. pkg. cream cheese, softened
1	cup sugar
2	Tbsp. all-purpose flour
1	tsp. vanilla
2	eggs
1	egg yolk
¼	cup milk
	Fresh strawberries, quartered (optional)

1. Preheat oven to 375°F. For the crust, in a medium bowl, combine crushed gingersnaps or graham crackers, walnuts, and cinnamon. Stir in melted butter. If desired, set aside ¼ *cup* of the crumb mixture for topping. Press the remaining crumb mixture onto bottom and 2 inches up side of an 8- or 9-inch springform pan. Set aside.

2. For filling, in a large bowl, combine cream cheese, sugar, flour, and vanilla; beat with an electric mixer on medium speed until combined. Add eggs and egg yolk, beating on low speed just until combined. Stir in milk.

3. Pour filling into crust-lined pan. If desired, sprinkle with reserved crumbs. Place on a shallow baking pan in oven. Bake for 40 to 45 minutes for the 8-inch pan, about 35 minutes for the 9-inch pan, or until a 2½-inch area around the outside edge appears set when gently shaken.

4. Cool in pan on a wire rack for 15 minutes. Loosen the crust from side of pan; cool 30 minutes more. Remove side of the pan. Cool completely on wire rack. Cover; chill for at least 4 hours or up to 24 hours. If desired, top with strawberries. Makes 12 to 16 servings.

Nutrition facts per serving: 463 cal., 33 g total fat (19 g sat. fat), 138 mg chol., 406 mg sodium, 36 g carbo., 1 g fiber, 8 g pro.

Lower-Fat Best-Ever Cheesecake: Prepare as directed through step 3, except reduce gingersnaps or graham crackers to ⅓ cup and omit walnuts, cinnamon, and butter. Sprinkle gingersnaps onto bottom and side of a well-buttered 8- or 9-inch springform pan. Substitute three 8-ounce packages fat-free cream cheese for regular cream cheese and ½ cup refrigerated or frozen egg product (thawed) for eggs and egg yolk. Bake for 40 to 45 minutes for the 8-inch pan, 30 to 35 minutes for the 9-inch pan, or until a 2½-inch area around the outside edge appears set when gently shaken. Continue as directed in step 4.

Nutrition facts per serving: 142 cal., 1 g total fat (0 g sat. fat), 9 mg chol., 49 mg sodium, 24 g carbo., 0 g fiber, 10 g pro.

White-Chocolate Cheesecake With Triple-Raspberry Sauce

Prep: 30 min. Bake: 45 min. Cool: 2 hr. Chill: 4 to 24 hr.

Remember the Triple-Raspberry Sauce when you're looking for a fabulous way to top off angel food cake or ice cream.

- 1 cup crushed shortbread cookies (about 3 oz.)
- 3 Tbsp. finely chopped slivered almonds, toasted (tip, page 102)
- ¼ cup butter, melted
- 2 8-oz. pkg. cream cheese, softened
- 1 6-oz. pkg. white chocolate baking squares (with cocoa butter), melted and cooled
- ⅔ cup sugar
- ⅔ cup dairy sour cream
- 1 tsp. vanilla
- 3 eggs
- 1 recipe Triple-Raspberry Sauce (below)

1. Preheat oven to 350°F. For crust, in a small bowl, combine crushed cookies and the almonds. Stir in melted butter. Press crushed cookie mixture onto the bottom of an 8-inch springform pan. Set aside.

2. For filling, in a large bowl, combine cream cheese and cooled white chocolate; beat with an electric mixer on medium-high speed until combined. Beat in sugar, sour cream, and vanilla until mixture is fluffy.

3. Add the eggs; beat on low speed just until combined. Pour into the crust. Place on a shallow baking pan.

4. Bake about 45 minutes or until center is nearly set when you shake the cheesecake gently. Cool on a wire rack for 15 minutes. Loosen from side of pan. Cool for 30 minutes more; remove side of pan. Cool completely.* Cover and chill for at least 4 hours or up to 24 hours.

5. To serve, cut into wedges and drizzle some of the Triple-Raspberry Sauce over each serving. Serves 12.

Triple-Raspberry Sauce: In a small saucepan, melt one 10-ounce jar seedless raspberry preserves over low heat. Add 1 cup fresh red raspberries or loose-pack frozen lightly sweetened red raspberries. Heat gently just until sauce simmers. Cool. If desired, stir in 1 to 2 tablespoons raspberry liqueur. Cover and chill until serving time. Makes 1⅔ cups.

*Test Kitchen Tip: This cheesecake puffs during baking, then settles as it cools.

Nutrition facts per serving: 451 cal., 28 g total fat (16 g sat. fat), 115 mg chol., 230 mg sodium, 43 g carbo., 1 g fiber, 7 g pro.

Today

Every so often, our editors have the delightful task of coming up with a new and different cheesecake. This ultra-rich version with a shortbread crust, white chocolate filling, and raspberry sauce is one of our finest efforts. It wins accolades from editors and readers alike.

Peppermint Candy Cane Cookies

Peppermint Candy Cane Cookies

Prep: 25 min. Bake: 7 min. per batch

Here's the ultimate approval rating: These cookie canes are good enough to stuff into Christmas stockings. Just tuck them into small resealable plastic bags before adding them to the other treats.

- ⅓ cup butter, softened
- ⅓ cup shortening
- ¾ cup sugar
- 1 tsp. baking powder
  Dash salt
- 1 egg
- 1 Tbsp. milk
- ½ tsp. vanilla
- ½ tsp. peppermint extract
- 2 cups all-purpose flour
  Red or green paste food coloring
  Sugar (optional)

1. In a medium mixing bowl, beat butter and shortening with an electric mixer on medium to high speed for 30 seconds. Add the ¾ cup sugar, the baking powder, and salt. Beat until combined, scraping side of bowl. Beat in egg, milk, vanilla, and peppermint extract. Beat in as much of the flour as you can with the mixer. Using a wooden spoon, stir in any remaining flour.

2. Divide dough in half. Stir red or green paste food coloring into *half* of the dough. If necessary, cover and chill dough for 30 minutes to 1 hour or until dough is easy to handle.

3. Preheat oven to 375°F. Divide *each half* of the dough into six pieces. Roll *each piece* into a 12-inch-long rope. Lay ropes side by side on a lightly floured surface, alternating plain and colored dough. With a rolling pin, roll assembled ropes into a 14×9-inch rectangle. Using a pastry cutter, pizza wheel, or long sharp knife, cut the rectangle diagonally into ½-inch-wide strips. Cut strips into pieces 5 to 7 inches long. (Press shorter strips together end to end to reach desired length.) Place on an ungreased cookie sheet. Curve *one end* of *each* piece to form a candy cane shape. If desired, sprinkle lightly with additional sugar.

4. Bake for 7 to 8 minutes or until edges are firm and bottoms are very lightly browned. Transfer cookies to wire racks and let cool. Makes 36 cookies.

Nutrition facts per cookie: 74 cal., 4 g total fat (2 g sat. fat), 10 mg chol., 33 mg sodium, 9 g carbo., 0 g fiber, 1 g pro.

Kris Kringles

Prep: 25 min. Chill: 1 hr. Bake: 20 min. per batch

Named after Santa himself, these buttery rich morsels flecked with citrus peel and coated with walnuts date back to our 1953 holiday issue.

- ½ cup butter
- ¼ cup sugar
- 1 egg yolk
- 1 tsp. finely shredded lemon peel (set aside)
- 1 tsp. lemon juice
- 1 cup all-purpose flour
- 1 Tbsp. finely shredded orange peel
  Dash salt
- 1 egg white, slightly beaten
- ⅔ cup finely chopped walnuts
- 13 whole candied red or green cherries, halved

1. In a medium mixing bowl, beat butter with an electric mixer on medium to high speed for 30 seconds. Add sugar and beat until combined. Beat in egg yolk and lemon juice until combined. Stir in flour, orange peel, salt, and lemon peel. Cover and chill about 1 hour or until easy to handle.

2. Preheat oven to 325°F. Grease cookie sheets; set aside. Shape dough into 1-inch balls. Dip balls into egg white; roll in walnuts. Place balls about 2 inches apart on prepared cookie sheets. Press a cherry half into each ball. Bake about 20 minutes or until lightly browned. Transfer to wire racks and let cool. Makes about 26 cookies.

Nutrition facts per cookie: 85 cal., 6 g total fat (2 g sat. fat), 18 mg chol., 46 mg sodium, 8 g carbo., 0 g fiber, 1 g pro.

At *Better Homes and Gardens*® we love to bring young cooks into the kitchen, and we know publishing kid-friendly cookies at holiday time is a surefire way to do it.

Chocolate-Mint Creams

Prep: 25 min. Chill: 1 to 2 hr. Bake: 10 min. per batch

Bite into one of these crackly delights and you'll discover fudgy chocolate flavor under the dab of mint "frosting."

1¼ **cups all-purpose flour**
½ **tsp. baking soda**
⅔ **cup packed brown sugar**
6 **Tbsp. butter**
1 **Tbsp. water**
1 **cup semisweet chocolate pieces (6 oz.)**
1 **egg**
8 **to 12 oz. pastel cream mints**

1. In a small bowl, stir together flour and baking soda; set aside. In a medium saucepan, cook and stir brown sugar, butter, and the water over low heat until butter is melted. Add chocolate pieces. Cook and stir until chocolate is melted. Pour into a large bowl; let stand for 10 to 15 minutes or until cool.

2. Using a wooden spoon, beat egg into chocolate mixture. Stir in the flour mixture until well mixed. (Dough will be soft.) Cover and chill for 1 hour to 2 hours or until dough is easy to handle.

3. Preheat oven to 350°F. Shape dough into 1-inch balls. Place balls 2 inches apart on ungreased cookie sheets. Bake for 8 minutes. Remove from oven and immediately top each cookie with a cream mint. Bake about 2 minutes more or until edges are set.

Chocolate-Mint Creams

4. Swirl the melted mints with a knife to "frost" cookies. Transfer to wire racks; cool. Makes about 48.

Nutrition facts per cookie: 76 cal., 4 g total fat (2 g sat. fat), 8 mg chol., 34 mg sodium, 10 g carbo., 0 g fiber, 1 g pro.

Swirled Mint Cookies

Prep: 25 min. Chill: 1 hr. + 30 min.
Bake: 8 min. per batch

If you bake cookies to give away at holiday time, be sure to include these dainty peppermint thins as part of the assortment. We first featured them in 1985.

2 **cups all-purpose flour**
½ **tsp. baking powder**
1 **cup butter**
1 **cup sugar**
1 **egg**
1 **tsp. vanilla**
½ **tsp. peppermint extract**
10 **drops red food coloring**
10 **drops green food coloring**
 Sugar

1. In a small bowl, stir together flour and baking powder; set aside. In a large mixing bowl, beat butter with an electric mixer on medium to high speed for 30 seconds. Add the 1 cup sugar; beat until fluffy. Add egg, vanilla, and peppermint extract; beat well. Add flour mixture; beat until well mixed. Divide into three equal portions. Stir red food coloring into one portion, stir green food coloring into another portion, and leave remaining portion plain. Cover; chill about 1 hour or until easy to handle.

2. Divide each color of dough into four equal portions. On a lightly floured surface, roll each portion into a ½-inch-diameter rope. Place one red, one green, and one plain rope side by side. Twist together. Repeat with remaining ropes. Chill for 30 minutes.

3. Preheat oven to 375°F. Cut ropes into ½-inch-thick slices for large cookies. (Or cut into ¼-inch-thick slices for small cookies.) Carefully roll into balls, blending colors as little as possible. Place balls about 2 inches apart on ungreased cookie sheets. Flatten to ¼-inch thickness with the bottom of a glass dipped in sugar.

4. Bake until edges are set. Allow 8 to 10 minutes for large cookies or 6 to 8 minutes for small ones. Transfer to wire racks and let cool. Makes about 72 (2½-inch) or 144 (1¼-inch) cookies.

Nutrition facts per large cookie: 46 cal., 3 g total fat (2 g sat. fat), 10 mg chol., 29 mg sodium, 5 g carbo., 0 g fiber, 0 g pro.

Cranberry-Orange
Pinwheels

Cranberry-Orange Pinwheels

Prep: 25 min. Chill: 1 hr. + 4 to 24 hr.
Bake: 8 min. per batch

When everyone comes in from caroling or sledding,
celebrate with hot cocoa and these soft, chewy slices.

- 1   cup fresh cranberries
- 1   cup pecans
- ¼   cup packed brown sugar
- 1   cup butter, softened
- 1½ cups granulated sugar
- ½   tsp. baking powder
- ½   tsp. salt
- 2   eggs
- 2   tsp. finely shredded orange peel
- 3   cups all-purpose flour

1. For filling, in a blender or food processor, combine
cranberries, pecans, and brown sugar. Cover and blend
or process until cranberries and nuts are finely chopped.

2. In a large mixing bowl, beat butter with an electric
mixer on medium to high speed for 30 seconds. Add
granulated sugar, baking powder, and salt. Beat until
combined, scraping side of bowl occasionally. Beat in
eggs and orange peel until combined. Beat in as much
of the flour as you can with the mixer. Stir in any
remaining flour. Divide dough in half. Cover and chill
about 1 hour or until easy to handle.

3. Place *half* of the dough between pieces of waxed
paper; roll into a 10-inch square. Spread *half* of the
filling over dough square to within ½ inch of the edges;
roll up dough. Moisten edges; pinch to seal. Wrap in
plastic wrap. Repeat with remaining dough and filling.
Chill for at least 4 hours or up to 24 hours.

4. Preheat oven to 375°F. Cut rolls into ¼-inch-thick
slices. Place slices 2 inches apart on ungreased cookie
sheets. Bake for 8 to 10 minutes or until edges are firm
and bottoms are lightly browned. Cool on cookie sheets
for 1 minute. Transfer to wire racks; cool. Makes about 60.

Nutrition facts per cookie: 89 cal., 5 g total fat (2 g sat. fat), 16 mg chol.,
58 mg sodium, 11 g carbo., 0 g fiber, 1 g pro.

Chocolate-Caramel Bars

Prep: 30 min. Bake: 15 + 25 min. Stand: 10 min.

Layers of pecans, coconut, caramels, and milk
chocolate on a rich crust add up to an irresistible bar
that will satisfy just about any Yuletide sweet tooth.

- 1   cup all-purpose flour
- ½   cup packed brown sugar
- ½   cup butter
- 1   14-oz. can (1¼ cups) sweetened
      condensed milk
- 2   tsp. vanilla
- 2   cups coarsely chopped pecans
- 1   cup flaked coconut
- 20 vanilla caramels
- 2   Tbsp. milk
- 6   oz. semisweet chocolate, coarsely
      chopped

1. Preheat oven to 350°F. For crust, in a medium bowl,
stir together flour and brown sugar. Using a pastry blender,
cut in butter until mixture resembles coarse crumbs.

2. Press crumb mixture onto the bottom of an
ungreased 13×9×2-inch baking pan. Bake for 15 minutes.

3. Meanwhile, for filling, combine sweetened
condensed milk and the vanilla. Sprinkle pecans and
coconut over partially baked crust. Pour filling over
pecans and coconut.

4. Bake for 25 to 30 minutes more or until filling is
set. Place pan on a wire rack; let stand for 10 minutes.

5. Meanwhile, in a small saucepan, combine
unwrapped caramels and milk. Cook and stir over
medium-low heat just until caramels are melted. Drizzle
caramel mixture over baked filling. Sprinkle top with
chopped chocolate. Cool completely. Makes 48 bars.

Nutrition facts per bar: 142 cal., 8 g total fat (3 g sat. fat), 10 mg chol.,
46 mg sodium, 16 g carbo., 1 g fiber, 2 g pro.

Santa's Cookie Jar Baking
cookies is a treasured way to celebrate
the holidays. Keep a supply on hand to
serve when guests drop by or to swap at
a neighborhood cookie exchange. To ease
the holiday time crunch, make several
batches ahead and store them in the
freezer. For storing information, refer
to the tip on page 237.

Pecan Balls

*Test Kitchen Tip: To make colored fine granulated sugar, place ⅔ cup fine granulated sugar in a small bowl. Fill a ¼-teaspoon measuring spoon with water. Add 1 or 2 drops liquid food coloring to the water. Sprinkle colored water over sugar in bowl. Stir until combined and color is evenly distributed. Do not overmoisten or the sugar will begin to dissolve.

Nutrition facts per cookie: 52 cal., 4 g total fat (2 g sat. fat), 7 mg chol., 33 mg sodium, 5 g carbo., 0 g fiber, 0 g pro.

White Chocolate Fudge

Prep: 15 min. Cook: 15 min.

In 1972, we published this prizewinning recipe for white fudge. It wasn't until the late 1970s and early 1980s, however, that white chocolate reached celebrity status with the introduction of a trendy dessert—white chocolate mousse.

2   cups sugar
1   cup evaporated milk
½   cup butter
8   oz. white chocolate baking squares (with cocoa butter) or white chocolate, cut up
1   cup tiny marshmallows
1   tsp. vanilla
½   cup flaked coconut
½   cup chopped unblanched almonds, toasted (tip, page 102)
    Unblanched almonds, toasted and chopped (optional) (tip, page 102)

1. Line an 8×8×2-inch baking pan with foil, extending foil over edges of pan. Butter the foil; set pan aside.

2. Butter side of a heavy, 3-quart saucepan. In the saucepan, combine sugar, evaporated milk, and the ½ cup butter. Cook and stir over medium heat until mixture boils. Clip a candy thermometer to side of pan. Cook until thermometer registers 234°F, soft-ball stage (about 15 minutes), stirring frequently. Remove from heat. Add white chocolate, marshmallows, and vanilla; stir vigorously with a wooden spoon until mixture is melted. Quickly stir in coconut and the ½ cup chopped almonds. Pour into prepared pan. If desired, sprinkle with additional chopped almonds. Score into squares while warm.

3. When fudge is firm, use foil to lift it out of pan. Cut into squares. Store, tightly covered, for up to 1 week. Makes 2 pounds (36 squares).

Nutrition facts per square: 132 cal., 7 g total fat (4 g sat. fat), 10 mg chol., 43 mg sodium, 17 g carbo., 0 g fiber, 1 g pro.

Pecan Balls

Prep: 35 min. Bake: 12 min. per batch

Favorites from the 1930s and 1940s, these melt-in-your-mouth butter cookies, also called sandies or Mexican wedding cakes, disappear like magic from holiday tables.

1   cup butter, softened
½   cup granulated sugar
¼   tsp. salt
2   tsp. vanilla
2   cups all-purpose flour
1   cup finely chopped pecans
    Fine granulated sugar, colored fine granulated sugar,* and/or powdered sugar

1. Preheat oven to 350°F. In a large mixing bowl, beat butter with an electric mixer on medium to high speed for 30 seconds. Add granulated sugar and salt; beat until combined. Beat in vanilla. Beat in as much of the flour as you can with the mixer. Stir in any remaining flour. Stir in pecans.

2. Shape slightly rounded teaspoons of dough into balls the size of large grapes. Place balls 1 inch apart on ungreased cookie sheets. Bake about 12 minutes or until bottoms just begin to brown.

3. While cookies are still warm, roll them in fine granulated sugar, colored fine granulated sugar, and/or powdered sugar. Transfer to wire racks and let cool. Makes about 72 cookies.

Mocha and Pecan Divinity

Prep: 30 min. Cook: 5 + 15 min.

Long before flavored coffees became hip, this prizewinning recipe from 1985 used coffee powder to give divinity a delightful flavor.

    2   egg whites
 2½   cups sugar
   ½   cup light-colored corn syrup
   ½   cup water
   ¼   cup instant Swiss-style coffee powder
    1   cup chopped pecans

1. Allow egg whites to stand at room temperature. In a heavy, 2-quart saucepan, combine sugar, corn syrup, the water, and coffee powder. Cook and stir over medium-high until mixture boils (5 to 7 minutes). Clip a candy thermometer to the side of pan. Reduce heat to medium; continue cooking, without stirring, until the thermometer registers 260°F, hard-ball stage (about 15 minutes). (Adjust heat to maintain a steady boil.)

2. Remove saucepan from heat; remove thermometer. In a large mixing bowl, immediately beat egg whites with a freestanding electric mixer on medium speed until stiff peaks form (tips stand straight). Gradually pour hot mixture in a thin stream into egg whites, beating on high speed and scraping the side of the bowl occasionally (this will take about 3 minutes). Continue beating on high speed just until candy mixture starts to lose its gloss (5 to 6 minutes). When beaters are lifted, the candy mixture should fall in a ribbon that mounds on itself.

Mocha and Pecan Divinity

3. Drop a spoonful of candy mixture onto waxed paper. If it stays mounded, the mixture has been beaten sufficiently. If mixture flattens, beat for 30 seconds to 1 minute more; check again. If mixture is too stiff to spoon, beat in a few drops hot water until mixture is a softer consistency.

4. Immediately fold in nuts. Quickly drop candy mixture onto waxed paper. Store, tightly covered, for up to 1 week. Makes about 36 pieces.

Nutrition facts per piece: 90 cal., 2 g total fat (0 g sat. fat), 0 mg chol., 12 mg sodium, 18 g carbo., 0 g fiber, 0 g pro.

Buttery Cashew Brittle

Prep: 10 min. Cook: 35 + 10 min.

This recipe was part of our "Favorites Forever" series that ran in 1997 to celebrate the 75th anniversary of *Better Homes and Gardens*® magazine. Originally published in 1974, this modern take on brittle substitutes cashews for the usual peanuts.

    2   cups sugar
    1   cup light-colored corn syrup
   ½   cup water
    1   cup butter
    3   cups raw cashews (about 12 oz.)
    1   tsp. baking soda, sifted

1. Butter 2 large baking sheets or two 15×10×1-inch pans. Set aside. Butter the side of a heavy, 3-quart saucepan. In saucepan, combine sugar, corn syrup, and the water. Cook and stir until sugar is dissolved. Bring mixture to boiling; add the 1 cup butter and stir until butter is melted. Clip a candy thermometer to side of pan. Reduce heat to medium-low; continue boiling at a moderate, steady rate, stirring occasionally, until thermometer registers 280°F, soft-crack stage (about 35 minutes).

2. Stir in cashews; continue cooking over medium-low heat, stirring frequently, until thermometer registers 300°F, hard-crack stage (10 to 15 minutes more).

3. Remove saucepan from heat; remove thermometer. Quickly sprinkle baking soda over mixture, stirring constantly. Pour mixture onto prepared baking sheets or pans.

4. Use 2 forks to lift and pull candy as it cools. Loosen from pans as soon as possible; pick up sections and break them into bite-size pieces. Store, tightly covered, for up to 1 week. Makes about 2½ pounds (72 servings).

Nutrition facts per serving: 90 cal., 5 g total fat (2 g sat. fat), 7 mg chol., 47 mg sodium, 11 g carbo., 0 g fiber, 1 g pro.

From the cocktail parties of the fifties to today's impromptu

grazing get-togethers, our ideas about party appetizers have

changed significantly during the span of *Better Homes and*

Gardens® magazine. Yet one thing has

remained constant: Decade to decade,

Party Bites

our editors have created great can't-eat-just-one delicacies,

giving readers bite-size morsels that are the talk of the party.

This chapter highlights our hors d'oeuvre and snack favorites.

155

165

167

158

161

156

Shrimp Rounds

2. For each serving, place a round on an ungreased baking sheet; brush with milk. Using a round hors d'oeuvre cutter, cut a 1-inch circle out of the center of 2 more dough rounds. Place on top of first round, making 3 layers in all and brushing with milk between layers. Repeat with remaining dough, rerolling and cutting dough scraps to make a total of 32 layered rounds.

3. Bake layered rounds for 22 to 25 minutes or until golden. Transfer to wire racks; let cool.

4. Meanwhile, for the filling, set aside 32 shrimp for garnish. Chop remaining shrimp. In a medium bowl, combine cream cheese, lemon juice, Worcestershire sauce, dill weed, and garlic powder; beat with an electric mixer on medium speed until smooth. Gradually beat in the ¼ cup milk. Stir in the chopped shrimp.

5. Spoon filling into pastry rounds. Top with reserved shrimp. If desired, garnish with fresh herb sprigs. Makes 32 appetizers.

Cheddar Cheese Pastry: Using a pastry blender, in a large bowl, cut 1 cup butter into 1½ cups all-purpose flour until mixture resembles coarse crumbs. Stir in ½ cup dairy sour cream and ½ cup shredded sharp cheddar cheese (2 ounces). Divide mixture in half; wrap and chill about 1 hour or until dough is firm.

Make-ahead directions: Prepare as directed. Cover filled rounds and chill for up to 2 hours. Remove from refrigerator 10 minutes before serving and let stand at room temperature. (Or prepare and bake rounds as directed; place in a single layer in a freezer container. Cover and freeze for up to 1 week. Thaw overnight in refrigerator before using.) The filling may be made up to 24 hours ahead; cover and chill filling and shrimp for garnish separately.

Nutrition facts per appetizer: 124 cal., 10 g total fat (6 g sat. fat), 48 mg chol., 123 mg sodium, 5 g carbo., 0 g fiber, 4 g pro.

Shrimp Rounds
Prep: 50 min. Chill: 1 hr. Bake: 22 min.

With their Cheddar Cheese Pastry, these captivating rounds from our December 1976 issue suit any type of party, from an informal after-work gathering to an elegant holiday open house.

     1   recipe Cheddar Cheese Pastry (right)
         Milk
    48   peeled, deveined, and cooked small
         shrimp (about 12 oz.)
     1   8-oz. pkg. cream cheese, softened
     1   tsp. lemon juice
     1   tsp. Worcestershire sauce
    ¼   tsp. dried dill weed
         Dash garlic powder
    ¼   cup milk
         Fresh herb sprigs (optional)

1. Prepare Cheddar Pastry. Preheat oven to 350°F. On a floured surface, roll out *half* of the pastry to ¹⁄₁₆-inch thickness. Using a floured 2-inch biscuit cutter, cut pastry into rounds.

Sizing Up Shrimp

You can buy shrimp in the shell fresh or frozen in a variety of sizes. Here are some of the most common: colossal (fewer than 15 per pound), jumbo (20 or 21 per pound), extra-large (26 to 30 per pound), large (31 to 40 per pound), medium (41 to 50 per pound), and small (51 to 60 per pound).

Chicken-Spinach Phyllo Rolls

Prep: 25 min. Bake: 15 min. Stand: 5 min.

A winner in the Festive Finger Foods category of our Prize Tested Recipes® contest in 1995, these flaky phyllo rolls won a thumbs-up from our staff because they're luscious and easy to make.

- 1 10-oz. pkg. frozen chopped spinach, thawed
- 1 5-oz. can chunk-style chicken, drained and flaked
- 1 cup shredded cheddar or provolone cheese (4 oz.)
- ½ of an 8-oz. tub cream cheese with chive and onion
- ½ cup chopped walnuts, toasted (tip, page 102)
- 1 Tbsp. dry sherry
- ½ tsp. Worcestershire sauce
- ¼ tsp. ground nutmeg
- 15 sheets frozen phyllo dough (14×9-inch rectangles), thawed
- ⅓ cup butter or margarine, melted

1. Drain spinach well, pressing out excess liquid. For filling, in a medium bowl, combine spinach, chicken, cheddar or provolone cheese, cream cheese, walnuts, sherry, Worcestershire sauce, and nutmeg; set aside.

2. Preheat oven to 400°F. Unfold phyllo dough; remove *1 sheet* of the phyllo dough. (As you work, cover the remaining phyllo dough with plastic wrap to prevent it from drying out.) Brush with *some* of the melted butter. Place another phyllo sheet on top; brush with butter. Repeat once more.

3. Spoon *½ cup* of the filling evenly lengthwise down the buttered phyllo dough, about 2 inches from one long side and 1 inch from the short sides. Fold 2 inches of the long side over filling; fold in the short sides. Starting from the side with the filling, loosely roll up into a spiral. Place roll, seam side down, on an ungreased baking sheet. Repeat with remaining phyllo, butter, and filling to make 5 rolls.

4. Brush tops of rolls with any remaining butter. Using a sharp knife, score rolls at 1½-inch intervals. Bake about 15 minutes or until golden. Let stand for 5 minutes before slicing rolls where scored. Serve warm. Makes 40 appetizers.

Make-ahead directions: Prepare as directed through step 3. Cover and chill up to 6 hours. Continue as directed in step 4.

Nutrition facts per appetizer: 66 cal., 5 g total fat (2 g sat. fat), 12 mg chol., 95 mg sodium, 3 g carbo., 0 g fiber, 2 g pro.

Sweet, Hot, and Sour Meatballs

Prep: 20 min. Bake: 30 min.

These sassy sausage-and-beef morsels simmered in an apple jelly, brown mustard, and whiskey sauce will keep your guests coming back for more.

- 2 eggs
- ½ cup fine dry bread crumbs
- ½ cup finely chopped onion
- ¼ cup milk
- ½ tsp. salt
- ½ tsp. pepper
- 1 lb. bulk pork sausage
- 1 lb. ground beef
- ¾ cup apple jelly
- ⅓ cup spicy brown mustard
- ⅓ cup whiskey or apple juice
- 1½ tsp. Worcestershire sauce
    Few dashes bottled hot pepper sauce

1. Preheat oven to 375°F. In a large bowl, beat eggs with a fork. Add bread crumbs, onion, milk, salt, and pepper. Add sausage and beef; mix well. Shape into about forty-eight 1¼- to 1½-inch meatballs. Place in a shallow baking pan. Bake, uncovered, about 30 minutes or until cooked through (160°F). Drain.

2. Meanwhile, in a large saucepan, stir together jelly, mustard, whiskey or apple juice, Worcestershire sauce, and bottled hot pepper sauce; heat and stir until jelly melts and mixture bubbles. Add meatballs. Cook, stirring gently, for 3 to 5 minutes or until sauce thickens slightly and meatballs are coated. Makes about 48 meatballs.

Make-ahead directions: Prepare as directed in step 1. Place in an airtight container; cover. Chill for up to 24 hours. To serve, continue as directed in step 2.

Nutrition facts per meatball: 78 cal., 4 g total fat (2 g sat. fat), 20 mg chol., 115 mg sodium, 5 g carbo., 0 g fiber, 3 g pro.

Sausage Bites

Start to finish: 30 min.

Just about everyone has a favorite recipe for little sausages in barbecue sauce. Here's the *Better Homes and Gardens*® version—it mixes a trio of sausages with a citrus-accented sauce.

1½	cups bottled barbecue sauce
⅔	cup orange marmalade
½	tsp. dry mustard
⅛	tsp. ground allspice
12	oz. cooked bratwurst, cut into ½-inch-thick slices
12	oz. cooked kielbasa, cut diagonally into ½-inch-thick slices
8	oz. small cooked smoked sausage links
1	8-oz. can pineapple chunks, drained

1. In a large saucepan, combine barbecue sauce, marmalade, dry mustard, and allspice. Cook and stir until bubbly. Stir in bratwurst, kielbasa, smoked sausage links, and pineapple. Cover and cook over medium-low heat about 20 minutes more or until heated through, stirring occasionally. Makes 20 servings.

Slow-cooker directions: In a 3½- or 4-quart slow cooker, combine barbecue sauce, orange marmalade, dry mustard, and allspice. Stir in bratwurst, kielbasa, and smoked sausage links. Cover and cook on high-heat setting for 2½ to 3 hours. Stir in pineapple chunks. Serve immediately or keep warm on the low-heat setting for up to 2 hours.

Nutrition facts per appetizer serving: 194 cal., 13 g total fat (5 g sat. fat), 25 mg chol., 511 mg sodium, 13 g carbo., 1 g fiber, 6 g pro.

> You may think the move toward no-hassle entertaining is new, but *Better Homes and Gardens*® has been preaching "keep it simple" for more than 50 years. In a 1947 article, we pointed out, "Notice how folks relax, have more fun at your house, when you entertain casually without a lot of fuss?"

Salmon Mousse

Prep: 25 min. Chill: 5 hr.

Salmon and tuna team up for this spunky spread that's been popular with readers for decades. If you like, serve it on melba rounds, party rye bread, or toasted bagel chips.

1	14¾-oz. can red salmon
2	envelopes unflavored gelatin
2	cups mayonnaise or salad dressing
½	cup bottled chili sauce
2	Tbsp. lemon juice
1	Tbsp. Worcestershire sauce
½	tsp. dried dill weed
¼	tsp. pepper
1	6½-oz. can tuna, drained and finely flaked
4	hard-cooked eggs, chopped
½	cup pimiento-stuffed olives, finely chopped
¼	cup finely chopped onion

1. Lightly oil a 6-cup mold; set aside. Drain salmon, reserving liquid; add water, if needed, to equal ½ cup total liquid. Remove salmon skin and bones; discard. Finely flake salmon; set aside.

2. In a small saucepan, stir together reserved salmon liquid and the gelatin. Let stand for 5 minutes. Cook and stir over medium heat until gelatin is dissolved; transfer to a large bowl. Gradually stir in mayonnaise. Stir in the chili sauce, lemon juice, Worcestershire sauce, dill weed, and pepper. Fold in salmon, tuna, hard-cooked eggs, finely chopped olives, and onion.

3. Turn mousse mixture into prepared mold. Cover surface with plastic wrap. Chill about 5 hours or until firm. Unmold to serve. Makes 6 cups (96 servings).

Make-ahead directions: Prepare as directed. Cover and chill for up to 24 hours.

Nutrition facts per tablespoon spread: 48 cal., 4 g total fat (1 g sat. fat), 15 mg chol., 92 mg sodium, 1 g carbo., 0 g fiber, 2 g pro.

Greek Croustade

Prep: 30 min. Bake: 30 min. Stand: 15 min.

Readers first eyed this phyllo pastry when it appeared on our cover in March 1983. The flaky dough wraps around a puffed spinach and feta cheese filling.

- ¼ **cup chopped onion**
- 2 **Tbsp. butter**
- 2 **Tbsp. all-purpose flour**
- ½ **tsp. dried tarragon or fennel seeds, crushed**
- ¼ **tsp. pepper**
- ½ **cup milk**
- 1 **egg, slightly beaten**
- ½ **of a 10-oz. pkg. frozen chopped spinach, thawed and well drained**
- ⅔ **cup crumbled feta cheese**
- ⅓ **cup butter, melted**
- 10 **sheets frozen phyllo dough (14×9-inch rectangles), thawed**

1. For filling, in a small saucepan, cook onion in the 2 tablespoons butter until tender. Stir in flour, tarragon, and pepper. Add milk all at once. Cook and stir until mixture is thickened and bubbly. Stir *about half* of the hot mixture into egg; return all to saucepan. Cook and stir 1 minute more (do not boil). Remove from heat. Stir in spinach and feta cheese. Set aside.

2. Preheat oven to 375°F. Brush a 12-inch pizza pan with *some* of the ⅓ cup melted butter; set aside. Unroll the phyllo dough; remove *1 sheet* of the phyllo dough at a time. (As you work, cover the remaining phyllo dough with plastic wrap to prevent it from drying out.) Lightly brush the first sheet with *some* of the remainder of the ⅓ cup melted butter. Fold phyllo in thirds lengthwise to form a strip; brush the top with butter.

3. Place one end of the strip in the center of the prepared pan, extending it over the side of the pan. Repeat with the remaining phyllo dough and butter, arranging strips spoke-fashion evenly around pan. (The ends of the strips will overlap in the center and be about 3 inches apart at outer ends.)

4. Spread the spinach mixture in a 6-inch circle in the center of the pastry. Starting with the last phyllo strip placed in the pan, lift the end of the strip up and bring it in toward the center of filling. Holding end with both hands, twist end several times; coil and tuck end under to form a rosette. Lay rosette over filling, leaving a 2- to 3-inch circle in center (filling should be visible).

5. Repeat with the remaining phyllo strips in the reverse order in which they were placed in the pan. Drizzle any remaining butter over all. Bake for 30 to 35 minutes or until golden. Let stand 15 minutes before serving. To serve, cut into wedges. Makes 10 servings.

Nutrition facts per appetizer serving: 163 cal., 12 g total fat (7 g sat. fat), 55 mg chol., 288 mg sodium, 9 g carbo., 1 g fiber, 4 g pro.

Greek Croustade

Creamy Onion Dip

1. Arrange lettuce on a platter, leaving a 2-inch open rim at edge of platter. In a small bowl, stir together bean dip and picante sauce. Spread bean mixture onto lettuce, making a layer ¼ inch thick. Spread avocado dip over bean mixture; spread sour cream over avocado dip. Top with cheese, green onions, and olives. Cover and chill for at least 4 hours or up to 24 hours.

2. Before serving, sprinkle with chopped tomato. Makes 16 servings.

Nutrition facts per appetizer serving: 105 cal., 8 g total fat (3 g sat. fat), 14 mg chol., 195 mg sodium, 5 g carbo., 1 g fiber, 4 g pro.

Lower-Fat Mexican Eight-Layer Dip: Prepare as directed, except substitute light dairy sour cream and reduced-fat cheddar cheese for the regular dairy sour cream and cheddar cheese.

Nutrition facts per appetizer serving: 87 cal., 5 g total fat (1 g sat. fat), 10 mg chol., 218 mg sodium, 5 g carbo., 1 g fiber, 5 g pro.

White Bean Dip

Prep: 20 min. Chill: 4 to 24 hr.

White kidney beans and toasted almonds are party-perfect partners in this tangy whirl-together dip. If you like, serve it in a bowl lined with lettuce; arrange vegetable dippers alongside.

- ¼   cup soft bread crumbs
- 2   Tbsp. dry white wine or water
- 1   15- to 19-oz. can white kidney beans (cannellini beans) or Great Northern beans, rinsed and drained
- ¼   cup slivered almonds, toasted (tip, page 102)
- 2   Tbsp. lemon juice
- 2   Tbsp. olive oil
- 3   cloves garlic, minced
- ¼   tsp. salt
- ⅛   tsp. cayenne pepper
- 2   tsp. snipped fresh oregano or basil or ½ tsp. dried oregano or basil, crushed

1. In a small bowl, combine bread crumbs and wine or water; set aside to soak for 10 minutes.

2. In a food processor or blender, combine beans, almonds, lemon juice, olive oil, garlic, salt, and cayenne pepper. Cover and process or blend until almost smooth. Add bread crumb mixture; process or blend until smooth. Stir in the snipped or dried oregano or basil. Transfer to bowl. Cover and chill for at least 4 hours or up to 24 hours. Makes about 2 cups dip (32 servings).

Nutrition facts per tablespoon dip: 57 cal., 2 g total fat (0 g sat. fat), 0 mg chol., 86 mg sodium, 8 g carbo., 1 g fiber, 2 g pro.

Creamy Onion Dip

Prep: 10 min. Chill: 4 to 48 hr.

Now here's a blast from the past! When onion soup mix was new back in the 1950s, the dip recipe quickly became the rage at parties. It's still popular because it's so easy. Be sure to have plenty of vegetable dippers or potato chips on hand.

- 1½   cups dairy sour cream
- 2   Tbsp. dry onion soup mix
- ½   cup crumbled blue cheese (2 oz.)

1. In a medium bowl, stir together sour cream and dry onion soup mix. Stir in blue cheese. Cover and chill for at least 4 hours or up to 48 hours. Makes 1¾ cups dip (28 servings).

Nutrition facts per tablespoon dip: 34 cal., 3 g total fat (2 g sat. fat), 6 mg chol., 79 mg sodium, 2 g carbo., 0 g fiber, 1 g pro.

Mexican Eight-Layer Dip

Prep: 15 min. Chill: 4 to 24 hr.

From the base of shredded lettuce on up to the colorful tomato topper, these luscious layers will delight all the Mexican food lovers in your crowd. Serve the dip with tortilla chips or crackers.

- 2   to 3 cups shredded lettuce
- 1   9-oz. can bean dip
- ¼   cup bottled picante or taco sauce
- 1   6-oz. container frozen avocado dip, thawed
- 1   8-oz. carton dairy sour cream
- 1   cup shredded cheddar or taco cheese (4 oz.)
- ¼   cup sliced green onions
- 2   Tbsp. sliced pitted ripe olives
- ⅔   cup chopped, seeded tomato (1 medium)

Pecan-Crusted Artichoke Spread

Prep: 25 min. Bake: 40 + 10 min.

This spread is our jazzy version of the spinach dip popular in the 1990s. Slather it onto toasted baguette-style French bread slices.

 1   **Tbsp. butter**
 ½   **cup finely chopped onion**
 3   **cloves garlic, minced**
 4   **cups coarsely chopped fresh spinach**
 1   **14-oz. can artichoke hearts,
     drained and chopped**
 1   **8-oz. pkg. reduced-fat cream cheese
     (Neufchâtel), softened**
 ½   **cup fat-free mayonnaise dressing or
     salad dressing**
 2   **cups shredded reduced-fat cheddar
     cheese (8 oz.)**
 ½   **cup grated Parmesan cheese (2 oz.)**
 2   **dashes bottled hot pepper sauce**
 ¼   **cup finely chopped pecans**

1. Preheat oven to 350°F. In a medium saucepan, melt butter over medium-high heat. Add onion and garlic; cook for 3 minutes. Add spinach; cook for 3 to 5 minutes more or until onion is tender and spinach is cooked, stirring frequently. Remove from heat.

2. Stir in chopped artichoke hearts, cream cheese, mayonnaise dressing, cheddar cheese, Parmesan cheese, and hot pepper sauce. Transfer artichoke mixture to an ungreased 1½-quart casserole. Bake for 40 minutes. Top with pecans; bake for 10 minutes more. Makes 4 cups spread (64 servings).

Nutrition facts per tablespoon spread: 23 cal., 2 g total fat (1 g sat. fat), 4 mg chol., 71 mg sodium, 1 g carbo., 0 g fiber, 1 g pro.

> As entertaining became more and more informal in the 1970s, participation parties blossomed. Gatherings where each person cooks to some extent, such as fondue suppers, progressive dinners, and cooking clubs, became imaginative ways to have fun with friends.

Pecan-Crusted
Artichoke Spread

Chicken Wontons

4. Fry wontons, 3 or 4 at a time, in hot shortening or oil about 2 minutes or until golden and no pink remains in filling, turning once. Drain wontons on paper towels. Keep warm in a 300°F oven while frying remaining wontons. If desired, serve with sweet-and-sour sauce. Makes 32 wontons.

Make-ahead directions: Prepare as directed through step 2. Place wontons in a single layer in a refrigerator container. Seal and chill for up to 24 hours. To serve, continue as directed in step 3.

Nutrition facts per wonton: 60 cal., 3 g total fat (0 g sat. fat), 1 mg chol., 89 mg sodium, 5 g carbo., 0 g fiber, 2 g pro.

Egg Rolls
Prep: 35 min. Cook: 2 min. per batch

- 1   **recipe Pork Filling (below)**
- 8   **egg roll wrappers**
    Shortening or cooking oil for deep-fat frying
- 1⅓   **cups bottled sweet-and-sour sauce or ½ cup purchased Chinese-style hot mustard**

1. Prepare Pork Filling. For each egg roll, place an egg roll wrapper on a flat surface with a corner pointing toward you. Spoon *about ¼ cup* of the filling across and just below center of egg roll wrapper. Fold bottom corner over filling, tucking it under on the other side. Fold side corners over filling, forming an envelope shape. Roll egg roll toward remaining corner. Moisten top corner with water; press firmly to seal.

2. In a heavy saucepan or deep-fat fryer, heat 2 inches melted shortening or cooking oil to 365°F. Fry egg rolls, a few at a time, in hot shortening or oil for 2 to 3 minutes or until golden and filling is cooked through. Drain on paper towels. Keep warm in a 300°F oven while frying remaining egg rolls. Serve with sweet-and-sour sauce or hot mustard. Makes 8 egg rolls.

Pork Filling: In a medium skillet, combine 8 ounces ground pork, 2 teaspoons grated fresh ginger, and 1 clove garlic, minced; cook for 2 to 3 minutes or until meat is brown. Drain off fat. Add ½ cup finely chopped bok choy or cabbage, ½ cup chopped water chestnuts, ½ cup shredded carrot, and ¼ cup finely chopped onion to pork mixture. Cook and stir for 2 minutes more. In a small bowl, stir together 2 tablespoons soy sauce, 2 teaspoons cornstarch, ½ teaspoon sugar, and ¼ teaspoon salt; add to skillet. Cook and stir for 1 minute. Cool filling slightly before using.

Chicken Wontons
Prep: 50 min. Cook: 2 min. per batch

When Asian restaurants sprang up all across the U.S.A., Americans fell in love with the bold flavors. Before long, home cooks were preparing Far East specialties, and we provided the recipes and know-how, including the recipe for these crispy tidbits.

- 1   **green onion, finely chopped**
- 2   **small shallots, finely chopped**
- 2   **Tbsp. finely chopped crystallized ginger**
- 2   **Tbsp. soy sauce or reduced-sodium soy sauce**
- 2   **Tbsp. peanut butter**
- 1   **Tbsp. snipped fresh cilantro**
- 1   **Tbsp. honey**
- ¼   **tsp. finely shredded lime peel**
- 2   **tsp. lime juice**
- ½   **tsp. crushed red pepper**
- 8   **oz. uncooked ground chicken**
- ¼   **cup chopped peanuts**
- 32   **wonton wrappers**
    Shortening or cooking oil for deep-fat frying
    Bottled sweet-and-sour sauce (optional)

1. In a bowl, combine green onion, shallots, ginger, soy sauce, peanut butter, cilantro, honey, lime peel, lime juice, and red pepper. Stir in chicken and peanuts.

2. For each wonton, place a wonton wrapper with a point toward you. Spoon *about 2 teaspoons* of the chicken mixture just below the center of the wrapper. Lightly moisten edges of wrapper with water. Fold wrapper over filling to make a triangle; press edges to seal. Grasp the right- and left-hand corners of the wrapper; bring corners together and press to seal.

3. In a heavy saucepan or deep-fat fryer, heat 2 inches melted shortening or cooking oil to 365°F.

Make-ahead directions: Prepare as directed through step 1. Place egg rolls in a single layer in a refrigerator container. Seal and chill for up to 24 hours. To serve, continue as directed in step 2.

Nutrition facts per egg roll: 276 cal., 16 g total fat (3 g sat. fat), 16 mg chol., 535 mg sodium, 27 g carbo., 1 g fiber, 6 g pro.

Red-Hot Pita Chips

Prep: 15 min. Bake: 13 min.

Our readers know how to turn on the heat at a party, as shown by this winner from our March 2000 Prize Tested Recipes® Knack for Snacks contest.

- 1 egg white
- 2 Tbsp. olive oil
- 2 tsp. Dijon-style mustard
- 2 cloves garlic, minced
- 1 tsp. ground cumin
- ½ tsp. salt
- ½ tsp. chili powder
- ½ tsp. paprika
  Dash cayenne pepper
- 3 pita bread rounds, halved horizontally

1. Preheat oven to 350°F. In a small bowl, whisk together all ingredients except pita rounds. Brush cut surfaces of bread with the spice mixture. Cut each into 8 wedges. Place wedges, spice sides up, on ungreased baking sheet. Bake for 13 to 15 minutes or until crisp. Cool on baking sheet. Makes 6 servings (48 wedges).

Nutrition facts per serving: 132 cal., 5 g total fat (1 g sat. fat), 0 mg chol., 376 mg sodium, 18 g carbo., 1 g fiber, 4 g pro.

Savory Nuts

Prep: 5 min. Bake: 12 min.

Set out a bowl of these herb-accented nuts at your next party, and they'll disappear in no time.

- 2 cups macadamia nuts or broken walnuts
- 2 Tbsp. white wine Worcestershire sauce
- 1 Tbsp. olive oil
- ½ tsp. dried thyme, crushed
- ¼ tsp. salt
- ¼ tsp. dried rosemary, crushed
- ⅛ tsp. cayenne pepper

1. Preheat oven to 350°F. Spread the nuts in a 13×9×2-inch baking pan. In a small bowl, combine Worcestershire sauce, olive oil, thyme, salt, rosemary, and cayenne pepper; drizzle over nuts. Toss to coat.

2. Bake for 12 to 15 minutes or until nuts are toasted, stirring occasionally. Spread on foil; cool. Store in an airtight container for up to 2 weeks. Makes 2 cups nuts.

Nutrition facts per 2-tablespoon serving: 258 cal., 27 g total fat (4 g sat. fat), 0 mg chol., 193 mg sodium, 5 g carbo., 3 g fiber, 3 g pro.

Crunchy Party Mix

Prep: 15 min. Bake: 45 min.

Cereal-based snack mixes have been making the party circuit since the 1970s. Our zesty version of the eat-by-the-fistful mix based on pretzels, nuts, and three kinds of cereal dates back to 1981.

- 5 cups pretzel sticks
- 4 cups round toasted oat cereal
- 4 cups bite-size wheat or bran square cereal
- 4 cups bite-size rice or corn square cereal
  or bite-size shredded wheat biscuits
- 3 cups mixed nuts
- 1 cup butter or margarine
- 3 Tbsp. Worcestershire sauce
- ½ tsp. garlic powder
  Several drops bottled hot pepper sauce

1. Preheat oven to 300°F. In a very large roasting pan, combine pretzels, oat cereal, wheat or bran cereal, rice or corn cereal, and nuts. Set aside.

2. In small saucepan, combine butter, Worcestershire sauce, garlic powder, and hot pepper sauce. Heat and stir until butter is melted. Drizzle butter mixture over cereal mixture; stir gently to coat.

3. Bake for 45 minutes, stirring every 15 minutes. Spread on a large piece of foil to cool. Store in an airtight container for up to 1 week. Makes 20 cups.

Make-ahead directions: Prepare as directed. Place in freezer bags. Seal, label, and freeze for up to 1 month.

Nutrition facts per ½-cup serving: 168 cal., 11 g total fat (4 g sat. fat), 13 mg chol., 309 mg sodium, 15 g carbo., 2 g fiber, 3 g pro.

Cajun-Style Party Mix: Prepare as directed, except increase the bottled hot pepper sauce to 1 tablespoon and substitute 3 cups pecan halves for the mixed nuts.

Nutrition facts per ½-cup serving: 158 cal., 11 g total fat (4 g sat. fat), 13 mg chol., 250 mg sodium, 14 g carbo., 2 g fiber, 2 g pro.

Tex-Mex Shrimp Cocktail
Prep: 20 min. Chill: 2 to 4 hr.

The 1937 edition of the *Better Homes and Gardens®
Cook Book* included grapefruit, crab, oyster, and, of
course, shrimp cocktails. Since then, the shrimp
medley has been reinvented time and time again.
One of our favorites is this Tex-Mex version.

1	**lb. fresh or frozen shrimp**
¼	**cup ketchup**
¼	**cup lime juice**
1	**to 2 tsp. bottled hot pepper sauce**
½	**cup chopped tomato**
¼	**cup chopped onion**
¼	**cup snipped fresh cilantro**
2	**avocados, seeded, peeled, and chopped**
	Lime wedges (optional)
	Purple flowering kale (optional)

1. Thaw shrimp, if frozen. Peel and devein shrimp.
Cook shrimp in a large amount of boiling water for 1 to
2 minutes or until shrimp are opaque, stirring
occasionally. Drain; rinse under cold running water.

2. In a large bowl, stir together ketchup, lime juice,
and hot pepper sauce. Add shrimp, tomato, onion, and
cilantro; toss to coat. Cover and chill for at least 2 hours
or up to 4 hours.

3. Just before serving, add avocados; toss to coat. If
desired, garnish with lime wedges and flowering kale.
Makes 8 servings.

Nutrition facts per appetizer serving: 113 cal., 6 g total fat (1 g sat. fat),
65 mg chol., 183 mg sodium, 9 g carbo., 2 g fiber, 8 g pro.

> **When hostesses planned parties
> during the late 1940s, shrimp
> showed up on the buffet table,
> as long as it was affordable.**

Buffalo Wings
Prep: 25 min. Chill: 30 min. Broil: 10 + 10 min.

Originally created by the folks at the Anchor Bar in Buffalo, New York, fiery-sauced chicken wings now star on menus coast to coast. This *Better Homes and Gardens*® adaptation of the burning bites first appeared in 1992.

12 chicken wings (about 2 lb.)
 2 Tbsp. butter or margarine, melted
 2 to 3 Tbsp. bottled hot pepper sauce
 1 tsp. paprika
 1 recipe Blue Cheese Dip or Lower-Fat Blue Cheese Dip (below)
    Salt (optional)
    Pepper (optional)

1. Preheat broiler. Meanwhile, cut off and discard tips of chicken wings. Cut wings at joints to form 24 pieces. Place chicken wing pieces in a shallow nonmetal pan.

2. For sauce, in a small bowl, stir together the melted butter, bottled hot pepper sauce, and paprika. Pour mixture over chicken wings, stirring to coat. Cover chicken; chill for 30 minutes. Prepare Blue Cheese Dip.

3. Drain chicken, reserving sauce. Place the chicken wing pieces on the unheated rack of a broiler pan. If desired, sprinkle the chicken with salt and pepper. Brush with some of the reserved sauce.

4. Broil chicken 4 to 5 inches from the heat about 10 minutes or until lightly browned. Turn the chicken pieces; brush again with the reserved sauce. Discard any remaining sauce. Broil for 10 to 15 minutes more or until the chicken is tender and no longer pink. Serve with dip. Makes 12 servings.

Blue Cheese Dip: In a blender or a food processor, combine ½ cup dairy sour cream; ½ cup mayonnaise or salad dressing; ½ cup crumbled blue cheese (2 ounces); 1 clove garlic, minced; and 1 tablespoon white wine vinegar or white vinegar. Cover and blend or process until smooth. To store dip, cover and refrigerate for up to 2 weeks. If desired, top with additional crumbled blue cheese before serving.
Nutrition facts per appetizer with 2 tablespoons dip: 208 cal., 19 g total fat (6 g sat. fat), 49 mg chol., 168 mg sodium, 1 g carbo., 0 g fiber, 9 g pro.

Lower-Fat Blue Cheese Dip: Prepare as directed, except substitute fat-free dairy sour cream and fat-free mayonnaise dressing or salad dressing for the regular dairy sour cream and mayonnaise or salad dressing.
Nutrition facts per appetizer with 2 tablespoons dip: 140 cal., 10 g total fat (1 g sat. fat), 11 mg chol., 206 mg sodium, 3 g carbo., 0 g fiber, 9 g pro.

Mushrooms 101
To keep mushrooms at their best, store them unwashed in the refrigerator for up to 2 days. Leave prepackaged mushrooms in their package and store loose mushrooms or those in open containers in a paper sack or a damp cloth bag.

Stuffed Mushrooms
Prep: 25 min. Bake: 8 min.

Take your choice of a garlic-seasoned cheddar cheese filling or an Italian-seasoned prosciutto filling for these mouthwatering appetizers.

24 large fresh mushrooms, 1½ to 2 inches in diameter
¼ cup sliced green onions
 1 clove garlic, minced
¼ cup butter or margarine
⅔ cup fine dry bread crumbs
½ cup shredded cheddar cheese or smoked Gouda cheese or crumbled blue cheese (2 oz.)

1. Preheat oven to 425°F. Rinse and drain the mushrooms. Remove stems; set caps aside. Chop enough of the stems to measure 1 cup.

2. In a medium saucepan, cook the chopped stems, the green onions, and garlic in butter until tender. Stir in bread crumbs and cheese. Spoon crumb mixture into mushroom caps.

3. Arrange stuffed mushrooms in a 15×10×1-inch baking pan. Bake for 8 to 10 minutes or until heated through. Makes 24 mushrooms.
Nutrition facts per mushroom: 42 cal., 3 g total fat (1 g sat. fat), 8 mg chol., 97 mg sodium, 2 g carbo., 0 g fiber, 2 g pro.

Prosciutto-Stuffed Mushrooms: Prepare as directed, except omit cheese. Stir ⅓ cup chopped prosciutto, ¼ cup shredded provolone cheese, and ½ teaspoon dried Italian seasoning, crushed, into the crumb mixture.
Nutrition facts per mushroom: 39 cal., 3 g total fat (2 g sat. fat), 7 mg chol., 112 mg sodium, 2 g carbo., 0 g fiber, 2 g pro.

Yesterday

When cheese balls first hit the entertaining scene in the 1950s, they were a shoo-in for the party food popularity contest since they were easy to adapt to almost any flavor. The fact that they tasted better when made ahead won them the congeniality award, too.

Smoky Cheese Ball

Prep: 30 min. Stand: 30 + 15 min. Chill: 4 to 24 hr.

We think the smoky cheddar cheese in this easy-fixing spread makes it a cut above other versions. Try it on party-size bread or crackers.

- 2 8-oz. pkg. cream cheese
- 2 cups finely shredded smoked cheddar cheese, Swiss cheese, or Gouda cheese (8 oz.)
- ½ cup butter or margarine
- 2 Tbsp. milk
- 2 tsp. bottled steak sauce
- 1 cup finely chopped nuts, toasted (tip, page 102)
- 2 Tbsp. finely snipped fresh parsley

1. Place the cream cheese, shredded cheese, and butter in a large mixing bowl; let stand at room temperature for 30 minutes. Add milk and steak sauce; beat with an electric mixer on medium speed until fluffy. Cover and chill for at least 4 hours or up to 24 hours.

2. In a shallow dish, combine nuts and parsley. Shape cheese mixture into a ball; roll in nut mixture. Let stand for 15 minutes. Makes 1 large ball (80 servings).

Make-ahead directions: Prepare as directed through step 1. Wrap cheese ball in moisture- and vaporproof freezer wrap. Freeze for up to 1 month. To serve, thaw in refrigerator overnight. Continue with step 2, except let stand for 30 minutes at room temperature before serving.

Nutrition facts per tablespoon spread: 51 cal., 5 g total fat (3 g sat. fat), 12 mg chol., 50 mg sodium, 0 g carbo., 0 g fiber, 1 g pro.

Over the years, both our editors and our readers wanted more flavorful cheese balls and spreads. This robust version from 1998 is a delicious example. It includes garlic-and-herb feta cheese.

Herbed Feta Spread

Start to finish: 15 min.

Team this ready-when-you-are spread with crackers, party-size bread, or even fresh apple or pear slices.

- 1 **8-oz. pkg. reduced-fat cream cheese (Neufchâtel)**
- 1 **4-oz. pkg. crumbled garlic-and-herb feta cheese**
- 1 **Tbsp. milk**
  Pepper
- 2 **Tbsp. snipped fresh parsley**
- ½ **tsp. snipped fresh rosemary**

1. In a small mixing bowl, combine cream cheese, feta cheese, and milk. Season to taste with pepper. Beat with an electric mixer on medium speed until mixture is well mixed and of spreading consistency. Divide in half.

2. In a shallow bowl, combine parsley and rosemary. Shape *each half* of cheese mixture into a 5-inch-long roll. Roll in parsley mixture. Serve immediately or wrap in plastic wrap and chill until serving time. Makes about 1¼ cups (20 servings).

Make-ahead directions: Prepare as directed through step 2. Wrap in plastic wrap. Chill for up to 3 days. Serve as directed.

Nutrition facts per tablespoon spread: 44 cal., 4 g total fat (3 g sat. fat), 14 mg chol., 108 mg sodium, 1 g carbo., 0 g fiber, 2 g pro.

Praline-Topped Brie

Prep: 10 min. Bake: 15 min.

All you need are four simple ingredients for this elegant appetizer. Scoop up the warm, buttery cheese with toasted baguette slices or sturdy crackers.

  1 **13- to 15-oz. round Brie or Camembert cheese**
  ½ **cup orange marmalade**
  2 **Tbsp. packed brown sugar**
  ⅓ **cup coarsely chopped pecans**

1. Preheat oven to 350°F. Place the round of cheese in a shallow ovenproof serving dish or pie plate. In a small bowl, stir together orange marmalade and brown sugar. Spread on top of cheese. Sprinkle with pecans.

2. Bake about 15 minutes for smaller round, about 20 minutes for larger round, or until cheese is slightly softened and topping is bubbly. Makes 10 to 12 servings.

Nutrition facts per appetizer serving: 192 cal., 13 g total fat (7 g sat. fat), 36 mg chol., 239 mg sodium, 13 g carbo., 0 g fiber, 8 g pro.

Praline-Topped Brie

Appetizer Cheesecake

Prep: 35 min. Bake: 9 + 40 min. Chill: 6 to 24 hr.

In November 1993, we ran a story showcasing America's 15 favorite appetizers. This savory cheesecake with a Greek accent was on the list.

  ¼ **cup butter or margarine, melted**
  6 **sheets frozen phyllo dough (14×9-inch sheets), thawed**
  ½ **of a 6-oz. jar marinated artichoke hearts**
  3 **8-oz. pkg. cream cheese, softened**
  1¼ **cups crumbled feta cheese (5 oz.)**
  ½ **tsp. dried oregano, crushed**
  ¼ **tsp. garlic powder**
  3 **eggs**
  ¼ **cup sliced green onions**

1. Preheat oven to 400°F. For crust, brush bottom and side of a 9-inch springform pan with some of the melted butter. Unfold phyllo dough; remove *1 sheet* of the phyllo. (As you work, cover the remaining phyllo dough with plastic wrap to prevent it from drying out.) Ease the sheet into the prepared pan off-center so phyllo extends evenly up side of pan. Brush with melted butter. Repeat with remaining phyllo and butter, placing sheets off-center to cover bottom and side of pan. Trim off phyllo that extends beyond edge of pan. Make 2 slits in center of phyllo for steam to escape.

2. Bake 9 to 10 minutes or until light golden brown. Cool on a wire rack. Lower oven temperature to 325°F.

3. Meanwhile, drain and chop artichokes, reserving *2 tablespoons* of the marinade; set aside.

4. In a large mixing bowl, beat cream cheese with an electric mixer on medium speed until smooth. Add feta cheese, oregano, and garlic powder; beat well. Add eggs; beat just until combined (do not overbeat). Stir in artichoke hearts, reserved 2 tablespoons marinade, and the green onions. Pour into crust. Bake for 40 to 50 minutes or until center is soft-set and outside stays firm when gently shaken. Cool.

5. Cover and chill for at least 6 hours or up to 24 hours. To serve, remove from pan. (If desired, let stand to bring to room temperature.) Makes 16 servings.

Nutrition facts per appetizer serving: 239 cal., 21 g total fat (13 g sat. fat), 103 mg chol., 317 mg sodium, 6 g carbo., 0 g fiber, 6 g pro.

Lower-Fat Appetizer Cheesecake: Prepare as directed, except substitute fat-free cream cheese for regular cream cheese.

Nutrition facts per appetizer serving: 119 cal., 6 g total fat (4 g sat. fat), 63 mg chol., 178 mg sodium, 6 g carbo., 0 g fiber, 9 g pro.

Herbed Leek Tart

2. Unfold piecrust according to package directions. On a lightly floured surface, roll *1 piecrust* into a 12-inch circle. Transfer piecrust to a baking sheet. Spread *half* of the filling onto the center of the piecrust, leaving a 1½-inch border. Fold border up and over filling, pleating as necessary. Sprinkle *1 tablespoon* of the nuts over the filling. Repeat with remaining piecrust, filling, and nuts.

3. Bake about 25 minutes or until crusts are golden. Cool on baking sheets on wire racks for 10 minutes. Cut each tart into 12 wedges. Serve warm, or cool to room temperature. Makes 2 tarts (24 servings).

Make-ahead directions: Prepare as directed through step 2. Cover and chill assembled tarts for up to 4 hours. Uncover and bake as directed in step 3.

Nutrition facts per appetizer serving: 133 cal., 9 g total fat (4 g sat. fat), 11 mg chol., 100 mg sodium, 11 g carbo., 0 g fiber, 3 g pro.

Herbed Leek Tart

Prep: 20 min. Bake: 25 min. Cool: 10 min.

When it comes to inventing unique appetizers, our readers are real pros. This beguiling Gruyère tart was one of the top-notch entries in our Easy Holiday Appetizers contest in December 1998. It features herbes de Provence. Look for this ingredient in the herb and spice aisle of larger supermarkets.

    9   medium leeks, thinly sliced (3 cups)
    4   cloves garlic, minced
    2   Tbsp. olive oil
    ½   cup coarsely chopped red sweet pepper
    2   Tbsp. Dijon-style mustard
    1   tsp. dried herbes de Provence or dried
        basil, crushed
    6   oz. Gruyère cheese or Swiss cheese,
        shredded (1½ cups)
    1   15-oz. pkg. (2 crusts) folded refrigerated
        unbaked piecrust
    2   Tbsp. sliced almonds or chopped walnuts

1. Preheat oven to 375°F. For filling, in a large skillet, cook leeks and garlic in hot oil about 5 minutes or until tender. Remove from heat; stir in sweet pepper, mustard, and herbes de Provence. Cool slightly; stir in shredded cheese. Set filling aside.

Monterey Jack Fondue

Start to finish: 15 min.

Although long a favorite in California, Monterey Jack cheese didn't hit the national scene until the late 1960s. Just about then, *Better Homes and Gardens*® magazine featured the cheese in this fondue.

    3   Tbsp. butter
    1   clove garlic, minced
    3   Tbsp. all-purpose flour
    ⅛   tsp. cayenne pepper
    ¾   cup chicken broth
    1   5-oz. can (⅔ cup) evaporated milk
    1¼ cups shredded Monterey Jack cheese (5 oz.)
        French bread cubes or sweet pepper strips

1. In a 1½-quart saucepan, melt butter over medium heat. Add garlic; cook and stir for 30 seconds. Stir in flour and cayenne pepper. Stir in broth and evaporated milk all at once. Cook and stir until thickened and bubbly. Gradually add cheese, stirring until cheese is melted. Transfer to a fondue pot placed over fondue burner.

2. Serve with bread cubes or sweet pepper strips. (Stir in additional chicken broth, as necessary, for desired consistency.) Makes 8 servings.

Nutrition facts per ¼-cup fondue and 1 cup bread cubes: 228 cal., 12 g total fat (7 g sat. fat), 33 mg chol., 443 mg sodium, 20 g carbo., 1 g fiber, 9 g pro.

Deviled Eggs

Start to finish: 35 min.

Our first deviled egg recipe in the 1937 *Better Homes and Gardens*₀ *Cook Book* was only six lines long and started with the direction "Cook as many eggs as desired." This 2002 update gives cooks more guidance and the choice of five flavor variations.

    7 hard-cooked eggs
    ¼ cup mayonnaise or salad dressing
    1 to 2 tsp. Dijon-style mustard, balsamic
       herb mustard, honey mustard, or other
       favorite prepared mustard
    ½ tsp. dry mustard
       Salt
       Pepper
       Several leaves fresh flat-leaf parsley
       or paprika (optional)

1. Cut 6 eggs in half lengthwise. Carefully remove yolks; set whites aside. Coarsely chop the remaining whole egg.

2. In a resealable plastic bag, combine the 6 egg yolks, the chopped egg, mayonnaise, prepared mustard, and dry mustard. Seal bag; gently squeeze to combine ingredients. Season to taste with salt and pepper.

3. Snip one corner of the bag. Squeeze bag, pushing egg yolk mixture through hole into egg white halves. If desired, top with fresh parsley or paprika. Makes 12 halves.

Make-ahead directions: Prepare as directed. Cover and chill for up to 12 hours.

Nutrition facts per egg half: 79 cal., 7 g total fat (1 g sat. fat), 125 mg chol., 95 mg sodium, 0 g carbo., 0 g fiber, 4 g pro.

Italian-Style Deviled Eggs: Prepare as directed, except omit mayonnaise, mustards, and salt. Add ¼ cup bottled creamy Italian salad dressing and 2 tablespoons grated Parmesan cheese to mashed yolks and chopped egg; mix well.

Nutrition facts per egg half: 66 cal., 5 g total fat (1 g sat. fat), 124 mg chol., 92 mg sodium, 1 g carbo., 0 g fiber, 4 g pro.

Greek-Style Deviled Eggs: Prepare as directed, except add 2 tablespoons crumbled feta cheese, 1 tablespoon finely chopped pitted kalamata olives or other pitted ripe olives, and 2 teaspoons snipped fresh oregano to yolk mixture; mix well.

Nutrition facts per egg half: 85 cal., 7 g total fat (2 g sat. fat), 127 mg chol., 120 mg sodium, 0 g carbo., 0 g fiber, 4 g pro.

Mexican-Style Deviled Eggs: Prepare as directed, except omit mayonnaise and mustards. Add 3 tablespoons dairy sour cream, 1 tablespoon bottled salsa, and ½ teaspoon ground cumin to mashed yolks and chopped egg; mix well. Sprinkle filled egg halves with snipped fresh cilantro.

Nutrition facts per egg half: 52 cal., 4 g total fat (1 g sat. fat), 125 mg chol., 41 mg sodium, 1 g carbo., 0 g fiber, 4 g pro.

Indian-Style Deviled Eggs: Prepare as directed, except omit the mayonnaise and mustards. Add 3 tablespoons plain low-fat yogurt; 1 tablespoon chutney, chopped; and ½ teaspoon curry powder to mashed yolks and chopped egg; mix well. Sprinkle filled egg halves with chopped peanuts.

Nutrition facts per egg half: 57 cal., 4 g total fat (1 g sat. fat), 124 mg chol., 44 mg sodium, 2 g carbo., 0 g fiber, 4 g pro.

Nutty Blue Cheese Rolls

Prep: 20 min. Bake: 15 min.

These walnut-studded pastry rolls start with refrigerated piecrust and can be chilled overnight.

    ⅔ cup finely chopped walnuts
    ⅓ cup crumbled blue cheese
    1 Tbsp. finely snipped fresh parsley
    ¼ tsp. pepper
    ½ of a 15-oz. pkg. (1 crust) folded
       refrigerated unbaked piecrust
    1 Tbsp. milk
    2 tsp. grated Parmesan cheese
       Finely snipped fresh parsley

1. Preheat oven to 425°F. Grease baking sheets; set aside. For filling, in a medium bowl, stir together walnuts, blue cheese, the 1 tablespoon parsley, and the pepper.

2. On a lightly floured surface, unfold piecrust according to package directions. Spread filling evenly over the crust. Cut pastry circle into 12 wedges. Starting at wide ends, loosely roll up wedges. Place rolls, tips down, on prepared baking sheet.

3. Brush rolls lightly with milk. Sprinkle with Parmesan and additional parsley. Bake about 15 minutes or until golden. Transfer to wire rack. Serve warm. Makes 12 rolls.

Make-ahead directions: Prepare as directed in step 1. Cover and chill for up to 24 hours. Continue as directed in step 2.

Nutrition facts per roll: 139 cal., 10 g total fat (1 g sat. fat), 8 mg chol., 130 mg sodium, 9 g carbo., 3 g fiber, 3 g pro.

Italian Pepperoni-Cheese Puffs

Prep: 30 min. Bake: 15 min.

These prizewinning snack-size cream puffs from our November 1999 issue are loaded with pepperoni and Romano cheese. Beware: They're easy to gobble down one after another.

- 1¼   **cups water**
- ⅓   **cup shortening**
- 1½   **cups all-purpose flour**
- 4   **eggs**
- ¾   **cup finely chopped pepperoni (3 oz.)**
- ¾   **cup finely shredded Pecorino Romano cheese or Parmesan cheese (3 oz.)**
- 2   **Tbsp. snipped fresh parsley**
- ⅛   **tsp. garlic powder**
- ⅛   **tsp. pepper**

1. Preheat oven to 450°F. Grease 2 large baking sheets; set aside. In a large saucepan, combine the water and shortening. Bring to boiling. Add flour all at once, stirring vigorously. Cook and stir until mixture forms a ball. Remove from heat. Cool for 10 minutes. Add eggs, one at a time, beating well with a wooden spoon after each addition. Stir in pepperoni, cheese, parsley, garlic powder, and pepper.

2. Drop dough by rounded teaspoons 2 inches apart onto prepared baking sheets. Bake for 15 to 17 minutes or until golden. Transfer to a wire rack. Serve warm. Makes 48 puffs.

Nutrition facts per puff: 48 cal., 3 g total fat (1 g sat. fat), 21 mg chol., 62 mg sodium, 3 g carbo., 0 g fiber, 2 g pro.

Bruschetta

Start to finish: 40 min.

In cooking, it's funny how necessity and thrift become the mother of invention. These tasty tomato-topped slices were originally some cook's creative attempt to use up day-old bread.

- 1   **cup pitted ripe olives**
- 2   **cloves garlic, minced**
- 2   **tsp. balsamic vinegar or red wine vinegar**
- 1   **tsp. capers, drained**
- 1   **tsp. olive oil**
- 1⅓   **cups chopped red and/or yellow tomato**
- ⅓   **cup thinly sliced green onions**
- 1   **Tbsp. snipped fresh basil or oregano or 1 tsp. dried basil or oregano, crushed**
- 1   **Tbsp. olive oil**
- ⅛   **tsp. pepper**
- 1   **8-oz. loaf baguette-style French bread**
- 2   **Tbsp. olive oil**
- ½   **cup finely shredded Parmesan cheese (2 oz.)**

1. Preheat oven to 425°F. For olive paste, in a food processor or blender, combine olives, garlic, vinegar, capers, and the 1 teaspoon oil. Cover and process or blend until a slightly chunky paste forms, stopping and scraping the side as necessary.

2. For tomato topping, in small bowl, combine tomato, green onions, basil, the 1 tablespoon oil, and the pepper.

3. For the toast, cut bread into ½-inch-thick slices. Using the 2 tablespoons olive oil, lightly brush both sides of each bread slice. Place on an ungreased baking sheet. Bake about 5 minutes or until crisp and light brown, turning once.

4. To assemble, spread each piece of toast with *about 1 teaspoon* of the olive paste. Top each piece with *about 1 tablespoon* of the tomato topping; sprinkle with Parmesan cheese. Return slices to the ungreased baking sheet. Bake for 3 to 4 minutes or until cheese starts to melt and toppings are heated through. Serve warm. Makes 24 servings.

Make-ahead directions: Prepare as directed through step 3, except cover and chill the olive paste and tomato topping separately for up to 24 hours. Place the cooled toast in an airtight container and store at room temperature for up to 24 hours. Assemble and bake as directed in step 4.

Nutrition facts per appetizer serving: 60 cal., 3 g total fat (1 g sat. fat), 1 mg chol., 142 mg sodium, 6 g carbo., 1 g fiber, 2 g pro.

Soft Pretzels with Three Mustards

Prep: 50 min. Rise: 1¼ hr. Bake: 4 + 10 min.

With this foolproof recipe, you won't need to head to the mall or a brew pub to enjoy fresh baked pretzels. Make them at home and serve them with one or more of these marvelous mustards.

    4   to 4½ cups all-purpose flour
    1   pkg. active dry yeast
 1½   cups milk
    ¼   cup sugar
    2   Tbsp. cooking oil
    1   tsp. salt
    1   egg white, slightly beaten
    1   Tbsp. water
        Coarse salt, sesame seeds, or poppy seeds
    1   recipe Black and Tan Mustard, Mole Mustard, and/or Pecan Mustard (right)

1. In a large mixing bowl, stir together *1½ cups* of the flour and the yeast; set aside. In a medium saucepan, heat and stir milk, sugar, oil, and the 1 teaspoon salt until warm (120°F to 130°F). Add milk mixture to flour mixture. Beat with an electric mixer on low to medium speed for 30 seconds, scraping side of bowl constantly. Beat on high speed for 3 minutes. Using a wooden spoon, stir in as much of the remaining flour as you can.

2. Turn out dough onto a lightly floured surface. Knead in enough of the remaining flour to make a moderately stiff dough that is smooth and elastic (6 to 8 minutes total). Shape into a ball. Place in a lightly greased bowl, turning once to grease surface. Cover and let rise in a warm place until double in size (about 1¼ hours).

> **As Americans gravitated to the television set during the 1950s, many of the foods we ate changed. Perhaps the most well-known innovation was the TV dinner, but easy-to-munch finger foods, such as pretzels, party mixes, and popcorn, also made crumbs on the couch.**

3. Punch down dough. Turn out dough onto a lightly floured surface. Cover and let rest for 10 minutes. In a small bowl, stir together egg white and the water; set aside.

4. Preheat oven to 475°F. To make diamond-shaped pretzels, roll dough into a 14×12-inch rectangle. Cut into sixteen 7×1½-inch strips. With a sharp knife or pizza cutter, make a slit lengthwise down center of each strip, beginning ¾ inch from one end and ending ¾ inch from the other end. Place strips 3 inches apart on ungreased baking sheet. Pull center apart to form a diamond shape; gently push ends toward one another to form final shape.

5. Bake for 4 minutes. Remove from oven. Reduce oven temperature to 350°F. Brush pretzels with the egg white mixture. Sprinkle pretzels lightly with coarse salt, sesame seeds, or poppy seeds. Bake about 10 minutes more or until golden. Transfer to wire racks and let cool. Serve with desired mustard(s). Makes 16 pretzels.

Nutrition facts per pretzel without mustard: 145 cal., 2 g total fat (1 g sat. fat), 2 mg chol., 148 mg sodium, 26 g carbo., 1 g fiber, 4 g pro.

Black and Tan Mustard: In a small bowl, stir together 2 tablespoons Dijon-style mustard, 2 tablespoons packed brown sugar, 1 tablespoon dry mustard, and 1 tablespoon stout or dark beer until smooth.

Nutrition facts per 1-tablespoon serving: 19 cal., 0 g total fat, 0 mg chol., 95 mg sodium, 3 g carbo., 0 g fiber, 0 g pro.

Mole Mustard: In a small bowl, stir 2 tablespoons purchased mole sauce into ¼ cup coarse-grain mustard. Add 3 tablespoons water, 1 tablespoon sugar, and 1 teaspoon unsweetened cocoa powder; stir until combined. Cover and chill for at least 8 hours or up to 24 hours. To serve, bring mustard to room temperature.

Nutrition facts per 1-tablespoon serving: 15 cal., 1 g total fat (0 g sat. fat), 0 mg chol., 124 mg sodium, 2 g carbo., 0 g fiber, 1 g pro.

Pecan Mustard: In small bowl, stir together: ¼ cup coarse-grain brown mustard; ¼ cup pecans, chopped and toasted (tip, page 102); 2 teaspoons water; and 1 teaspoon lemon juice. Season to taste with salt and pepper.

Nutrition facts per 1-tablespoon serving: 48 cal., 4 g total fat (0 g sat. fat), 0 mg chol., 188 mg sodium, 2 g carbo., 0 g fiber, 1 g pro.

Make-ahead directions: Prepare mustards as directed, except do not add pecans to Pecan Mustard. Cover and chill for up to 2 weeks. For Pecan Mustard, stir in chopped pecans immediately before serving.

Caramel Corn

Prep: 20 min. Bake: 20 min.

This best-loved version of the golden popcorn treat gets its irresistible flavor from the right mix of brown sugar, butter, and vanilla.

7	to 8 cups popped popcorn
¾	cup packed brown sugar
6	Tbsp. butter
3	Tbsp. light-colored corn syrup
¼	tsp. baking soda
¼	tsp. vanilla

1. Butter a large piece of foil; set aside. Preheat oven to 300°F. Remove all unpopped kernels from popped popcorn. Put popcorn into a 17×12×2-inch baking pan or roasting pan. Keep popcorn warm in the oven while making caramel mixture.

2. For carmel mixture, in a medium saucepan, combine brown sugar, butter, and corn syrup. Cook and stir over medium heat until mixture boils. Continue boiling at a moderate, steady rate, without stirring, for 5 minutes more. Remove saucepan from heat. Stir in baking soda and vanilla.

3. Pour caramel mixture over popcorn; stir gently to coat. Bake for 15 minutes. Stir mixture; bake for 5 minutes more. Spread caramel corn on prepared foil to cool. Makes 7 to 8 cups.

Make-ahead directions: Prepare as directed. Place in an airtight container. Cover and store at room temperature for up to 1 week.

Nutrition facts per 1-cup serving: 236 cal., 11 g total fat (7 g sat. fat), 28 mg chol., 171 mg sodium, 36 g carbo., 1 g fiber, 1 g pro.

Yesterday

Sweetened popcorn has been around for a long time on the pages of our magazine. First came white popcorn balls, then popcorn peanut brittle (a mixture of peanuts and popcorn), and, of course, caramel corn.

Sesame-Ginger Popcorn

Prep: 20 min. Bake: 20 min.

For a rich, nutty flavor, it's important to use deep-brown toasted sesame oil, not golden sesame oil. Made from toasted sesame seeds, the brown oil has a bold flavor. Look for it in the Asian section of your supermarket or at Asian specialty stores.

5	cups popped popcorn
1½	cups lightly salted cashews
⅔	cup packed brown sugar
2	Tbsp. butter
2	Tbsp. light-colored corn syrup
1	Tbsp. grated fresh ginger
2	tsp. toasted sesame oil
2	Tbsp. sesame seeds
1	tsp. vanilla
⅛	tsp. baking soda

1. Butter a large piece of foil; set aside. Preheat oven to 300°F. Grease a 17×12×2-inch baking pan or roasting pan. Remove all unpopped kernels from popped popcorn. Put popcorn and cashews in prepared baking or roasting pan.

2. In a medium saucepan, combine brown sugar, butter, corn syrup, grated ginger, and sesame oil. Cook and stir over medium heat until mixture boils. Continue boiling at a moderate, steady rate, without stirring, for 5 minutes more.

3. Remove saucepan from heat. Stir in sesame seeds, vanilla, and baking soda. Pour mixture over popcorn mixture; stir gently to coat. Bake for 20 to 25 minutes or until golden, stirring twice. Spread popcorn mixture on prepared foil to cool. Makes about 8 cups.

Make-ahead directions: Prepare as directed. Place in an airtight container. Cover and store at room temperature for up to 1 week.

Nutrition facts per 1-cup serving: 287 cal., 16 g total fat (4 g sat. fat), 8 mg chol., 107 mg sodium, 33 g carbo., 2 g fiber, 5 g pro.

Today

Caramel corn underwent an Asian makeover in this top-prize entry in our March 2000 Knack for Snacks contest. Grated fresh ginger, toasted sesame oil, and sesame seeds add exotic flavor notes to the mix.

Since 1922, our food editors have made it a high priority to help readers prepare delicious, nutritious meals for their families. That means including fresh salad and vegetable recipes to round out meals. Dip into this colorful collection and you'll find green, potato, pasta, and fruit salads (main dish and side dish), plus suggestions for a variety of vegetable sides you can cook in the oven or on the range.

Splendid Salads & Vegetables

175

189

191

180

183

Asian Chicken Salad

Start to finish: 35 min.

Tossed lettuce salad first appeared in *Better Homes and Gardens*® magazine in the 1930s. Since then, we've paired lettuce with an astounding array of ingredients. In the 1980s, when Asian flavors were especially in vogue, we created this tossed noodle salad.

- 1 lb. skinless, boneless chicken breast halves
- 3 Tbsp. soy sauce
- 2 tsp. grated fresh ginger
- 1 recipe Asian Salad Dressing (below)
- 5 cups torn mixed salad greens
- 3 cups assorted vegetables (such as fresh pea pods, halved crosswise; red sweet pepper strips; shredded carrot; and/or bite-size cucumber strips)
- 1 cup coarsely chopped red cabbage
- ¼ cup sliced green onions
- 1 3-oz. pkg. chicken-flavored ramen noodles
- 2 tsp. sesame seeds, toasted

1. Preheat broiler. Grease the unheated rack of a broiler pan. Place chicken breasts on prepared rack. In a small bowl, combine soy sauce and ginger; brush some of the mixture onto *one side* of *each* chicken breast half. Broil 4 inches from heat for 12 to 15 minutes or until chicken is tender and no longer pink (170°F), turning once and brushing once with the remaining soy mixture halfway through broiling. Discard any remaining soy mixture. Remove from heat; cool slightly. Cut chicken into bite-size strips. Set aside.

2. Meanwhile, prepare Asian Salad Dressing. In a large bowl, toss together the mixed greens, assorted vegetables, red cabbage, and green onions. Break dry ramen noodles into small pieces; add to salad. (Reserve flavor package, if present, for another use.)

3. Shake Asian Salad Dressing well; pour *about ½ cup* of the dressing over salad. Toss lightly to coat. Divide salad among four salad plates. Top *each* salad with *one-fourth* of the chicken strips; pour remaining dressing over chicken. Top with sesame seeds. Makes 4 servings.

Asian Salad Dressing: In a screw-top jar, combine ⅓ cup unsweetened pineapple juice, ¼ cup rice vinegar or white vinegar, 3 tablespoons salad oil, 1 tablespoon soy sauce, 2 teaspoons sugar, 1½ teaspoons toasted sesame oil, and ¼ teaspoon pepper. Cover; shake well.

Nutrition facts per main-dish serving: 411 cal., 15 g total fat (3 g sat. fat), 66 mg chol., 1,477 mg sodium, 32 g carbo., 4 g fiber, 33 g pro.

Taco Salad

Prep: 30 min. Bake: 15 min.

In the 1960s, Americans began experimenting with south-of-the-border flavors. One delicious result was the taco salad. We first published our version in 1968. It's as hearty and satisfying today as it was then.

- 1 recipe Tortilla Cups (below) or 6 purchased tortilla bowls
- 8 oz. lean ground beef or uncooked ground turkey
- 3 cloves garlic, minced
- 1 15-oz. can dark red kidney beans, rinsed and drained
- 1 8-oz. jar taco sauce
- ¾ cup frozen whole kernel corn, thawed (optional)
- 6 cups shredded leaf or iceberg lettuce
- 2 medium tomatoes, chopped
- 1 large green sweet pepper, chopped
- ½ cup thinly sliced green onions
- 1 medium avocado, pitted, peeled, and chopped
- ¾ cup shredded sharp cheddar cheese (3 oz.)
  Dairy sour cream (optional)
  Bottled taco sauce or salsa (optional)

1. If using, prepare Tortilla Cups. In a medium saucepan, cook ground meat and garlic until meat is brown. Drain off fat. Stir in kidney beans, the 8-ounce jar taco sauce, and, if desired, the corn. Bring to boiling; reduce heat. Cover and simmer for 10 minutes.

2. Meanwhile, in a very large bowl, combine lettuce, tomatoes, sweet pepper, and green onions. To serve, divide lettuce mixture among Tortilla Cups. Top lettuce mixture with the meat mixture and avocado. Sprinkle with cheese. If desired, serve with sour cream and additional taco sauce or salsa. Makes 6 servings.

Tortilla Cups: Preheat oven to 350°F. Lightly brush *one side* of *each* of six 9- or 10-inch flour tortillas with a small amount of water or lightly coat with nonstick cooking spray. Coat six small oven-safe bowls or six 16-ounce individual casseroles with nonstick cooking spray. Press tortillas, coated sides up, into prepared bowls or casseroles. Place a ball of foil in each tortilla cup. Bake for 15 to 20 minutes or until light brown. Transfer to a wire rack. Remove the foil; let tortilla cups cool. Remove cups from the bowls. Use immediately or store in an airtight container for up to 5 days.

Nutrition facts per main-dish serving: 412 cal., 18 g total fat (6 g sat. fat), 35 mg chol., 632 mg sodium, 45 g carbo., 8 g fiber, 21 g pro.

Cobb Salad

Start to finish: 20 min.

We originally featured this eye-catching salad from Hollywood's Brown Derby restaurant in 1964. When we updated it in 1997, we substituted French dressing for the original Derby dressing.

½   **of a large head lettuce, shredded (about 6 cups)**

4   **skinless, boneless chicken breast halves (1¼ lb. total), cooked, chilled, and cubed, or 3 cups diced cooked chicken**

2   **medium tomatoes, chopped**

3   **hard-cooked eggs, chopped**

6   **slices bacon, crisp-cooked, drained, and crumbled**

¾   **cup crumbled blue cheese (3 oz.)**

1   **or 2 medium avocados, pitted, peeled, and cut into wedges**

1   **small Belgian endive**

1   **Tbsp. snipped fresh chives or thinly sliced green onion tops (optional)**

½   **cup bottled French salad dressing**

1. On four individual salad plates or on a large platter, arrange the shredded lettuce. On top of the lettuce, arrange piles of chicken, tomatoes, eggs, bacon, and blue cheese.

2. Just before serving, tuck avocado wedges and endive leaves at the edges of the plates or platter. If desired, sprinkle with chives or green onion tops. Serve with dressing. Makes 6 servings.

Nutrition facts per main-dish serving: 490 cal., 32 g total fat (12 g sat. fat), 186 mg chol., 825 mg sodium, 10 g carbo., 3 g fiber, 33 g pro.

Lower-Fat Cobb Salad: Prepare as directed, except omit the bacon and avocado and substitute a reduced-calorie or fat-free bottled French salad dressing for the regular salad dressing.

Nutrition facts per main-dish serving: 236 cal., 8 g total fat (4 g sat. fat), 171 mg chol., 447 mg sodium, 9 g carbo., 1 g fiber, 29 g pro.

Creamy Potato Salad (recipe, page 176)

Yesterday

Summertime entertaining 1950s-style often involved a backyard barbecue on the patio. To round out those grilled steaks, burgers, or hot dogs, *Better Homes and Gardens*® published side dishes galore, including everybody's favorite—creamy potato salad.

Today

For a novel take on traditional potato salad, try this colorful combo of red potatoes, purple potatoes, and green beans. The tangy rosemary-and-wine vinegar dressing tossed with the taters gives them a lighter, livelier flavor.

Kaleidoscope Potato Salad (recipe, page 176)

Creamy Potato Salad

Prep: 35 min. Chill: 2 to 24 hr.

In 1955, we called this salad Perfect Potato Salad. Although it's as perfect as ever, we changed the name to reflect its velvety coating. (Photo on page 174.)

- 3 medium potatoes (about 1 lb.)
- ½ cup sliced celery
- ⅓ cup thinly sliced green onions
- 2 Tbsp. chopped sweet pickle
  or sweet pickle relish
- 1 tsp. celery seeds
- ½ tsp. salt
- ⅔ cup mayonnaise or salad dressing
- 2 hard-cooked eggs, coarsely chopped
  Hard-cooked egg wedges (optional)
  Celery leaves (optional)

1. If desired, peel potatoes. Quarter and slice potatoes. In a medium saucepan, cover potatoes with water. Bring to boiling; reduce heat. Cover and simmer for 25 to 30 minutes or until tender. Drain; cool.

2. In a large bowl, combine potatoes, celery, green onions, pickle, celery seeds, and salt; toss gently to mix.

3. Add mayonnaise; toss gently to coat. Carefully fold in chopped eggs. Cover and chill for at least 2 hours or up to 24 hours. If desired, garnish with egg wedges and celery leaves. Makes 6 servings.

Nutrition facts per serving: 265 cal., 21 g total fat (3 g sat. fat), 85 mg chol., 401 mg sodium, 15 g carbo., 2 g fiber, 4 g pro.

Lower-Fat Creamy Potato Salad: Prepare as directed, except use light or fat-free mayonnaise dressing or salad dressing in place of regular mayonnaise or salad dressing.

Nutrition facts per serving: 166 cal., 11 g total fat (2 g sat. fat), 80 mg chol., 422 mg sodium, 15 g carbo., 1 g fiber, 4 g pro.

Kaleidoscope Potato Salad

Prep: 25 min. Cook: 10 min.

Purple potatoes vary in color from lavender to deep blue. Inside, they range from white to beige with hints of purple. (Photo on page 175.)

- 8 oz. small, red new potatoes, quartered
- 8 oz. purple potatoes, quartered
- 8 oz. fresh green beans, trimmed
- 3 Tbsp. olive oil
- 3 Tbsp. white wine vinegar
- 1 Tbsp. snipped fresh rosemary
  or ½ tsp. dried rosemary, crushed
- ¼ tsp. salt
- ¼ tsp. ground white pepper
- ¼ cup sliced green onions
  or 3 Tbsp. snipped fresh chives

1. In a covered Dutch oven, cook potatoes in a small amount of boiling, lightly salted water for 10 to 15 minutes or until tender. Add beans to Dutch oven for the last 3 to 5 minutes of cooking. Drain; rinse with cold water until vegetables are cooled. Drain.

2. In a medium bowl, stir together oil, vinegar, rosemary, salt, and white pepper. Add potato mixture and green onions or chives. Toss mixture gently. Serve immediately. Makes 6 to 8 servings.

Nutrition facts per serving: 146 cal., 7 g total fat (1 g sat. fat), 0 mg chol., 96 mg sodium, 20 g carbo., 2 g fiber, 2 g pro.

Summer Fruit with Sesame Dressing

Start to finish: 25 min.

We gave the ordinary spinach-and-fruit salad a fresh spin when we tossed the leafy greens with the summer's finest fruits, a honey dressing, and mint.

- 2 cups sliced peeled peaches or
  sliced nectarines
- 1 cup sliced peeled papaya or mango
- ½ cup sliced fresh strawberries
- ½ cup fresh raspberries
- ¼ cup rice vinegar
- 1 tsp. honey
- ½ tsp. toasted sesame oil
- 6 cups torn fresh spinach
- 2 Tbsp. snipped fresh mint

1. In a large bowl, combine the peaches, papaya, strawberries, and raspberries. Set aside.

2. For vinaigrette, in a small bowl, whisk together rice vinegar, honey, and sesame oil. Pour vinaigrette over fruit; toss gently to coat.

3. To serve, line six salad plates with spinach. Top with fruit mixture. Top with mint. Makes 6 servings.

Nutrition facts per serving: 80 cal., 1 g total fat (0 g sat. fat), 0 mg chol., 40 mg sodium, 18 g carbo., 7 g fiber, 2 g pro.

Wilted Greens Salad With Port Dressing

Start to finish: 30 min.

Fresh spinach drizzled with dressing was part of our salad repertoire from early on. But this salad from the turn of the millennium takes a different approach. It wilts spinach in a dressing of port wine and dried cherries and tosses it with pancetta and nuts.

⅓ cup dried tart red cherries
¼ cup port wine
4 oz. pancetta or 3 slices bacon, cut into small pieces
1 Tbsp. walnut oil or almond oil
⅓ cup sliced green onions
1 clove garlic, minced
3 Tbsp. red raspberry vinegar or balsamic vinegar
1 tsp. sugar
1 10-oz. pkg. prewashed fresh spinach, torn (10 to 12 cups)
¼ cup broken walnuts, toasted (tip, page 102)

1. In a small saucepan, combine cherries and port. Bring to boiling; remove from heat. Let stand for 10 minutes.

2. Meanwhile, in a 12-inch skillet, cook pancetta or bacon over medium heat until crisp. With a slotted spoon, remove pancetta or bacon pieces, reserving *1 tablespoon* drippings in skillet. Add oil to skillet. Add green onions and garlic; cook until onion is tender. Stir in cherry mixture, vinegar, and sugar. Bring just to boiling; reduce heat.

3. Add spinach to skillet, *half* at a time, tossing for 30 to 60 seconds or just until wilted. Add pancetta or bacon and walnuts; toss to combine. Serve immediately. Makes 4 servings.

Nutrition facts per serving: 207 cal., 14 g total fat (3 g sat. fat), 7 mg chol., 163 mg sodium, 14 g carbo., 7 g fiber, 5 g pro.

Cranberry-Walnut Cabbage Slaw

Cranberry-Walnut Cabbage Slaw

Prep: 25 min. Chill: 1 to 6 hr.

When we went looking for favorite slaws and potato salads, we couldn't overlook this garden-fresh entry from a reader in West Virginia.

1 recipe Creamy Honey Mustard Dressing (below)
5 cups coarsely shredded cabbage
⅓ cup chopped walnuts
¼ cup finely chopped celery
¼ cup finely chopped onion
¼ cup finely chopped red sweet pepper
¼ cup dried cranberries

1. Prepare Creamy Honey Mustard Dressing. In a large bowl, combine cabbage, walnuts, celery, onion, sweet pepper, and cranberries.

2. Add dressing to cabbage mixture; toss to coat. Cover and chill for at least 1 hour or up to 6 hours. Makes 8 to 10 servings.

Creamy Honey Mustard Dressing: In a small bowl, combine ¼ cup mayonnaise or salad dressing, 1 tablespoon sweet pickle relish, 1 tablespoon honey mustard, 1 tablespoon honey, ¼ teaspoon ground white or black pepper, ⅛ teaspoon salt, and ⅛ teaspoon celery seeds.

Nutrition facts per serving: 124 cal., 9 g total fat (1 g sat. fat), 4 mg chol., 104 mg sodium, 12 g carbo., 2 g fiber, 2 g pro.

Yesterday

In the 1960s, when cooks wanted an easy salad, a triple-bean combo was a popular solution. It was great tasting and went together in minutes. This version appeared in *Better Homes and Gardens*® magazine in 1968 and still wins the trifecta.

Three-Bean Salad

Prep: 15 min. Chill: 4 to 24 hr.

If you like, substitute about ½ cup of your favorite bottled vinaigrette for the Mustard Vinaigrette.

- 1 **recipe Mustard Vinaigrette (right)**
- 1 **16-oz. can cut wax beans or black beans, rinsed and drained**
- 1 **8-oz. can cut green beans or lima beans, rinsed and drained**
- 1 **8-oz. can red kidney beans, rinsed and drained**
- ½ **cup chopped green sweet pepper**
- ⅓ **cup chopped red onion**

1. Prepare Mustard Vinaigrette. In a large bowl, combine wax beans or black beans, green beans or lima beans, red kidney beans, sweet pepper, and red onion.

2. Pour vinaigrette over vegetables; gently stir. Cover and chill for at least 4 hours or up to 24 hours, stirring often. Makes 6 servings.

Mustard Vinaigrette: In a screw-top jar, combine ¼ cup vinegar, 2 tablespoons sugar, 2 tablespoons salad oil, ½ teaspoon celery seeds, ½ teaspoon dry mustard, and 1 clove garlic, minced. Cover and shake well.

Test Kitchen Tip: The tangy dressing will work with just about any combination of beans. Just make sure you use between 3½ and 4 cups of vegetables.

Nutrition facts per serving: 120 cal., 5 g total fat (1 g sat. fat), 0 mg chol., 419 mg sodium, 17 g carbo., 5 g fiber, 4 g pro.

Today

For the 21st century, we updated three-bean salad. We replaced the wax beans with chickpeas and tossed in some fresh herbs—basil, cilantro, and tarragon.

Mixed Bean Salad with Herbs

Prep: 25 min. Stand: 30 min.

If you like, substitute cider or white vinegar for the red wine vinegar.

- 1 **15-oz. can black beans or red kidney beans, rinsed and drained**
- 1 **15-oz. can chickpeas (garbanzo beans), rinsed and drained**
- 1 **10-oz. pkg. frozen cut green beans, thawed and drained**
- ¼ **cup olive oil**
- ½ **cup chopped onion**
- ½ **cup red sweet pepper cut into strips**
- 2 **Tbsp. snipped fresh basil**
- 2 **Tbsp. snipped fresh cilantro**
- 2 **Tbsp. snipped fresh tarragon or oregano**
- ¼ **cup red wine vinegar**
- 1 **Tbsp. Dijon-style mustard**
- ¼ **tsp. ground black pepper**
- ⅛ **tsp. salt**

1. In a large bowl, combine black beans, chickpeas, and green beans. In a large skillet, heat oil over medium heat. Add onion and sweet pepper; cook about 5 minutes or just until tender. Add to beans. Stir in basil, cilantro, and tarragon.

2. In a small bowl, whisk together vinegar, mustard, black pepper, and salt. Pour over bean mixture; toss gently to coat. Cover and let stand at room temperature for 30 minutes. Makes 8 to 10 servings.

Make-ahead directions: Prepare as directed. Cover and chill salad for up to 24 hours. Let stand at room temperature for 30 minutes before serving.

Nutrition facts per serving: 182 cal., 8 g total fat (1 g sat. fat), 0 mg chol., 370 mg sodium, 24 g carbo., 6 g fiber, 7 g pro.

Lemon-Tarragon Asparagus Salad

1. In a large saucepan, bring a large amount of lightly salted water to boiling. Meanwhile, wash asparagus. Snap off and discard woody bases. Cut spears into 1½-inch pieces. Add to boiling water; return to boiling. Cover; cook 2 minutes. Drain and rinse with cold water.

2. Transfer asparagus to a salad bowl. Add radishes, oil, green onion, tarragon, lemon peel, and salt; toss to combine. Cover and chill for at least 2 hours or up to 3 hours.

3. To serve, stir in almonds and vinegar. Makes 6 to 8 servings.

Nutrition facts per serving: 100 cal., 8 g total fat (1 g sat. fat), 0 mg chol., 112 mg sodium, 6 g carbo., 3 g fiber, 4 g pro.

Fresh Mozzarella Salad

Prep: 15 min. Bake: 20 min. Stand: 30 min.

Fresh mozzarella cheese was a darling of the 1990s. Serve it with roasted peppers and greens, as in this memorable salad from our March 1999 issue.

- 2   **medium red and/or yellow sweet peppers**
- 2   **cups fresh arugula or spinach**
- 8   **oz. smoked fresh mozzarella cheese or fresh mozzarella cheese, thinly sliced**
- ¼   **cup olive oil**
- ¼   **cup balsamic vinegar**
- ¼   **tsp. ground black pepper**
- ⅛   **tsp. salt (optional)**

1. Preheat oven to 425°F. Halve sweet peppers lengthwise; remove stems, seeds, and membranes. Place peppers, cut sides down, on a foil-lined baking sheet. Bake for 20 to 25 minutes or until skins are blistered and dark. Remove from oven; immediately cover tightly with foil. Let stand for 30 minutes to steam.

2. Remove skin from peppers; discard. Cut roasted peppers into 3×1½-inch strips. On four chilled salad plates, arrange arugula or spinach. Loosely overlap sweet pepper strips and mozzarella slices on top. Drizzle with oil and vinegar. Sprinkle with black pepper and, if desired, salt. Makes 6 servings.

Nutrition facts per serving: 211 cal., 17 g total fat (6 g sat. fat), 29 mg chol., 144 mg sodium, 7 g carbo., 1 g fiber, 8 g pro.

Lemon-Tarragon Asparagus Salad

Prep: 20 min. Chill: 2 to 3 hr.

When the new spring crop of asparagus comes in, use some to make this snappy salad.

- 1½   **lb. fresh asparagus spears**
- 1   **cup sliced radishes**
- 2   **Tbsp. olive oil**
- 1   **Tbsp. thinly sliced green onion**
- 2   **tsp. snipped fresh tarragon or ½ tsp. dried tarragon, crushed**
- 1   **tsp. finely shredded lemon peel**
- ¼   **tsp. salt**
- ¼   **cup slivered almonds, toasted (tip, page 102)**
- 2   **Tbsp. white balsamic vinegar or white wine vinegar**

Crunchy Pea and Cashew Salad

Crunchy Pea and Cashew Salad

Prep: 20 min. Chill: 1 to 24 hr.

You still see creamed pea salads on many restaurant salad bars. This 2002 recipe gives the classic a modern look and taste with cauliflower, ranch dressing, and cashews.

1   10-oz. pkg. frozen peas, thawed
1   cup cauliflower florets
1   cup sliced celery
¼   cup sliced green onions
½   cup bottled fat-free ranch salad dressing
¼   cup light dairy sour cream
½   tsp. dried dill weed
    Salt
    Pepper
⅓   cup broken cashews

1. In a large bowl, combine peas, cauliflower, celery, and green onions.

2. In a small bowl, combine ranch dressing, sour cream, and dill weed. Add dressing mixture to vegetable mixture; toss to coat. Season to taste with salt and pepper.

3. Cover and chill in the refrigerator for at least 1 hour or up to 24 hours. To serve, sprinkle with cashews. Makes 8 servings.

Nutrition facts per serving: 93 cal., 4 g total fat (1 g sat. fat), 3 mg chol., 286 mg sodium, 11 g carbo., 2 g fiber, 4 g pro.

According to *Better Homes and Gardens*® folklore, Myrna Johnston, the food editor of the magazine for decades, was the person who coined the phrase "tossed salad."

Italian-Style Pasta Salad

Prep: 25 min. Chill: 4 to 24 hr.

In 1983, our readers sent us their best ideas for picnic salads. This recipe from a California cook won top prize. It's a tasty example of the chilled pasta combos that crop up at picnics everywhere.

4   oz. dried spaghetti or vermicelli
1   6-oz. jar marinated artichoke hearts
1   small zucchini, halved lengthwise and sliced crosswise
1   carrot, sliced
1   cup shredded mozzarella cheese (4 oz.)
2   oz. sliced salami, cut into strips
2   Tbsp. grated Parmesan cheese
2   Tbsp. white wine vinegar
1½   tsp. snipped fresh basil or ½ tsp. dried basil, crushed
1   tsp. snipped fresh oregano or ¼ tsp. dried oregano, crushed
¾   tsp. dry mustard
1   clove garlic, minced

1. Break pasta in half. Cook pasta according to package directions; drain. Rinse with cold water; drain again. Set aside.

2. Drain artichoke hearts, reserving marinade; coarsely chop artichoke hearts. In a large bowl, combine the cooked pasta, the artichokes, zucchini, carrot, mozzarella cheese, salami, and Parmesan cheese.

3. In a screw-top jar, combine the reserved artichoke marinade, the vinegar, basil, oregano, mustard, and garlic. Cover and shake well. Pour dressing over pasta mixture; toss to coat evenly.

4. Cover; chill in the refrigerator for at least 4 hours or up to 24 hours. Makes 8 to 10 servings.

Nutrition facts per serving: 148 cal., 7 g total fat (3 g sat. fat), 15 mg chol., 318 mg sodium, 15 g carbo., 1 g fiber, 8 g pro.

Yesterday

Vinaigrette has reigned supreme with home cooks and classic chefs for more than a century. The versatile vinegar-and-oil dressing has been part of the *Better Homes and Gardens*® recipe collection from the earliest days. In the beginning, however, we called it French dressing instead of vinaigrette.

Fresh Herb Vinaigrette
Start to finish: 10 min.

Mix and match your favorite salad ingredients with any of these five vinaigrette flavor variations.

- ⅓   cup olive oil or salad oil
- ⅓   cup white or red wine vinegar, rice vinegar, or white vinegar
- 1   Tbsp. snipped fresh thyme, oregano, or basil, or ½ tsp. dried thyme, oregano, or basil, crushed
- 1   to 2 tsp. sugar
- 1   clove garlic, minced
- ¼   tsp. dry mustard or 1 tsp. Dijon-style mustard
- ⅛   tsp. pepper

1. In a screw-top jar, combine oil, vinegar, herb, sugar, garlic, mustard, and pepper. Cover and shake well. Makes about ¾ cup.

Make-ahead directions: Prepare as directed. If using fresh herb, cover and store in the refrigerator for up to 3 days. If using dried herbs, cover and store in the refrigerator for up to 1 week. Shake before serving.

Nutrition facts per tablespoon: 57 cal., 6 g total fat (1 g sat. fat), 0 mg chol., 0 mg sodium, 1 g carbo., 0 g fiber, 0 g pro.

Balsamic Vinaigrette: Prepare Fresh Herb Vinaigrette as directed, except use regular or white balsamic vinegar instead of the listed vinegar options.

Nutrition facts per tablespoon: 64 cal., 6 g total fat (1 g sat. fat), 0 mg chol., 1 mg sodium, 2 g carbo., 0 g fiber, 0 g pro.

Orange Balsamic Vinaigrette: Prepare Balsamic Vinaigrette as directed, except add ½ teaspoon finely shredded orange peel and ¼ cup orange juice.

Nutrition facts per tablespoon: 66 cal., 6 g total fat (1 g sat. fat), 0 mg chol., 1 mg sodium, 3 g carbo., 0 g fiber, 0 g pro.

Ginger Vinaigrette: Prepare Fresh Herb Vinaigrette as directed, except use rice vinegar, substitute 2 teaspoons honey for the sugar, and use 1 teaspoon grated fresh ginger instead of the herb. Add 2 teaspoons soy sauce.

Nutrition facts per tablespoon: 60 cal., 6 g total fat (1 g sat. fat), 0 mg chol., 52 mg sodium, 1 g carbo., 0 g fiber, 0 g pro.

Apricot Vinaigrette: Prepare Fresh Herb Vinaigrette as directed, except use white wine vinegar and reduce amount to 2 tablespoons; add ⅓ cup apricot nectar.

Nutrition facts per tablespoon: 59 cal., 6 g total fat (1 g sat. fat), 0 mg chol., 0 mg sodium, 1 g carbo., 0 g fiber, 0 g pro.

Oil-Free Herb Dressing

Prep: 15 min. Chill: 30 min.

Chilling the mixture gives the pectin time to
set up and thicken the dressing.

- 2 **Tbsp. powdered fruit pectin***
- 1½ **tsp. snipped fresh oregano, basil, thyme, tarragon, savory, or dill, or ¼ tsp. dried oregano, basil, thyme, tarragon, savory, or dill weed, crushed**
- 1 **tsp. sugar**
- ¼ **tsp. salt**
- ¼ **tsp. dry mustard**
- ⅛ **tsp. pepper**
- ½ **cup water**
- 2 **Tbsp. vinegar**
- 1 **clove garlic, minced**

1. In a small bowl, stir together pectin, desired herb,
sugar, salt, dry mustard, and pepper. Stir in the water,
vinegar, and garlic. Cover and chill for 30 minutes before
serving. Makes about ¾ cup.

***Test Kitchen Tip:** Look for powdered fruit pectin
with the canning and jelly-making supplies in your
supermarket.

Nutrition facts per tablespoon: 12 cal., 0 g total fat, 0 mg chol.,
49 mg sodium, 3 g carbo., 0 g fiber, 0 g pro.

Oil-Free Creamy Onion Dressing: Prepare as
directed, except increase the sugar to 2 tablespoons. Stir
in ½ cup thinly sliced green onions and ½ cup plain
yogurt with the water, vinegar, and garlic. Makes about
1½ cups.

Nutrition facts per tablespoon: 13 cal., 0 g total fat, 1 mg chol.,
27 mg sodium, 3 g carbo., 0 g fiber, 0 g pro.

Today

During the 1990s, Americans began
to pay more attention to the amount
of fat in their diets. In response to
readers' interest in low-fat recipes,
we developed this fat-free adaptation
of a vinaigrette.

2. In a small bowl, combine bread crumbs, butter, and parsley. Press mixture onto bottom and up side of prepared casserole. Set aside.

3. In a medium bowl, slightly beat egg yolks; stir in the ¼ cup basil, the shredded lemon peel, the lemon juice, salt, and white pepper; stir in milk and *1 cup* of the cheese. Stir milk mixture into mashed potatoes.

4. In a medium mixing bowl, beat egg whites with an electric mixer on medium speed until stiff peaks form (tips stand straight); fold into potato mixture.

5. Transfer to prepared casserole; top with remaining ½ cup cheese. Bake, uncovered, about 45 minutes or until a knife inserted in center comes out clean. If desired, garnish with additional snipped basil and lemon peel strips. Makes 10 servings.

Nutrition facts per serving: 242 cal., 14 g total fat (8 g sat. fat), 99 mg chol., 387 mg sodium, 19 g carbo., 2 g fiber, 10 g pro.

Volcano Potatoes

Prep: 35 min. Bake: 20 min.

In 1953, we took this playful approach to mashed potatoes. It's a volcano-shaped cone of spuds filled with whipped cream and American cheese. Now that's comfort food!

1 ½ **lb. baking potatoes (4 or 5 medium), peeled and quartered**
1 **to 3 Tbsp. milk**
½ **tsp. salt**
⅛ **tsp. pepper**
½ **cup whipping cream**
½ **cup shredded sharp American or American cheese (2 oz.)**
  Snipped fresh chives

1. Preheat oven to 350°F. In covered large saucepan, cook potatoes in a large amount of boiling water for 20 to 25 minutes or until tender; drain. Mash with potato masher or beat with an electric mixer on low speed until smooth. Gradually beat in enough of the milk to make light and fluffy. Beat in salt and pepper.

2. Grease a 9-inch pie plate. Pile potatoes in plate, forming a pyramid 3 inches tall and 5 inches across at the base. (Leave a 1-inch space between potato and edge of plate.) Make a deep hole or crater in the center.

3. In a chilled bowl, whip cream with chilled beaters of an electric mixer until soft peaks form (tips curl); fold in cheese. Spoon into the hole or crater, allowing excess to flow down sides of potatoes. Bake, uncovered, about 20 minutes or until bubbly. Top with chives Serves 5.

Nutrition facts per serving: 211 cal., 13 g total fat (8 g sat. fat), 45 mg chol., 319 mg sodium, 19 g carbo., 2 g fiber, 6 g pro.

Lemon-Basil Potato Puff

Prep: 40 min. Bake: 45 min.

We asked our readers to send us their best-tasting tater tempters in 1998. This herb-laced casserole took top honors in our Hot Potatoes contest.

2 **lb. potatoes, peeled and quartered**
¾ **cup fine dry bread crumbs**
⅓ **cup butter or margarine, melted**
1 **Tbsp. snipped fresh parsley**
3 **egg yolks**
¼ **cup snipped fresh basil or lemon basil**
1 **tsp. finely shredded lemon peel**
1 **tsp. lemon juice**
¾ **tsp. salt**
¼ **tsp. ground white pepper**
1 **cup milk**
1 ½ **cups shredded Swiss cheese (6 oz.)**
3 **egg whites**
  Snipped fresh basil (optional)
  Lemon peel strips (optional)

1. In a covered Dutch oven, cook potatoes in a large amount of boiling water for 20 to 25 minutes or until tender; drain. Mash with potato masher or beat with an electric mixer on low speed until smooth; set aside. Preheat oven to 350°F. Lightly grease a 1½-quart casserole; set aside.

Stuffed Zucchini

Prep: 30 min. Bake: 20 + 5 min.

When this recipe first appeared in 1937, many of our readers were unfamiliar with zucchini, so we explained that it was Italian squash. Now it's an All-American garden crop.

- **6 medium zucchini**
- **1½ cups soft bread crumbs**
- **¼ cup finely shredded cheddar cheese or Parmesan cheese (1 oz.)**
- **¼ cup finely chopped onion**
- **1 Tbsp. snipped fresh parsley**
- **¼ tsp. salt**
- **⅛ tsp. pepper**
- **1 egg, slightly beaten**
- **¼ cup finely shredded cheddar cheese or Parmesan cheese (1 oz.)**

1. Wash zucchini and trim ends; do not peel. In a covered Dutch oven, cook whole zucchini in lightly salted boiling water for 5 minutes; drain and cool slightly. Cut a lengthwise slice off the top of each zucchini. Remove pulp, leaving about a ¼-inch-thick shell; reserve the pulp.

2. Preheat oven to 350°F. Chop enough of the zucchini pulp to measure 2 cups; place chopped pulp in a medium bowl. (Save remaining pulp for another use.) Stir the bread crumbs, ¼ cup cheese, the onion, parsley, salt, pepper, and egg into chopped pulp until well mixed. Fill zucchini shells with pulp mixture.

3. Place stuffed zucchini in a shallow baking pan. Bake for 20 minutes. Sprinkle with ¼ cup cheese; bake for 5 to 10 minutes more or until golden brown and heated through. Makes 6 servings.

Nutrition facts per serving: 93 cal., 4 g total fat (2 g sat. fat), 45 mg chol., 229 mg sodium, 8 g carbo., 1 g fiber, 5 g pro.

Ginger-Glazed Carrots

Start to finish: 15 min.

Looking for a way to dress up buttered carrots? Try these ginger-and-orange slices that won top prize in our Swift Side Dishes contest in October 2000.

- **2½ cups ½-inch-thick crinkle-cut and/or plain sliced carrots**
- **3 Tbsp. ginger preserves or orange marmalade**
- **2 Tbsp. frozen orange juice concentrate, thawed**
- **1 Tbsp. butter or margarine**
- **1 tsp. grated fresh ginger**

1. In a covered medium saucepan, cook carrots in a small amount of lightly salted boiling water for 3 minutes. Drain and set aside.

2. In the same saucepan, combine preserves, orange juice concentrate, butter, and fresh ginger; cook and stir over medium heat until butter is melted. Return carrots to saucepan. Cook, uncovered, over medium heat for 5 to 6 minutes or just until carrots are tender and glazed, stirring occasionally. Makes 4 servings.

Nutrition facts per serving: 108 cal., 3 g total fat (0 g sat. fat), 0 mg chol., 65 mg sodium, 21 g carbo., 3 g fiber, 1 g pro.

Swiss Corn Bake

Prep: 25 min. Bake: 30 min. Stand: 10 min.

We published this simple, yet scrumptious, casserole in 1968 as a tasty alternative to scalloped corn.

- **3½ cups cut fresh corn kernels or one 16-oz. pkg. frozen whole kernel corn**
- **¼ cup finely chopped onion**
- **2 eggs**
- **2 5-oz. cans (1⅓ cups) evaporated milk**
- **½ tsp. garlic salt**
- **¼ tsp. pepper**
- **1 cup shredded process Swiss or Gruyère cheese (4 oz.)**

1. Preheat oven to 350°F. Grease a 2-quart square baking dish; set aside. In a covered medium saucepan, cook fresh corn and onion in a small amount of boiling lightly salted water for 6 minutes. (Or cook frozen corn, with onion, according to package directions.) Drain well.

2. In medium bowl, beat eggs with a fork. Stir in drained corn and onion, evaporated milk, garlic salt, and pepper. Stir in ¾ *cup* of the cheese. Pour into prepared dish.

3. Sprinkle remaining ¼ cup cheese onto corn mixture. Bake, uncovered, for 30 minutes. Let stand for 10 minutes before serving. Makes 6 servings.

Nutrition facts per serving: 247 cal., 11 g total fat (7 g sat. fat), 104 mg chol., 437 mg sodium, 26 g carbo., 2 g fiber, 13 g pro.

Eyeing the Ears When buying corn on the cob, look for ears with a healthy-looking husk. Also, peel back the husk to check the appearance of the kernels. They should be plump and fresh looking.

Broccoli and Peppers with Walnuts

Broccoli and Peppers With Walnuts

Start to finish: 25 min.

Although stir-fries usually are main dishes, these Asian-style veggies go well with grilled fish.

- ¼ cup chicken broth
- 2 Tbsp. bottled oyster sauce
- 1 tsp. finely shredded lemon peel
- ⅛ tsp. cayenne pepper
- 4 tsp. cooking oil
- ½ cup coarsely chopped walnuts
- 1 clove garlic, minced
- 1 lb. broccoli florets, cut into 1-inch pieces
- 1 medium red sweet pepper, cut into bite-size strips

1. For sauce, in a small bowl, combine broth, oyster sauce, lemon peel, and cayenne pepper; set aside.

2. In a large nonstick skillet, heat *2 teaspoons* of the oil over medium heat; add walnuts and garlic. Cook and stir for 2 to 3 minutes or until nuts are lightly toasted; transfer to a small bowl. Set aside.

3. Heat remaining 2 teaspoons oil in the same skillet over medium-high heat; add broccoli and sweet pepper. Stir-fry for 2 to 3 minutes or until crisp-tender.

4. Stir sauce mixture; add to skillet. Cook and stir for 1 minute more. Transfer to a serving bowl. Sprinkle with walnut mixture. Makes 6 servings.

Nutrition facts per serving: 124 cal., 10 g total fat (1 g sat. fat), 0 mg chol., 199 mg sodium, 7 g carbo., 3 g fiber, 4 g pro.

Fried Green Tomatoes

Prep: 25 min. Cook: 8 min. per batch

Compared to other produce, tomatoes are a relative culinary newcomer. It wasn't until the early 1900s that Americans took to them. These fried slices started out as a way to use up the autumn stragglers.

- 3 medium firm green tomatoes
- ½ tsp. salt
- ¼ tsp. pepper
- ½ cup all-purpose flour
- ¼ cup milk
- 2 eggs, beaten
- ⅔ cup fine dry bread crumbs or cornmeal
- ¼ cup cooking oil
  Salt (optional)
  Pepper (optional)

1. Remove stem ends from tomatoes. Cut unpeeled tomatoes into ½-inch-thick slices; sprinkle slices with the ½ teaspoon salt and ¼ teaspoon pepper. Let tomato slices stand for 15 minutes. Meanwhile, place flour, milk, eggs, and bread crumbs in separate shallow dishes.

2. Dip tomato slices into milk; coat with flour. Dip into eggs; coat with bread crumbs. In a large skillet, heat oil over medium heat. Add tomato slices, *half* at a time; cook for 8 to 12 minutes or until browned, turning once. (If tomatoes begin to brown too quickly, reduce heat to medium-low. If necessary, add additional oil.) If desired, season to taste with additional salt and pepper. Makes 6 servings.

Nutrition facts per serving: 194 cal., 12 g total fat (2 g sat. fat), 72 mg chol., 465 mg sodium, 18 g carbo., 1 g fiber, 5 g pro.

Skillet Okra and Vegetables

Start to finish: 30 min.

This tomato, okra, and corn skillet is Southern-style cooking at its best. The crumbled bacon on top gives it a rich smoky flavor.

- ¾ cup chopped green sweet pepper
- ½ cup chopped onion
- 2 cloves garlic, minced
- 2 Tbsp. butter or margarine
- 2 large tomatoes, peeled and chopped (2½ cups)
- 8 oz. whole fresh okra, cut into ½-inch-thick pieces (2 cups)
- 1 cup cut fresh corn kernels or frozen whole kernel corn
- ¼ tsp. salt
- ⅛ tsp. paprika
- ⅛ tsp. cayenne pepper
- 3 slices bacon, crisp-cooked, drained, and crumbled

1. In a large skillet, cook sweet pepper, onion, and garlic in hot butter until onion is tender. Stir in the tomatoes, okra, corn, salt, paprika, and cayenne pepper. Cover and cook over medium-low heat about 20 minutes or until okra is tender. Sprinkle with crumbled bacon. Makes 4 servings.

Nutrition facts per serving: 165 cal., 9 g total fat (4 g sat. fat), 19 mg chol., 306 mg sodium, 20 g carbo., 5 g fiber, 5 g pro.

Yesterday

The combination of green beans and cream of mushroom soup topped with French-fried onions has been a treasured serve-along at family gatherings for decades. Our version gives the old standby a slight twist by including soup options and adding wax beans.

Home-Style Green Bean Bake (recipe, page 190)

Green Bean and Sweet Onion Gratin (recipe, page

Today

In 2001, one of our readers contributed this recipe, saying it was her attempt to update the popular green bean-and-mushroom casserole. We thought she'd accomplished her mission deliciously.

Yesterday

Home-Style Green Bean Bake

Prep: 15 min. Bake: 35 + 5 min.

Although the original version of this side dish used French-cut green beans, any cut works well. (Photo on page 188.)

1	10¾-oz. can condensed cream of celery soup or cream of mushroom soup
½	cup shredded cheddar cheese or American cheese (2 oz.)
1	2-oz. jar diced pimiento, drained (optional)
2	9-oz. pkg. frozen cut green beans, thawed and drained, or two 16-oz. cans cut green beans, drained
1	16-oz. can cut wax beans, drained
½	of a 2.8-oz. can (¾ cup) french-fried onions

1. Preheat oven to 350°F. In a large bowl, combine soup, cheese, and, if desired, pimiento. Stir in green beans and wax beans. Transfer to an ungreased 1½-quart casserole. Bake for 35 minutes.

2. Remove from oven; stir. Sprinkle with onions. Bake about 5 minutes more or until heated through. Serves 6.

Nutrition facts per serving: 155 cal., 8 g total fat (3 g sat. fat), 15 mg chol., 686 mg sodium, 14 g carbo., 3 g fiber, 5 g pro.

Today

Green Bean and Sweet Onion Gratin

Prep: 20 min. Bake: 30 min. Stand: 10 min.

Vidalia, Maui, and Walla Walla are three of the most popular varieties of super sweet onions. Look for sweet onions from late spring to early autumn. (Photo on page 189.)

1	16-oz. pkg. frozen cut green beans
1	lb. sweet onions (such as Vidalia, Maui, or Walla Walla), halved and thinly sliced
¼	cup butter or margarine
¼	cup all-purpose flour
½	tsp. salt
¼	tsp. pepper
⅛	tsp. ground nutmeg
1	cup chicken broth
1	cup half-and-half, light cream, or milk
1½	cups soft bread crumbs (2 slices)
3	Tbsp. grated Parmesan cheese
2	Tbsp. olive oil
	Fresh thyme sprigs (optional)

1. Preheat oven to 325°F. Cook frozen green beans according to package directions; drain well and set aside.

2. Meanwhile, in a covered medium saucepan, cook onion slices in a small amount of boiling water for 4 to 5 minutes or until tender. Drain in a colander; set aside.

3. For sauce, in the same saucepan, melt butter. Stir in flour, salt, pepper, and nutmeg. Add broth and half-and-half. Cook and stir until mixture is thickened and bubbly.

4. In an ungreased 2-quart baking dish, layer *half* of the beans, all of the onions, and the remaining beans. Spoon sauce over all.

5. In a medium bowl, toss together bread crumbs, Parmesan cheese, and oil; sprinkle over vegetables. Bake, uncovered, for 30 to 35 minutes or until bubbly. Let stand for 10 minutes before serving. If desired, garnish with fresh thyme sprigs. Makes 6 servings.

Make-ahead directions: Prepare as directed, except do not top with the bread crumb mixture. Cover baking dish; chill for up to 24 hours. Store bread crumb mixture separately; chill. To serve, preheat oven to 325°F. Sprinkle casserole with bread crumb mixture. Bake, uncovered, for 50 to 55 minutes or until heated through.

Nutrition facts per serving: 278 cal., 19 g total fat (9 g sat. fat), 39 mg chol., 575 mg sodium, 23 g carbo., 4 g fiber, 6 g pro.

East-West Veggies

Start to finish: 20 min.

This Canned and Frozen Vegetable Ideas prizewinner takes the Tex-Mex duo of corn and beans and combines it with an Asian-inspired sauce.

1	Tbsp. butter or margarine
1	Tbsp. olive oil
1	medium onion, cut into thin wedges
6	green onions, cut into 1-inch pieces
3	Tbsp. bottled hoisin sauce
1	tsp. paprika
1	15¼-oz. can whole kernel corn, drained
1	15-oz. can black beans, rinsed and drained
¾	cup thinly sliced celery
½	cup chopped red sweet pepper

1. In a large skillet, heat butter and oil over medium heat. Add onion wedges; cook and stir about 4 minutes or until tender. Stir in green onions, hoisin sauce, and paprika. Cook and stir for 1 minute more.

2. Add corn, beans, celery, and sweet pepper. Cook and stir until heated through. Makes 6 servings.

Nutrition facts per serving: 166 cal., 5 g total fat (2 g sat. fat), 5 mg chol., 574 mg sodium, 28 g carbo., 5 g fiber, 6 g pro.

Risotto Primavera

Prep: 25 min. Cook: 25 min. Stand: 5 min.

Classic risotto takes time and patience, so we looked for a way to make it easier. Our result was this no-stir method.

¼   cup thinly sliced celery
¼   cup thinly sliced shallots or green onions
2   cloves garlic, minced
⅛   tsp. pepper
1   Tbsp. butter or margarine
1   cup arborio or long grain rice
1   14-oz. can reduced-sodium chicken broth
1¾ cups water
½   cup loose-pack frozen peas
½   cup coarsely chopped yellow summer squash and/or zucchini
½   tsp. finely shredded lemon peel
2   Tbsp. grated Parmesan cheese
1   tsp. snipped fresh dill or ¼ tsp. dried dill weed, crushed (optional)
     Fresh dill sprigs (optional)

1. In a 3-quart saucepan, cook celery, shallots or green onions, garlic, and pepper in hot butter until tender. Add uncooked rice. Cook and stir for 2 minutes more.

2. Carefully stir in broth and the water. Bring to boiling; reduce heat. Cover and simmer for 25 minutes. (Do not lift cover.) Remove from heat.

3. Stir in peas, squash, and lemon peel. Cover and let stand for 5 minutes. Stir in cheese and, if desired, snipped or dried dill. If desired, garnish with fresh dill sprigs. Serve immediately. Makes 6 servings.

Traditional method: Cook celery mixture as directed. Add uncooked rice. Cook and stir for 2 minutes more. In a medium saucepan, bring broth and the water to boiling. Add broth mixture, ¾ *cup* at a time, to rice mixture, stirring constantly until rice is almost tender but still firm to the bite. (It should have a creamy consistency.) This should take about 20 minutes. During cooking, adjust the heat as necessary to keep the broth at a gentle simmer. Stir in peas, squash, and lemon peel. Remove from heat. Cover and let stand for 5 minutes. Stir in Parmesan and, if desired, snipped or dried dill. If desired, garnish with fresh dill sprigs. Serve immediately.

Nutrition facts per serving: 123 cal., 3 g total fat (2 g sat. fat), 7 mg chol., 243 mg sodium, 22 g carbo., 1 g fiber, 4 g pro.

Risotto Primavera

Homebaked Breads

The alluring aroma of freshly baked bread inevitably conjures up a feeling of coziness. Whether you're making hearty loaves of yeast bread, delicately sweet nut breads, buttery rich coffee cakes, flaky biscuits, or fluffy pancakes, taking the time to bake bread for your family shows how much you care. This chapter is filled with dozens of scrumptious old-fashioned, bread machine, and quick bread ideas to help you rise to the occasion.

Homebaked Breads

215

212

200

209

203

205

Cinnamon Swirl Bread

Two-Way Egg Bread
Prep: 30 min. Rise: 1 hr. + 30 min. Bake: 25 min.

Basic yeast breads have been in our *Better Homes and Gardens*® bread basket since the 1920s. Back then, fresh cake yeast was the common form used. This modern cousin of a 1930 recipe uses the more convenient package of active dry yeast.

4¾ to 5¼ cups all-purpose flour
  1 pkg. active dry yeast
1⅓ cups milk
  3 Tbsp. sugar
  3 Tbsp. butter
  ¾ tsp. salt
  2 eggs

1. In a large mixing bowl, stir together *2 cups* of the flour and the yeast; set aside. In a medium saucepan, heat and stir milk, sugar, butter, and salt just until warm (120°F to 130°F) and butter almost melts.

2. Add milk mixture to flour mixture along with eggs. Beat with an electric mixer on low to medium speed for 30 seconds, scraping side of bowl constantly. Beat on high speed for 3 minutes. Using a wooden spoon, stir in as much of the remaining flour as you can.

3. Turn out dough onto a lightly floured surface. Knead in enough of the remaining flour to make a moderately stiff dough that is smooth and elastic (6 to 8 minutes total). Shape dough into a ball. Place in a lightly greased bowl, turning once to grease surface. Cover; let rise in a warm place until double in size (about 1 hour).

4. Punch down dough. Turn out dough onto a lightly floured surface. Divide dough in half. Cover; let rest for 10 minutes. Meanwhile, lightly grease two 8×4×2-inch loaf pans. Shape each half of the dough into a loaf by patting or rolling. Place shaped dough in prepared pans. Cover and let rise in a warm place until nearly double in size (about 30 minutes).

5. Preheat oven to 375°F. Bake for 25 to 30 minutes or until bread sounds hollow when lightly tapped. If necessary to prevent overbrowning, cover loosely with foil for last 10 minutes of baking. Immediately remove bread from pans. Cool on wire racks. Makes 2 loaves (28 servings).

Nutrition facts per serving: 99 cal., 2 g total fat (1 g sat. fat), 20 mg chol., 86 mg sodium, 17 g carbo., 1 g fiber, 3 g pro.

Cinnamon Swirl Bread: Prepare Two-Way Egg Bread as directed, except instead of shaping into loaves, on a lightly floured surface, roll each half of dough into a 12×7-inch rectangle. Brush lightly with water. In a small bowl, combine ½ cup granulated sugar and 2 teaspoons ground cinnamon; sprinkle *half* of the sugar-cinnamon mixture over *each* rectangle. Starting from a short side, roll up into a spiral. Pinch seam to seal. Place, seam sides down, in prepared pans. Rise and bake as directed. If desired, for icing, combine 1 cup sifted powdered sugar, 1 tablespoon milk, and ¼ teaspoon vanilla; stir in additional milk, 1 teaspoon at a time, until drizzling consistency. Drizzle over warm loaves. Cool.

Nutrition facts per serving (without icing): 119 cal., 2 g total fat (1 g sat. fat), 20 mg chol., 86 mg sodium, 22 g carbo., 1 g fiber, 3 g pro.

Bread Machine Egg Bread

Prep: 10 min. Bake: per bread machine directions

When bread machines came along, everyone wanted to try the new devices. Once our readers had these appliances, they asked us for new ideas, and we were glad to oblige with such wonders as this golden loaf.

- ¾ cup milk
- 1 egg
- ¼ cup water
- 2 Tbsp. butter, cut up
- 3 cups bread flour
- 2 Tbsp. sugar
- ¾ tsp. salt
- 1 tsp. active dry yeast or bread machine yeast

1. Add all the ingredients to a bread machine according to the manufacturer's directions. Select the basic white bread cycle. Remove hot bread from machine as soon as it is done. Cool on a wire rack. Makes one 1½-pound loaf (20 servings).

Test Kitchen Tip: For this bread, the bread machine pan must have a capacity of 10 cups or more.

Nutrition facts per serving: 98 cal., 2 g total fat (1 g sat. fat), 11 mg chol., 102 mg sodium, 17 g carbo., 1 g fiber, 3 g pro.

Try It in Your Machine

Want to make your grandma's favorite yeast bread in your bread machine? Just follow these tips for converting the recipe.

• For a 1½-pound loaf, reduce the flour to 3 cups. Reduce all ingredients by the same proportion, including the yeast (1 package equals 2¼ teaspoons). For example, for a 1½-pound loaf, cut 4½ cups flour and 1 package yeast to 3 cups flour and 1½ teaspoons yeast.

• To use more than one type of flour, total the flour amounts and use that total as the basis for reducing the recipe.

• Use bread flour instead of all-purpose flour. (Rye bread also needs 1 tablespoon of gluten flour—available at health food stores and larger supermarkets.)

• Make sure the liquid ingredients are at room temperature before starting.

• Add ingredients in the order specified by your bread machine manufacturer.

• Do not use light-colored dried fruits, such as apricots or light raisins. The preservative in them inhibits yeast.

• For breads containing whole wheat or rye flour, use the whole grain cycle. For sweet breads, use the light-color setting.

• The first time you try a recipe, check after 3 to 5 minutes of kneading. If your machine is working too hard, the dough looks crumbly, or two or more balls of dough form, add 1 to 2 tablespoons of liquid. If the dough looks too soft and doesn't form a ball, add flour, a tablespoon at a time, until a ball forms.

Honey-Oatmeal Bread

Prep: 30 min. Rise: 45 + 35 min. Bake: 35 min.

Some think that the interest in whole grain breads was revived with the hearty loaves of the 1970s or the artisan breads of the 1990s, but in truth, these loaves never went out of fashion, as this 1959 recipe attests.

4¾ to 5¼ cups whole wheat flour
  3 pkg. active dry yeast
  2 cups milk
  ⅓ cup honey
  ¼ cup cooking oil
  2 tsp. salt
  ½ cup quick-cooking rolled oats
     Quick-cooking rolled oats
  1 egg white
  1 Tbsp. water

1. In a large mixing bowl, combine *2 cups* of the flour and the yeast. In a saucepan, heat milk, honey, oil, and salt just until warm (120°F to 130°F). Add to flour mixture. Beat with an electric mixer on low speed for 30 seconds, scraping side of bowl constantly. Beat on high speed for 3 minutes. Using a wooden spoon, stir in the ½ cup oats and as much of the remaining flour as you can.

2. Turn out onto a lightly floured surface. Knead in enough of the remaining flour to make a moderately stiff dough that is smooth and elastic (6 to 8 minutes total). Shape into a ball. Place in a lightly greased bowl, turning once to grease surface. Cover; let rise in a warm place until double in size (45 to 60 minutes).

3. Punch down dough. Turn out onto a lightly floured surface. Divide dough in half. Cover; let rest for 10 minutes.

4. Meanwhile, generously grease two 8×4×2-inch loaf pans. Sprinkle *each* pan with an *additional 2 tablespoons* rolled oats. Shape each half of the dough into a loaf. Place in prepared pans. Cover; let rise in a warm place until double in size (35 to 45 minutes).

5. Preheat oven to 375°F. Using a fork, in a small bowl, beat together egg white and the water; brush onto loaves. Sprinkle loaves lightly with rolled oats.

6. Bake for 35 to 40 minutes or until bread sounds hollow when lightly tapped. If necessary to prevent overbrowning, cover loosely with foil for the last 15 minutes of baking. Immediately remove from pans. Cool on wire racks. Makes 2 loaves (24 servings).

Nutrition facts per serving: 135 cal., 3 g total fat (1 g sat. fat), 2 mg chol., 208 mg sodium, 24 g carbo., 3 g fiber, 5 g pro.

Swedish Rye Bread

Prep: 30 min. Rise: 1¼ hr. + 40 min. Bake: 35 min.

A reader from Iowa sent us her grandmother's recipe for this molasses-sweetened loaf.

  1 pkg. active dry yeast
  ¼ cup warm water (105°F to 115°F)
  ½ cup butter, cut up
  ⅓ cup sugar
  ¼ cup light-flavored molasses
  2 tsp. salt
  2 cups boiling water
  2 cups rye flour
4¾ to 5½ cups all-purpose flour
     Butter, softened

1. In a small bowl, dissolve yeast in the warm water. Set aside.

2. Meanwhile, in a large mixing bowl, combine the ½ cup butter, the sugar, molasses, and salt. Add the boiling water; stir until butter is melted. Add rye flour. Beat with an electric mixer on low speed until combined; beat on medium speed for 3 minutes. Gradually beat in yeast mixture. Using a wooden spoon, stir in as much of the all-purpose flour as you can.

3. Turn out dough onto a lightly floured surface. Knead in enough of the remaining all-purpose flour to make a moderately stiff dough that is smooth and elastic (6 to 8 minutes total). Shape dough into a ball. Place in a greased bowl, turning dough once to grease surface. Cover; let rise in a warm place until double in size (1¼ to 1½ hours).

4. Grease two 8×4×2-inch or 9×5×3-inch loaf pans; set aside. Punch down dough. Turn out dough onto a lightly floured surface. Divide dough in half. Cover; let rest for 10 minutes. Shape each half of the dough into a loaf. Place in prepared pans. Cover and let rise in a warm place until nearly double in size (40 to 50 minutes).

5. Preheat oven to 350°F. Bake for 35 to 45 minutes or until bread sounds hollow when lightly tapped. Remove from pans. Brush tops of warm loaves with a little softened butter. Cool on wire racks. Makes 2 loaves (24 servings).

Nutrition facts per serving: 171 cal., 5 g total fat (3 g sat. fat), 11 mg chol., 230 mg sodium, 29 g carbo., 2 g fiber, 3 g pro.

Sunflower Seed Bread

Prep: 30 min. Rise: 1¼ hr. + 30 min. Bake: 40 min.

Homemade loaves made from unbleached or whole wheat flour and laced with wheat germ, nuts, or seeds were hip in the 1970s. Keeping up with the times, we published recipe after recipe for hearty loaves like this. Decades later, the sweet citrus-flecked slices are still terrific.

3¼ **to 3¾ cups all-purpose flour**
  1 **pkg. active dry yeast**
  ½ **cup milk**
  3 **Tbsp. sugar**
  2 **Tbsp. butter**
  ½ **tsp. salt**
  1 **egg**
  1 **tsp. finely shredded orange peel (set aside)**
  ½ **cup orange juice**
  ⅔ **cup shelled sunflower seeds**
     Melted butter (optional)
     Honey (optional)

1. In a large mixing bowl, combine *1½ cups* of the flour and the yeast. In a small saucepan, heat and stir milk, sugar, the 2 tablespoons butter, and the salt just until warm (120°F to 130°F) and butter almost melts.

2. Add butter mixture to flour mixture; add egg and orange juice. Beat with an electric mixer on low speed for 30 seconds, scraping side of bowl constantly. Beat on high speed for 3 minutes. Using a wooden spoon, stir in orange peel, sunflower seeds, and as much of the remaining flour as you can.

3. Turn out dough onto a lightly floured surface. Knead in enough of the remaining flour to make a moderately stiff dough that is smooth and elastic (6 to 8 minutes total). Shape into a ball. Place in a lightly greased bowl, turning once to grease surface. Cover; let rise in a warm place until double in size (1¼ to 1½ hours).

4. Punch down dough. Cover; let rest for 10 minutes. Meanwhile, grease an 8×4×2-inch loaf pan. Shape dough into loaf; place in prepared pan. Cover; let rise in a warm place until double in size (30 to 45 minutes). If desired, brush top with melted butter.

5. Preheat oven to 375°F. Bake about 40 minutes or until bread sounds hollow when lightly tapped. If necessary to prevent overbrowning, cover loosely with foil for the last 15 minutes of baking. Immediately remove from pan. Cool on wire rack. If desired, serve with honey. Makes 1 loaf (16 servings).

Nutrition facts per serving: 155 cal., 5 g total fat (1 g sat. fat), 18 mg chol., 97 mg sodium, 23 g carbo., 1 g fiber, 5 g pro.

Potato Bread with Sour Cream and Chives

Prep: 30 min. Rise: 45 + 30 min. Bake: 20 min.

No need to peel, boil, and mash potatoes for this easy loaf. The captivating flavor of this light-textured bread comes from cream of potato soup, sour cream, chives, and a hint of herb.

- 6¼ to 6¾ cups all-purpose flour
- 2 pkg. active dry yeast
- 1½ cups milk
- 2 Tbsp. sugar
- 2 Tbsp. butter
- 2 tsp. salt
- 1 10¾-oz. can condensed cream of potato soup
- ½ cup dairy sour cream
- ¼ cup snipped fresh chives
- 1 tsp. dried tarragon, crushed, or 1 tsp. dried dill weed

1. In a large mixing bowl, combine *2½ cups* of the flour and the yeast. In a medium saucepan, heat and stir milk, sugar, butter, and salt just until warm (120°F to 130°F) and butter almost melts. Add milk mixture to flour mixture along with condensed soup, sour cream, chives, and tarragon or dill weed. Beat with an electric mixer on low speed for 30 seconds, scraping side of bowl constantly. Beat on high speed for 3 minutes. Using a wooden spoon, stir in as much of the remaining flour as you can.

2. Turn out dough onto a lightly floured surface. Knead in enough of the remaining flour to make a moderately stiff dough that is smooth and elastic (6 to 8 minutes total). Shape dough into a ball. Place in a lightly greased bowl, turning once to grease surface. Cover; let rise in a warm place until double in size (45 to 60 minutes).

3. Punch down dough. Divide dough in half. Cover; let rest 10 minutes. Meanwhile, lightly grease two 9×5×3-inch loaf pans. Shape each half of the dough into a loaf. Place in prepared pans. Cover; let rise in a warm place until nearly double in size (30 to 40 minutes).

4. Preheat oven to 400°F. Bake for 20 to 25 minutes or until bread sounds hollow when lightly tapped. Immediately remove bread from pans. Cool on wire racks. Makes 2 loaves (24 servings).

Nutrition facts per serving: 150 cal., 3 g total fat (2 g sat. fat), 7 mg chol., 309 mg sodium, 26 g carbo., 1 g fiber, 4 g pro.

Favorite Cheese Bread

Prep: 10 min. Bake: per bread machine directions

Ranch salad dressing mix and cheddar cheese make this bread machine loaf a natural for sandwiches.

- 1 cup water
- 3 cups white bread flour
- 1 Tbsp. sugar
- 1 tsp. salt
- 1 Tbsp. buttermilk powder
- ¼ cup dairy sour cream
- ½ cup shredded cheddar cheese
- 1 Tbsp. dried chives
- 1 Tbsp. dry ranch salad dressing mix
- 1 tsp. active dry yeast or bread machine yeast

1. Add all ingredients to bread machine according to manufacturer's directions. Select basic white bread cycle. Remove bread from machine as soon as it is done. Cool on a wire rack. Makes one 1½-pound loaf (16 servings).

Test Kitchen Tip: For this bread, the bread machine pan must have a capacity of 10 cups or more.

Nutrition facts per serving: 120 cal., 2 g total fat (1 g sat. fat), 5 mg chol., 208 mg sodium, 20 g carbo., 1 g fiber, 4 g pro.

Butter Them Up! It's hard to beat homemade bread slathered with flavored butter. Chill to blend the flavors.

Nut Butter: Combine ½ cup finely chopped almonds or walnuts; ¼ cup butter, softened; and ¼ cup apricot or peach preserves. Makes 1 cup.

Citrus Butter: Combine ½ cup butter, softened; 1 tablespoon powdered sugar; and 1 teaspoon finely shredded orange peel or lemon peel. Makes ½ cup.

Herb Butter: Combine ½ cup butter, softened, and 1½ teaspoons *each* snipped fresh thyme and marjoram or 1 tablespoon snipped fresh basil. Makes ½ cup.

Sage-Olive Baguettes

Prep: 30 min. Rise: 45 + 35 min. Bake: 20 + 10 min.

Although it's hard to improve on classic French bread, we thought we'd give the crusty baguette an artisan spin by dressing it up with fresh sage and kalamata olives.

3½   **to 4 cups bread flour**
     or unbleached all-purpose flour
1   **pkg. active dry yeast**
½   **tsp. salt**
1¼   **cups warm water (120°F to 130°F)**
½   **cup coarsely chopped pitted**
     kalamata olives
2   **to 3 Tbsp. snipped fresh sage**
     or 2 to 3 tsp. dried sage, crushed
     Cornmeal
1   **egg white**
1   **Tbsp. water**

1. In a large mixing bowl, stir together *1 cup* of the flour, the yeast, and salt; add the 1¼ cups warm water. Beat with an electric mixer on low speed for 30 seconds, scraping side of bowl constantly. Beat on high speed for 3 minutes. Stir in olives and sage. Using a wooden spoon, stir in as much of the remaining flour as you can.

2. Turn out dough onto a lightly floured surface. Knead in enough of the remaining flour to make a stiff dough that is smooth and elastic (8 to 10 minutes total). Shape dough into a ball; place in a lightly greased bowl, turning once to grease surface. Cover; let rise in a warm place until double in size (45 minutes to 1 hour).

3. Punch down dough; turn out onto a lightly floured surface. Divide dough in half. Shape into balls. Cover; let rest for 10 minutes.

4. Meanwhile, lightly grease 1 large baking sheet or 2 baguette pans; sprinkle with cornmeal. Roll each portion of dough into a 14×5-inch rectangle. Starting from a long side, roll up into a spiral; seal seam. Pinch ends and pull slightly to taper. Place, seam sides down, on prepared baking sheet or in baguette pans.

5. In a small bowl, stir together egg white and the 1 tablespoon water; brush some onto loaves. Cover; let rise until nearly double in size (35 to 45 minutes). With a sharp knife, make 3 or 4 diagonal cuts about ¼ inch deep across top of each loaf.

6. Preheat oven to 375°F. Bake for 20 minutes. Brush again with egg white mixture. Bake for 10 to 15 minutes more or until bread sounds hollow when lightly tapped. Immediately remove the bread from baking sheet or pans. Cool on wire racks. Makes 2 baguettes (14 servings).

Nutrition facts per serving: 132 cal., 1 g total fat (0 g sat. fat), 0 mg chol., 103 mg sodium, 25 g carbo., 1 g fiber, 5 g pro.

Sage-Olive Baguettes

Sourdough Bread

Prep: 30 min. Stand: 30 min.
Rise: 45 + 30 min. Bake: 30 min.

It's hard to resist the tart flavor and tuggy texture that old-fashioned sourdough starter adds.

- 1 cup Sourdough Starter (right)
- 5½ to 6 cups all-purpose flour
- 1 pkg. active dry yeast
- 1½ cups water
- 3 Tbsp. sugar
- 3 Tbsp. butter
- 1½ tsp. salt
- ½ tsp. baking soda

1. Measure Sourdough Starter; let stand at room temperature for 30 minutes. In a large mixing bowl, combine 2½ cups of the flour and the yeast; set aside. Heat and stir the water, sugar, butter, and salt just until warm (120°F to 130°F) and butter almost melts. Add water mixture to flour mixture. Add Sourdough Starter. Beat with an electric mixer on low to medium speed for 30 seconds, scraping side of bowl constantly. Beat on high speed for 3 minutes.

2. Combine 2½ cups of the remaining flour and the baking soda; add to yeast mixture. Using a wooden spoon, stir until combined. Stir in as much of the remaining flour as you can.

3. Turn out dough onto a lightly floured surface. Knead in enough of the remaining flour to make a moderately stiff dough that is smooth and elastic (6 to 8 minutes total). Shape dough into a ball. Place in a lightly greased bowl, turning once to grease surface. Cover; let rise in a warm place until double in size (45 to 60 minutes).

4. Punch down dough. Turn out dough onto a lightly floured surface. Divide dough in half. Cover; let rest for 10 minutes. Meanwhile, lightly grease 2 baking sheets.

5. Shape dough by gently pulling each portion into a ball, tucking edges under. Place on prepared baking sheets. Flatten each dough ball slightly to about 6 inches in diameter. Using a sharp knife, make crisscross slashes across tops of loaves. Cover and let rise in a warm place until nearly double in size (about 30 minutes).

6. Preheat oven to 375°F. Bake for 30 to 35 minutes or until bread sounds hollow when lightly tapped. If necessary to prevent overbrowning, cover loosely with foil for the last 10 minutes of baking. Immediately remove bread from baking sheets. Cool on wire racks. Makes 2 loaves (24 servings).

Nutrition facts per serving: 131 cal., 2 g total fat (1 g sat. fat), 4 mg chol., 133 mg sodium, 25 g carbo., 1 g fiber, 3 g pro.

Sourdough Starter

Prep: 10 min. Stand: 5 to 10 days

Old-time bread bakers valued their starters so much, they gave them names and hoarded them as prized possessions.

- 1 pkg. active dry yeast
- 2½ cups warm water (105°F to 115°F)
- 2 cups all-purpose flour
- 1 Tbsp. sugar or honey

1. In a large bowl, dissolve yeast in ½ cup of the warm water. Stir in the remaining warm water, the flour, and sugar or honey. Using a wooden spoon, beat until smooth. Cover bowl with 100%-cotton cheesecloth*. Let stand at room temperature (75°F to 85°F) for 5 to 10 days or until mixture has a fermented aroma and vigorous bubbling stops, stirring two or three times a day. (Fermentation time depends on room temperature; a warmer room will hasten the fermentation process.)

2. To store, transfer Sourdough Starter to a 1-quart plastic container. Cover and chill.

3. *To use,* stir starter. Measure desired amount of cold starter; bring to room temperature. Replenish starter after each use by stirring ¾ cup all-purpose flour, ¾ cup water, and 1 teaspoon sugar or honey into remaining starter *for each 1 cup removed.* Cover with cheesecloth*; let stand at room temperature for 1 day or until bubbly. Cover with lid; chill for later use.

4. *If starter is not used within 10 days,* stir in 1 teaspoon sugar or honey. Continue to add an additional 1 teaspoon sugar or honey every 10 days unless starter is replenished. Makes about 2½ cups.

*Test Kitchen Tip: Do not tightly cover the starter when it stands at room temperature.

> **Sourdough bread is a part of America's culinary tradition. Using a version of sourdough starter has been a fact of life for bread bakers from the Colonists and pioneers to chuckwagon cooks and gold rush miners to today's hobby bakers.**

Granary Bread

Prep: 15 min. Bake: per bread machine directions

The chewy texture of this multigrain bread machine loaf makes it just right for club sandwiches or BLTs.

- ¼ cup cracked wheat
- 2 Tbsp. millet
- 1 cup boiling water
- 1¼ cups water
- 2 Tbsp. molasses or honey
- 2 tsp. shortening
- 2 cups whole wheat flour
- 1 cup bread flour
- ¼ cup rolled oats
- 3 Tbsp. cornmeal
- 2 Tbsp. toasted wheat germ or unprocessed wheat bran
- 1 Tbsp. gluten flour*
- ¾ tsp. salt
- 1 tsp. active dry yeast or bread machine yeast

1. In a small bowl, combine the cracked wheat and millet. Add the 1 cup boiling water. Let stand for 5 minutes; drain well.

2. Add all the ingredients to bread machine according to the manufacturer's directions, adding the cracked wheat mixture with the 1¼ cups water. If available, select the whole grain cycle, or select the basic white bread cycle. Remove hot bread from machine as soon as it is done. Cool on a wire rack. Makes one 1½-pound loaf (16 servings).

*Test Kitchen Tip: Look for gluten flour at health food stores or larger supermarkets.

Nutrition facts per serving: 124 cal., 1 g total fat (0 g sat. fat), 0 mg chol., 112 mg sodium, 25 g carbo., 3 g fiber, 4 g pro.

> In the old days, the granary was where grains were stored once they had been threshed. Home bakers often went there to get the grains they needed to make bread. Because the loaf above uses so many different grains, we called it Granary Bread.

Dill Bread

Prep: 40 min. Rise: 1 hr. + 30 min. Bake: 35 min.

The cottage cheese in this casserole bread from a 1973 issue makes it moist and tender.

- 1 pkg. active dry yeast
- ¼ cup warm water (105°F to 115°F)
- 1 Tbsp. sugar
- 1 cup cream-style cottage cheese
- 1 Tbsp. sugar
- 1 Tbsp. dried minced onion
- 1 Tbsp. butter
- 2 tsp. dill seeds
- 1 tsp. salt
- ¼ tsp. baking soda
- 1 egg, slightly beaten
- 2¼ to 2¾ cups bread flour or all-purpose flour
- 1 tsp. butter, melted
- ½ tsp. dill seeds

1. In a large bowl, combine yeast, the warm water, and 1 tablespoon sugar. Set aside to dissolve yeast.

2. Meanwhile, in a small saucepan, combine cottage cheese, 1 tablespoon sugar, the dried onion, the 1 tablespoon butter, the 2 teaspoons dill seeds, the salt, and baking soda. Heat and stir just until mixture is warm (120°F to 130°F) and butter almost melts. Remove from heat. Stir cheese mixture and egg into yeast mixture. Using a spoon, stir in as much of the flour as you can.

3. Turn out dough onto a lightly floured surface. Knead in enough of the remaining flour to make a moderately soft dough that is smooth and elastic (3 to 5 minutes total); dough may be sticky. Shape dough into a ball. Place dough in a lightly greased bowl, turning once to grease entire surface.

4. Cover; let rise in a warm place until double in size (about 1 hour). Grease a 1½-quart casserole. Punch down dough. Turn out dough onto a lightly floured surface. Shape dough by patting or rolling it into a 7-inch round loaf. Place dough in prepared casserole. Cover and let rise in a warm place until nearly double in size (30 to 40 minutes).

5. Preheat oven to 350°F. Brush with the 1 teaspoon melted butter. Sprinkle brushed surface with the ½ teaspoon dill seeds. Bake for 35 to 40 minutes or until browned and bread sounds hollow when lightly tapped. If necessary to prevent overbrowning, cover loosely with foil for the last 10 to 15 minutes of baking. Immediately remove bread from casserole. Cool on wire rack. Makes 1 loaf (16 servings).

Nutrition facts per serving: 106 cal., 2 g total fat (1 g sat. fat), 18 mg chol., 233 mg sodium, 16 g carbo., 1 g fiber, 5 g pro.

Swiss Cheese-Walnut Focaccia

Prep: 30 min. Rise: 1 hr. + 20 min. Bake: 25 min.

Italian focaccia usually is brushed with olive oil and sprinkled with salt and, sometimes, snipped herb. In 1999, we took the old-world bread a step further and topped it with walnuts, Swiss cheese, and pepper.

Swiss Cheese-Walnut Foccacia

3¼	to 3¾ cups bread flour or all-purpose flour
1	pkg. active dry yeast
1¼	cups warm water (120°F to 130°F)
1	Tbsp. olive oil
1	tsp. salt
2	Tbsp. olive oil
1	cup coarsely chopped walnuts
⅔	cup shredded Swiss cheese
½	tsp. cracked black pepper

1. In a large mixing bowl, stir together *1¼ cups* of the flour and the yeast. Add the warm water, the 1 tablespoon oil, and the salt to the flour mixture. Beat with an electric mixer on low to medium speed for 30 seconds, scraping side of bowl constantly. Beat on high speed for 3 minutes. Using a wooden spoon, stir in as much of the remaining flour as you can.

2. Turn out dough onto a lightly floured surface. Knead in enough of the remaining flour to make a stiff dough that is smooth and elastic (8 to 10 minutes total). Shape dough into a ball. Place in a lightly greased bowl, turning once to grease surface. Cover and let rise in a warm place until double in size (about 1 hour).

3. Lightly grease 2 baking sheets. Punch down dough. Turn out onto a lightly floured surface. Divide dough in half. Shape each half into a ball. Place on prepared baking sheets. Cover and let rest for 10 minutes.

4. Flatten each ball into a circle about 9 inches in diameter. Dust your fingers lightly with flour; using your fingertips, press ½-inch-deep indentations all over the surface of each dough round, spacing them about 2 inches apart. Brush rounds with the 2 tablespoons oil. Sprinkle with walnuts, cheese, and pepper. Cover and let rise in a warm place until nearly double in size (about 20 minutes).

5. Preheat oven to 375°F. Bake about 25 minutes or until golden. Remove from baking sheets; cool on wire racks. Makes 2 rounds (24 servings).

Make-ahead directions: Prepare and bake as directed. Wrap in plastic wrap or foil. Store at room temperature up to 3 days. (Or wrap in freezer wrap; freeze up to 3 months.)

Nutrition facts per serving: 87 cal., 2 g total fat (0 g sat. fat), 0 mg chol., 90 mg sodium, 15 g carbo., 1 g fiber, 3 g pro.

Stir Things Up

Old-time recipes routinely called for sifted all-purpose flour. But because most of the all-purpose flour sold today is presifted, we've eliminated the sifting from our bread recipes. However, flour does tend to settle, so our Test Kitchen suggests you stir through the bag or canister just before measuring to lighten the flour. To get an accurate measure, gently spoon the flour into a dry measuring cup and level it off with a spatula or table knife.

Almond Twirl Bread

Prep: 40 min. Rise: 1 hr. + 30 min.
Bake: 30 min. Cool: 15 min.

Ground almonds, a rich sweet dough, and an eye-catching shape make this luscious 1974 recipe a truly exceptional coffee cake.

3¾ to 4¼ cups all-purpose flour
  1 pkg. active dry yeast
  1 cup milk
  ⅓ cup granulated sugar
  ⅓ cup butter
  ½ tsp. salt
  2 eggs
  1 recipe Almond Filling (below right)
  ½ cup sifted powdered sugar
  ½ tsp. vanilla
  1 to 2 tsp. milk
  ¼ cup sliced almonds, toasted (tip, page 102)

1. In a large mixing bowl, combine *2 cups* of the flour and the yeast. In a small saucepan, heat and stir milk, granulated sugar, butter, and salt just until warm (120°F to 130°F) and butter almost melts.

Almond Twirl Bread

2. Add milk mixture to flour mixture; add eggs. Beat on low speed for 30 seconds, scraping bowl constantly. Beat on high speed for 3 minutes. Using a wooden spoon, stir in as much remaining flour as you can.

3. Turn out dough onto a lightly floured surface. Knead in enough of the remaining flour to make a moderately soft dough that is smooth and elastic (3 to 5 minutes total). Shape into a ball. Place in a lightly greased bowl, turning once to grease surface. Cover and let rise in a warm place until double in size (about 1 hour).

4. Punch down dough. Turn out dough onto a lightly floured surface. Cover; let rest for 10 minutes. Meanwhile, lightly grease a large baking sheet.

5. Prepare Almond Filling. Roll the dough to an 16×12-inch rectangle. Sprinkle with filling. Starting from a long side, roll up into a spiral. Seal seam. Place, seam side down, on prepared baking sheet. Shape into a ring; press ends together to seal. Using kitchen scissors, snip at 1-inch intervals, making each cut two-thirds of the way from outer edge toward center. Gently turn each section slightly to one side. Cover; let rise in a warm place until nearly double in size (about 30 minutes).

6. Preheat oven to 350°F. Bake for 30 to 35 minutes or until bread sounds hollow when lightly tapped. Transfer to a wire rack and cool for 15 minutes.

7. For icing, in a bowl, combine powdered sugar, vanilla, and 1 to 2 teaspoons milk to make of drizzling consistency. Drizzle onto bread. Top with almonds. Serve warm or cool. Makes 1 ring (18 servings).

Almond Filling: In a small mixing bowl, beat ⅓ cup granulated sugar and 2 tablespoons butter with an electric mixer on medium speed until mixed. Stir in ½ cup ground almonds.*

*Test Kitchen Tip: When you're grinding nuts, take extra care not to overgrind them, or you may end up with nut butter. If you're using a blender or food processor, add 1 tablespoon of the sugar to the ½ cup nuts to help absorb some of the oil. Use a quick start-and-stop motion for better control of the fineness.

Nutrition facts per serving: 218 cal., 9 g total fat (4 g sat. fat), 38 mg chol., 129 mg sodium, 30 g carbo., 1 g fiber, 5 g pro.

Our test kitchen buys more than $100,000 worth of groceries annually, including 6,000 cups of flour, 4,000 cups of sugar, 4,800 eggs, and 600 pounds of butter. Now, that's a lot of baking!

Lemon Drop Bread

Lemon Drop Bread

Prep: 15 min. Bake: per bread machine directions

This moist bread machine loaf owes its spunky citrus flavor to crushed lemon drops, frozen lemonade concentrate, and a lemon glaze.

- ¼ cup coarsely crushed lemon drops
- ¾ cup milk
- 1 egg
- 2 Tbsp. frozen lemonade concentrate, thawed
- 2 Tbsp. butter, cut up
- 3 cups bread flour
- 2 Tbsp. sugar
- 1½ tsp. finely shredded lemon peel
- ¾ tsp. salt
- 1 tsp. active dry yeast or bread machine yeast
- 1 recipe Lemon Icing (below)

1. Reserve *1 tablespoon* of the crushed lemon drops. Add the milk, egg, lemonade concentrate, butter, flour, remaining lemon drops, sugar, lemon peel, salt, and yeast to bread machine according to the manufacturer's directions. Select the basic white bread cycle.

2. Remove hot bread from machine as soon as it is done. Cool on a wire rack. Prepare Lemon Icing; drizzle over the cooled loaf. Sprinkle with the reserved crushed lemon drops. Makes one 1½-pound loaf (16 servings).

Lemon Icing: In a small bowl, combine ½ cup sifted powdered sugar, 1 teaspoon lemon juice, and ¼ teaspoon vanilla. Stir in enough milk (1 to 2 teaspoons) to make an icing of drizzling consistency.

Nutrition facts per serving: 168 cal., 2 g total fat (1 g sat. fat), 18 mg chol., 139 mg sodium, 32 g carbo., 1 g fiber, 4 g pro.

Brioche

Prep: 1 hr. Rise: 2 hr. + 45 min.
Chill: 6 hr. Bake: 15 min.

Rich with butter and eggs, this *Better Homes and Gardens®* version of the traditional French rolls dates back to the 1950s. Serve them with soup for supper or with honey butter for a continental breakfast.

- 1 pkg. active dry yeast
- ¼ cup warm water (105°F to 115°F)
- ½ cup butter
- ⅓ cup sugar
- ¾ tsp. salt
- 4 cups all-purpose flour
- ½ cup milk
- 4 eggs
- 1 Tbsp. water

1. In a small bowl, dissolve yeast in the ¼ cup warm water. Let stand for 5 to 10 minutes to soften. In a large mixing bowl, beat butter, sugar, and salt with an electric mixer on medium to high speed until fluffy. Add *1 cup* of the flour and the milk. Separate *1* of the eggs. Add the yolk and remaining 3 whole eggs to beaten mixture (refrigerate egg white to use later). Add softened yeast; beat well. Stir in remaining 3 cups flour until smooth. Place in a greased bowl. Cover; let rise in a warm place until double in size (about 2 hours). Chill dough for 6 hours.

2. Grease twenty-four 2½-inch muffin cups; set aside. Stir down dough. Turn out dough onto a lightly floured surface. Divide dough into 4 portions; set 1 portion aside. Divide each of the remaining 3 portions into 8 pieces (24 pieces total).

3. To shape, form each piece into a ball, tucking edges under to make smooth tops. Place in prepared muffin cups, smooth sides up. Divide reserved dough portion into 24 pieces; shape into small balls. Using a floured finger, make an indentation in each large ball. Press a small ball into each indentation. In a small bowl, combine reserved egg white and the 1 tablespoon water; brush onto rolls. Cover; let rise in a warm place until double in size (45 to 55 minutes).

4. Preheat oven to 375°F. Bake about 15 minutes or until golden, brushing again with egg white mixture after 7 minutes. Remove from pans. Cool on wire racks. Makes 24 rolls.

Make-ahead directions: Prepare as directed in step 1, except omit the 2-hour rising time, and chill dough for at least 12 hours or up to 24 hours. Continue as directed from step 2.

Nutrition facts per roll: 138 cal., 5 g total fat (3 g sat. fat), 47 mg chol., 128 mg sodium, 19 g carbo., 1 g fiber, 4 g pro.

Dinner Rolls

Prep: 45 min. Rise: 1 hr. + 30 min. Bake: 15 min.

You can prepare the dough in your bread machine, shape the rolls ahead of time, then bake them right before dinner to serve fresh from the oven.

3¼   **to 3¾ cups all-purpose flour**
  1   **pkg. active dry yeast**
  1   **cup milk**
¼   **cup sugar**
⅓   **cup butter or shortening**
¾   **tsp. salt**
  1   **egg**

1. In a large mixing bowl, stir together *1¼ cups* of the flour and the yeast. In a medium saucepan, heat and stir milk, sugar, butter, and salt just until warm (120°F to 130°F) and butter almost melts. Beat egg with a fork. Add milk mixture to flour mixture along with egg. Beat with an electric mixer on low to medium speed for 30 seconds, scraping side of bowl constantly. Beat on high speed for 3 minutes. Using a wooden spoon, stir in as much of the remaining flour as you can.

2. Turn out dough onto a lightly floured surface. Knead in enough of the remaining flour to make a moderately stiff dough that is smooth and elastic (6 to 8 minutes total). Shape dough into a ball. Place in a lightly greased bowl, turning dough once to grease surface. Cover; let rise in a warm place until double in size (about 1 hour).

Better Homes and Gardens® editors have always offered friendly advice to readers. As an example, take this recommendation from the 1930s: "No matter how plain the fare, nor how elaborate, if accompanied by a delicious hot bread, the homemaker may know the success of her meal is assured."

3. Punch down dough. Turn out dough onto a lightly floured surface. Divide dough in half. Cover; let rest for 10 minutes. Meanwhile, lightly grease a 13×9×2-inch baking pan or, if making Cloverleaf Rolls (below), twenty-four 2½-inch muffin cups.

4. Shape the dough into 24 balls. Place balls in prepared baking pan. (Or shape dough into Cloverleaf Rolls. Place in prepared muffin cups.) Cover and let rise in a warm place until nearly double in size (about 30 minutes).

5. Preheat oven to 375°F. Bake for 15 to 18 minutes or until rolls sound hollow when lightly tapped. Immediately remove rolls from pan. Cool on wire racks. Makes 24 rolls.

Cloverleaf Rolls: Divide *each half* of the dough into 36 pieces. Shape each piece into a ball, pulling edges under to make a smooth top. Place 3 balls in each prepared muffin cup, smooth sides up.

Make-ahead directions: Prepare as directed through step 4, except do not let shaped rolls rise. Cover rolls loosely with plastic wrap, leaving room for rolls to rise. Chill for at least 2 hours or up to 24 hours. Uncover; let stand at room temperature for 30 minutes. Continue as directed in step 5.

Nutrition facts per roll: 97 cal., 3 g total fat (2 g sat. fat), 17 mg chol., 108 mg sodium, 15 g carbo., 0 g fiber, 2 g pro.

Batter Dinner Rolls: Prepare as directed through step 1, except reduce the all-purpose flour to 3 cups. Lightly grease eighteen 2½-inch muffin cups. Spoon batter into prepared muffin cups, filling each half full. Cover and let rise in a warm place until nearly double in size (about 45 minutes). Preheat oven to 375°F. Brush roll tops with milk and, if desired, sprinkle with poppy seeds or sesame seeds. Bake about 15 minutes or until golden brown. Makes 18 rolls.

Nutrition facts per roll: 123 cal., 4 g total fat (3 g sat. fat), 33 mg chol., 144 mg sodium, 18 g carbo., 1 g fiber, 3 g pro.

Bread Machine Dinner Rolls: For a bread machine with 2-pound capacity, use ingredients as directed, except use 3½ cups all-purpose flour. Add ingredients to the machine according to the manufacturer's directions. Select the dough cycle. Watch dough carefully during the first kneading. If dough looks too dry and crumbly, add milk, *1 teaspoon* at a time, until a smooth ball forms. When cycle is complete, remove dough from machine. Punch down. Cover and let rest for 10 minutes. Continue as directed in steps 4 and 5.

Nutrition facts per roll: 102 cal., 3 g total fat (2 g sat. fat), 17 mg chol., 108 mg sodium, 15 g carbo., 1 g fiber, 2 g pro.

Cornmeal Yeast Rolls

Prep: 20 min. Cool: 45 min. Stand: 30 min.
Rise: 1 hr. + 30 min. Bake: 18 min.

Our staff loves these tender rolls because they combine the down-home flavor of corn bread with the light texture of a yeast bread.

- 2   cups milk
- ½   cup sugar
- ½   cup shortening
- ⅓   cup yellow cornmeal
- 1½ tsp. salt
- 1   pkg. active dry yeast
- ¼   cup warm water (105°F to 115°F)
- 2   eggs, beaten
- 5¼ to 5¾ cups all-purpose flour
      Butter or margarine, melted

1. In a medium saucepan, combine milk, sugar, shortening, cornmeal, and salt. Cook and stir over medium heat until thickened and bubbly. Remove from heat. Cool for 45 minutes to 1 hour or until lukewarm (105°F to 115°F).

2. In a large bowl, dissolve yeast in warm water. Add cornmeal mixture, stirring until smooth. Cover; let stand about 30 minutes or until bubbly. Stir in eggs. Using a wooden spoon, stir in as much of the flour as you can.

3. Turn out dough onto a floured surface. Knead in enough of the remaining flour to make a moderately soft dough that is smooth and elastic (3 to 5 minutes total). Dough will be slightly sticky. Shape dough into a ball. Place in a greased bowl, turning once to grease surface. Cover; let rise in a warm place until double in size (about 1 hour).

4. Punch down dough. Turn out onto a floured surface. Divide dough in half. Cover; let rest for 10 minutes. Lightly grease two 9×1½-inch round baking pans or two 9×9×2-inch baking pans.

5. Divide each half of the dough into 16 equal pieces; shape into even balls. Place in prepared pans. Cover and let rise in a warm place until nearly double in size (30 to 40 minutes).

6. Preheat oven to 375°F. Bake for 18 to 20 minutes or until golden. Remove from oven; brush with melted butter. Serve warm. Makes 32 rolls.

Nutrition facts per roll: 127 cal., 4 g total fat (1 g sat. fat), 15 mg chol., 121 mg sodium, 19 g carbo., 1 g fiber, 3 g pro.

Quaker Bonnet Biscuits

Prep: 20 min. + bread machine dough cycle
Rise: 30 min. Bake: 15 min.

A few years ago, when looking through a 1915 cookbook, we ran across a recipe for these whimsical biscuits, so named because they resemble the hats worn by Quaker women in the early 1800s. We were so charmed that we updated the recipe and converted it for the bread machine.

- ¾   cup milk
- 2   eggs
- ⅓   cup butter, cut up
- 2   Tbsp. water
- 4   cups bread flour
- 1   Tbsp. sugar
- 1   tsp. salt
- 1½ tsp. active dry yeast or bread
      machine yeast
- 1   egg yolk
- 2   tsp. milk

1. Add the ¾ cup milk, the 2 eggs, the butter, the water, flour, sugar, salt, and yeast to bread machine according to the manufacturer's directions. Select the dough cycle. When cycle is complete, remove dough. Punch down. Cover and let rest for 10 minutes. Lightly grease baking sheets; set aside.

2. On a lightly floured surface, roll the dough to ¼-inch thickness. Cut dough with floured 2- and 2½-inch round cutters, making an equal number of each. Place the larger rounds on the prepared baking sheets.

3. In a small bowl, combine egg yolk and the 2 teaspoons milk. Brush larger rounds with some of the egg yolk mixture. Top each with a smaller round, stacking slightly off-center. Cover and let rise in a warm place until nearly double in size (about 30 minutes).

4. Preheat oven to 350°F. Brush tops of biscuits with the remaining egg yolk mixture. Bake about 15 minutes or until tops are golden. Remove from baking sheets; cool slightly on wire racks. Serve warm. Makes about 20 biscuits.

Nutrition facts per biscuit: 146 cal., 5 g total fat (2 g sat. fat), 41 mg chol., 161 mg sodium, 21 g carbo., 1 g fiber, 5 g pro.

Yesterday

Cinnamon rolls are ever popular with *Better Homes and Gardens*® families. This basic recipe is our gold standard—light, tender rolls with an irresistible buttery cinnamon filling.

Old-Fashioned Cinnamon Rolls

Prep: 45 min. Rise: 1 hr. Chill: 2 to 24 hr.
Stand: 30 min. Bake: 20 min.

4¾ to 5¼ cups all-purpose four
   1 pkg. active dry yeast
   1 cup milk
   ⅓ cup butter
   ⅓ cup sugar
   3 eggs
   3 Tbsp. butter, melted
   ⅔ cup sugar
   2 tsp. ground cinnamon
   1 recipe Creamy Glaze (below)

1. In a large bowl, combine *2¼ cups* flour and yeast. In a saucepan, heat and stir milk, ⅓ cup butter, ⅓ cup granulated sugar, and ½ teaspoon *salt* just until warm (120°F to 130°F) and butter almost melts. Add to flour mixture; add eggs. Beat on low speed for 30 seconds, scraping bowl. Beat on high speed for 3 minutes. Stir in as much of the remaining flour as you can.

2. On a lightly floured surface, knead in enough of the remaining flour to make a moderately soft dough that is smooth and elastic (3 to 5 minutes total). Shape into a ball. Place in a greased bowl; turning once. Cover; let rise in a warm place until double in size (1 hour).

3. Punch down dough. Turn out onto a lightly floured surface; divide in half. Cover; let rest 10 minutes. Lightly grease 2 baking sheets or two 9×1½-inch round baking pans. Roll each half of the dough into a 12×8-inch rectangle. Brush with melted butter. Combine the ⅔ cup sugar and the cinnamon; sprinkle over rectangles. Starting from a long side, roll up each rectangle into a spiral. Seal seams. Cut each spiral into 12 slices. Place slices, cut sides down, on prepared baking sheets or in pans.

4. Cover dough loosely with plastic wrap, leaving room for rolls to rise. Chill for at least 2 hours or up to 24 hours. Uncover; let stand at room temperature for 30 minutes.

5. Preheat oven to 375°F. Break any surface bubbles with a greased toothpick. Bake for 20 to 25 minutes or until light brown. If necessary to prevent overbrowning, cover rolls loosely with foil for the last 5 to 10 minutes of baking. Remove from oven. Cool for 1 minute. Transfer rolls to a wire rack. (If using baking pans, carefully invert rolls onto rack. Cool slightly. Invert again onto a serving platter.) Drizzle with Creamy Glaze. Serve warm. Makes 24 rolls.

Creamy Glaze: Mix 1¼ cups sifted powdered sugar, 1 teaspoon light-colored corn syrup, and ½ teaspoon vanilla. Stir in enough half-and-half or light cream (1 to 2 tablespoons) to make of drizzling consistency.

Nutrition facts per roll: 197 cal., 5 g total fat (3 g sat. fat), 39 mg chol., 106 mg sodium, 33 g carbo., 1 g fiber, 4 g pro.

Creamy Caramel-Pecan Rolls

Prep: 25 min. Rise: 30 min. Bake: 20 min. Cool: 5 min.

The golden pecan glaze on the bottom becomes the top as you turn out these rolls onto a platter.

1¼	cups sifted powdered sugar
⅓	cup whipping cream
1	cup coarsely chopped pecans
½	cup packed brown sugar
1	Tbsp. ground cinnamon
2	16-oz. loaves frozen white bread dough or sweet roll dough, thawed
3	Tbsp. butter, melted
¾	cup raisins (optional)

1. Grease two 9×1½-inch round baking pans; set pans aside. For topping, in a small bowl, stir together powdered sugar and whipping cream; divide evenly between prepared baking pans. Sprinkle pecans evenly over sugar mixture.

2. In another small bowl, stir together brown sugar and cinnamon; set aside. On a lightly floured surface, roll each loaf of dough into a 12×8-inch rectangle. Brush with melted butter; sprinkle with brown sugar-cinnamon mixture. If desired, sprinkle with raisins.

3. Starting from a long side, roll up each rectangle into a spiral. Seal seams. Cut each spiral into 12 slices. Place slices, cut sides down, on topping in pans.

4. Cover and let rise in a warm place until nearly double in size (about 30 minutes). Break any surface bubbles with a greased toothpick.

5. Preheat oven to 375°F. Bake for 20 to 25 minutes or until golden. If necessary to prevent overbrowning, cover rolls loosely with foil for the last 10 minutes of baking. Cool in pans on wire racks for 5 minutes. Carefully invert rolls onto platters. Serve warm. Makes 24 rolls.

Make-ahead directions: Prepare as directed through step 3. Cover with oiled waxed paper, then with plastic wrap. Chill for at least 2 hours or up to 24 hours. Before baking, let chilled rolls stand, covered, for 30 minutes at room temperature. Preheat oven to 375°F. Uncover and bake rolls for 25 to 30 minutes or until golden. If necessary to prevent overbrowning, cover rolls loosely with foil for the last 10 minutes of baking. Cool in pans on wire racks for 5 minutes. Carefully invert rolls onto platters. Serve warm.

Nutrition facts per roll: 172 cal., 6 g total fat (2 g sat. fat), 9 mg chol., 19 mg sodium, 25 g carbo., 1 g fiber, 3 g pro.

Today

How do you make a good thing even better? Take some of the work out of cinnamon rolls. This recipe, from October 1992, starts with frozen dough. You can assemble the rolls ahead, chill the pans overnight, and bake the rolls for breakfast or brunch.

Orange Bowknots

Orange Bowknots

Prep: 45 min. Rise: 1 hr. + 30 min. Bake: 12 min.

This prizewinning recipe from 1946 reappeared when we compiled a cookbook in honor of our 75th anniversary.

- 5¼ to 5¾ cups all-purpose flour
- 1 pkg. active dry yeast
- 1¼ cups milk
- ½ cup butter or shortening
- ⅓ cup sugar
- 1 tsp. salt
- 2 eggs
- 2 Tbsp. finely shredded orange peel
- ¼ cup orange juice
- 1 recipe Orange Powdered Sugar Icing (above right)

1. In a large mixing bowl, combine *2 cups* of the flour and the yeast; set aside. In a medium saucepan, heat and stir milk, butter or shortening, sugar, and salt just until warm (120°F to 130°F) and butter almost melts. Add milk mixture to flour mixture along with eggs. Beat with an electric mixer on low to medium speed for 30 seconds, scraping side of bowl constantly. Beat on high speed for 3 minutes. Using a wooden spoon, stir in the shredded orange peel, orange juice, and as much of the remaining flour as you can.

2. Turn out dough onto a lightly floured surface. Knead in enough of the remaining flour to make a moderately stiff dough that is smooth and elastic (6 to 8 minutes total). Shape dough into a ball. Place dough in a lightly greased bowl, turning once to grease surface. Cover and let rise in a warm place until double in size (about 1 hour).

3. Punch down dough. Turn out onto a lightly floured surface. Divide dough in half. Cover and let rest for 10 minutes. Meanwhile, lightly grease 2 baking sheets; set aside.

4. Roll each half of the dough to a 12×7-inch rectangle. Cut each rectangle into twelve 7-inch-long strips. Tie each strip into a loose knot. Place knots 2 inches apart on prepared baking sheets. Cover and let rise in a warm place until nearly double in size (about 30 minutes).

5. Preheat oven to 400°F. Bake about 12 minutes or until golden. Immediately remove from baking sheets. Cool on wire racks. Prepare Orange Powdered Sugar Icing; drizzle onto rolls. Makes 24 rolls.

Orange Powdered Sugar Icing: In a small bowl, stir together 1 cup sifted powdered sugar, 1 teaspoon finely shredded orange peel, and enough orange juice (1 to 2 tablespoons) to make of spreading consistency.

Nutrition facts per roll: 176 cal., 5 g total fat (1 g sat. fat), 19 mg chol., 101 mg sodium, 28 g carbo., 1 g fiber, 4 g pro.

Cinnamon Crisps

Prep: 50 min. Rise: 1½ hr. + 30 min. Bake: 10 min.

Sometimes nicknamed elephant ears, these flaky rounds were a best seller at bakeries long before *Better Homes and Gardens*® magazine published several versions for home cooks in the 1970s and 1980s.

- 3¼ to 3¾ cups all-purpose flour
- 1 pkg. active dry yeast
- 1¼ cups milk
- ¼ cup granulated sugar
- ¼ cup butter or shortening
- 1 tsp. salt
- 1 egg
- ½ cup granulated sugar
- ½ cup packed brown sugar
- ¼ cup butter, melted
- ½ tsp. ground cinnamon
- ¼ cup butter, melted
- 1 cup granulated sugar
- ½ cup chopped pecans
- 1 tsp. ground cinnamon

1. In a large mixing bowl, combine *2 cups* of the flour and the yeast. In a medium saucepan, heat and stir milk, the ¼ cup granulated sugar, ¼ cup butter or shortening, and the salt just until warm (120°F to 130°F) and butter almost melts. Add milk mixture to flour mixture along with egg. Beat with an electric mixer on low speed for 30 seconds, scraping side of bowl constantly. Beat for 3 minutes on high speed. Using a wooden spoon, stir in as much of the remaining flour as you can.

2. Turn out dough onto a lightly floured surface. Knead in enough of the remaining flour to make a moderately soft dough that is smooth and elastic (3 to 5 minutes total). Shape into a ball. Place dough in a lightly greased bowl, turning once to grease surface. Cover; let rise in warm place until double in size (1½ to 2 hours).

3. Punch down dough. Turn out onto a lightly floured surface. Divide in half. Cover; let rest 10 minutes.

4. Grease 3 or 4 large baking sheets; set aside. Roll each half of the dough to a 12-inch square. In a small bowl, combine the ½ cup granulated sugar, the brown sugar, ¼ cup melted butter, and the ½ teaspoon cinnamon; spread onto dough squares. Roll up each into a spiral; pinch to seal edges. Cut each spiral into 12 slices. Place slices on prepared baking sheets 3 to 4 inches apart. Flatten slices to about 3 inches in diameter.

5. Cover rolls loosely with plastic wrap. Let rise in a warm place until nearly double in size (about 30 minutes).

6. Preheat oven to 400°F. With the plastic wrap on rolls, roll over tops with a rolling pin to flatten each roll to about ⅛-inch thickness. Carefully remove plastic wrap. Brush tops of rolls with ¼ cup melted butter. In a medium bowl, combine the 1 cup granulated sugar, the pecans, and the 1 teaspoon cinnamon. Sprinkle pecan mixture over rolls. Cover with plastic wrap and roll flat again.

7. Bake for 10 to 12 minutes or until light brown. (If you don't have oven space to bake all the rolls at once, cover remaining unbaked rolls with plastic wrap and store in refrigerator until ready to bake.) Immediately transfer rolls to wire racks. Cool. Makes 24 rolls.

Nutrition facts per roll: 209 cal., 8 g total fat (4 g sat. fat), 26 mg chol., 170 mg sodium, 32 g carbo., 1 g fiber, 3 g pro.

> **Although we've helped our readers eat healthfully all along, we really focused on nutrition in the 1980s—case in point, the 1981 edition of the *New Cook Book* was our first book to offer a nutrition analysis of each recipe.**

Heart-Healthy Apple Coffee Cake

Prep: 25 min. Bake: 25 min. Cool: 10 min.

An Arizona reader won top honors in our September 1992 Coffee Cakes Prize Tested Recipes® contest with this low-fat apple round. By substituting applesauce for shortening and egg product for whole eggs, she created a coffee cake with only 5 grams of fat per serving.

	Nonstick cooking spray
⅔	cup all-purpose flour
½	cup whole wheat flour
1	tsp. baking soda
1	tsp. ground cinnamon
¼	tsp. salt
1½	cups finely chopped cored and peeled apple (such as Jonathan or Granny Smith) (about 2 small)
¼	cup refrigerated or frozen egg product, thawed
¾	cup granulated sugar
¼	cup chopped pecans or walnuts
¼	cup applesauce
¼	cup packed brown sugar
1	Tbsp. all-purpose flour
1	Tbsp. whole wheat flour
½	tsp. ground cinnamon
1	Tbsp. butter
¼	cup chopped pecans or walnuts

1. Preheat oven to 350°F. Lightly coat a 9×1½-inch round baking pan with nonstick cooking spray; set aside. In a small bowl, combine the ⅔ cup all-purpose flour, the ½ cup whole wheat flour, the baking soda, the 1 teaspoon cinnamon, and the salt; set aside. In a medium bowl, toss together chopped apple and egg product. Stir in granulated sugar, ¼ cup nuts, and the applesauce. Add flour mixture; stir just until combined. Pour batter into prepared pan.

2. For topping, in a small bowl, stir together brown sugar, the 1 tablespoon all-purpose flour, the 1 tablespoon whole wheat flour, and the ½ teaspoon cinnamon. Using a pastry blender, cut in butter until mixture resembles coarse crumbs. Stir in ¼ cup nuts. Sprinkle topping onto batter in pan. Bake for 25 to 30 minutes or until a wooden toothpick inserted near center comes out clean. Cool in pan for 10 minutes. Serve warm. Makes 10 servings.

Nutrition facts per serving: 203 cal., 5 g total fat (1 g sat. fat), 3 mg chol., 211 mg sodium, 38 g carbo., 3 g fiber, 3 g pro.

Cocoa Ripple Ring

Prep: 30 min. Bake: 45 min. Stand: 5 min. Cool: 30 min.

This nutty coffee cake caught the fancy of our readers when it first appeared in the 1950s because it used presweetened instant cocoa powder—a new ingredient at the time.

1½	**cups all-purpose flour**
1	**tsp. baking powder**
½	**tsp. salt**
½	**cup butter, softened**
¾	**cup sugar**
2	**eggs**
¾	**cup milk**
⅓	**cup presweetened instant cocoa powder**
⅓	**cup broken walnuts**
1	**recipe Satin Chocolate Glaze (right)**

1. Preheat oven to 350°F. Grease a 6-cup fluted tube pan or a 9×9×2-inch baking pan. Set aside. In a small bowl, stir together the flour, baking powder, and salt. Set aside.

2. In a large bowl, beat butter with an electric mixer on medium to high speed for 30 seconds. Add sugar; beat on medium speed until mixed. Add eggs; beat until light and fluffy. Add flour mixture and milk alternately to the egg mixture, beating well after each addition.

3. If using a fluted tube pan, spoon in *one-third* of the batter. In a small bowl, combine cocoa powder and walnuts; sprinkle *half* of the nut mixture over batter in pan. Repeat layers, ending with batter. (If using a 9×9×2-inch baking pan, spoon *half* of the batter into it. Sprinkle with all of the walnut mixture; top with remaining batter.)

4. Bake until a wooden toothpick comes out clean. Allow about 45 minutes for fluted tube pan or about 35 minutes for the 9×9×2-inch baking pan. Let stand 5 minutes; turn out of tube pan (leave in 9×9×2-inch pan). Cool 30 minutes. Prepare Satin Chocolate Glaze; drizzle onto ring. Makes 12 servings.

Satin Chocolate Glaze: In a small saucepan, combine ¼ cup semisweet chocolate pieces, 1 tablespoon half-and-half or light cream, 1½ teaspoons sugar, and ¼ teaspoon vanilla. Heat and stir over low heat until melted and smooth.

Nutrition facts per serving: 255 cal., 13 g total fat (6 g sat. fat), 59 mg chol., 239 mg sodium, 32 g carbo., 1 g fiber, 4 g pro.

Island-Style Banana Bread

Prep: 20 min. Bake: 50 min.

We thought banana bread was great without jazzing it up, until we tasted this tropical teaser from a 1998 issue.

2	cups all-purpose flour
1½	tsp. ground cinnamon
1	tsp. baking powder
½	tsp. baking soda
¼	tsp. salt
½	cup butter, softened
½	cup packed brown sugar
2	eggs
1	tsp. vanilla
1	cup mashed ripe banana (2 to 3 medium)
½	cup chopped pecans
1	8-oz. pkg. reduced-fat cream cheese (Neufchâtel)
1	egg
¼	cup packed brown sugar
½	cup coconut

1. Preheat oven to 350°F. Grease the bottom and ½ inch up the sides of two 7½×3½×2-inch loaf pans; set aside. In a large bowl, combine flour, cinnamon, baking powder, baking soda, and salt; set aside.

2. In a large mixing bowl, beat butter with an electric mixer on high speed for 30 seconds. Add the ½ cup brown sugar, the 2 eggs, and the vanilla; beat until combined. Add flour mixture and mashed banana alternately to beaten mixture, beating on low speed after each addition until combined. Stir in pecans.

3. In a medium mixing bowl, beat the cream cheese, the 1 egg, and the ¼ cup brown sugar with an electric mixer on medium speed until almost smooth. Stir in coconut.

4. Pour *one-fourth* of the banana mixture into *each* loaf pan. Spoon *one-fourth* of the cream cheese mixture over *each* loaf. Using a thin metal spatula or a table knife, cut through the batter to marble. Repeat layers, but do not marble.

5. Bake about 50 minutes or until a wooden toothpick inserted near the centers comes out clean. Cool in pans on wire racks for 10 minutes. Remove from pans. Cool completely on wire racks. Wrap in plastic wrap and store overnight before slicing. Makes 2 loaves (20 servings).

Nutrition facts per serving: 191 cal., 11 g total fat (5 g sat. fat), 53 mg chol., 180 mg sodium, 21 g carbo., 1 g fiber, 4 g pro.

Wheat and Honey Pumpkin Bread

Prep: 25 min. Bake: 50 min.

Nibble a piece of this honey-sweetened quick bread and discover how tantalizing pumpkin pie in a loaf can be. For a company-special tea, try it spread with cream cheese or orange curd.

2	cups all-purpose flour
1⅓	cups whole wheat flour
2½	tsp. pumpkin pie spice or apple pie spice
1½	tsp. baking powder
1½	tsp. salt
1	tsp. baking soda
1¾	cups granulated sugar
⅓	cup shortening
4	eggs
1	15-oz. can pumpkin
½	cup honey
⅓	cup water
1	cup chopped walnuts or pecans
1	cup sifted powdered sugar
3	to 4 tsp. orange juice

1. Preheat oven to 350°F. Grease the bottom and ½ inch up the sides of two 8×4×2 or 9×5×3-inch loaf pans; set aside. In a large mixing bowl, stir together the all-purpose flour, whole wheat flour, pie spice, baking powder, salt, and baking soda. Set aside.

2. In a very large mixing bowl, beat granulated sugar and shortening with an electric mixer on medium speed until well mixed. Beat in eggs, one at a time, beating well after each addition. On low speed, beat in pumpkin, honey, and the water just until combined. Using a wooden spoon, stir flour mixture into beaten mixture just until combined. Fold in nuts. Divide mixture evenly between the prepared pans.

3. Bake for 50 to 60 minutes or until a wooden toothpick inserted near centers comes out clean. Cool in pans on wire racks for 10 minutes. Remove loaves from pans. Cool completely on wire racks.

4. For icing, in a small bowl, stir together powdered sugar and enough of the orange juice to make an icing of drizzling consistency. Drizzle icing onto cooled loaves. Makes 2 loaves (32 servings).

Make-ahead directions: Prepare as directed through step 3. Place bread, without icing, in a freezer container or bag. Seal, label, and freeze up to 3 months. To serve, thaw the wrapped bread overnight in the refrigerator. Continue as directed in step 4.

Nutrition facts per serving: 171 cal., 5 g total fat (1 g sat. fat), 27 mg chol., 166 mg sodium, 29 g carbo., 1 g fiber, 3 g pro.

Classic Corn Bread (recipe, page 216)

Yesterday

Golden corn bread is another basic must-have recipe for *Better Homes and Gardens*® readers. A cast-iron skillet gives the corn bread a crispy crust.

Today

To add a little pizzazz to corn bread, we embellished the basic recipe with Parmesan cheese, basil, fennel seeds, sun-dried tomatoes, and green onions. Awesome!

Confetti Corn Bread (recipe, page 216)

Yesterday

Classic Corn Bread

Prep: 15 min. Bake: 20 min.

If you don't own a cast-iron skillet, a round baking pan works well, too. (Photo on page 214.)

    1   cup all-purpose flour
    ¾   cup cornmeal
    2   Tbsp. sugar
    1   Tbsp. baking powder
    ¾   tsp. salt
    2   eggs
    1   cup milk
    ¼   cup melted shortening or cooking oil

1. Preheat oven to 400°F. In a medium bowl, stir together flour, cornmeal, sugar, baking powder, and salt. In a small bowl, beat eggs with a whisk; whisk in milk and melted shortening. Add egg mixture all at once to the flour mixture. Stir just until moistened.

2. If using a cast-iron skillet, grease 10-inch cast-iron skillet; place skillet in the 400°F oven for 3 minutes. Remove from oven. Pour the batter into hot skillet. (Or grease a 9×1½-inch round baking pan; pour batter into unheated pan.) Bake about 20 minutes or until light brown. Cool slightly in skillet or pan on a wire rack. Serve warm. Makes 8 to 10 servings.

Nutrition facts per serving: 203 cal., 9 g total fat (2 g sat. fat), 56 mg chol., 368 mg sodium, 26 g carbo., 1 g fiber, 5 g pro.

Today

Confetti Corn Bread

Prep: 20 min. Bake: 50 min. Cool: 30 min.

This basil- and fennel-accented loaf is the perfect partner for pasta or salad. (Photo on page 215.)

    1   cup boiling water
    ¼   cup bulgur
         Yellow cornmeal
    1   cup yellow cornmeal
    1   cup all-purpose flour
    ⅓   cup grated Parmesan cheese
    2   Tbsp. sugar
    1   Tbsp. baking powder
    1½   tsp. snipped fresh basil
         or ½ tsp. dried basil, crushed
    ½   tsp. salt
    ½   tsp. fennel seeds, crushed
    2   eggs
    1   cup milk

    ¼   cup olive oil or cooking oil
    ⅓   cup oil-packed dried tomatoes, drained
         and chopped, or diced pimiento, drained
    ⅓   cup sliced green onions

1. Preheat oven to 375°F. In a small bowl, pour the boiling water over bulgur; let stand for 5 minutes. Drain. Meanwhile, grease bottom and ½ inch up sides of a 1½-quart soufflé dish or an 8×4×2-inch loaf pan. Sprinkle bottom and sides with cornmeal. Set aside.

2. In a large bowl, combine the 1 cup cornmeal, the flour, Parmesan cheese, sugar, baking powder, basil, salt, and fennel seeds. Make a well in the center of flour mixture.

3. In a medium bowl, beat eggs with a whisk; whisk in milk and oil. Stir in drained bulgur. Add bulgur mixture all at once to flour mixture. Stir just until moistened (batter should be lumpy). Fold in tomatoes or pimiento and green onions.

4. Pour batter into prepared dish or pan. Bake for 50 to 55 minutes or until a wooden toothpick inserted near center comes out clean. If necessary to prevent overbrowning, cover loosely with foil for the last 10 to 15 minutes of baking. Remove from dish or pan. Cool on a wire rack for 30 minutes. Serve warm. Makes 8 to 10 servings.

Nutrition facts per serving: 264 cal., 11 g total fat (2 g sat. fat), 58 mg chol., 403 mg sodium, 34 g carbo., 3 g fiber, 8 g pro.

Cowboy Coffee Cake

Prep: 15 min. Bake: 25 min.

This buttery breakfast bread recipe dates back to the 1930s. Although we haven't forgotten how mouthwatering it is, we have forgotten why it's called "cowboy."

    1½   cups all-purpose flour
    1   cup packed brown sugar
    ⅓   cup butter
    1   tsp. baking powder
    ¼   tsp. baking soda
    ¼   tsp. ground cinnamon
    ¼   tsp. ground nutmeg
    ½   cup buttermilk or sour milk*
    1   egg, beaten

1. Preheat oven to 375°F. Grease an 8×8×2-inch baking pan; set aside. In a medium bowl, stir together flour and brown sugar. Using a pastry blender, cut in butter until mixture resembles fine crumbs; set aside ½ *cup* of the crumb mixture to sprinkle over batter. To remaining crumb mixture, add baking powder, baking soda, cinnamon, and nutmeg; stir to combine. Stir in buttermilk and egg.

Cowboy Coffee Cake

2. Pour into prepared baking pan; spread evenly. Sprinkle with the reserved crumb mixture. Bake about 25 minutes or until a wooden toothpick inserted near the center comes out clean. Serve warm. Makes 9 servings.

*Test Kitchen Tip: To make ½ cup sour milk, place 1½ teaspoons lemon juice or vinegar in a glass measuring cup. Add enough milk to make ½ cup total liquid; stir. Let mixture stand for 5 minutes before using.

Nutrition facts per serving: 246 cal., 8 g total fat (5 g sat. fat), 43 mg chol., 184 mg sodium, 41 g carbo., 1 g fiber, 3 g pro.

Cheesy Supper Bread

Prep: 15 min. Bake: 20 min.

Even though we look with nostalgia to the 1950s, when things moved at a slower pace, cooks back then were trying to speed up time in the kitchen. This 1953 recipe was considered a real timesaver because it was based on packaged biscuit mix.

    2   Tbsp. butter
    1   large onion, thinly sliced
    ½   cup milk
    1   egg
    1½ cups packaged biscuit mix
    1   cup shredded sharp process American
        cheese or cheddar cheese (4 oz.)
    1   Tbsp. poppy seeds

1. Preheat oven to 400°F. Grease an 8×1½-inch round baking pan. Set aside.

2. In a medium skillet, melt *1 tablespoon* of the butter over medium heat. Add onion; cook until onion is tender, stirring occasionally. Remove *half* of the onion slices and chop; set aside remaining onion slices.

3. In a small bowl, whisk together milk and egg until mixed. In a large bowl, add milk mixture to biscuit mix; stir just until moistened. Add the chopped onion, *half* of the cheese, and *half* of the poppy seeds. Spread batter into prepared pan. Sprinkle with the remaining cheese and the remaining poppy seeds. Arrange reserved cooked, sliced onion on top.

4. Melt remaining 1 tablespoon butter; drizzle onto mixture in pan. Bake about 20 minutes or until a wooden toothpick inserted near the center comes out clean. Serve warm. Makes 8 servings.

Nutrition facts per serving: 207 cal., 12 g total fat (6 g sat. fat), 49 mg chol., 528 mg sodium, 17 g carbo., 1 g fiber, 7 g pro.

Cheddar Spoonbread

Prep: 25 min. Bake: 45 min.

It's always a debate: Is spoonbread a bread or a side dish? The confusion comes because it tastes like a bread but is baked in a casserole and is served with a spoon. No matter what you call it, the cornmeal concoction is a great addition to just about any menu.

    1½ cups milk
    ½   cup cornmeal
    2   cups shredded cheddar cheese or
        Monterey Jack cheese (8 oz.)
    1   Tbsp. butter or margarine
    1½ tsp. baking powder
    1   tsp. sugar
    ¼   tsp. salt
    4   eggs

1. Preheat oven to 325°F. In a large saucepan, stir together the milk and cornmeal. Cook, stirring constantly, over medium-high heat until mixture is thickened and bubbly; remove from heat. Add cheese, butter, baking powder, sugar, and salt; stir until cheese melts.

2. Separate eggs. Add yolks, *one* at a time, to cornmeal mixture, stirring after each addition just until combined (mixture will be thick).

3. In a large mixing bowl, beat egg whites with an electric mixer on high speed until stiff peaks form (tips stand straight). Stir *about one-third* of the beaten egg whites into the cornmeal mixture. Gently fold remaining beaten egg whites into cornmeal mixture until combined. Spoon into an ungreased 2-quart casserole or soufflé dish.

4. Bake for 45 to 50 minutes or until a knife inserted near the center comes out clean. Serve immediately. Makes 8 servings.

Nutrition facts per serving: 221 cal., 14 g total fat (8 g sat. fat), 143 mg chol., 393 mg sodium, 10 g carbo., 1 g fiber, 12 g pro.

French Breakfast Puffs

Prep: 15 min. Bake: 20 min.

Ribbon winners from state and county fairs across the country are some of the best recipes around. In 1972, these marvelous muffins turned heads at the Champlain Valley Exposition in Vermont. We were so dazzled, we included the recipe in our magazine.

1½   cups all-purpose flour
½   cup sugar
1½   tsp. baking powder
¼   tsp. ground nutmeg
⅛   tsp. salt
1   egg
½   cup milk
⅓   cup butter, melted
¼   cup sugar
½   tsp. ground cinnamon
¼   cup butter, melted

1. Preheat oven to 350°F. Grease twelve 2½-inch muffin cups; set aside.

French Breakfast Puffs

2. In a medium bowl, stir together flour, the ½ cup sugar, the baking powder, nutmeg, and salt. Make a well in the center of the flour mixture. In a small bowl, beat egg with a fork; stir in milk and the ⅓ cup melted butter. Add egg mixture to flour mixture; stir just until moistened (the batter may be lumpy).

3. Spoon batter into prepared muffin cups, filling each two-thirds full. Bake for 20 to 25 minutes or until golden.

4. In a small bowl, combine the ¼ cup sugar and the cinnamon. Remove muffins from oven; remove from muffin cups. Immediately dip baked muffins into the ¼ cup melted butter, then into sugar-cinnamon mixture. Serve warm. Makes 12 muffins.

Nutrition facts per muffin: 191 cal., 10 g total fat (6 g sat. fat), 42 mg chol., 169 mg sodium, 24 g carbo., 0 g fiber, 2 g pro.

Apple Bread

Prep: 30 min. Bake: 45 min.

Cooks in Washington state know their apples. In fact, Wenatchee calls itself the apple capital of the U.S. This recipe came to us from a 1980 princess of the town's Apple Blossom Festival.

3   cups all-purpose flour
1   tsp. baking soda
1   tsp. salt
1   tsp. ground cinnamon
¼   tsp. baking powder
3   eggs
3   cups shredded peeled cooking apples (such as Golden Delicious, Rome, Granny Smith, Jonathan, or Newtown Pippin) (about 4 medium)
2   cups sugar
⅔   cup cooking oil
1   tsp. vanilla

1. Preheat oven to 325°F. Grease and flour three 7½×3½×2-inch or two 8×4×2-inch pans. Set aside. In a medium bowl, combine flour, baking soda, salt, cinnamon, and baking powder; set aside.

2. In a large bowl, beat eggs; stir in apples, sugar, oil, and vanilla. Stir in flour mixture just until moistened. Pour into prepared pans. Bake for 45 to 55 minutes or until a wooden toothpick inserted in centers comes out clean. Cool in pans on wire racks for 10 minutes. Remove from pans. Cool on wire racks. Wrap in plastic wrap; store overnight before slicing. Makes 30 servings.

Nutrition facts per serving: 152 cal., 6 g total fat (1 g sat. fat), 21 mg chol., 129 mg sodium, 24 g carbo., 1 g fiber, 2 g pro.

Pat-a-Cake Scones

Pat-a-Cake Scones

Prep: 20 min. Bake: 18 min.

Kids will like patting out these English biscuits.

1½ cups all-purpose flour
⅓ cup sugar
2 tsp. baking powder
½ tsp. salt
¾ cup whipping cream
2 tsp. finely shredded lemon peel
 Whipping cream
 Sugar
 Whipped cream (optional)
 Strawberry jam (optional)

1. Preheat oven to 375°F. In a large bowl, stir together flour, the ⅓ cup sugar, the baking powder, and salt. Make a well in the center of the flour mixture. Add the ¾ cup whipping cream and the lemon peel.

2. Stir until mixture is crumbly. Knead dough by folding and gently pressing for 10 to 12 strokes or until it can be formed into a ball.

3. Turn out dough onto a lightly floured surface. Gently roll or pat the dough into a circle 7½ inches in diameter. Cut into 6 or 8 wedges. Place scones about 1 inch apart on an ungreased baking sheet.

4. Lightly brush scones with additional whipping cream; sprinkle with additional sugar. Bake about 18 minutes or until golden. Serve warm. If desired, serve with whipped cream and strawberry jam. Makes 6 to 8.

Nutrition facts per scone: 261 cal., 12 g total fat (7 g sat. fat), 43 mg chol., 340 mg sodium, 35 g carbo., 1 g fiber, 4 g pro.

Fruit Scones: Prepare as directed, except stir ¾ cup raisins, snipped dried cherries, currants, or other chopped dried fruit into the flour mixture before adding the ¾ cup whipping cream.

Nutrition facts per scone: 315 cal., 12 g total fat (7 g sat. fat), 43 mg chol., 342 mg sodium, 49 g carbo., 2 g fiber, 4 g pro.

Poppy-Seed-Topped Scones: Prepare as directed, except after brushing the wedges with additional whipping cream, sprinkle with 2 teaspoons poppy seeds or sesame seeds instead of sugar.

Nutrition facts per scone: 261 cal., 12 g total fat (7 g sat. fat), 43 mg chol., 340 mg sodium, 34 g carbo., 1 g fiber, 4 g pro.

Blueberry Buckle

Prep: 20 min. Bake: 50 min.

"Buckle" is an old-time term for a single-layer cake made with berries and sprinkled with streusel topping. You can serve it as a coffee cake for breakfast or as a dessert with dinner.

2 cups all-purpose flour
2½ tsp. baking powder
¼ tsp. salt
½ cup shortening
¾ cup sugar
1 egg
½ cup milk
2 cups fresh or frozen blueberries
½ cup all-purpose flour
½ cup sugar
½ tsp. ground cinnamon
¼ cup butter

1. Preheat oven to 350°F. Grease bottom and ½ inch up sides of a 9×9×2-inch or 8×8×2-inch baking pan; set aside. In a medium bowl, combine the 2 cups flour, the baking powder, and salt; set aside.

2. In a medium mixing bowl, beat shortening with an electric mixer on medium speed for 30 seconds. Add the ¾ cup sugar. Beat on medium to high speed until light and fluffy. Add egg; beat well. Add flour mixture and milk alternately to beaten mixture, beating until smooth after each addition.

3. Spoon batter into prepared pan. Sprinkle with blueberries. In a small bowl, combine the ½ cup flour, the ½ cup sugar, and the cinnamon. Using a pastry blender, cut in butter until mixture resembles coarse crumbs; sprinkle onto blueberries. Bake for 50 to 60 minutes or until golden. Serve warm. Makes 9 servings.

Nutrition facts per serving: 401 cal., 18 g total fat (7 g sat. fat), 39 mg chol., 247 mg sodium, 56 g carbo., 2 g fiber, 5 g pro.

Raspberry Buckle: Prepare as directed, except substitute fresh or frozen red raspberries for the blueberries.

Nutrition facts per serving: 397 cal., 18 g total fat (7 g sat. fat), 39 mg chol., 245 mg sodium, 55 g carbo., 2 g fiber, 5 g pro.

Yesterday

We used "supreme" in the recipe title for these flaky baking powder morsels from the 1960s because we think they're the best biscuits ever.

Biscuits Supreme

Prep: 20 min. Bake: 10 min.

The secret to tender biscuits lies in cutting as many as possible from the first rolling of dough. Those cut from a second rolling may be slightly tougher.

3	cups all-purpose flour
4	tsp. baking powder
1	Tbsp. sugar
1	tsp. salt
¾	tsp. cream of tartar
¾	cup butter or ½ cup butter plus ¼ cup shortening
1¼	cups buttermilk or 1 cup milk

1. Preheat oven to 450°F. In a large bowl, stir together flour, baking powder, sugar, salt, and cream of tartar. Using a pastry blender, cut in butter until mixture resembles coarse crumbs. Make a well in the center of the flour mixture. Add buttermilk or milk all at once. Using a fork, stir just until moistened.

2. Turn out dough onto a lightly floured surface. Knead dough by folding and gently pressing dough for 4 to 6 strokes or just until dough holds together. Pat or lightly roll dough to ¾-inch thickness. Cut dough with a floured 2½-inch biscuit cutter.

3. Place biscuits 1 inch apart on an ungreased baking sheet. Bake for 10 to 12 minutes or until golden. Remove the biscuits from baking sheet and serve immediately. Makes 10 biscuits.

Nutrition facts per biscuit: 273 cal., 15 g total fat (9 g sat. fat), 40 mg chol., 574 mg sodium, 29 g carbo., 1 g fiber, 5 g pro.

Drop Biscuits Supreme: Prepare as directed, except add ¼ cup whipping cream with the buttermilk or milk. Do not knead, roll, or cut dough. Drop dough by spoonfuls onto greased baking sheet. Bake as directed. Makes 12 biscuits.

Make-ahead directions: Prepare and bake biscuits as directed; cool completely. Place biscuits in a freezer container or freezer bag. Seal, label, and freeze for up to 3 months. To serve, preheat oven to 300°F. Wrap the frozen biscuits in foil and bake for 20 to 25 minutes or until warm.

Nutrition facts per biscuit: 293 cal., 17 g total fat (11 g sat. fat), 49 mg chol., 576 mg sodium, 29 g carbo., 1 g fiber, 5 g pro.

Peppery White Cheddar Biscuits

Prep: 25 min. Bake: 13 min.

Sharp white cheddar cheese and coarsely ground pepper perk up these light and luscious biscuits.

- 4 cups all-purpose flour
- 2 Tbsp. baking powder
- ½ tsp. salt
- ½ cup shortening
- ¼ cup butter
- 1½ cups finely crumbled or shredded sharp white cheddar cheese (6 oz.)
- 2 to 3 tsp. coarsely ground black pepper
- 1½ cups milk
- 1 egg
- 1 tsp. water

1. Preheat oven to 400°F. Lightly grease a large baking sheet; set aside. In a large bowl, stir together flour, baking powder, and salt. Using a pastry blender, cut in shortening and butter until mixture resembles coarse crumbs. Add cheese and pepper; mix well. Make a well in center of the flour mixture. Add milk all at once; stir just until moistened.

2. Turn out dough onto a lightly floured surface. Knead dough by folding and gently pressing dough for 10 to 12 strokes or until almost smooth. Divide dough in half. Roll or pat each half into a 6-inch square. Using a sharp knife, cut dough into 2-inch squares. In a small bowl, whisk together egg and the water; brush onto tops of biscuits. Place on prepared baking sheet.

3. Bake for 13 to 15 minutes or until golden. Transfer to a wire rack. Serve warm. Makes 18 biscuits.

Make-ahead directions: Prepare and bake biscuits as directed; cool completely. Place biscuits in a freezer container or freezer bag. Seal, label, and freeze for up to 3 months. To serve, preheat oven to 300°F. Wrap the frozen biscuits in foil and bake for 20 to 25 minutes or until warm.

Nutrition facts per biscuit: 247 cal., 14 g total fat (6 g sat. fat), 34 mg chol., 314 mg sodium, 24 g carbo., 1 g fiber, 7 g pro.

Today

This newcomer takes a no-fuss approach to biscuit making. Instead of cutting out individual rounds, the recipe calls for the dough to be patted into squares and cut into 2-inch pieces. No rerolling required!

Seven-Grain Cereal Muffins

5. Bake until golden. Allow about 20 minutes for 3¼-inch muffins, 15 to 18 minutes for 2½-inch muffins, or about 12 minutes for muffin-top cups. Cool in cups on a wire rack for 5 minutes. Remove from cups; serve immediately. Makes six 3¼-inch muffins, sixteen 2½-inch muffins, or 12 muffin tops.

*Test Kitchen Tip: To make 1¼ cups sour milk, place 4 teaspoons lemon juice or vinegar in a glass measuring cup. Add enough milk to make 1¼ cups total liquid; stir. Let mixture stand for 5 minutes before using.

Nutrition facts per 3¼-inch muffin: 397 cal., 12 g total fat (2 g sat. fat), 37 mg chol., 442 mg sodium, 67 g carbo., 5 g fiber, 9 g pro.

Seven-Grain Cereal Muffins
Prep: 15 min. Stand: 30 min. Bake: 20 min.

This cherry-studded muffin based on seven-grain cereal is a hearty grab-and-go treat to carry you through the morning rush hour.

1	**cup seven-grain cereal**
1	**cup dried tart red cherries**
½	**cup packed brown sugar**
¼	**cup cooking oil**
1¼	**cups buttermilk or sour milk***
1	**cup whole wheat flour**
1	**tsp. baking powder**
1	**tsp. ground ginger or 1 Tbsp. crystallized ginger, finely chopped**
½	**tsp. baking soda**
½	**tsp. salt**
½	**tsp. ground nutmeg**
1	**egg**

1. Grease six 3¼-inch (jumbo) muffin cups, sixteen 2½-inch muffin cups, or 12 muffin-top cups. (Or line the 2½-inch muffin cups with paper bake cups.) Set aside.

2. In a medium bowl, combine seven-grain cereal, dried cherries, brown sugar, and oil. Pour buttermilk over cereal mixture; let stand for 30 minutes.

3. Meanwhile, in a large bowl, stir together whole wheat flour, baking powder, ginger, baking soda, salt, and nutmeg. Make a well in the center of flour mixture; set aside.

4. Preheat oven to 400°F. Whisk egg into buttermilk mixture until mixed. Add buttermilk mixture all at once to flour mixture. Stir just until moistened. Spoon batter into prepared cups, filling muffin cups three-fourths full or muffin-top cups almost full.

Old-Fashioned Popovers
Prep: 15 min. Bake: 35 min. Stand: 5 min.

In the 1930s, we advised readers, "The time to eat a popover is when it has just popped over"—meaning straight from the oven. Because folks tend to prefer popovers a little crisper today, our recipe now calls for pricking the popovers and allowing them to stand in a warm oven so the steam can escape.

	Nonstick cooking spray
2	**eggs**
1	**cup milk**
1	**Tbsp. cooking oil**
¾	**cup all-purpose flour**
½	**tsp. salt**
	Butter (optional)

1. Preheat oven to 400°F. Generously coat the bottom and sides of 6 cups of a popover pan or five 6-ounce custard cups with nonstick cooking spray. Place the custard cups, if using, on a 15×10×1-inch baking pan. Set aside.

2. In a medium bowl, use a wire whisk or a rotary beater to beat eggs; beat in milk and oil. Add flour and salt; beat until combined but still slightly lumpy. Fill the prepared popover cups or custard cups half full.

3. Bake about 35 minutes or until the crusts are very firm. Turn off oven. Using the tines of a fork, immediately prick each popover to let steam escape. Return the popovers to the oven for 5 to 10 minutes more or until of desired crispness. (Be sure the oven is turned off.) Remove from cups and serve immediately. If desired, serve with butter. Makes 5 or 6 popovers.

Nutrition facts per popover: 141 cal., 6 g total fat (2 g sat. fat), 89 mg chol., 282 mg sodium, 16 g carbo., 0 g fiber, 6 g pro.

Pear-Walnut Muffins

Prep: 20 min. Bake: 20 min. Cool: 5 min.

These moist and nutty pear-filled muffins tickled our taste buds enough to win a prize in 1996.

1½	cups all-purpose flour
½	cup packed brown sugar
2	tsp. baking powder
1	tsp. ground cinnamon
½	tsp. ground ginger
⅛	tsp. salt
1	egg
½	cup cooking oil
½	cup plain low-fat yogurt
½	tsp. vanilla
1	pear, cored and finely chopped
3	Tbsp. finely chopped walnuts
2	Tbsp. packed brown sugar

1. Preheat oven to 400°F. Lightly grease twelve 2½-inch muffin cups or line with paper bake cups; set aside. In a medium bowl, stir together flour, the ½ cup brown sugar, the baking powder, cinnamon, ginger, and salt. Make a well in the center of the flour mixture.

2. In a small bowl, beat egg with a fork. Stir in oil, yogurt, and vanilla; add to flour mixture. Stir just until moistened (batter should be lumpy). Fold in pear.

3. Spoon batter into prepared muffin cups, filling each two-thirds full. For topping, in a small bowl, combine walnuts and the 2 tablespoons brown sugar. Sprinkle onto batter.

4. Bake about 20 minutes or until golden. Cool in muffin cups on a wire rack for 5 minutes. Remove from cups; serve warm. Makes 12 muffins.

Nutrition facts per muffin: 206 cal., 11 g total fat (2 g sat. fat), 18 mg chol., 77 mg sodium, 26 g carbo., 1 g fiber, 3 g pro.

Pear-Walnut Muffins

Stuffed French Toast

Start to finish: 35 min.

Brimming with cheese, nuts, and apricot preserves, this company-special French toast from the 1990s ranks as one of our readers' favorite breakfast treats.

1	8-oz. pkg. cream cheese, softened
1	cup apricot preserves
1	tsp. vanilla
½	cup chopped walnuts
1	16-oz. loaf French bread
4	eggs
1	cup whipping cream
½	tsp. ground nutmeg
½	tsp. vanilla
¼	cup orange juice
	Fresh or frozen raspberries (optional)

1. Preheat oven to 300°F. In a medium mixing bowl, combine cream cheese, *2 tablespoons* of the apricot preserves, and the 1 teaspoon vanilla; beat with an electric mixer on medium speed until fluffy. Stir in nuts; set aside. Cut bread into ten to twelve 1½-inch-thick slices; cut a pocket about 2 inches deep in the top of each bread slice, but not all the way to the sides. Fill *each* pocket with a *rounded tablespoon* of the cream cheese mixture.

2. In a medium bowl, whisk together eggs, whipping cream, nutmeg, and the ½ teaspoon vanilla. Using tongs, quickly dip the filled bread slices into the egg mixture, allowing excess mixture to drip off and being careful not to squeeze out the filling. Cook on a lightly greased griddle over medium heat about 4 minutes or until golden, turning once. Keep warm in preheated oven while cooking remaining slices.

3. Meanwhile, in a small saucepan, heat and stir the remaining apricot preserves and the orange juice until mixture is melted. To serve, drizzle the apricot preserves mixture over hot French toast. If desired, top with raspberries. Makes 10 to 12 slices.

Nutrition facts per slice: 449 cal., 24 g total fat (12 g sat. fat), 143 mg chol., 388 mg sodium, 49 g carbo., 2 g fiber, 10 g pro.

Lower-Fat Stuffed French Toast: Prepare as directed, except use reduced-fat cream cheese (Neufchâtel); substitute 1 cup refrigerated or frozen egg product, thawed, for the whole eggs; and use fat-free milk instead of whipping cream.

Nutrition facts per slice: 337 cal., 11 g total fat (4 g sat. fat), 18 mg chol., 430 mg sodium, 49 g carbo., 2 g fiber, 11 g pro.

Puffed Oven Pancake

Puffed Oven Pancake

Prep: 10 min. Bake: 20 min.

Whether you call it an oven pancake, a German pancake, or a Dutch baby, this tender puffed hotcake-in-a-skillet filled with fresh fruit is a great way to start the day.

 2   **Tbsp. butter or margarine**
 3   **eggs**
 ½   **cup all-purpose flour**
 ½   **cup milk**
 ¼   **tsp. salt**
 ¼   **cup orange marmalade**
 3   **cups sliced fresh fruit (such as strawberries, nectarines, pears, or peeled peaches)**
     Powdered sugar (optional)
     Whipped cream (optional)

1. Preheat oven to 400°F. Place butter in a 10-inch ovenproof skillet. Place skillet in oven for 3 to 5 minutes or until butter is melted.

2. Meanwhile, for batter, in a medium bowl, use a wire whisk or rotary beater to beat eggs. Add flour, milk, and salt; beat until smooth. Immediately pour into hot skillet. Bake for 20 to 25 minutes or until puffed and browned.

3. Meanwhile, in a small saucepan, melt the orange marmalade over low heat. To serve, top pancake with fruit; spoon melted marmalade over fruit. If desired, sift powdered sugar over top and serve with whipped cream. Cut into wedges and serve warm. Makes 6 servings.

Nutrition facts per serving: 176 cal., 7 g total fat (4 g sat. fat), 119 mg chol., 188 mg sodium, 23 g carbo., 2 g fiber, 5 g pro.

Lemon Soufflé Pancakes

Prep: 20 min. Cook: 4 min. per batch

In our early issues, pancakes were dubbed griddle cakes and were made with simple stir-together batters. In 2001, we lightened the batter by folding in beaten egg whites. The cloudlike texture of these flapjacks makes it worth pulling out the mixer.

 1   **recipe Raspberry Syrup (below)**
 1   **cup all-purpose flour**
 2   **tsp. baking powder**
 2   **tsp. finely shredded lemon peel**
 ¼   **tsp. salt**
 1   **egg yolk**
 ¾   **cup milk**
 ¼   **cup butter, melted**
 3   **egg whites**

1. Prepare Raspberry Syrup; set aside. To make pancakes, in a medium bowl, stir together flour, baking powder, lemon peel, and salt. Make a well in the center of flour mixture; set aside. In a small bowl, use a fork to beat egg yolk slightly. Stir in milk and melted butter. Add egg yolk mixture all at once to the flour mixture. Stir just until moistened (batter should be lumpy).

2. In a medium mixing bowl, beat egg whites with an electric mixer on medium speed until stiff peaks form (tips stand straight). Gently fold egg whites into flour mixture, leaving a few fluffs of egg white. Do not overmix.

3. For *each 4-inch* pancake, pour ¼ *cup* of the batter onto hot, lightly greased griddle or heavy skillet. (Or for *each dollar-size* [2-inch] pancake, pour about *1 tablespoon* of the batter onto hot, lightly greased griddle or heavy skillet.) Cook over medium heat about 2 minutes per side or until pancakes are golden brown. Turn to second side when pancakes have bubbly surfaces and edges are slightly dry. Repeat with remaining batter. Serve with Raspberry Syrup. Makes eight 4-inch pancakes or twenty 2-inch pancakes.

Raspberry Syrup: Thaw 2 cups frozen lightly sweetened red raspberries but do not drain. Place the berries in a blender or food processor; blend or process until smooth. Press berries through a fine-mesh sieve into a saucepan. Discard seeds. Cook and stir over medium heat just until heated through. Stir in 1 cup pure maple syrup or maple-flavored syrup.

Nutrition facts per 4-inch pancake: 249 cal., 7 g total fat (4 g sat. fat), 45 mg chol., 271 mg sodium, 42 g carbo., 1 g fiber, 4 g pro.

Peanut Waffles with Butterscotch Sauce

Prep: 25 min. Cook: per waffle baker's directions

In 1938 when these crisp peanut-flecked waffles were first published, they were probably served for dessert. Today, cooks are more likely to whip them up for an extra-special breakfast or brunch.

1	**recipe Butterscotch Sauce (right)**
1¾	**cups all-purpose flour**
2	**Tbsp. sugar**
1	**Tbsp. baking powder**
¼	**tsp. salt**
2	**egg yolks**
1¾	**cups milk**
½	**cup cooking oil**
½	**cup finely chopped peanuts**
2	**egg whites**
	Banana slices (optional)
	Chopped peanuts (optional)

1. Prepare Butterscotch Sauce; keep warm.

2. In a large bowl, stir together flour, sugar, baking powder, and salt. In a medium bowl, beat egg yolks with a fork; stir in milk and oil. Add egg mixture to flour mixture all at once, stirring just until combined but still slightly lumpy. Stir in the ½ cup peanuts. Set aside.

3. In a small bowl, beat egg whites with an electric mixer on medium to high speed until stiff peaks form (tips stand straight). Gently fold egg whites into batter, leaving a few fluffs of egg white. Do not overmix.

4. Pour *1 to 1¼ cups* of the batter onto grids of a preheated, lightly greased waffle baker. Close lid quickly; do not open during baking. Bake according to manufacturer's directions. When done, use a fork to lift waffle off grid. Repeat with remaining batter.

5. Serve hot with warm Butterscotch Sauce and, if desired, banana slices. If desired, sprinkle with additional peanuts. Makes 16 to 20 (4-inch) waffles.

Butterscotch Sauce: In a medium saucepan, combine 1¼ cups packed brown sugar, ⅔ cup light-colored corn syrup, ¼ cup milk, and ¼ cup butter. Bring just to boiling; reduce heat. Simmer, uncovered, for 20 minutes, stirring occasionally. Serve warm. (Refrigerate any remaining sauce; reheat in saucepan over low heat.)

Nutrition facts per waffle with 2 tablespoons sauce: 375 cal., 18 g total fat (1 g sat. fat), 47 mg chol., 279 mg sodium, 50 g carbo., 1 g fiber, 6 g pro.

Peanut Waffles with Butterscotch Sauce

With a glass of milk after school or as a tempting morsel on a dessert buffet, cookies are one of life's little pleasures. And *Better Homes and Gardens®* editors have been helping to fill our readers' cookie jars for decades. On these pages, we've pulled together a cookie collection worth bragging about. You'll find all of your favorites, plus a few surprises. Select from drop, rolled, cutout, bar, and shaped cookies and stock your cookie jar full!

Best-Loved Cookies

230

245

251

237

233

229

Chocolate Chip Cookies Three Ways

We've worked hard to come up with the "perfect" chocolate chip cookie. Problem is—perfect is a matter of preference. We've learned over the years that a few tweaks to chocolate chip cookies can dramatically change how the cookie crumbles. Our tinkering has resulted in three super versions; you choose which is best—or try all three.

Chewy Chocolate Chip Cookies

Prep: 25 min. Bake: 8 min. per batch

For a good and basic cookie that's a little bit crisp and a little bit chewy, we use equal parts shortening and butter and a blend of sugars.

- ½ **cup shortening**
- ½ **cup butter, softened**
- 1 **cup packed brown sugar**
- ½ **cup granulated sugar**
- ½ **tsp. baking soda**
- 2 **eggs**
- 1 **tsp. vanilla**
- 2½ **cups all-purpose flour**
- 2 **cups semisweet chocolate pieces, milk chocolate pieces, or white baking pieces**
- 1½ **cups chopped walnuts or pecans (optional)**

Chewy Chocolate Chip Cookies

1. Preheat oven to 375°F. In a large mixing bowl, beat shortening and butter on medium to high speed for 30 seconds. Add brown sugar, granulated sugar, and baking soda. Beat until combined, scraping side of bowl occasionally. Beat in eggs and vanilla until combined. Beat in as much of the flour as you can with the mixer. Using a wooden spoon, stir in any remaining flour. Stir in chocolate pieces and, if desired, nuts.

2. Drop by rounded teaspoons 2 inches apart onto ungreased cookie sheets. Bake for 8 to 10 minutes or until edges are lightly browned. Transfer to wire racks and let cool. Makes about 60 cookies.

Nutrition facts per cookie: 98 cal., 5 g total fat (2 g sat. fat), 11 mg chol., 31 mg sodium, 13 g carbo., 0 g fiber, 1 g pro.

Thin-and-Crispy Chocolate Chip Cookies

Prep: 25 min. Bake: 10 min. per batch

For a thin, crisp cookie, we opt for an all-butter dough because butter melts quicker than shortening, so the dough spreads more. We also include an equal mix of brown and granulated sugars.

- 1 **cup butter, softened**
- ¾ **cup packed brown sugar**
- ¾ **cup granulated sugar**
- ½ **tsp. baking soda**
- 1 **egg**
- 1 **tsp. vanilla**
- 2 **cups all-purpose flour**
- 2 **cups semisweet chocolate pieces, milk chocolate pieces, or white baking pieces**
- 1½ **cups chopped walnuts or pecans (optional)**

1. Preheat oven to 375°F. In a large mixing bowl, beat butter on medium to high speed for 30 seconds. Add brown sugar, granulated sugar, and baking soda. Beat until combined, scraping side of bowl occasionally. Beat in egg and vanilla until combined. Beat in as much of the flour as you can with the mixer. Using a wooden spoon, stir in any remaining flour. Stir in chocolate pieces and, if desired, nuts.

2. Drop dough by rounded teaspoons 2 inches apart onto ungreased cookie sheets. Bake for 10 to 12 minutes or until edges are lightly browned. Transfer to wire racks and let cool. Makes about 60 cookies.

Nutrition facts per cookie: 93 cal., 5 g total fat (3 g sat. fat), 12 mg chol., 46 mg sodium, 12 g carbo., 0 g fiber, 1 g pro.

Soft-and-Cakelike Chocolate
Chip Cookies

Soft-and-Cakelike Chocolate Chip Cookies

Prep: 25 min. Bake: 9 min. per batch

For a puffy cookie, we go for all shortening instead of butter; that way the dough stays mounded. We also use only brown sugar. Sour cream adds richness.

- ½ **cup shortening**
- 1½ **cups packed brown sugar**
- 2 **eggs**
- 1 **tsp. vanilla**
- 2½ **cups all-purpose flour**
- 1 **tsp. baking soda**
- ½ **tsp. baking powder**
- ¼ **tsp. salt**
- 1 **8-oz. carton dairy sour cream**
- 2 **cups white baking pieces, semisweet chocolate pieces, or milk chocolate pieces**
- 1½ **cup chopped macadamia nuts, walnuts, or pecans (optional)**

1. Preheat oven to 375°F. In a large mixing bowl, beat shortening and brown sugar on medium to high speed until combined. Add eggs and vanilla; beat until combined. In a medium bowl, stir together flour, baking soda, baking powder, and salt. Alternately add flour mixture and sour cream to shortening mixture, beating after each addition. Using a wooden spoon, stir in white baking pieces and, if desired, nuts.

2. Drop by rounded teaspoons 2 inches apart onto ungreased cookie sheets. Bake for 9 to 11 minutes or until edges are lightly browned. Transfer to wire racks and let cool. Makes about 60 cookies.

Nutrition facts per cookie: 97 cal., 4 g total fat (2 g sat. fat), 10 mg chol., 46 mg sodium, 13 g carbo., 0 g fiber, 1 g pro.

Orange-Pumpkin Cookies

Prep: 30 min. Bake: 9 min. per batch

Canned pumpkin is a true timesaver. Without it, cooking the pumpkin for these moist cookies would take hours.

- ½ **cup butter, softened**
- ½ **cup shortening**
- ½ **cup granulated sugar**
- ½ **cup packed brown sugar**
- ½ **tsp. baking powder**
- ¼ **tsp. baking soda**
- 1 **cup canned pumpkin**
- 1 **egg**
- 1 **tsp. finely shredded orange peel**
- 2 **cups all-purpose flour**
- 1 **recipe Orange-Butter Frosting (below)**

1. Preheat oven to 375°F. In a large mixing bowl, beat butter and shortening with an electric mixer on medium to high speed for 30 seconds. Add the granulated sugar, brown sugar, baking powder, and baking soda. Beat until combined, scraping side of bowl occasionally. Beat in pumpkin, egg, and orange peel. Beat in as much of the flour as you can with the mixer. Using a wooden spoon, stir in any remaining flour.

2. Drop dough by rounded teaspoons 2 inches apart onto ungreased cookie sheets. Bake for 9 to 11 minutes or until tops are firm. Transfer to wire racks and let cool.

3. Prepare Orange-Butter Frosting; frost cookies. Makes 36 cookies.

Orange-Butter Frosting: In a medium mixing bowl, beat ¼ cup butter until fluffy. Gradually add 2 cups sifted powdered sugar, beating well. Slowly beat in ¾ teaspoon finely shredded orange peel and 2 tablespoons orange juice. Beat in additional orange juice, if needed, to make a frosting of spreading consistency.

Nutrition facts per cookie: 128 cal., 7 g total fat (3 g sat. fat), 16 mg chol., 55 mg sodium, 16 g carbo., 0 g fiber, 1 g pro.

Oatmeal Cookies

Prep: 25 min. Bake: 8 min. per batch
Stand: 1 min. per batch

Everyone has opinions about what should be added to oatmeal cookies—raisins, nuts, chocolate, butterscotch chips, peanut butter pieces, or nothing at all. Our recipe gives you options aplenty.

¾	**cup butter, softened**
1	**cup packed brown sugar**
½	**cup granulated sugar**
1	**tsp. baking powder**
¼	**tsp. baking soda**
½	**tsp. ground cinnamon (optional)**
¼	**tsp. ground cloves (optional)**
2	**eggs**
1	**tsp. vanilla**
1¾	**cups all-purpose flour**
2	**cups rolled oats**

Oatmeal-Raisin Cookies

1. Preheat oven to 375°F. In a large mixing bowl, beat butter with an electric mixer on medium to high speed for 30 seconds. Add brown sugar, granulated sugar, baking powder, baking soda, and, if desired, cinnamon and cloves. Beat until combined, scraping side of bowl occasionally. Beat in eggs and vanilla until combined. Beat in as much of the flour as you can with the mixer. Using a wooden spoon, stir in any remaining flour. Stir in rolled oats.

2. Drop dough by rounded teaspoons 2 inches apart onto ungreased cookie sheets. Bake for 8 to 10 minutes or until edges are golden. Let stand on cookie sheets for 1 minute. Transfer to wire racks and let cool. Makes about 48 cookies.

Nutrition facts per cookie: 84 cal., 4 g total fat (2 g sat. fat), 17 mg chol., 51 mg sodium, 12 g carbo., 0 g fiber, 1 g pro.

Oatmeal-Raisin Cookies: Prepare as directed, except after stirring in oats, stir in 1 cup raisins or snipped dried tart cherries and, if desired, ½ cup chopped nuts. Makes about 54 cookies.

Nutrition facts per cookie: 83 cal., 3 g total fat (2 g sat. fat), 15 mg chol., 45 mg sodium, 13 g carbo., 0 g fiber, 1 g pro.

Oatmeal-Chip Cookies: Prepare as directed, except after stirring in oats, stir in 1 cup semisweet chocolate, butterscotch-flavored, or peanut butter-flavored pieces and ½ cup chopped walnuts or pecans. Makes about 54 cookies.

Nutrition facts per cookie: 97 cal., 5 g total fat (2 g sat. fat), 15 mg chol., 45 mg sodium, 13 g carbo., 1 g fiber, 1 g pro.

Oversize Oatmeal Cookies: Prepare as directed, except use a ¼-cup measure or scoop to drop mounds of dough 2 inches apart onto ungreased cookie sheets. Press into 3-inch circles. Bake in the 375°F oven for 8 to 10 minutes or until edges are golden. Let stand on cookie sheets for 1 minute. Transfer to wire racks and let cool. Makes about 10 cookies.

Nutrition facts per cookie: 404 cal., 17 g total fat (10 g sat. fat), 82 mg chol., 242 mg sodium, 59 g carbo., 2 g fiber, 6 g pro.

Before ovens had thermostats, a cook making a cake would bake a tiny one as a test to check the oven temperature. Those trial cakes evolved into what we call cookies. The word cookie comes from the Dutch word for cake—*koekje*.

Frosted Butterscotch Cookies

Prep: 40 min. Bake: 10 min. per batch

A Florida cook submitted this 1938 recipe when we solicited readers' favorites for our 75th anniversary. She says her now-grown grandchildren still fondly remember the cookies from their childhoods.

2½ cups all-purpose flour
1 tsp. baking soda
½ tsp. salt
½ tsp. baking powder
1½ cups packed brown sugar
½ cup shortening
2 eggs
1 tsp. vanilla
1 8-oz. carton dairy sour cream
⅔ cup chopped walnuts
1 recipe Browned Butter Frosting (below)
   Chopped walnuts or walnut
   halves (optional)

1. Preheat oven to 375°F. Grease cookie sheets. Set aside. In a medium bowl, stir together flour, baking soda, salt, and baking powder. Set aside.

2. In a large mixing bowl, beat the brown sugar and shortening with an electric mixer on medium speed until well mixed. Beat in eggs and vanilla. Alternately add flour mixture and sour cream to beaten mixture, beating until combined after each addition. Stir in the ⅔ cup nuts.

3. Drop dough by rounded teaspoons 2 inches apart onto prepared cookie sheets. Bake for 10 to 12 minutes or until edges are lightly browned. Transfer to wire racks and let cool.

4. Prepare Browned Butter Frosting; spread cooled cookies with frosting. If desired, top with additional chopped walnuts or walnut halves. Makes about 60 cookies.

Browned Butter Frosting: In a medium saucepan, heat and stir ½ cup butter over medium-low heat until golden brown. (Do not scorch.) Remove from heat. Stir in 3½ cups sifted powdered sugar, 5 teaspoons boiling water, and 1½ teaspoons vanilla. Using a wooden spoon, beat until frosting is easy to spread. Immediately spread on cookies. If frosting begins to set up, stir in a small amount of boiling water.

Nutrition facts per cookie: 105 cal., 5 g total fat (2 g sat. fat), 13 mg chol., 63 mg sodium, 14 g carbo., 0 g fiber, 1 g pro.

Hermits

Prep: 30 min. Bake: 8 min. per batch

These chewy spice cookies date back to Colonial New England, although Southerners claim them, too. Apparently they're called Hermits because they're better after hiding away for several days. They've been part of our cookie collection since the late 1920s.

¾ cup butter, softened
¾ cup packed brown sugar
1 tsp. ground cinnamon
½ tsp. baking soda
¼ tsp. ground cloves
¼ tsp. ground nutmeg
1 egg
¼ cup strong coffee, cooled
1 tsp. vanilla
1½ cups all-purpose flour
2 cups raisins
1 cup chopped pecans
   Pecan halves (optional)

1. Preheat oven to 375°F. In a large mixing bowl, beat butter with an electric mixer on medium to high speed for 30 seconds. Add brown sugar, cinnamon, baking soda, cloves, and nutmeg; beat until combined. Beat in egg, coffee, and vanilla. Beat in as much of the flour as you can with the mixer. Using a wooden spoon, stir in any remaining flour. Stir in raisins and chopped pecans.

2. Drop dough by rounded tablespoons 2 inches apart onto ungreased cookie sheets. If desired, lightly press a pecan half on top of each mound. Bake for 8 to 10 minutes or until edges are lightly browned. Transfer to wire racks and let cool. Makes about 30 cookies.

Nutrition facts per cookie: 144 cal., 8 g total fat (3 g sat. fat), 20 mg chol., 76 mg sodium, 18 g carbo., 1 g fiber, 2 g pro.

Chewy Coconut Macaroons

Prep: 15 min. Bake: 20 min. per batch

During the Great Depression, coconut was
a luxury; so macaroon recipes back then often
extended the precious ingredient with a cereal, such
as cornflakes. Today, coconut is more affordable, so
we can enjoy it solo in these moist, fluffy tempters.

- 1 **7-oz. bag flaked coconut (2⅔ cups total)**
- ⅔ **cup sugar**
- ⅓ **cup all-purpose flour**
- ¼ **tsp. salt**
- 4 **egg whites**
- ½ **tsp. almond extract**
- 2 **oz. semisweet chocolate (optional)**
- ½ **tsp. shortening (optional)**

1. Preheat oven to 325°F. Lightly grease and flour a
large cookie sheet; set aside.

2. In a medium bowl, combine coconut, sugar, flour,
and salt. Stir in egg whites and almond extract. Drop egg
white mixture by rounded teaspoons 2 inches apart onto
prepared cookie sheet. Bake for 20 to 25 minutes or until
edges are golden. Transfer to wire racks and let cool.

3. If desired, in a heavy, small saucepan, combine
chocolate and shortening; heat and stir over low heat until
melted. Drizzle onto cooled cookies. Makes 30 cookies.

Nutrition facts per cookie: 55 cal., 3 g total fat (2 g sat. fat), 0 mg chol.,
27 mg sodium, 8 g carbo., 0 g fiber, 1 g pro.

Lemon Drops

Prep: 25 min. Bake: 8 min. per batch

These dainty citrus sparklers were prizewinners in
our December 1952 issue.

- ½ **cup butter, softened**
- ¾ **cup sugar**
- 4 **tsp. finely shredded lemon peel**
- ½ **tsp. baking powder**
- ½ **tsp. baking soda**
- ⅛ **tsp. salt**
- 1 **egg**
- ½ **cup dairy sour cream**
- ⅓ **cup lemon juice**
- 2 **cups all-purpose flour**
- 1 **recipe Lemon Glaze (top right)**

1. Preheat oven to 375°F. In a large mixing bowl, beat
butter with an electric mixer on medium to high speed
for 30 seconds. Add sugar, lemon peel, baking powder,
soda, and salt. Beat until combined, scraping side often.

2. Beat in egg, sour cream, and lemon juice until
combined. Beat in as much of the flour as you can with
the mixer. Using a spoon, stir in any remaining flour.

3. Drop dough by slightly rounded tablespoons
3 inches apart onto ungreased cookie sheets. Bake
about 8 minutes or until tops are firm. Transfer to wire
racks. Prepare Lemon Glaze. Brush tops of the warm
cookies with glaze. Let cool. Makes 36 cookies.

Lemon Glaze: In a small bowl, stir together ¼ cup
sugar and 2 tablespoons lemon juice.

Nutrition facts per cookie: 71 cal., 3 g total fat (2 g sat. fat), 13 mg chol.,
61 mg sodium, 11 g carbo., 0 g fiber, 1 g pro.

Cranberry Jumbles

Prep: 20 min. Bake: 12 min. per batch

"Jumbals" were one of the earliest cookies baked in
the Colonies. The spelling may have changed but
these favorites are still loaded with fruit and nuts.

- 1¼ **cups all-purpose flour**
- ⅔ **cup packed brown sugar**
- ½ **cup whole wheat flour**
- ¾ **tsp. baking powder**
- ½ **tsp. ground cinnamon**
- ¼ **tsp. baking soda**
- ⅔ **cup shortening**
- 1 **egg**
- 3 **Tbsp. cranberry juice or orange juice**
- 1 **cup dried cranberries**
- ½ **cup slivered almonds**
- 1 **recipe Double Orange Icing (below)**

1. Preheat oven to 350°F. Stir together the all-purpose
flour, brown sugar, whole wheat flour, baking powder,
cinnamon, and baking soda. Using a pastry blender, cut
in shortening until mixture resembles fine crumbs.

2. In a small bowl, beat egg with a fork; stir in juice.
Add to flour mixture; using a wooden spoon, stir until all
is moistened. Stir in cranberries and almonds.

3. Drop dough by rounded teaspoons 2 inches apart
onto ungreased cookie sheets. Bake for 12 to
14 minutes or until bottoms are lightly browned. Transfer
to wire racks and let cool. Prepare Double Orange Icing;
drizzle onto cookies. Makes about 32 cookies.

Double Orange Icing: In a small bowl, stir together
1 cup sifted powdered sugar, ½ teaspoon finely shredded
orange peel, and enough orange juice (3 to 4 teaspoons)
to make an icing of drizzling consistency.

Nutrition facts per cookie: 119 cal., 6 g total fat (1 g sat. fat), 7 mg chol.,
24 mg sodium, 16 g carbo., 1 g fiber, 1 g pro.

Ranger Cookies

Prep: 25 min. Bake: 8 min. per batch
Stand: 1 min. per batch

The *Better Homes and Gardens*® version of the ever-popular ranger cookie includes crisp rice cereal, coconut, and dates or raisins.

½	cup butter, softened
½	cup granulated sugar
½	cup packed brown sugar
½	tsp. baking powder
¼	tsp. baking soda
1	egg
1	tsp. vanilla
1¼	cups all-purpose flour
2	cups crisp rice cereal
1⅓	cups coconut
1	cup snipped pitted whole dates or raisins

1. Preheat oven to 375°F. In a large mixing bowl, beat butter with an electric mixer on medium to high speed for 30 seconds. Add granulated sugar, brown sugar, baking powder, and baking soda. Beat until combined, scraping side of bowl occasionally. Beat in egg and vanilla until combined. Beat in as much of the flour as you can with the mixer. Using a wooden spoon, stir in any remaining flour. Stir in cereal, coconut, and dates.

2. Drop dough by rounded teaspoons 2 inches apart onto ungreased cookie sheets. Bake about 8 minutes or until edges are golden. Let stand on cookie sheets for 1 minute. Transfer to wire racks and let cool. Makes about 54 cookies.

Nutrition facts per cookie: 61 cal., 2 g total fat (2 g sat. fat), 8 mg chol., 40 mg sodium, 10 g carbo., 1 g fiber, 1 g pro.

Yesterday

Since their invention, breakfast cereals have become a favorite ingredient in cookies. The recipe for ranger cookies is one of the most popular cereal-based creations to ever make the recipe-swapping rounds. Here's our version from 1981.

Ranger Cookies in a Jar

Prep: 20 min. Bake: 8 min. per batch
Stand: 1 min. per batch

When it's gift-giving time, jot the baking directions for these delightful drop cookies on a decorative piece of paper, punch a hole in the paper, and tie it around the neck of the jar with a ribbon.

1¼	**cups all-purpose flour**
½	**tsp. baking powder**
¼	**tsp. baking soda**
½	**cup shortening**
2	**cups fruit-flavored crisp rice cereal**
⅔	**cup packed brown sugar**
⅓	**cup coconut**

1. In a medium bowl, stir together flour, baking powder, and baking soda. Using a pastry blender, cut in shortening until the mixture resembles coarse crumbs.

2. In a 1-quart glass jar or canister, layer ingredients in the following order: *one-third* of the cereal, the flour mixture, another *one-third* of the cereal, brown sugar, coconut, and remaining cereal. Tap jar gently on the counter to settle each layer before adding the next. Cover jar.

3. Attach baking directions and give as a gift. (Or store at room temperature for up to 1 month. Prepare and bake as directed below.)

Baking Directions

Preheat oven to 375°F. Empty contents of jar into a large bowl. Stir in: 1 egg, beaten; 2 tablespoons milk; and 1 teaspoon vanilla until combined. Drop by rounded teaspoons 2 inches apart onto ungreased cookie sheets. Bake for 8 to 9 minutes or until edges are golden. Let stand on cookie sheets for 1 minute. Transfer to wire racks and let cool. Makes 24 cookies.

Nutrition facts per cookie: 106 cal., 5 g total fat (1 g sat. fat), 9 mg chol., 48 mg sodium, 14 g carbo., 0 g fiber, 1 g pro.

Today

In recent years, attractive cookie and soup mixes in jars have become treasured homemade gift items at holiday time. Remember this updated in-a-jar version of ranger cookies any time of year.

Deluxe Dried Cherry Cookies

Prep: 30 min. Bake: 8 min. per batch

As dried cherries became the rage in the 1980s and 1990s, we showed cooks how to use them in everything from sauces to stuffings to cookies. These treats from 2000 feature a marvelous mix of cherries, oats, pecans, and white baking pieces.

- 1   **cup butter, softened**
- 1   **cup packed brown sugar**
- 2   **eggs**
- 1   **tsp. baking soda**
- ½   **tsp. salt**
- 1½   **cups all-purpose flour**
- 2   **cups dried tart cherries**
- 1½   **cups rolled oats**
- ⅔   **cup chopped pecans**
- ⅔   **cup white baking pieces**

1. Preheat oven to 375°F. In a large bowl, beat butter with an electric mixer on medium to high speed for 30 seconds. Add brown sugar, eggs, baking soda, and salt. Beat until combined, scraping side of bowl occasionally. Beat in flour. Using a wooden spoon, stir in cherries, oats, pecans, and white baking pieces,

2. Drop dough by rounded teaspoons 2 inches apart onto ungreased cookie sheets. Bake for 8 to 9 minutes or until edges are lightly browned. Transfer to wire racks and let cool. Makes 48 cookies.

Nutrition facts per cookie: 127 cal., 6 g total fat (3 g sat. fat), 20 mg chol., 101 mg sodium, 16 g carbo., 1 g fiber, 1 g pro.

Coffeehouses and espresso bars were just hitting their stride in the 1990s, and Americans were captivated by the pastries they sold along with their brews. To help our readers re-create them at home, we featured such Coffeehouse Pleasures as Toffee Triangles in a 1995 issue.

Toffee Triangles

Prep: 15 min. Bake: 20 + 12 + 1 min. Chill: 1 hr.

These irresistible bars are made up of four luscious layers: a buttery crust, a creamy vanilla filing, a sprinkling of chocolate, and almond toffee pieces on top.

- ¾   **cup butter, softened**
- ¾   **cup packed brown sugar**
- 1   **egg yolk**
- 1½   **cups all-purpose flour**
- ¼   **tsp. salt**
- 1   **14-oz. can (1¼ cups) sweetened condensed milk**
- 2   **Tbsp. butter**
- 2   **tsp. vanilla**
- 1   **12-oz. pkg. (2 cups) semisweet chocolate pieces***
- 1   **cup almond toffee pieces or 1 cup toasted chopped pecans (tip, page 102)**

1. Preheat oven to 350°F. Grease a 13×9×2-inch baking pan; set aside. For crust, in a large mixing bowl, combine the ¾ cup butter and the brown sugar; beat with an electric mixer on medium speed until combined. Beat in egg yolk. Using a wooden spoon, stir in the flour and salt until well mixed. Using floured hands, press the dough onto the bottom of the prepared baking pan. Bake about 20 minutes or until lightly browned. Cool on a wire rack.

2. For filling, in a heavy, small saucepan, cook and stir the sweetened condensed milk and the 2 tablespoons butter over medium heat until bubbly. Cook and stir for 5 minutes more. (Mixture will thicken and become smooth.) Stir in the vanilla. Spread filling onto the crust. Bake in the 350°F oven for 12 to 15 minutes more or until top layer is golden.

3. Sprinkle baked layers evenly with the chocolate pieces. Bake for 1 to 2 minutes more or until chocolate pieces melt. Remove from oven; set on a wire rack. Using a flexible spatula, immediately spread the chocolate evenly over baked layers. Sprinkle with almond toffee pieces or pecans. Cool on a wire rack. Cover and chill about 1 hour or until chocolate is set. Cut into triangles or squares. Makes about 36 triangles.

*Test Kitchen Tip: Be sure to use real semisweet chocolate pieces. Do not substitute products labeled imitation chocolate pieces or chocolate-flavored pieces.

Nutrition facts per triangle: 177 cal., 10 g total fat (3 g sat. fat), 23 mg chol., 95 mg sodium, 22 g carbo., 0 g fiber, 2 g pro.

Peanut Brittle Bars

Blondies

Prep: 20 min. Bake: 25 min.

According to an old story, a Southern cook swapped brown sugar for granulated sugar in a cookie recipe one day and created these butterscotch brownies.

- 2 **cups packed brown sugar**
- ⅔ **cup butter**
- 2 **eggs**
- 2 **tsp. vanilla**
- 2 **cups all-purpose flour**
- 1 **tsp. baking powder**
- ¼ **tsp. baking soda**
- 1 **cup semisweet chocolate pieces (6 oz.)**
- 1 **cup chopped nuts**

1. Preheat oven to 350°F. Grease a 13×9×2-inch baking pan; set aside. In a medium saucepan, combine brown sugar and butter; heat and stir over medium heat until butter melts and mixture is smooth. Cool slightly. Using a wooden spoon, stir in eggs, one at a time; stir in vanilla. Stir in flour, baking powder, and baking soda.

2. Spread batter in prepared baking pan. Sprinkle with chocolate pieces and nuts. Bake for 25 to 30 minutes or until a wooden toothpick inserted near center comes out clean (avoid chocolate pieces). Cool slightly on a wire rack. Cut into bars while warm. Makes 36 bars.

Nutrition facts per bar: 157 cal., 8 g total fat (4 g sat. fat), 21 mg chol., 65 mg sodium, 21 g carbo., 1 g fiber, 2 g pro.

The Storing Story

Grandma used to keep cookies in a cookie jar, knowing they'd be gone in no time. But today, bakers want to keep cookies longer. To store them well, cool the cookies completely *but don't frost them.* In a freezer container, arrange them in a single layer. Cover with waxed paper. Repeat layers, leaving enough airspace to close the container easily. Store at room temperature for up to 3 days or freeze for up to 8 months. Thaw at room temperature and frost, if you like.

Peanut Brittle Bars

Prep: 15 min. Bake: 12 + 12 min.

The New York reader who sent this recipe says her neighbors look forward to these bars at local gatherings, and her grown children always request a batch when they visit. We call that high praise!

- 2 **cups all-purpose flour**
- ½ **cup packed brown sugar**
- ⅔ **cup butter**
- 2 **cups cocktail peanuts**
- 1 **cup milk chocolate pieces**
- 1 **12-oz. jar caramel ice cream topping**
- 3 **Tbsp. all-purpose flour**

1. Preheat oven to 350°F. Line a 15×10×1-inch baking pan with foil. Grease foil; set aside. In a medium bowl, stir together the 2 cups flour and the brown sugar. Using a pastry blender, cut in butter until mixture is crumbly. Press mixture onto bottom of prepared pan. Bake about 12 minutes or until golden.

2. Sprinkle peanuts and milk chocolate pieces over top. In a small bowl, stir together caramel topping and the 3 tablespoons flour. Drizzle over top.

3. Bake for 12 to 15 minutes more or until caramel is bubbly. Cool on a wire rack. Carefully lift foil; gently peel away from edges. Cut into bars. Makes 36 bars.

Nutrition facts per bar: 169 cal., 9 g total fat (4 g sat. fat), 9 mg chol., 102 mg sodium, 20 g carbo., 1 g fiber, 3 g pro.

Oatmeal-Cheesecake-Cranberry Bars

Prep: 10 min. Bake: 15 + 40 min. Chill: 3 hr.

In March 1998, we published our readers' Best Brownies and Cookies. These colorful triple-layer bars were our hands-down choice for top honors.

2	**cups all-purpose flour**
1¼	**cups rolled oats**
¾	**cup packed brown sugar**
1	**cup butter**
12	**oz. cream cheese, softened**
½	**cup granulated sugar**
2	**eggs**
2	**tsp. lemon juice**
1	**tsp. vanilla**
1	**16-oz. can whole cranberry sauce**
2	**tsp. cornstarch**

1. Preheat oven to 350°F. Grease a 13×9×2-inch baking pan; set aside. In a large bowl, stir together flour, rolled oats, and brown sugar. Using a pastry blender, cut in butter until mixture resembles coarse crumbs. Set aside *1½ cups* of the crumb mixture. Press remaining crumbs into the bottom of the prepared baking pan. Bake for 15 minutes.

Oatmeal-Cheesecake-Cranberry Bars

2. Meanwhile, in a medium mixing bowl, combine cream cheese and granulated sugar; beat with an electric mixer on medium speed until light and fluffy. Beat in eggs, lemon juice, and vanilla. Spread cream cheese mixture onto baked crust.

3. In a small bowl, stir together cranberry sauce and cornstarch; spoon carefully over cream cheese layer. Sprinkle with reserved crumb mixture. Bake about 40 minutes or until set. Cool in pan on a wire rack. Cover and chill about 3 hours or until firm. Cut into bars. Makes 36 bars.

Nutrition facts per bar: 161 cal., 9 g total fat (5 g sat. fat), 36 mg chol., 88 mg sodium, 19 g carbo., 1 g fiber, 2 g pro.

Lemon Bars Deluxe

Prep: 25 min. Bake: 30 + 20 min.

We updated this 1969 classic to make it more lemony and a little less sweet. Pictured on page 246.

2	**cups all-purpose flour**
½	**cup sifted powdered sugar**
1	**cup butter**
4	**eggs**
1½	**cups granulated sugar**
1	**Tbsp. finely shredded lemon peel (set aside)**
⅓	**cup lemon juice**
¼	**cup all-purpose flour**
	Powdered sugar

1. Preheat oven to 350°F. In a large bowl, stir together the 2 cups flour and the ½ cup sifted powdered sugar. Using a pastry blender, cut in butter until mixture clings together. Press onto the bottom of an ungreased 13×9×2-inch baking pan. Bake about 30 minutes or until lightly browned.

2. In a medium bowl, beat eggs with a whisk; whisk in granulated sugar and lemon juice until well mixed. Whisk in the ¼ cup flour and the lemon peel. Pour over baked crust.

3. Bake about 20 minutes more or until edges begin to brown and center is set. Cool in pan on a wire rack. Sift additional powdered sugar over top. Cut into bars or into 2×1¾-inch diamonds. Store, covered, in refrigerator. Makes 30 bars.

Nutrition facts per bar: 144 cal., 7 g total fat (4 g sat. fat), 46 mg chol., 75 mg sodium, 18 g carbo., 0 g fiber, 2 g pro.

Toasted Hazelnut Bars

Toasted Hazelnut Bars

Prep: 20 min. Bake: 15 + 35 min.

A cream cheese crust and an old-fashioned buttermilk filling combine with toasty hazelnuts in this prizewinning 1997 Cookie Jar Favorite.

2⅓   cups all-purpose flour
½   cup butter, softened
2   3-oz. pkg. cream cheese, softened
½   cup packed brown sugar
2   cups granulated sugar
1½   cups buttermilk or sour milk*
4   eggs
½   cup butter, melted
2   tsp. vanilla
¼   tsp. salt
2   cups chopped hazelnuts (filberts), toasted (tip, page 102)
    Sifted powdered sugar

   1. Preheat oven to 350°F. In a large mixing bowl, combine *2 cups* of the flour, the ½ cup butter, cream cheese, and brown sugar; beat with an electric mixer on medium speed until well mixed. With lightly floured hands, pat mixture onto bottom and up sides of a 15×10×1-inch baking pan. Bake for 15 minutes.

   2. Meanwhile, in a medium bowl, combine the remaining ⅓ cup flour, the granulated sugar, buttermilk, eggs, melted butter, vanilla, and salt; beat with an electric mixer on low speed until combined. Stir in nuts. Pour onto baked crust.

   3. Bake about 35 minutes or until golden. Cool in pan; cut into bars. Sprinkle with powdered sugar. Store, covered, in the refrigerator. Makes 48 bars.

   *Test Kitchen Tip: To make 1½ cups sour milk, place 4½ teaspoons lemon juice or vinegar in a glass measuring cup. Add enough milk to make 1½ cups total liquid; stir. Let mixture stand for 5 minutes before using.

Nutrition facts per bar: 146 cal., 9 g total fat (4 g sat. fat), 32 mg chol., 75 mg sodium, 16 g carbo., 1 g fiber, 2 g pro.

Top Banana Bars

Prep: 15 min. Bake: 20 min.

Toasted wheat germ and whole wheat flour give these fruity bars a wholesome down-home flavor.

½   cup all-purpose flour
½   cup whole wheat flour
1   Tbsp. toasted wheat germ
1   tsp. baking powder
½   tsp. ground cinnamon
⅛   tsp. salt
1   egg
½   cup packed brown sugar
⅓   cup milk
¼   cup cooking oil
½   tsp. vanilla
1   ripe medium banana, mashed
⅓   cup mixed dried fruit bits
1   recipe Vanilla Icing (below)

   1. Preheat oven to 350°F. Grease an 11×7×1½-inch baking pan; set aside. In a large bowl, combine all-purpose flour, whole wheat flour, wheat germ, baking powder, cinnamon, and salt; set aside.

   2. In a medium bowl, beat egg,; stir in brown sugar, milk, oil, and vanilla. Stir in banana and fruit bits. Add banana mixture to flour mixture, stirring to combine. Spread batter evenly in the prepared pan.

   3. Bake for 20 to 25 minutes or until a wooden toothpick inserted near center comes out clean. Cool in pan on a wire rack. Drizzle with Vanilla Icing. Makes 20 bars.

   Vanilla Icing: In a small bowl, combine ⅓ cup sifted powdered sugar and ¼ teaspoon vanilla. Stir in enough milk to make an icing of drizzling consistency (1 to 2 teaspoons total).

Nutrition facts per bar: 91 cal., 3 g total fat (1 g sat. fat), 11 mg chol., 27 mg sodium, 15 g carbo., 1 g fiber, 1 g pro.

Skip the Squares

Think outside the box when cutting bar cookies. Instead of squares or rectangles, make triangles by cutting 2-inch squares in half diagonally. Or make diamonds by cutting lines 1 to 1½ inches apart down the length of the pan. Then cut lines 1 to 1½ inches apart diagonally across.

Carrot and Zucchini Bars

Prep: 30 min. Bake: 25 min.

The reader who sent in this recipe in 1991 told us she added the flavors of carrot cake to zucchini bars to create these moist, cream cheese-frosted cookies.

1½ **cups all-purpose flour**
¾ **cup packed brown sugar**
1 **tsp. baking powder**
½ **tsp. ground ginger**
¼ **tsp. baking soda**
2 **eggs**
1½ **cups shredded carrot**
1 **medium zucchini, shredded (1 cup)**
½ **cup raisins**
½ **cup chopped walnuts**
½ **cup cooking oil**
¼ **cup honey**
1 **tsp. vanilla**
1 **recipe Citrus-Cream Cheese Frosting (below)**

1. Preheat oven to 350°F. In a large bowl, stir together flour, brown sugar, baking powder, ginger, and baking soda. In another large bowl, beat eggs with a fork; stir in carrot, zucchini, raisins, walnuts, oil, honey, and vanilla. Add carrot mixture to flour mixture, stirring just until combined. Spread batter into an ungreased 13×9×2-inch baking pan.

2. Bake about 25 minutes or until a wooden toothpick inserted in center comes out clean. Cool in pan on a wire rack. Prepare Citrus-Cream Cheese Frosting; frost baked layer. Store, covered, in the refrigerator. Cut into bars. Makes 36 bars.

Citrus-Cream Cheese Frosting: In a medium mixing bowl, combine one 8-ounce package cream cheese, softened, and 1 cup sifted powdered sugar; beat with an electric mixer on medium speed until fluffy. Stir in 1 teaspoon finely shredded lemon peel or orange peel.

Nutrition facts per bar: 125 cal., 7 g total fat (2 g sat. fat), 19 mg chol., 46 mg sodium, 16 g carbo., 0 g fiber, 2 g pro.

Lime Zingers

Prep: 40 min. Bake: 8 min. per batch

Better Homes and Gardens® magazine sponsored a holiday cookie contest in 1994, and after combing through thousands of entries, our editors chose 12 winners. These citrus cutouts laced with Brazil nuts were among the delicious dozen.

1 **cup butter, softened**
½ **cup granulated sugar**
2 **tsp. finely shredded lime peel**
¼ **cup lime juice (about 2 limes)**
1 **tsp. vanilla**
2¼ **cups all-purpose flour**
¾ **cup finely chopped Brazil nuts or hazelnuts (filberts)**
1 **recipe Lime Cream Cheese Frosting (below)**

1. In a large mixing bowl, beat butter with an electric mixer on medium to high speed for 30 seconds. Add granulated sugar and beat until combined. Beat in lime peel, the ¼ cup lime juice, and vanilla. Beat in as much of the flour as you can with the mixer. Using a wooden spoon, stir in any remaining flour and the nuts. Divide dough in half.

2. Preheat oven to 350°F. On a lightly floured surface, roll each half of the dough to ¼-inch thickness. Using 1- to 2-inch cookie cutters, cut into desired shapes. Place cutouts on ungreased cookie sheets. Bake for 8 to 10 minutes or until edges are lightly browned. Transfer to wire racks and let cool. Prepare Lime Cream Cheese Frosting; spread onto cookies. Makes 72 cookies.

Lime Cream Cheese Frosting: In a medium mixing bowl, combine: ½ of an 8-ounce package cream cheese, softened; 1 cup sifted powdered sugar; 1 tablespoon lime juice; and 1 teaspoon vanilla. Beat with an electric mixer on medium speed until smooth. Tint with green food coloring.

Nutrition facts per cookie: 62 cal., 4 g total fat (2 g sat. fat), 9 mg chol., 31 mg sodium, 6 g carbo., 0 g fiber, 1 g pro.

> **Throughout the decades, our readers have told us they see baking as a way to express their love and creativity. Shaped, drop, and cutout cookies continue to be beloved family favorites.**

Lemon-Pistachio Biscotti

Prep: 35 min. Bake: 20 + 8 + 8 min.
Cool: 30 min. to 1 hr.

- ⅓ cup butter, softened
- ⅔ cup granulated sugar
- 2 tsp. baking powder
- 2 eggs
- 1 tsp. vanilla
- 4 tsp. finely shredded lemon peel
- 2 cups all-purpose flour
- 1½ cups unsalted pistachio nuts (6 oz.)
- 1 recipe Tangy Lemon Icing (below)

1. Preheat oven to 375°F. Line an extra-large cookie sheet or 2 cookie sheets with parchment paper or lightly grease the cookie sheet(s); set aside.

2. In a large mixing bowl, beat butter with an electric mixer on medium to high speed for 30 seconds. Add granulated sugar, baking powder, and ½ teaspoon *salt;* beat until combined, scraping side of bowl occasionally. Beat in eggs and vanilla. Beat in lemon peel and as much of the flour as you can with the mixer. Using a wooden spoon, stir in any remaining flour and the pistachio nuts.

3. On a lightly floured surface, divide dough into 3 equal portions. Shape each portion into an 8-inch-long loaf. Flatten loaves to about 2½ inches wide. Place flattened loaves at least 3 inches apart on prepared cookie sheet(s). Bake for 20 to 25 minutes or until golden and tops are cracked. (Loaves will spread slightly.) Cool on cookie sheet(s) for at least 30 minutes or up to 1 hour.

4. Preheat oven to 325°F. Transfer loaves to a cutting board. Cut each loaf diagonally into ½-inch-thick slices. Place slices, cut sides down, on the same cookie sheet(s). Bake for 8 minutes. Turn over slices and bake for 8 to 10 minutes more or until dry and crisp. Transfer to wire racks and let cool. Prepare Tangy Lemon Icing. Dip ends of cookies into icing or drizzle on top. Makes about 36 cookies.

Tangy Lemon Icing: In a bowl, stir together 1 cup sifted powdered sugar and 1 teaspoon finely shredded lemon peel. Stir in enough milk or lemon juice (1 to 2 tablespoons) to make an icing of drizzling consistency.

Nutrition facts per cookie: 99 cal., 5 g total fat (1 g sat. fat), 16 mg chol., 71 mg sodium, 13 g carbo., 1 g fiber, 2 g pro.

Lemon-Pistachio Biscotti

New Cookie Sheets

Cooks used to bake cookies on pans they'd had for years, but then cookie sheets went hi-tech. Are they for you? See our cookie sheet tips below.

• Choose heavy aluminum sheets with low sides or no sides at all. Generally, dull-finish, light-colored sheets brown cookie bottoms more evenly.

• If you use nonstick cookie sheets, you may get thicker cookies because the dough may not spread as much.

• Insulated cookie sheets give cookies soft-set centers, but you may have trouble using them for high-butter cookies. The butter may melt before the dough sets, causing it to spread and the cookies to have thin edges.

Brown Sugar Icebox Cookies

Prep: 30 min. Chill: 4 hr. Bake: 10 min. per batch

½	cup shortening
½	cup butter, softened
1¼	cups packed brown sugar
½	tsp. baking soda
¼	tsp. salt
1	egg
1	tsp. vanilla
2½	cups all-purpose flour
¾	cup toasted ground hazelnuts (filberts) or pecans (tip, page 102)
⅔	cup toasted finely chopped hazelnuts (filberts) or pecans (optional)
1	to 1½ cups semisweet or milk chocolate pieces (optional)*
1	Tbsp. shortening (optional)

1. In a large mixing bowl, beat the ½ cup shortening and the butter with an electric mixer on medium to high speed for 30 seconds. Add brown sugar, baking soda, and salt. Beat until combined, scraping side of bowl.

2. Beat in egg and vanilla. Beat in as much of the flour as you can with the mixer. Using a wooden spoon, stir in any remaining flour and the ¾ cup ground nuts.

3. Divide dough in half. On waxed paper, shape each half into a 10-inch-long log. Lift and smooth the waxed paper to help shape the logs. If desired, roll logs in the ⅔ cup finely chopped nuts. Wrap each log in plastic wrap. Chill about 4 hours or until firm enough to slice.

4. Preheat oven to 375°F. Cut logs into ¼-inch-thick slices. Place slices 1 inch apart on ungreased cookie sheets. Bake for 10 to 12 minutes or until edges are firm. Transfer to wire racks and let cool.

5. If desired, in a small saucepan, combine chocolate pieces and the 1 tablespoon shortening; heat and stir over low heat until melted. Drizzle chocolate mixture onto the cookies. Place cookies on waxed paper-lined cookie sheet. Chill until set. Makes 72 cookies.

*Test Kitchen Tip: Be sure to use real semisweet chocolate pieces. Do not substitute products labeled imitation chocolate pieces or chocolate-flavored pieces.

Nutrition facts per cookie: 65 cal., 4 g total fat (1 g sat. fat), 7 mg chol., 33 mg sodium, 7 g carbo., 0 g fiber, 1 g pro.

In the 1990s, we gave icebox cookies a new look and taste by creating checkered slices with alternating rolls of orange and chocolate cookie dough.

Today

Orange-Chocolate Rounds

Prep: 30 min. Chill: 2 hr. + 30 min.
Bake: 7 min. per batch

1	cup butter, softened
1½	cups sugar
1½	tsp. baking powder
¼	tsp. salt
1	egg
1	tsp. vanilla
2½	cups all-purpose flour
2	tsp. finely shredded orange peel
2	oz. unsweetened chocolate, melted and cooled slightly

1. In a large mixing bowl, beat butter with an electric mixer on medium to high speed for 30 seconds. Add sugar, baking powder, and salt. Beat until combined, scraping side of bowl occasionally. Beat in egg and vanilla. Beat in as much of the flour as you can with the mixer. Using a wooden spoon, stir in any remaining flour.

2. Divide dough in half. Stir orange peel into one half of the dough; stir melted chocolate into the other half of the dough. If necessary, cover and chill about 1 hour or until dough is easy to handle.

3. Shape each half of the dough into a 10-inch-long roll. Wrap each roll in plastic wrap or waxed paper. Chill about 2 hours or until firm.

4. Cut each chilled roll lengthwise into quarters; reassemble into 2 rolls, alternating chocolate and orange quarters. Wrap and chill about 30 minutes more or until firm.

5. Preheat oven to 375°F. Using a sharp knife, cut dough into ¼-inch-thick slices. Place slices 1 inch apart on ungreased cookie sheets.

6. Bake for 7 to 9 minutes or until edges are firm and bottoms are lightly browned. Transfer to wire racks and let cool. Makes about 60 cookies.

Nutrition facts per cookie: 70 cal., 4 g total fat (2 g sat. fat), 12 mg chol., 50 mg sodium, 9 g carbo., 0 g fiber, 1 g pro.

Date Pinwheels

Prep: 40 min. Chill: 1 + 2 to 24 hr.
Bake: 8 min. per batch

Some readers are diehard date fans. To please them, we've published date cookies in a variety of forms—everything from drop cookies to bars to sandwich cookies. But by far, the best-loved are these pinwheels.

1	**8-oz. pkg. (1⅓ cups) pitted whole dates, finely snipped**
½	**cup water**
⅓	**cup granulated sugar**
2	**Tbsp. lemon juice**
½	**tsp. vanilla**
½	**cup shortening**
½	**cup butter, softened**
½	**cup granulated sugar**
½	**cup packed brown sugar**
½	**tsp. baking soda**
¼	**tsp. salt**
1	**egg**
3	**Tbsp. milk**
1	**tsp. vanilla**
3	**cups all-purpose flour**

1. For filling, in a small saucepan, combine the dates, the water, and the ⅓ cup granulated sugar. Bring to boiling; reduce heat. Cook and stir about 2 minutes or until thick. Stir in lemon juice and the ½ teaspoon vanilla; set filling aside to cool.

2. In a large mixing bowl, beat shortening and butter with an electric mixer on medium to high speed for 30 seconds. Add the ½ cup granulated sugar, the brown sugar, baking soda, and salt. Beat until combined, scraping side of bowl occasionally. Beat in egg, milk, and the 1 teaspoon vanilla. Beat in as much of the flour as you can with the mixer. Using a wooden spoon, stir in any remaining flour. Divide dough in half. Cover and chill about 1 hour or until easy to handle.

3. Place *half* of the dough between pieces of waxed paper; roll into a 12×10-inch rectangle. Remove waxed paper and spread top of dough with *half* of the filling. Starting from a long side, roll up dough into a spiral. Moisten edges; pinch to seal. Wrap in waxed paper or plastic wrap. Repeat with remaining dough and filling. Chill for at least 2 hours or up to 24 hours.

4. Preheat oven to 375°F. Grease cookie sheets; set aside. Cut rolls into ¼-inch-thick slices. Place slices 1 inch apart on prepared cookie sheets. Bake for 8 to 10 minutes or until edges are lightly browned. Transfer to wire racks and let cool. Makes about 64 cookies.

Nutrition facts per cookie: 76 cal., 3 g total fat (1 g sat. fat), 7 mg chol., 37 mg sodium, 11 g carbo., 0 g fiber, 1 g pro.

Coconut-Pecan Pinwheels

Prep: 20 min. Chill: 2 hr. Bake: 10 min. per batch

Originally called Santa's Whiskers because the shredded coconut around the edge of each slice resembles whiskers, these easy cherry rounds are ideal for holiday gift trays. They won first place in our December 1970 Fancy Holiday Cookies contest.

¾	**cup butter, softened**
¾	**cup sugar**
1	**Tbsp. milk**
1	**tsp. vanilla**
2	**cups all-purpose flour**
¾	**cup finely chopped candied red or green cherries**
⅓	**cup finely chopped pecans**
¾	**cup shredded coconut**

1. In a large mixing bowl, beat butter with an electric mixer on medium to high speed for 30 seconds. Add sugar. Beat until combined, scraping side of bowl occasionally. Beat in milk and vanilla until combined. Beat in as much of the flour as you can with the mixer. Stir in any remaining flour. Stir in cherries and pecans.

2. Divide dough in half. Shape each half into an 8-inch-long roll; roll in coconut. Wrap in plastic wrap or waxed paper. Chill about 2 hours or until firm enough to slice.

3. Preheat oven to 375°F. Cut rolls into ¼-inch-thick slices. Place slices 1 inch apart on ungreased cookie sheets. Bake for 10 to 12 minutes or until edges are golden. Transfer to wire racks and let cool. Makes about 60 cookies.

Make-ahead directions: Prepare as directed through step 2. Chill for up to 48 hours. Continue as directed in step 3.

Nutrition facts per cookie: 65 cal., 3 g total fat (2 g sat. fat), 7 mg chol., 30 mg sodium, 8 g carbo., 0 g fiber, 1 g pro.

Birds' Nests

Birds' Nests

Prep: 25 min. Bake: 10 min. per batch

This 1938 prizewinning recipe features a dollop of raspberry jam cradled in a buttery walnut cookie crust or "nest." If you like, substitute other fruit flavors of jam or preserves.

  1   **cup butter, softened**
  ½   **cup packed brown sugar**
  2   **egg yolks**
  2   **cups all-purpose flour**
  2   **egg whites, slightly beaten**
  2   **cups finely chopped walnuts or pecans**
  ½   **cup seedless raspberry jam or preserves**
  1   **recipe Powdered Sugar Drizzle (below) (optional)**

1. Preheat oven to 375°F. Grease cookie sheets; set aside. In a large mixing bowl, beat butter with an electric mixer on medium to high speed for 30 seconds. Add brown sugar and beat until combined, scraping side of bowl occasionally. Beat in egg yolks. Beat in as much of the flour as you can with the mixer. Using a wooden spoon, stir in any remaining flour.

2. Shape dough into 1¼-inch balls. Dip each ball into egg whites; roll in chopped nuts. Place balls 1 inch apart on prepared cookie sheets. Press your thumb into the center of each ball. Bake for 10 to 12 minutes or until edges are lightly browned. Transfer to wire racks; let cool.

3. To serve, fill centers with jam or preserves (about ½ teaspoon each). If desired, prepare Powdered Sugar Drizzle; drizzle over cookies. Makes 36 cookies.

Powdered Sugar Drizzle: In a small bowl, combine 1 cup sifted powdered sugar and enough milk (1 to 2 tablespoons) to make of drizzling consistency.

Nutrition facts per cookie: 144 cal., 10 g total fat (4 g sat. fat), 26 mg chol., 61 mg sodium, 12 g carbo., 1 g fiber, 2 g pro.

Lemon-Almond Tea Cookies

Prep: 20 min. Chill: 4 to 24 hr. Bake: 8 min. per batch

Looking for an easy party cookie? These nutty slice-and-bake rounds are eye-catching and loaded with lemon flavor. They're a natural with a cup of tea.

  ½   **cup butter, softened**
  ½   **cup granulated sugar**
  ⅛   **tsp. baking soda**
  1   **egg yolk**
  1   **Tbsp. milk**
  2   **tsp. finely shredded lemon peel**
  1   **tsp. almond extract**
  ½   **tsp. vanilla**
1½   **cups all-purpose flour**
  1   **recipe Lemon-Butter Frosting (below)**
  ½   **cup sliced almonds, toasted (tip, page 102)**

1. In a medium bowl, beat butter with an electric mixer on medium to high speed for 30 seconds. Add granulated sugar and baking soda. Beat until combined. Beat in egg yolk, milk, lemon peel, almond extract, and vanilla. Beat in as much of the flour as you can with the mixer. Using a wooden spoon, stir in any remaining flour.

2. Shape dough into an 8-inch-long roll. Wrap in waxed paper or plastic wrap. Chill for at least 4 hours or up to 24 hours.

3. Preheat oven to 375°F. Cut dough into ¼-inch-thick slices. Place slices 2 inches apart on ungreased cookie sheets. Bake for 8 to 10 minutes or until edges are firm and bottoms are lightly browned. Transfer to wire racks and let cool.

4. Prepare Lemon-Butter Frosting. Spread onto cookies. Sprinkle with almonds. Makes 64 cookies.

Lemon-Butter Frosting: In a small bowl, beat 2 tablespoons butter with an electric mixer on medium to high speed for 30 seconds. Beat in ½ cup sifted powdered sugar. Beat in 1 tablespoon milk and ½ teaspoon lemon juice. Gradually beat in an additional ½ cup sifted powdered sugar.

Nutrition facts per cookie: 45 cal., 2 g total fat (1 g sat. fat), 8 mg chol., 21 mg sodium, 5 g carbo., 0 g fiber, 1 g pro.

**Lemon Bars DeLuxe
(recipe, page 238)
Cranberry-Pecan Tassies**

Cranberry-Pecan Tassies
Prep: 25 min. Bake: 30 min.

These mini cream cheese-pastry tarts have appeared time and again in *Better Homes and Gardens*®, each version holding a different filling. This festive 1978 recipe showcases a sweet-tart cranberry-laced filling.

  1 **3-oz. pkg. cream cheese, softened**
 ½ **cup butter, softened**
  1 **cup all-purpose flour**
  1 **egg**
 ¾ **cup packed brown sugar**
  1 **tsp. vanilla**
    Dash salt
 ⅓ **cup finely chopped fresh cranberries**
  3 **Tbsp. chopped pecans**

1. Preheat oven to 325°F. In a medium bowl, combine cream cheese and butter. Stir in flour. Shape dough into 24 balls; place one ball in each of 24 cups of an ungreased 1¾-inch muffin pan(s). Press dough evenly against bottom and side of each muffin cup.

2. For filling, in a small mixing bowl, combine egg, brown sugar, vanilla, and salt; beat with an electric mixer on medium speed just until smooth. Stir in cranberries and pecans. Spoon filling into pastry-lined muffin cups.

3. Bake for 30 to 35 minutes or until pastry is golden. Cool in pan on wire rack. Remove from pan by running a knife around the edge of each cup. Makes 24 cookies.

Nutrition facts per cookie: 94 cal., 6 g total fat (3 g sat. fat), 23 mg chol., 59 mg sodium, 10 g carbo., 0 g fiber, 1 g pro.

Shortbread
Prep: 15 min. Bake: 25 min.

Shortbread has only three ingredients, but what buttery flavor! Although now enjoyed year-round, shortbread started out as a Scottish holiday favorite.

1¼ **cups all-purpose flour**
 3 **Tbsp. sugar**
 ½ **cup butter**

1. Preheat oven to 325°F. In a medium mixing bowl, combine flour and sugar. Using a pastry blender, cut in butter until mixture resembles fine crumbs and starts to cling. Form mixture into a ball; knead until smooth.

2. *For wedges*, on an ungreased cookie sheet, pat or roll dough into an 8-inch circle. Use your fingers to make a scalloped edge. Cut the circle into 16 wedges, leaving them in a circle.

3. *For rounds*, on a lightly floured surface, roll dough to ½-inch thickness. Using 1½-inch round cookie cutter, cut into rounds. Place 1 inch apart on an ungreased cookie sheet.

4. *For strips*, on a lightly floured surface, roll dough into an 8×6-inch rectangle. Cut into twenty-four 2×1-inch strips. Place 1 inch apart on an ungreased cookie sheet.

5. *For all shapes,* bake just until bottoms start to brown and centers are set. Allow 25 to 30 minutes for wedges or 20 to 25 minutes for rounds or strips. Makes 16 wedges or 24 rounds or strips.

Nutrition facts per wedge: 98 cal., 6 g total fat (4 g sat. fat), 16 mg chol., 62 mg sodium, 10 g carbo., 0 g fiber, 1 g pro.

Bet on Butter
Before World War II, bakers always made cookies with butter, and our Test Kitchen still recommends butter for tenderness and rich flavor. However, if you prefer to use margarine, select a stick brand that contains 80 percent vegetable oil. If the package doesn't state the percentage of oil, check the nutrition label to see that it has at least 100 calories per tablespoon. You may need to chill doughs made with margarine longer than doughs made with butter.

Butter-Pecan Shortbread: Prepare as directed, except substitute brown sugar for the granulated sugar. After cutting in butter, stir in 2 tablespoons finely chopped pecans. Sprinkle mixture with ½ teaspoon vanilla before kneading.

Nutrition facts per wedge: 102 cal., 7 g total fat (4 g sat. fat), 16 mg chol., 63 mg sodium, 9 g carbo., 0 g fiber, 1 g pro.

Lemon-Poppy Seed Shortbread: Prepare as directed, except stir 1 tablespoon poppy seeds into flour mixture and add 1 teaspoon finely shredded lemon peel with the butter.

Nutrition facts per wedge: 101 cal., 6 g total fat (4 g sat. fat), 16 mg chol., 62 mg sodium, 10 g carbo., 0 g fiber, 1 g pro.

Oatmeal Shortbread: Prepare as directed, except reduce flour to 1 cup. After cutting in butter, stir in ⅓ cup rolled oats.

Nutrition facts per wedge: 99 cal., 6 g total fat (4 g sat. fat), 16 mg chol., 62 mg sodium, 10 g carbo., 0 g fiber, 1 g pro.

Spiced Shortbread: Prepare as directed, except substitute brown sugar for the granulated sugar and stir ½ teaspoon ground cinnamon, ¼ teaspoon ground ginger, and ⅛ teaspoon ground cloves into the flour mixture.

Nutrition facts per wedge: 96 cal., 6 g total fat (4 g sat. fat), 16 mg chol., 63 mg sodium, 9 g carbo., 0 g fiber, 1 g pro.

Giant Snickerdoodle Cookies

Prep: 20 min. Chill: 4 hr. Bake: 12 min. per batch

This fun-to-eat cookie with a fun name is distinguished by its crackly surface and a dusting of cinnamon sugar.

4½	cups all-purpose flour
2	tsp. baking powder
1	tsp. baking soda
¾	tsp. salt
1¼	cups shortening
2	cups sugar
2	eggs
1½	tsp. vanilla
½	tsp. lemon extract or 1 tsp. finely shredded lemon peel
1	cup buttermilk or sour milk*
½	cup sugar
2	Tbsp. ground cinnamon

1. In a medium bowl, stir together flour, baking powder, baking soda, and salt. .

2. In a large mixing bowl, beat shortening with an electric mixer on medium to high speed for 30 seconds. Add the 2 cups sugar. Beat mixture until combined, scraping side of bowl occasionally. Beat in eggs, *one* at a time, beating well after each addition. Stir in vanilla and lemon extract or peel.

3. Alternately add flour mixture and buttermilk to shortening mixture, scraping down side of bowl as necessary. Cover and chill for 4 hours.

4. Preheat oven to 375°F. In a small bowl, combine the ½ cup sugar and the cinnamon. Lightly grease cookie sheets; set aside. For each cookie, use a ¼-cup measure or ¼-cup ice cream scoop.** Roll each scoop of dough in the sugar-cinnamon mixture to coat. Place 3 inches apart on prepared cookie sheets. With the palm of your hand, gently press cookie to a ½-inch thickness.

5. Bake for 12 to 14 minutes or until bottoms are golden. Transfer to wire racks; cool. The cookies bake more evenly if you bake one batch at a time. Makes about 24.

***Test Kitchen Tip:** To make 1 cup sour milk, place 1 tablespoon lemon juice or vinegar in a glass measuring cup. Add enough milk to make 1 cup total liquid; stir. Let mixture stand for 5 minutes before using.

****Test Kitchen Tip:** If using an ice cream scoop, lightly coat the scoop with nonstick cooking spray to help prevent dough from sticking.

Nutrition facts per cookie: 263 cal., 11 g total fat (3 g sat. fat), 18 mg chol., 175 mg sodium, 37 g carbo., 1 g fiber, 3 g pro.

Chill Out Making shaped cookies used to be a cold-weather activity since the dough had to be thoroughly chilled. Our Test Kitchen still recommends ample chilling time because chilled dough is easier to handle and holds its shape better during baking. If your kitchen is warm, return the dough to the refrigerator between batches. If the dough sticks to your hands, even when chilled, dust your hands with flour occasionally.

Peanut Butter Blossoms

Peanut Butter Blossoms

Prep: 25 min. Bake: 10 min. per batch

In this recipe treasure, nuggets of chocolate add a touch of class to peanut butter cookies. These can't-stop-eating-them morsels are sometimes called black-eyed Susans.

- ½ cup shortening
- ½ cup peanut butter
- ½ cup granulated sugar
- ½ cup packed brown sugar
- 1 tsp. baking powder
- ⅛ tsp. baking soda
- 1 egg
- 2 Tbsp. milk
- 1 tsp. vanilla
- 1¾ cups all-purpose flour
- ¼ cup granulated sugar
  Milk chocolate kisses or stars

1. Preheat oven to 350°F. In a large mixing bowl, beat the shortening and peanut butter with an electric mixer on medium speed for 30 seconds. Add the ½ cup granulated sugar, the brown sugar, baking powder, and baking soda. Beat until combined, scraping side of bowl occasionally. Beat in egg, milk, and vanilla. Beat in as much of the flour as you can with the mixer. Using a wooden spoon, stir in any remaining flour.

2. Shape dough into 1-inch balls. Roll balls in the ¼ cup granulated sugar. Place balls 2 inches apart on ungreased cookie sheets. Bake for 10 to 12 minutes or until edges are firm and bottoms are lightly browned. Immediately press a chocolate kiss or star into center of each cookie. Transfer to wire racks and let cool. Makes 54 cookies.

Nutrition facts per cookie: 94 cal., 5 g total fat (2 g sat. fat), 5 mg chol., 28 mg sodium, 11 g carbo., 0 g fiber, 2 g pro.

Big Soft Ginger Cookies

Prep: 25 min. Bake: 10 min. per batch
Stand: 2 min. per batch

A Salt Lake City grandma shared this triple-spice molasses cookie with us in the 1989 story "Holiday Sweets—With Love from Grandma's Kitchen."

- 2¼ cups all-purpose flour
- 2 tsp. ground ginger
- 1 tsp. baking soda
- ¾ tsp. ground cinnamon
- ½ tsp. ground cloves
- ¾ cup butter, softened
- 1 cup sugar
- 1 egg
- ¼ cup molasses
- 2 Tbsp. sugar

1. Preheat oven to 350°F. In a bowl, combine flour, ginger, baking soda, cinnamon, and cloves. Set aside.

2. In a large mixing bowl, beat butter with an electric mixer on medium to high speed for 30 seconds. Gradually add the 1 cup sugar, beating on low speed until fluffy. Add the egg and molasses; beat well. Using a wooden spoon, stir flour mixture into egg mixture.

3. Shape dough into 1½-inch balls (1 heaping tablespoon dough each). Roll balls in the 2 tablespoons sugar. Place about 2½ inches apart on ungreased cookie sheets. Bake about 10 minutes or until lightly browned but still puffed. *Do not overbake*. Let stand on cookie sheets for 2 minutes. Transfer to wire rack; cool. Makes 24.

Nutrition facts per cookie: 141 cal., 6 g total fat (4 g sat. fat), 25 mg chol., 119 mg sodium, 20 g carbo., 0 g fiber, 1 g pro.

Cutout cookies hold a special place in our readers' hearts. We've had many a letter from now-grown kids telling us how they cherish the time they spent with their mothers or grandmothers making gingerbread men or other cookies. And they're making sure the children in their lives have the same fond cookie-baking memories.

Gingerbread People Cutouts

Prep: 35 min. Chill: 3 hr. Bake: 6 min. per batch for
5-inch cookies; 10 min. per batch for 7½-inch cookies

In America, the custom of making gingerbread
people originated in the colonial city of New
Amsterdam, now known as New York City.

½	**cup shortening**
½	**cup granulated sugar**
1	**tsp. baking powder**
1	**tsp. ground ginger**
½	**tsp. baking soda**
½	**tsp. ground cinnamon**
½	**tsp. ground cloves**
½	**cup molasses**
1	**egg**
1	**Tbsp. vinegar**
2½	**cups all-purpose flour**
1	**recipe Orange Glaze (below)**

1. In a large mixing bowl, beat shortening with an
electric mixer on medium to high speed for 30 seconds.
Add granulated sugar, baking powder, ginger, baking
soda, cinnamon, and cloves. Beat until combined,
scraping side of bowl frequently. Beat in the molasses,
egg, and vinegar. Beat in as much of the flour as you can
with the mixer. Using a wooden spoon, stir in any
remaining flour. Divide dough in half. Cover and chill
about 3 hours or until easy to handle.

2. Preheat oven to 375°F. Grease cookie sheets; set
aside. On a lightly floured surface, roll half of the dough
to a ¼-inch thickness. Using a 5- or 7½-inch gingerbread
person cookie cutter, cut into people shapes. Place 1 inch
apart on the prepared cookie sheets. Bake for 6 to
8 minutes for 5-inch cookies or 10 to 12 minutes for
7½-inch cookies or until edges are lightly browned. Cool
on cookie sheets for 1 minute. Transfer to wire racks and
let cool. Repeat with remaining dough.

3. Prepare Orange Glaze; decorate cookies with icing.
Makes about twenty-four 5-inch cookies or eleven
7½-inch cookies.

Orange Glaze: Combine 2 cups sifted powdered
sugar, 2 tablespoons orange juice or milk, and ½ teaspoon
vanilla. Stir in enough additional juice or milk, 1 teaspoon
at a time, to make an icing of drizzling consistency.

Nutrition facts per 5-inch cookie: 151 cal., 5 g total fat (1 g sat. fat),
9 mg chol., 45 mg sodium, 26 g carbo., 0 g fiber, 2 g pro.

Sugar Cookie Cutouts

Prep: 30 min. Bake: 7 min. per batch

Other cookies may take center stage for a while,
but bakers always seem to return to sugar cookies
when they want colorful cutouts for Christmas,
Valentine's Day, or other occasions. This recipe
is our unbeatable version of the old standby.

⅔	**cup butter, softened**
¾	**cup granulated sugar**
1	**tsp. baking powder**
¼	**tsp. salt**
1	**egg**
1	**Tbsp. milk**
1	**tsp. vanilla**
2	**cups all-purpose flour**
1	**recipe Vanilla Powdered Sugar Icing (below) (optional)**

1. In a large mixing bowl, beat butter with an electric
mixer on medium to high speed for 30 seconds. Add
granulated sugar, baking powder, and salt. Beat until
combined, scraping side of bowl occasionally. Beat in egg,
milk, and vanilla. Beat in as much of the flour as you can
with the mixer. Using a wooden spoon, stir in any
remaining flour. Divide dough in half. If necessary, cover
and chill dough about 30 minutes or until easy to handle.

2. Preheat oven to 375°F. On a lightly floured surface,
roll half of the dough to an ⅛-inch thickness. Using
2½-inch cookie cutters, cut into desired shapes. Place
1 inch apart on ungreased cookie sheets. Bake for 7 to
8 minutes or until edges are firm and bottoms are very
lightly browned. Transfer to wire racks and let cool.
Repeat with remaining dough. If desired, frost with
Vanilla Powdered Sugar Icing. Makes about 36 cookies.

Vanilla Powdered Sugar Icing: In a medium
mixing bowl, combine 4 cups sifted powdered sugar,
¼ cup milk, and 1 teaspoon vanilla; beat with an electric
mixer on medium speed until smooth. Stir in additional
milk if needed, 1 teaspoon at a time, to make an icing of
spreading consistency. If desired, tint with food coloring.

Nutrition facts per cookie: 73 cal., 4 g total fat (2 g sat. fat), 16 mg chol.,
66 mg sodium, 9 g carbo., 0 g fiber, 1 g pro.

Candy Windowpane Cutouts: Prepare as
directed, except place cutout dough on foil-lined cookie
sheets. Cut small shapes out of cookie centers. Finely
crush 3 ounces hard candy (about ½ cup). Fill each
center cutout with crushed candy. When baked, cool
cookies on foil.

Nutrition facts per cookie: 83 cal., 4 g total fat (2 g sat. fat), 16 mg chol.,
67 mg sodium, 11 g carbo., 0 g fiber, 1 g pro.

Buttery Spritz

Prep: 30 min. Bake: 8 min. per batch

Originally from Scandinavia (an early version in our magazine called them Swedish Spritz), these rich butter cookies have become an American standard.

1½ **cups butter, softened**
1 **cup sugar**
1 **tsp. baking powder**
1 **egg**
1 **tsp. vanilla**
3½ **cups all-purpose flour**
  Decorative sugars or candies (optional)

1. Preheat oven to 375°F. In a large mixing bowl, beat butter with an electric mixer on medium to high speed for 30 seconds. Add sugar and baking powder; beat until combined, scraping side of bowl occasionally. Beat in egg and vanilla. Beat in as much of the flour as you can with the mixer. Using a wooden spoon, stir in any remaining flour. *Do not chill dough*.

2. Pack dough into a cookie press. Force dough through press onto ungreased cookie sheets. If desired, decorate with decorative sugars or candies. Bake for 8 to 10 minutes or until edges of cookies are firm but not brown. Transfer to wire racks; let cool. Makes about 84.

Nutrition facts per cookie: 58 cal., 4 g total fat (2 g sat. fat), 12 mg chol., 41 mg sodium, 6 g carbo., 0 g fiber, 1 g pro.

Chocolate Spritz: Prepare as directed, except add ¼ cup unsweetened cocoa powder with the sugar and reduce flour to 3¼ cups.

Nutrition facts per cookie: 58 cal., 4 g total fat (2 g sat. fat), 12 mg chol., 41 mg sodium, 6 g carbo., 0 g fiber, 1 g pro.

Clever Gizmos
Cookware stores boomed in the 1960s and 70s as cooks demanded the latest kitchen gadgets, such as these handy helpers:
• Cookie scoops help ensure drop cookies are uniform in size and shape.
• Cookie stamps make quick work of adding a decorative touch to cookies.
• Slightly bent offset spatulas allow you to frost cookies easily without getting your fingers in the frosting.

Chocolate Pizzelles

Prep: 20 min. Bake: per manufacturer's directions

Crisp pizzelles, traditional Italian cookies, are made with an intricately designed iron similar to a waffle iron. At cookware stores, you'll find electric models and irons that must be heated on the range top.

1½ **cups hazelnuts (filberts), toasted (tip, page 102)**
2¼ **cups all-purpose flour**
3 **Tbsp. unsweetened cocoa powder**
1 **Tbsp. baking powder**
3 **eggs**
1 **cup granulated sugar**
⅓ **cup butter, melted and cooled**
2 **tsp. vanilla**
1 **recipe Cocoa Powder Glaze (below)**

1. Finely chop *1 cup* of the hazelnuts; set aside. Place remaining ½ cup hazelnuts in a blender or food processor. Cover and blend or process until very fine but dry and not oily.

2. In a medium bowl, stir together the ground hazelnuts, the flour, cocoa powder, and baking powder; set aside.

3. In a large mixing bowl, beat eggs with an electric mixer on high speed about 4 minutes or until thick and lemon colored. Gradually add granulated sugar, beating on medium speed. Beat in butter and vanilla. Add flour mixture, beating on low speed until combined.

4. Heat an electric pizzelle iron according to manufacturer's directions. (Or heat a pizzelle iron on range top over medium heat until a drop of water sizzles on the grid. Reduce heat to medium-low.)

5. For each pizzelle, place a slightly rounded tablespoon of batter on pizzelle grid, slightly off-center toward the back. Close lid. Bake according to manufacturer's directions. (For a nonelectric iron, bake about 2 minutes or until golden, turning once.) Turn warm pizzelle onto a cutting board; cut in half or into quarters. Transfer to a paper towel to cool. Repeat with remaining batter.

6. Prepare Cocoa Powder Glaze. Dip the rounded edge of each pizzelle piece into glaze; dip into finely chopped hazelnuts. Place on wire racks until glaze is set. Makes 36 pizzelle halves.

Cocoa Powder Glaze: In a small bowl, stir together 1½ cups sifted powdered sugar, 3 tablespoons unsweetened cocoa powder, and ½ teaspoon vanilla. Stir in enough milk (2 to 3 tablespoons) to make an icing of glazing consistency.

Nutrition facts per pizzelle half: 120 cal., 5 g total fat (1 g sat. fat), 22 mg chol., 54 mg sodium, 17 g carbo., 1 g fiber, 2 g pro.

Brandy Snaps

Prep: 40 min. Bake: 9 min. per batch
Stand: 1 min. per batch

Although these elegant cookies have been served at gatherings as far back as Colonial times, this version was sent to us by a reader in 1993 who said it was a favorite in her Welsh family.

½ cup **sugar**
½ cup **butter**
⅓ cup **golden syrup* or dark-colored corn syrup**
¾ cup **all-purpose flour**
½ tsp. **ground ginger**
1 Tbsp. **brandy**
   Whipped cream (optional)

1. Preheat oven to 350°F. Line a cookie sheet with foil. Lightly grease the foil; set aside.

2. In a medium saucepan, combine sugar, butter, and syrup. Cook mixture over low heat until butter melts; remove from heat. In a small bowl, stir together flour and ginger. Add flour mixture to butter mixture, stirring until well mixed. Stir in brandy.

3. Drop batter by rounded teaspoonfuls 3 to 4 inches apart onto the prepared cookie sheet. *Bake only 2 or 3 cookies at a time.* Bake for 9 to 10 minutes or until bubbly and golden brown. Let cookies stand on the cookie sheet for 1 to 2 minutes. Quickly invert cookies onto another cookie sheet; wrap each cookie around the greased handle of a wooden spoon or a metal cone.

4. When cookie is set, slide cookie off spoon or cone; cool on a wire rack. If desired, fill cookies with whipped cream. Makes about 30 cookies.

*Test Kitchen Tip: Golden syrup, popular in England, is available in specialty stores and larger supermarkets.

Nutrition facts per cookie: 63 cal., 3 g total fat (2 g sat. fat), 9 mg chol., 39 mg sodium, 8 g carbo., 0 g fiber, 0 g pro.

All-American Desserts

Whether you're treating your family at suppertime or capping

off an elegant dinner party, a homemade dessert is a surefire

way to make a meal memorable. We have been tempting our

readers with luscious desserts for more

than seven decades. The pages that

follow are brimming with our most successful sweets. No matter

which desserts are your weakness—cakes, pies, crisps,

puddings, or ice creams—you'll find a reason to indulge here.

266

274

263

270

277

258

Ginger Carrot Cake

Prep: 40 min. Bake: 30 min.

In our February 1995 issue, we boldly proclaimed this recipe to be the best-ever carrot cake. What makes it stand out from the competition is the addition of fresh ginger and dried fruit bits.

  2   **cups all-purpose flour**
  2   **cups granulated sugar**
  2   **tsp. baking powder**
  ½   **tsp. baking soda**
  4   **eggs**
  3   **cups finely shredded carrot**
  ¾   **cup cooking oil**
  ¾   **cup mixed dried fruit bits**
  2   **tsp. grated fresh ginger or ¾ tsp. ground ginger**
  1   **recipe Orange-Cream Cheese Frosting (right)**
  1   **cup finely chopped pecans, toasted (optional) (tip, page 102)**
      Finely shredded orange peel (optional)

  1. Preheat oven to 350°F. Grease and flour two 9×1½-inch round cake pans.* Set aside.
  2. In a large bowl, stir together flour, sugar, baking powder, and baking soda. Set aside.

  3. In a medium bowl, beat eggs; stir in carrot, oil, dried fruit bits, and ginger. Stir egg mixture into flour mixture. Pour batter into prepared pans.
  4. Bake for 30 to 35 minutes or until a wooden toothpick inserted near centers come out clean. Cool in pans on wire racks for 10 minutes. Remove from pans. Cool completely on wire racks.
  5. Prepare Orange-Cream Cheese Frosting. Fill and frost cake layers. If desired, press toasted pecans onto the side of the cake and sprinkle with orange peel.
  6. Cover loosely and store cake or any leftovers in the refrigerator for up to 2 days. Makes 16 servings.

Orange-Cream Cheese Frosting: In a medium mixing bowl, combine: two 3-ounce packages cream cheese, softened; ½ cup butter, softened; and 1 tablespoon apricot brandy or orange juice. Beat with an electric mixer on medium speed until smooth. Gradually add 2 cups sifted powdered sugar, beating until mixed. Gradually beat in enough of an additional 2½ to 2¾ cups sifted powdered sugar to make of spreading consistency. Stir in ½ teaspoon finely shredded orange peel.

Make-ahead directions: Prepare as directed through step 5, assembling cake on the base of a cake container with a tight-fitting lid or on a baking sheet. Freeze about 1 hour or just until frosting is firm. Cover with cake container lid or moisture- and vaporproof wrap. Label and freeze for up to 1 week. Thaw cake overnight in the refrigerator.

*Test Kitchen Tip: To prepare Ginger Carrot Cake as a layer cake, the 9-inch round cake pans need to be at least 1½ inches deep or the batter could flow over the sides of the pans during baking. If your round pans aren't deep enough, use one greased 13×9×2-inch baking pan. Prepare batter as directed; pour into prepared pan. Bake in a 350°F oven about 40 minutes or until a wooden toothpick inserted near the center comes out clean. Place pan on wire rack; cool completely. Frost with Cream Cheese-Orange Frosting. (Some frosting may be left over if using the rectangular pan.) If desired, sprinkle with nuts.

Nutrition facts per serving: 489 cal., 22 g total fat (8 g sat. fat), 81 mg chol., 211 mg sodium, 71 g carbo., 1 g fiber, 4 g pro.

Orange-Raisin Cake

Prep: 30 min. Bake: 40 min.

When this cake first appeared on *Better Homes and Gardens*® pages in the 1930s, it was considered to be a timesaver because the orange glaze eliminated the need to make a frosting.

1	cup raisins
1¾	cups all-purpose flour
1	tsp. baking soda
½	tsp. salt
1	cup sugar
½	cup butter
2	eggs
1	tsp. vanilla
1	cup buttermilk or sour milk (tip, page 116)
½	cup chopped walnuts
2	tsp. finely shredded orange peel
¾	cup sugar
¼	cup orange juice

1. Preheat oven to 350°F. In a small bowl, combine the raisins and *2 tablespoons* of the flour. Set aside. In a bowl, stir together the remaining flour, the baking soda, and salt. Grease a 9×9×2-inch baking pan. Set aside.

2. In a large mixing bowl, combine the 1 cup sugar and the butter. Beat with an electric mixer on medium speed for 30 seconds. Add eggs and vanilla; beat well. Alternately add flour mixture and buttermilk or sour milk to egg mixture, beating after each addition until combined. Stir in raisin mixture, walnuts, and orange peel. Pour batter into prepared pan.

3. Bake for 40 to 45 minutes or until a wooden toothpick inserted near the center comes out clean. In a small saucepan, combine the ¾ cup sugar and the orange juice; cook and stir until the sugar is dissolved. Prick top of warm cake all over with tines of a fork; spoon sugar mixture over cake. Cool in pan on wire rack. Serves 9.

Nutrition facts per serving: 446 cal., 17 g total fat (8 g sat. fat), 78 mg chol., 425 mg sodium, 70 g carbo., 2 g fiber, 6 g pro.

Busy-Day Cake with Broiled Coconut Topping

Prep: 25 min. Bake: 25 min. Broil: 3 min. Cool: 30 min.

In the 1930s, busy home bakers relied on this easy one-bowl cake and its simple broiled brown sugar frosting when they didn't have time to make a full layer cake.

1⅓	cups all-purpose flour
⅔	cup granulated sugar
2	tsp. baking powder
⅔	cup milk
¼	cup butter, softened
1	egg
1	tsp. vanilla
1	recipe Broiled Coconut Topping (below)

1. Preheat oven to 350°F. Grease an 8×1½-inch round cake pan; set the pan aside.

2. In a large mixing bowl, stir together flour, sugar, and baking powder. Add milk, butter, egg, and vanilla. Beat with an electric mixer on low speed until combined. Beat on medium speed for 1 minute. Pour batter into prepared pan.

3. Bake for 25 to 30 minutes or until a wooden toothpick comes out clean. Meanwhile, prepare Broiled Coconut Topping; spread onto warm cake. Broil about 4 inches from heat for 3 to 4 minutes or until golden. Cool in pan on a wire rack for 30 minutes. Serve immediately. Makes 8 servings.

Broiled Coconut Topping: In a small bowl, stir together ¼ cup packed brown sugar and 2 tablespoons softened butter until combined. Stir in 1 tablespoon milk. Stir in ½ cup coconut and, if desired, ¼ cup chopped nuts.

Nutrition facts per serving: 300 cal., 13 g total fat (9 g sat. fat), 53 mg chol., 238 mg sodium, 43 g carbo., 1 g fiber, 4 g pro.

How many tests does it take to pass? Some *Better Homes and Gardens®* recipes fly through our Test Kitchen with just one taste-test, while others take three or more tries to perfect.

Orange-Almond Cake

Stand: 30 min. Prep: 30 min. Bake: 20 min.

When you're looking for a spectacular cake to celebrate a birthday or other special occasion, try this citrus-flavored layer cake.

¾   **cup butter**
3   **eggs**
1   **cup milk**
2½   **cups all-purpose flour**
2½   **tsp. baking powder**
½   **tsp. salt**
1¾   **cups granulated sugar**
1½   **tsp. vanilla**
¼   **cup orange liqueur, rum, or milk**
1   **Tbsp. finely shredded orange peel**
1   **recipe Easy Crème Fraîche Frosting (right)**
⅔   **cup whole cranberry sauce**
½   **cup orange marmalade**
¼   **cup coarsely chopped slivered almonds, toasted (tip, page 102)**

1. Allow butter, eggs, and 1 cup milk to stand at room temperature for 30 minutes. Meanwhile, grease and lightly flour three 8×1½- or 9×1½-inch round cake pans; set aside. In medium bowl, combine flour, baking powder, and salt; set aside. Preheat oven to 375°F.

2. In a large mixing bowl, beat butter with an electric mixer on medium to high speed for 30 seconds. Gradually add granulated sugar, *about ¼ cup* at a time, beating on medium speed until combined. Beat on medium speed for 2 minutes more. Add eggs, *one* at a time, beating after each. Beat in vanilla. Combine the 1 cup milk and the orange liqueur. Alternately add flour mixture and milk mixture to beaten mixture, beating on low speed after each addition just until combined. (Batter may appear curdled after each addition of milk.) Fold in orange peel. Pour batter into prepared pans; spread evenly.

3. Bake for 20 to 25 minutes for 8-inch cakes, 15 to 18 minutes for 9-inch cakes, or until a wooden toothpick inserted near the centers comes out clean. Cool in pans on wire racks for 10 minutes. Remove from pans. Cool completely on racks. Prepare Easy Crème Fraîche Frosting.

4. To assemble, place *one* cake layer on a platter. Spread with cranberry sauce. Top with another cake layer. In a small bowl, stir together orange marmalade and almonds; spread onto second cake layer. Top with the third cake layer. Frost top and side of cake with frosting. Cover loosely and store cake or any leftovers in the refrigerator for up to 24 hours. Makes 16 servings.

Easy Crème Fraîche Frosting: In a medium mixing bowl, combine one 8-ounce carton dairy sour cream, 1 cup whipping cream, and ¾ cup sifted powdered sugar. Beat with an electric mixer on medium speed until mixture thickens and forms soft peaks (tips curl).

Nutrition facts per serving: 419 cal., 20 g total fat (12 g sat. fat), 92 mg chol., 270 mg sodium, 54 g carbo., 1 g fiber, 5 g pro.

Oatmeal Cake

Prep: 45 min. Bake: 40 min. Cool: 20 min. + 1 hr.
Broil: 2 min.

Broiled nut topping plus a sturdy oatmeal cake add up to a mighty fine old-fashioned dessert. Serve this family-pleaser with a scoop of vanilla ice cream.

½   **cup butter**
2   **eggs**
1¼   **cups boiling water**
1   **cup rolled oats**
2   **cups all-purpose flour**
2   **tsp. baking powder**
¾   **tsp. ground cinnamon**
½   **tsp. baking soda**
½   **tsp. salt**
¼   **tsp. ground nutmeg**
¾   **cup granulated sugar**
½   **cup packed brown sugar**
1   **tsp. vanilla**
1   **recipe Broiled Nut Topping (opposite)**

1. Allow butter and eggs to stand at room temperature for 30 minutes. Meanwhile, grease and lightly flour a 9-inch springform pan; set pan aside. In a small bowl, pour boiling water over oats. Stir until combined; let stand for 20 minutes. In a medium bowl, stir together flour, baking powder, cinnamon, baking soda, salt, and nutmeg; set aside.

2. Preheat oven to 350°F. In a large mixing bowl, beat butter with an electric mixer on medium to high speed for 30 seconds. Add granulated sugar, brown sugar, and vanilla; beat until well mixed. Add eggs, *one* at a time, beating well after each addition. Alternately add flour mixture and oatmeal mixture to beaten mixture, beating on low speed after each addition just until combined. Pour batter into prepared pan.

3. Bake for 40 to 45 minutes or until a wooden toothpick inserted in the center comes out clean. Cool cake in pan on a wire rack for 20 minutes. Remove side of pan; cool on wire rack for at least 1 hour more.

4. Prepare Broiled Nut Topping. Transfer cake to a baking sheet. Spread topping onto warm cake. Broil about 4 inches from heat for 2 to 3 minutes or until topping is bubbly and golden. Cool on a wire rack before serving. Makes 12 servings.

Broiled Nut Topping: In a medium saucepan, combine ¼ cup butter and 2 tablespoons half-and-half, light cream, or milk. Cook and stir until butter melts. Add ½ cup packed brown sugar; stir until sugar dissolves. Remove from heat. Stir in ¾ cup chopped pecans or walnuts and ⅓ cup coconut.

Nutrition facts per serving: 410 cal., 20 g total fat (10 g sat. fat), 70 mg chol., 273 mg sodium, 54 g carbo., 2 g fiber, 5 g pro.

Make-Ahead Solution

With today's busy schedules, making a cake the same day you plan to serve it can be next to impossible. Rather than settling for store-bought, bake a cake ahead and freeze it. For best results, freeze cakes unfrosted. Place the cooled cakes on baking sheets and freeze just until firm. Transfer each frozen cake or layer to a large freezer bag or wrap and seal in freezer wrap. Freeze layer cakes for up to 4 months; angel food, sponge, and chiffon cakes for up to 3 months. Thaw frozen cakes at room temperature for several hours before serving or filling and frosting.

Peanut Butter Cupcakes

Prep: 25 min. Bake: 18 min.

This 1939 recipe for chocolate-frosted peanut butter cupcakes is delicious proof that the peanut-chocolate combo has been around for a long time.

    2   cups all-purpose flour
    2½   tsp. baking powder
    ½   tsp. salt
    2   eggs
    ½   cup packed brown sugar
    1   cup packed brown sugar
    ⅓   cup shortening
    ½   cup creamy peanut butter
    1   tsp. vanilla
    ¾   cup milk
    1½   cups canned chocolate or chocolate
         fudge frosting
         Chopped peanuts (optional)

1. Preheat oven to 350°F. Grease twenty-four 2½-inch muffin cups or line with paper bake cups; set aside. In a small bowl, stir together flour, baking powder, and salt; set aside.

2. In a medium mixing bowl, combine eggs and the ½ cup brown sugar; beat with an electric mixer on medium-high speed about 5 minutes or until thick and smooth. Set aside.

3. In a large mixing bowl, combine the 1 cup brown sugar and the shortening; beat with an electric mixer on low to medium speed until well mixed. Beat in the peanut butter and vanilla. Add the egg mixture, beating on low speed until combined. Alternately add flour mixture and milk to beaten mixture, beating on low speed after each addition just until combined.

4. Spoon into prepared muffin cups, filling each about two-thirds full. Bake for 18 to 20 minutes or until cupcakes spring back when lightly touched. Cool in pans on wire racks for 5 minutes. Transfer cupcakes to wire racks; cool completely. Spread tops with chocolate or fudge frosting. If desired, sprinkle with chopped peanuts. Makes 24 cupcakes.

Nutrition facts per cupcake: 219 cal., 9 g total fat (2 g sat. fat), 18 mg chol., 177 mg sodium, 33 g carbo., 1 g fiber, 3 g pro.

Walnut Mocha Torte

Prep: 40 min. Bake: 20 min. Chill: 4 to 24 hr.

This Prize Tested Recipes® winner is so easy because it's made in a blender or food processor. The whirled-together batter results in a moist, nutty, and spectacular dessert.

1	**cup walnuts or pecans**
2	**Tbsp. all-purpose flour**
2½	**tsp. baking powder**
4	**eggs**
¾	**cup sugar**
1	**recipe Mocha Frosting (right)**
	Chocolate curls (optional)
	Edible rose petals (optional)

1. Preheat oven to 350°F. Grease and lightly flour two 8×1½-inch round cake pans; set aside. In a medium bowl, stir together nuts, flour, and baking powder.

2. In a blender or food processor, combine eggs and sugar; cover and blend or process until smooth. Add nut mixture. Cover and blend or process until smooth. Spread batter evenly in prepared pans.

3. Bake for 20 to 25 minutes or until cakes spring back when lightly touched (centers may dip slightly). Cool in pans on wire racks for 10 minutes. Remove from pans. Cool on wire racks. Prepare Mocha Frosting.

4. Split each cake layer in half horizontally to make 4 layers. Spread frosting between layers; stack layers. Spread frosting on top and side of cake. Chill frosted cake for at least 4 hours or up to 24 hours. If desired, top with chocolate curls and garnish with rose petals. Makes 8 servings.

Mocha Frosting: In a chilled small mixing bowl, dissolve 1 teaspoon instant coffee crystals, crushed, in 1 cup whipping cream; beat with chilled beaters of an electric mixer on low speed until slightly thickened. Add ⅓ cup sugar and ¼ cup unsweetened cocoa powder; beat just until stiff peaks form (tips stand straight).

Nutrition facts per serving: 360 cal., 23 g total fat (8 g sat. fat), 147 mg chol., 158 mg sodium, 34 g carbo., 1 g fiber, 7 g pro.

Sour Cream Pound Cake

Prep: 45 min. Bake: 1 hr.

Recipes for old-time pound cakes were easy to remember because they called for a pound of each of the major ingredients. Although the proportions of this enchanting cake deviate a little, we've yet to find a pound cake we like better.

- ½ **cup butter**
- 3 **eggs**
- ½ **cup dairy sour cream**
- 1½ **cups all-purpose flour**
- ¼ **tsp. baking powder**
- ⅛ **tsp. baking soda**
- 1 **cup sugar**
- ½ **tsp. vanilla**

1. Allow butter, eggs, and sour cream to stand at room temperature for 30 minutes. Meanwhile, grease and lightly flour an 8×4×2-inch or 9×5×3-inch loaf pan; set aside. In a small bowl, stir together flour, baking powder, and baking soda; set aside.

2. Preheat oven to 325°F. In a large mixing bowl, beat butter with an electric mixer on medium to high speed for 30 seconds. Gradually add sugar, beating about 10 minutes or until very light and fluffy. Beat in vanilla. Add eggs, *one* at a time, beating 1 minute after each addition and scraping side of bowl frequently. Alternately add flour mixture and sour cream to beaten mixture, beating on low to medium speed after each addition just until combined. Pour batter into prepared pan.

3. Bake for 60 to 75 minutes or until a wooden toothpick inserted in center comes out clean. Cool in pan on a wire rack for 10 minutes. Remove from pan. Cool completely on wire rack. Makes 10 servings.

Nutrition facts per serving: 267 cal., 13 g total fat (8 g sat. fat), 94 mg chol., 149 mg sodium, 33 g carbo., 0 g fiber, 4 g pro.

Lemon-Poppy Seed Pound Cake: Prepare as directed, except substitute ½ cup lemon yogurt for the sour cream. Add 1 teaspoon finely shredded lemon peel, 2 tablespoons lemon juice, and 2 tablespoons poppy seeds to batter.

Nutrition facts per serving: 269 cal., 12 g total fat (7 g sat. fat), 91 mg chol., 154 mg sodium, 35 g carbo., 1 g fiber, 5 g pro.

Orange-Rosemary Pound Cake: Prepare as directed, except stir 1¼ teaspoons finely shredded orange peel and 1 teaspoon snipped fresh rosemary into the batter.

Nutrition facts per serving: 267 cal., 13 g total fat (8 g sat. fat), 94 mg chol., 149 mg sodium, 33 g carbo., 1 g fiber, 4 g pro.

Hot Milk Sponge Cake

Prep: 45 min. Bake: 20 min.

This fantastically foolproof fifities sponge cake is so versatile you can serve it with anything—from a simple dusting of powdered sugar and fresh fruit to the richest frosting.

- 2 **eggs**
- 1 **cup all-purpose flour**
- 1 **tsp. baking powder**
- 1 **cup sugar**
- ½ **cup milk**
- 2 **Tbsp. butter**

1. Allow eggs to stand at room temperature for 30 minutes. Meanwhile, grease a 9×9×2-inch square baking pan. Combine flour and baking powder; set aside.

2. Preheat oven to 350°F. In a large mixing bowl, beat eggs with an electric mixer on high speed about 4 minutes or until thick. Gradually add sugar, beating on medium speed for 4 to 5 minutes or until light and fluffy. Add the flour mixture; beat on low to medium speed just until combined.

3. In a small saucepan, heat and stir milk and butter until butter melts; add to batter, beating until combined. Pour batter into the prepared pan.

4. Bake for 20 to 25 minutes or until a wooden toothpick inserted in center comes out clean. Cool cake in pan on a wire rack. Makes 9 servings.

Nutrition facts per serving: 180 cal., 4 g total fat (2 g sat. fat), 56 mg chol., 93 mg sodium, 33 g carbo., 0 g fiber, 3 g pro.

It's All in the Pan

Our readers often write wondering why their cakes get too brown. We ask about their bakeware. Glass, dark, or dull-finish bakeware, such as tin and many nonstick pans, absorbs more heat than shiny aluminum or stainless-steel bakeware. So, if you're using a dark or dull-finish pan or a glass baking dish, reduce the oven temperature by 25°F and check the cake's doneness about 3 to 5 minutes before the end of the suggested baking time.

Lemonade Roll

Prep: 25 min. Bake: 18 min. Chill: 1 to 24 hr.

An Illinois reader sent us the recipe for this luscious lemon cake roll in 1971.

- ¾ **cup all-purpose flour**
- 1 **tsp. baking powder**
- 4 **egg yolks**
- ¾ **cup granulated sugar**
- ½ **cup frozen lemonade concentrate, thawed**
- 4 **egg whites**
  Sifted powdered sugar
- 1 **tsp. finely shredded lemon peel**
- ⅔ **of an 8-oz. container frozen whipped dessert topping, thawed (about 2 cups)**

1. Preheat oven to 375°F. Lightly grease a 15×10×1-inch baking pan. Line pan with waxed paper; grease and flour paper. Set aside. In a small bowl, stir together flour, baking powder, and ½ teaspoon *salt*.

2. In a medium mixing bowl, beat egg yolks with an electric mixer on high speed about 5 minutes or until thick and lemon colored. Gradually add ½ *cup* of the granulated sugar, beating on high speed until sugar is almost dissolved. Add flour mixture and lemonade concentrate alternately to beaten mixture, beating after each addition just until combined.

Lemonade Roll

3. Wash and dry beaters. In a large bowl, beat egg whites with electric mixer on medium speed until soft peaks form (tips curl); gradually add the remaining ¼ cup granulated sugar, beating until stiff peaks form (tips stand straight). Fold egg yolk mixture into whites.

4. Spread batter evenly into prepared pan. Bake for 18 to 20 minutes or until cake springs back when lightly touched. Immediately loosen the edges of cake from pan. Turn out onto a towel sprinkled with powdered sugar. Remove waxed paper. Starting from a short side, roll up warm cake and towel together; cool on a wire rack.

5. Fold lemon peel into dessert topping. Unroll cake; remove towel. Spread dessert topping mixture onto cake to within 1 inch of edges. Roll up cake. Chill for at least 1 hour or up to 24 hours. To serve, if desired, sprinkle with additional powdered sugar. Makes 10 servings.

Nutrition facts per serving: 189 cal., 5 g total fat (3 g sat. fat), 85 mg chol., 182 mg sodium, 32 g carbo., 0 g fiber, 3 g pro.

Caramel Angel Food Cake

Prep: 45 min. Bake: 40 min.

In 1936 when we first published this heavenly treat, we boasted it was "the" cake that Sigma Nu fraternity housemothers made for homesick college students. It's still a sure cure for the blues.

- 1½ **cups egg whites (10 to 12 large)**
- 1 **recipe Burnt-Sugar Syrup (above, right)**
- 2 **cups sugar**
- 1½ **cups sifted cake flour or all-purpose flour**
- ¼ **tsp. cream of tartar**
- 1 **tsp. vanilla**
  Sweetened whipped cream (optional)
  Fresh berries, peaches, and/or kiwifruit (optional)

1. In a very large mixing bowl, allow egg whites to stand at room temperature for 30 minutes. Meanwhile, prepare Burnt-Sugar Syrup. Sift sugar and flour together two times; set aside.

2. Preheat oven to 375°F. Add cream of tartar and vanilla to egg whites. Beat with an electric mixer on high speed until stiff peaks form (tips stand straight). Sift *one-fourth* of the sugar mixture over beaten egg whites; fold in gently. Repeat, folding in the remaining sugar mixture by fourths. Carefully fold in ¼ *cup* of the Burnt-Sugar Syrup; discard remaining syrup. Spoon batter into ungreased 10-inch tube pan, spreading evenly.

3. Bake about 40 minutes or until top springs back when touched. Immediately invert cake (leave in pan); cool. Loosen from pan; remove cake. If desired, serve with whipped cream and fresh fruit. Makes 16 servings.

Burnt-Sugar Syrup: In a heavy, small skillet, cook ¾ cup sugar over medium-high heat until sugar begins to melt, shaking skillet occasionally to heat the sugar evenly. Do not stir. Once the sugar starts to melt, reduce heat to low. Cook about 5 minutes more or until all of the sugar is melted and golden, stirring as needed with a wooden spoon. When a deep golden brown, remove syrup from heat. Slowly add 1 cup boiling water. Return to medium heat; cook and stir about 8 minutes or until sugar is dissolved and syrup is reduced to ½ cup. Cover with plastic wrap and let cool.

Nutrition facts per serving: 159 cal., 0 g total fat, 0 mg chol., 35 mg sodium, 37 g carbo., 0 g fiber, 3 g pro.

Tropical Isle Chiffon Cake

Prep: 30 min. Bake: 1 hr.

Chiffon cake (a cross between a regular cake and sponge cake) didn't make a big splash on the home baking scene until the late 1940s, when the recipe was used to promote cake flour. This coconut version was sent to us by an Arizona reader in 1965.

2¼	**cups sifted cake flour or 2 cups sifted all-purpose flour**
1½	**cups granulated sugar**
1	**Tbsp. baking powder**
¼	**tsp. salt**
½	**cup cooking oil**
7	**egg yolks**
1	**tsp. finely shredded orange peel (set aside)**
¾	**cup orange juice**
7	**egg whites**
½	**tsp. cream of tartar**
1	**3½-oz. can (1⅓ cups) flaked coconut**
	Sifted powdered sugar (optional)
	Chopped fresh tropical fruit (such as mango, papaya, and pineapple) (optional)
	Fresh mint sprigs (optional)

1. Preheat oven to 325°F. In a large mixing bowl, combine flour, sugar, baking powder, and salt. Make a well in the center of flour mixture. Add oil, egg yolks, and orange juice. Beat with an electric mixer on low speed until combined. Beat on high speed about 5 minutes more or until smooth. Stir in orange peel.

2. Wash and dry beaters thoroughly. In a very large mixing bowl, beat egg whites and cream of tartar with an electric mixer on high speed until stiff peaks form (tips stand straight). Pour egg yolk-flour mixture in a thin stream over beaten egg whites. Sprinkle with coconut; fold in gently. Pour into an ungreased 10-inch tube pan, spreading evenly.

3. Bake for 60 to 65 minutes or until top springs back when lightly touched. Immediately invert cake (leave in pan); cool completely. Loosen cake from pan; remove cake. If desired, sprinkle with sifted powdered sugar. If desired, serve with tropical fruit and garnish with mint. Makes 12 servings.

Nutrition facts per serving: 337 cal., 15 g total fat (5 g sat. fat), 124 mg chol., 210 mg sodium, 45 g carbo., 1 g fiber, 6 g pro.

Lemon Pudding Cake

Prep: 20 min. Bake: 40 min.

Pudding cakes were popular in the 1940s because the batter separates into pudding and cake, making two desserts in one pan—slick!

3	**egg whites**
½	**cup sugar**
¼	**cup all-purpose flour**
1	**tsp. finely shredded lemon peel**
3	**Tbsp. lemon juice**
2	**Tbsp. butter, melted**
3	**egg yolks**
1	**cup milk**

1. Allow egg whites to stand at room temperature. Preheat oven to 350°F. In a medium bowl, combine sugar and flour. Stir in lemon peel, lemon juice, and melted butter. Beat egg yolks; stir in milk. Add to flour mixture; stir just until combined.

2. In a medium mixing bowl, beat egg whites with an electric mixer on high speed until stiff peaks form (tips stand straight). Gently fold egg whites into lemon batter.

3. Transfer batter to a 1½-quart casserole. Place the casserole in a large pan on an oven rack. Pour hot water into the large pan around the casserole to a depth of 1 inch. Bake about 40 minutes or until golden and top springs back when lightly touched near the center. Serve warm. Makes 4 servings.

Nutrition facts per serving: 266 cal., 11 g total fat (6 g sat. fat), 181 mg chol., 139 mg sodium, 34 g carbo., 0 g fiber, 8 g pro.

Strawberry Chiffon Pie

Prep: 30 min. Chill: 4 to 24 hr.

- 1   **recipe Baked Pastry Shell (below)**
- 1   **envelope unflavored gelatin**
- ¾   **to 1 cup sugar•**
- 3   **egg yolks**
- 3   **Tbsp. lemon juice**
- 2½ **cups fresh strawberries, crushed (about 1½ cups after crushing)**
-    **Dried egg whites equivalent to 3 fresh egg whites** or 1 cup whipping cream**
-    **Strawberry fans (optional)**
-    **Whipped cream (optional)**

1. Prepare Baked Pastry Shell; set aside. In a small saucepan, stir gelatin into ⅓ cup *cold water*. Let stand 1 minute. Add sugar, egg yolks, lemon juice, and dash *salt*. Cook and stir mixture over medium heat until mixture begins to boil; remove from heat. Transfer to a medium bowl; stir in crushed strawberries. Cover and chill until mixture mounds when spooned; stir occasionally.

2. Prepare and beat dried egg whites to stiff peaks (tips stand straight) according to package directions, or whip the 1 cup cream to soft peaks (tips curl). Gently fold egg white mixture or whipped cream into strawberry mixture. Spoon into pastry shell. Cover; chill for at least 4 hours or up to 24 hours. If desired, garnish with strawberry fans and whipped cream. Serves 8.

Baked Pastry Shell: Preheat oven to 450°F. In a medium bowl, stir together 1¼ cups all-purpose flour and ¼ teaspoon salt. Using a pastry blender, cut in ⅓ cup shortening until pieces are pea-size. Sprinkle with 1 tablespoon cold water; gently toss with a fork. Push to side of bowl. Repeat with additional cold water, 1 tablespoon at a time (4 to 5 tablespoons total), until all is moistened. Form into a ball. On a lightly floured surface, slightly flatten dough. Roll from center to edge into a circle about 12 inches in diameter. Wrap pastry around rolling pin; unroll into a 9-inch pie plate. Ease into pie plate, being careful not to stretch. Trim pastry to ½ inch beyond edge of pie plate. Fold under extra pastry. Crimp edge. Do not prick. Line with a double thickness of foil. Bake for 8 minutes. Remove foil. Bake 5 to 6 minutes more or until golden. Cool on a wire rack.

*Test Kitchen Tip: Taste a strawberry before you start. If it is nicely sweet, use the lesser amount of sugar.

**Test Kitchen Tip: Look in the baking section of the supermarket for dried egg whites.

Nutrition facts per serving: 252 cal., 11 g total fat (3 g sat. fat), 80 mg chol., 103 mg sodium, 35 g carbo., 2 g fiber, 4 g pro.

Yesterday

In earlier times, cooks made desserts using raw egg whites, such as chiffon pie, without a qualm. But now, food safety experts caution that eating raw eggs may be hazardous for some people. We thought it would be a shame to give up chiffon pie, so we revamped our version to use pasteurized dried egg whites or whipping cream.

Today's French Silk Pie

Prep: 40 min. Chill: 5 to 24 hr.

- 1 **recipe Baked Pastry Shell (opposite)**
- 1 **cup whipping cream**
- 1 **cup semisweet chocolate pieces (6 oz.)***
- ⅓ **cup butter**
- ⅓ **cup sugar**
- 2 **egg yolks, beaten**
- 3 **Tbsp. crème de cacao or whipping cream**
- ½ **cup whipping cream, whipped**
- 1 **recipe Double-Chocolate Curls (below)
  (optional)**

1. Prepare Baked Pastry Shell; set aside. In a heavy, medium saucepan, combine the 1 cup whipping cream, the chocolate pieces, butter, and sugar. Cook over low heat, stirring constantly, until chocolate is melted (about 10 minutes). Remove from heat.

2. Gradually stir *half* of the hot mixture into egg yolks. Return egg yolk mixture to chocolate mixture in saucepan. Cook over medium-low heat, stirring constantly, until mixture is slightly thickened and begins to bubble (about 5 minutes). Remove from heat. (Mixture may appear to separate.) Stir in the crème de cacao. Place saucepan in a bowl of ice water; stir occasionally until the mixture stiffens and becomes hard to stir (about 20 minutes).

3. Transfer cooled mixture to a medium mixing bowl. Beat with an electric mixer on medium to high speed for 2 to 3 minutes or until light and fluffy. Spread in the cooled pastry shell. Cover and chill for at least 5 hours or up to 24 hours. To serve, top with whipped cream. If desired, garnish with Double-Chocolate Curls. Serves 8.

Double-Chocolate Curls: Line a 4½×2½×2-inch or 6×3×2-inch loaf pan with heavy foil; set aside. Melt 3 ounces semisweet chocolate and 3 ounces white chocolate separately according to package directions. Spread *half* of the semisweet chocolate in prepared pan. Drizzle with *half* of the white chocolate. With a spatula, carefully smooth white chocolate over semisweet chocolate layer in pan. Repeat layers with remaining semisweet chocolate and white chocolate, carefully smoothing each layer. Cover and let stand at room temperature for 3 to 4 hours or until completely set. (The white chocolate may set up more quickly than the semisweet chocolate.) When chocolate is set, grasp foil and remove block from pan. Pull back foil to expose one side of the block. Run a vegetable peeler over the side of the block. To store the block, wrap in foil and place in an airtight container. Store in the refrigerator for up to 1 month or in the freezer for up to 3 months. Bring chocolate to room temperature before making curls.

Today

Another recipe traditionally made with uncooked eggs—in this case the yolks—is French silk pie. Because we wanted to enjoy this ultra-rich dessert without worry, we reworked our recipe to completely cook the egg yolks. It's still every bit as decadent as the classic.

***Test Kitchen Tip:** Be sure to use real semisweet chocolate pieces. Do not substitute products labeled imitation chocolate pieces or chocolate-flavored pieces.

Nutrition facts per serving: 533 cal., 41 g total fat (21 g sat. fat), 137 mg chol., 168 mg sodium, 31 g carbo., 3 g fiber, 4 g pro.

The introduction of the refrigerator into America's kitchens in the 1930s changed the way folks shopped and cooked. It also opened the door to all sorts of new chilled pies and other desserts.

Double-Coconut Cream Pie

Prep: 40 min. Bake: 15 min. Cool: 1 hr. Chill: 3 to 6 hr.

Cream of coconut and flaked coconut give this Decadent Dessert Prize Tested Recipes® winner from 1994 an exquisite double dose of flavor.

1	recipe Baked Pastry Shell (page 262)
1	recipe Meringue for Pie (page 265)
¼	cup cornstarch
2	cups milk
¾	cup cream of coconut
3	egg yolks, beaten
2	Tbsp. butter
1	cup coconut
2	tsp. vanilla
2	Tbsp. coconut

1. Prepare Baked Pastry Shell; set aside. Let egg whites for Meringue for Pie stand as directed.

2. Meanwhile, for filling, in a medium saucepan, combine cornstarch and ¼ teaspoon *salt;* add ¼ cup of the milk, stirring until smooth. Stir in remaining 1¾ cups milk and the cream of coconut. Cook and stir over medium heat until thickened. Cook and stir for 2 minutes more. Remove from heat.

3. Gradually add *about 1 cup* of the hot filling to egg yolks, stirring constantly. Pour egg yolk mixture into remaining hot filling in saucepan. Bring to a gentle boil. Reduce heat; cook and stir for 2 minutes more. Remove from heat. Stir in butter until melted. Stir in the 1 cup coconut and vanilla. Keep warm. Preheat oven to 350°F.

4. Prepare Meringue for Pie. Spoon warm filling into cooled Baked Pastry Shell. Immediately spread meringue over warm filling, carefully sealing to edge of pastry to prevent shrinkage. Sprinkle with the 2 tablespoons coconut. Bake for 15 minutes. Cool on a wire rack for 1 hour. Chill for at least 3 hours or up to 6 hours before serving. Makes 8 servings.

Nutrition facts per serving: 416 cal., 25 g total fat (15 g sat. fat), 93 mg chol., 223 mg sodium, 40 g carbo., 2 g fiber, 8 g pro.

Paradise Pumpkin Pie

Prep: 30 min. Chill: 30 min. Bake: 25 + 40 min.

Candied nuts are the crowning touch to this twin-layered cream cheese and pumpkin dessert. Long a reader favorite, this captivating combo will tempt even guests only lukewarm about pumpkin pie.

1	8-oz. pkg. cream cheese, softened
1	egg
¼	cup granulated sugar
½	tsp. vanilla
1	recipe Pastry for a Single-Crust Pie (page 54)
2	eggs, beaten
1¼	cups canned pumpkin
1	cup evaporated milk
¼	cup packed brown sugar
¼	cup granulated sugar
1	tsp. ground cinnamon
¼	tsp. salt
¼	tsp. ground nutmeg
1	recipe Buttery Candied Pecans (below) or toasted chopped pecans (tip, page 102)

1. In a small mixing bowl, combine cream cheese, the 1 egg, ¼ cup granulated sugar, and the vanilla; beat with an electric mixer on medium speed until smooth. Chill in the refrigerator for 30 minutes. Meanwhile, prepare Pastry for a Single-Crust Pie; set aside.

2. Preheat oven to 350°F. Turn cream cheese mixture into pastry-lined pie plate. In a medium bowl, beat the 2 eggs; stir in pumpkin, evaporated milk, the brown sugar, ¼ cup granulated sugar, the cinnamon, salt, and nutmeg. Carefully pour over cream cheese mixture.

3. Cover edge of pie with foil. Bake for 25 minutes. Remove foil; bake for 40 to 50 minutes more or until a knife inserted near the center comes out clean. Cool on a wire rack. If desired, prepare Candied Pecans. Before serving, sprinkle the pie with Candied Pecans or toasted chopped pecans. Makes 8 servings.

Buttery Candied Pecans: Butter a baking sheet or sheet of foil; set aside. In a heavy, 8-inch skillet, combine ½ cup coarsely chopped pecans, ¼ cup granulated sugar, and 1 tablespoon butter. Heat mixture over medium heat, stirring constantly, for 6 to 8 minutes or until sugar melts and turns a rich brown color. Remove from heat and spread nuts on prepared baking sheet or foil; separate into clusters. Cool. Break clusters into small chunks.

Nutrition facts per serving: 482 cal., 29 g total fat (12 g sat. fat), 124 mg chol., 307 mg sodium, 47 g carbo., 2 g fiber, 10 g pro.

Lemon Meringue Pie

Lemon Meringue Pie

Prep: 40 min. Bake: 15 min. Cool: 1 hr. Chill: 3 to 6 hr.

Lemon meringue pie has been one of our standards since the 1950s. Then, as now, we thought the blend of tart and sweet was sublime.

1	recipe Baked Pastry Shell (page 262)
1	recipe Meringue for Pie (right)
1½	cups sugar
3	Tbsp. all-purpose flour
3	Tbsp. cornstarch
	Dash salt
1½	cups water
3	eggs yolks
2	Tbsp. butter
1	to 2 tsp. finely shredded lemon peel
⅓	cup lemon juice

1. Prepare Baked Pastry Shell; set aside. Let egg whites for Meringue for Pie stand as directed.

2. Preheat oven to 350°F. For filling, in a medium saucepan, stir together sugar, flour, cornstarch, and salt. Gradually stir in the water. Cook and stir over medium-high heat until mixture is thickened and bubbly. Reduce heat; cook and stir for 2 minutes more. Remove from heat.

3. Slightly beat egg yolks with a rotary beater or fork. Gradually add *about 1 cup* of the hot filling to egg yolks, stirring constantly. Pour egg yolk mixture into remaining hot filling in saucepan. Bring to a gentle boil. Reduce heat; cook and stir for 2 minutes more. Remove from heat. Stir in butter and lemon peel. Gently stir in lemon juice. Keep filling warm.

4. Prepare Meringue for Pie. Pour warm filling into cooled Baked Pastry Shell. Immediately spread meringue over warm filling, carefully sealing to edge of pastry to prevent shrinkage. Bake for 15 minutes. Cool on a wire rack for 1 hour. Chill in the refrigerator for at least 3 hours or up to 6 hours before serving. Makes 8 servings.

Meringue for Pie: Allow 3 egg whites to stand at room temperature for 30 minutes. In a large mixing bowl, combine egg whites, ½ teaspoon vanilla, and ¼ teaspoon cream of tartar. Beat with an electric mixer on medium speed about 1 minute or until soft peaks form (tips curl). Gradually add 6 tablespoons sugar, 1 tablespoon at a time, beating on high speed about 4 minutes more or until mixture forms stiff, glossy peaks (tips stand straight) and sugar is dissolved.

Nutrition facts per serving: 395 cal., 14 g total fat (5 g sat. fat), 88 mg chol., 182 mg sodium, 65 g carbo., 1 g fiber, 5 g pro.

Tropical Fruit Pie

Prep: 30 min. Bake: 8 + 10 min. Chill: 1 to 4 hr.

When votes were tallied for Glorious Spring Pies in our May 2001 issue, this eye-catching medley of cream cheese filling and fresh fruit was the victor.

- 1 **recipe Rich Pastry (below right)**
- 12 **oz. cream cheese (1½ 8-oz. pkg. or four 3-oz. pkg.), softened**
- ⅔ **cup sifted powdered sugar**
- ¼ **cup whipping cream**
- 1 **Tbsp. orange liqueur or orange juice**
- 1 **tsp. vanilla**
- 2 **to 2½ cups assorted fresh fruit (peeled and cut-up kiwifruit or papaya, whole raspberries, and/or cut-up strawberries)**
- 2 **Tbsp. apricot preserves**
- ½ **tsp. orange liqueur or orange juice**

1. Preheat oven to 400°. Prepare Rich Pastry. On a lightly floured surface, roll dough from center to edge into a circle about 12 inches in diameter. To transfer pastry, wrap it around the rolling pin. Unroll pastry into a 9-inch pie plate, being careful not to stretch pastry. Trim pastry to ½ inch beyond edge of pie plate. Fold under pastry edge. Crimp edge.

2. Generously prick bottom and side of pastry with a fork. Line pastry with a double thickness of foil. Bake for 8 minutes; remove foil. Bake about 10 minutes more or until golden. Cool on wire rack.

3. For filling, in a large mixing bowl, combine cream cheese and powdered sugar; beat with an electric mixer on medium speed until combined. Add whipping cream, the 1 tablespoon liqueur, and the vanilla. Beat until combined. Spoon filling into baked pastry shell. Cover and chill for at least 1 hour or up to 4 hours.

4. To serve, arrange fruit on top of filling. In a small saucepan, combine preserves and the ½ teaspoon liqueur; heat and stir until melted. Drizzle onto pie. Makes 8 servings.

Rich Pastry: In a medium bowl, stir together 1¼ cups all-purpose flour, 3 tablespoons granulated sugar, and ¼ teaspoon salt. Using a pastry blender, cut in 6 tablespoons butter until mixture resembles coarse crumbs. Stir in 1 egg yolk and enough cold water to moisten (use 3 to 4 tablespoons total). Knead gently until mixture forms a ball.

Nutrition facts per serving: 427 cal., 28 g total fat (17 g sat. fat), 108 mg chol., 298 mg sodium, 38 g carbo., 3 g fiber, 6 g pro.

Tropical Fruit Pie

Candy-Sugar Creme Tart

Candy-Sugar Creme Tart

Prep: 30 min. Bake: 30 min. Cool: 1 hr. Chill: 4 to 8 hr.

At her grandmother's urging, 10-year-old Samantha set out to create a cake for our November 1999 Winter Wonderful Desserts category. Destiny must have been at work because this remarkable tart was the prizewinning result.

- ¾ cup finely crushed shortbread cookies (about 12 cookies)
- ¼ cup finely crushed graham crackers
- 1 Tbsp. butter, melted
- 1 8-oz. pkg. cream cheese, softened
- 3 eggs
- ½ cup half-and-half or light cream
- ¼ cup sugar
- 3 Tbsp. butter, softened
- 1 tsp. vanilla
- 3 1.4-oz. bars chocolate-covered English toffee, coarsely chopped
- 1 1.55-oz. bar white chocolate with chocolate cookie bits, coarsely chopped
- 15 malted milk balls, coarsely chopped (about ⅓ cup)
  Additional chopped candy (optional)

1. Preheat oven to 350°F. For the crust, in a small bowl, stir together crushed cookies, crushed graham crackers, and the 1 tablespoon melted butter (mixture will be crumbly). Press onto the bottom and up the side of a 9-inch tart pan with a removable bottom. Bake about 10 minutes or until lightly browned. Set aside to cool.

2. For filling, in a blender or food processor, mix cream cheese, eggs, half-and-half, sugar, the 3 tablespoons softened butter, and the vanilla. Cover and blend or process until smooth. In a large bowl, place the chopped toffee, white chocolate, and malted milk balls. Stir in the cream cheese mixture. Place crust-lined pan in a shallow baking pan. Pour filling into crust-lined pan. (Pan will be full.)

3. Bake about 30 minutes or until center appears nearly set when tart is shaken. Cool in pan on a wire rack for 1 hour. Remove side of tart pan. Place on a platter. Cover; chill for at least 4 hours or up to 8 hours. If desired, top with additional chopped candy. Serves 12.

Nutrition facts per serving: 268 cal., 19 g total fat (8 g sat. fat), 93 mg chol., 195 mg sodium, 20 g carbo., 0 g fiber, 4 g pro.

Sour Cream-Apple Pie

Prep: 30 min. Bake: 25 + 20 min.

This twist on apple pie made waves when it appeared in 1953 because it called for the latest new ingredient—commercially produced dairy sour cream. Before then, cooks had to sour their own cream.

- 1 recipe Pastry for a Single-Crust Pie (page 54)
- 1 egg
- 1 8-oz. carton dairy sour cream
- ¾ cup granulated sugar
- 2 Tbsp. all-purpose flour
- 1 tsp. vanilla
- ¼ tsp. salt
- 4 cups coarsely chopped peeled tart apples (such as Granny Smith or Rome Beauty)
- ½ cup all-purpose flour
- ⅓ cup packed brown sugar
- 3 Tbsp. butter

1. Preheat oven to 400°F. Prepare Pastry for a Single-Crust Pie; set aside. In a large bowl, beat egg with a fork; stir in sour cream, granulated sugar, the 2 tablespoons flour, the vanilla, and salt. Stir in chopped apple. Pour mixture into the pastry-lined pie plate. Cover edge with foil. Bake for 25 minutes.

2. Meanwhile, in a small bowl, combine the ½ cup flour and the brown sugar. Using a pastry blender, cut in butter until crumbly. Remove foil from pie. Sprinkle brown sugar mixture over pie. Bake about 20 minutes more or until top is golden. Cool on a wire rack. Refrigerate within 2 hours. Makes 8 to 10 servings.

Nutrition facts per serving: 424 cal., 20 g total fat (9 g sat. fat), 51 mg chol., 219 mg sodium, 58 g carbo., 2 g fiber, 5 g pro.

Lower-Fat Sour Cream-Apple Pie: Prepare as directed, except substitute light dairy sour cream for regular dairy sour cream.

Nutrition facts per serving: 400 cal., 16 g total fat (7 g sat. fat), 48 mg chol., 223 mg sodium, 58 g carbo., 2 g fiber, 6 g pro.

Banana-Pecan Streusel Bread Pudding

Prep: 20 min. Bake: 40 min. Stand: 30 min.

We assumed it was hard to beat old-fashioned bread pudding, until we tasted this winner. It updates grandma's favorite by replacing regular bread with croissants and adding mashed banana to the creamy custard.

> 3 **eggs**
> 1 **12-oz. can (1½ cups) evaporated milk**
> 1⅓ **cups mashed ripe banana (4 medium)**
> ½ **cup granulated sugar**
> 1 **Tbsp. vanilla**
> 1 **tsp. ground cinnamon**
> ¼ **to ½ tsp. almond extract**
> 2 **large croissants, cut or torn into 1-inch pieces (5 oz. total)**
> ¼ **cup packed brown sugar**
> 2 **Tbsp. all-purpose flour**
> 1 **Tbsp. butter, melted**
> 1 **tsp. ground cinnamon**
> ½ **cup chopped pecans**
> **Whipped cream or ice cream (optional)**

1. Preheat oven to 350°F. Lightly grease a 2-quart rectangular baking dish; set aside. In a medium bowl, beat eggs; stir in evaporated milk, banana, granulated sugar, vanilla, 1 teaspoon cinnamon, and the almond extract. Place croissant pieces in prepared baking dish. Pour egg mixture evenly over croissants, pressing pieces down to be sure they are all moistened.

2. In a small bowl, combine brown sugar, flour, melted butter, and 1 teaspoon cinnamon. Stir in pecans. Sprinkle over croissant mixture. Bake for 40 to 45 minutes or until a knife inserted near center comes out clean. Let stand for 30 minutes. Serve warm. If desired, top with whipped cream or ice cream. Makes 10 to 12 servings.

Nutrition facts per serving: 280 cal., 12 g total fat (6 g sat. fat), 96 mg chol., 141 mg sodium, 38 g carbo., 1 g fiber, 7 g pro.

Musician's Tart

Musician's Tart

Prep: 30 min. Bake: 10 + 8 + 20 min. Cool: 1 hr.

According to legend, dried fruit and nuts were the currencies used to pay Spanish musicians long ago, hence the name for this fruit-and-nut tart.

> 1 **recipe Tart Pastry (opposite)**
> 1 **cup dried pears, cut up**
> 1 **cup pitted dates, cut up**
> ⅓ **cup pear nectar**
> ¼ **cup packed brown sugar**
> ¼ **cup butter**
> ¼ **cup packed brown sugar**
> 2 **Tbsp. light-colored corn syrup**
> ⅓ **cup pine nuts**
> ⅓ **cup whole almonds**
> ⅓ **cup cashews**
> 2 **Tbsp. whipping cream**
> **Whipped cream (optional)**
> **Grated chocolate (optional)**

1. Preheat oven to 350°F. Prepare Tart Pastry.

2. On a lightly floured surface, roll dough from center to edge into an 11-inch circle. Transfer to a 9-inch tart pan with a removable bottom, being careful not to stretch pastry. Press into bottom and up side of pan. Trim even with edge of pan. Line pastry with a double thickness of foil. Bake for 10 minutes. Remove foil; bake for 8 minutes more. Cool crust on a wire rack for 1 hour.

3. Preheat oven to 375°F. For filling, in a medium saucepan, combine pears, dates, pear nectar, and ¼ cup brown sugar. Bring to boiling over medium heat. Cook, uncovered, for 1 minute. Remove from heat. Cool slightly. Transfer to food processor. Cover and process until a thick paste forms and fruit is nearly smooth.

4. For nut topping, in a small saucepan, combine butter, ¼ cup brown sugar, and the corn syrup. Bring to boiling over medium heat. Cook, uncovered, for 1 minute. Remove from heat. Stir in pine nuts, almonds, cashews, and the 2 tablespoons whipping cream. Set aside.

5. To assemble, spread fruit filling onto bottom of cooled crust. Pour nut topping evenly over filling. Place tart pan on a baking sheet. Bake for 20 minutes. Cool. If desired, serve with whipped cream and grated chocolate. Makes 12 servings.

Tart Pastry: In a food processor, combine 1¼ cups all-purpose flour and 3 tablespoons granulated sugar. Cover and process until combined. Add ½ cup cold butter. Process until mixture resembles coarse crumbs. Add 1 egg yolk and ½ teaspoon vanilla. Process until combined. With the food processor running, add 2 tablespoons water through feed tube, processing just until a soft dough forms. Shape into a ball. If necessary, wrap in plastic wrap or waxed paper and chill in refrigerator for 30 to 60 minutes or until easy to handle.

Nutrition facts per serving: 406 cal., 22 g total fat (10 g sat. fat), 59 mg chol., 159 mg sodium, 53 g carbo., 3 g fiber, 5 g pro.

Blackberry Gingerbread

Prep: 25 min. Bake: 50 min. Cool: 5 + 20 min.

Cold weather season is the ideal time to enjoy gingerbread—which is why we chose this homey dessert as the top prizewinner in our Winter Wonderful Desserts contest in November 1999.

- 2 **cups all-purpose flour**
- 2 **tsp. ground ginger**
- 1 **tsp. baking powder**
- 1 **tsp. ground cinnamon**
- ¼ **tsp. baking soda**
- ⅓ **cup butter, softened**
- ½ **cup packed brown sugar**
- 1 **egg**
- ½ **cup mild-flavored molasses**
- ¾ **cup warm water**
- 1½ **cups frozen blackberries or boysenberries**
- 1 **Tbsp. all-purpose flour**
  Powdered sugar (optional)
- 1 **recipe Butter Sauce (right)**
  Frozen blackberries or boysenberries, thawed

1. Preheat oven to 325°F. Grease and flour a 2-quart square baking dish; set aside. In a medium bowl, stir together the 2 cups flour, the ginger, baking powder, cinnamon, and baking soda; set aside.

2. In a large mixing bowl, beat butter with an electric mixer on medium speed for 30 seconds. Add brown sugar; beat until combined. Add egg and molasses; beat for 1 minute.

3. Add the flour mixture and the warm water alternately to beaten mixture, beating on low speed after each addition until combined. Toss the 1½ cups berries with the 1 tablespoon flour; fold into molasses mixture. Pour batter into prepared baking dish.

4. Bake about 50 minutes or until a wooden toothpick inserted near the center comes out clean. Cool in pan on a wire rack for 5 minutes. Remove from pan. Cool for 20 minutes more. If desired, sift powdered sugar onto gingerbread. Prepare Butter Sauce. Serve gingerbread with sauce and additional berries. Serves 9.

Butter Sauce: In a small saucepan, combine ⅓ cup granulated sugar, ¼ cup butter, and ¼ cup half-and-half or light cream. Bring to boiling, stirring constantly. Reduce heat. Boil gently, uncovered, for 2 minutes, stirring constantly. Serve warm.

Nutrition facts per serving: 350 cal., 14 g total fat (8 g sat. fat), 58 mg chol., 214 mg sodium, 55 g carbo., 2 g fiber, 4 g pro.

Blackberry Gingerbread

The earliest recipes for gingerbread came to the New England colonies from England. It was one of the most popular foods sold "at muster," when state militia assembled for a week's drill. The event was almost like a country fair as wives and children watched the men drill.

Mixed Berry Shortcake

2. Using a pastry blender, cut butter into flour mixture until mixture resembles coarse crumbs. Make a well in the center of the flour mixture. Add buttermilk all at once to flour mixture. Using a fork, stir just until moistened.

3. Drop the dough into 2 mounds on the prepared baking sheet. If desired, sprinkle with coarse sugar. Bake for 10 to 12 minutes or until golden.

4. In a chilled small bowl, beat the whipping cream and 2 teaspoons granulated sugar with chilled beaters of an electric mixer on medium speed or with a rotary beater until soft peaks form (tips curl).

5. Split each shortcake horizontally into 2 layers. Place the bottom layers in 2 dessert bowls. Spoon some of the berries and whipped cream over bottom layers. Top with the remaining shortcake layers, berries, and whipped cream. Makes 2 servings.

*Test Kitchen Tip: To make ¼ cup sour milk, place 1 teaspoon lemon juice or vinegar in a glass measuring cup. Add enough milk to make ¼ cup total liquid; stir. Let stand for 5 minutes before using.

Nutrition facts per serving: 406 cal., 21 g total fat (13 g sat. fat), 71 mg chol., 346 mg sodium, 49 g carbo., 6 g fiber, 6 g pro.

Mixed Berry Shortcake
Prep: 20 min. Bake: 10 min.

Shortcake has always gone a long way with our readers. In 2002, we scaled down our recipe to serve just two.

- ½   cup all-purpose flour
- 2   tsp. granulated sugar
- ¾   tsp. baking powder
- ⅛   tsp. cream of tartar
- ⅛   tsp. baking soda
- 1   Tbsp. butter
- ¼   cup buttermilk or sour milk*
      Coarse sugar (optional)
- ⅓   cup whipping cream
- 2   tsp. granulated sugar
- 2   cups mixed fresh berries (such as raspberries, blueberries, and/or sliced strawberries)

1. Preheat oven to 450°F. Grease a baking sheet; set aside. In a medium bowl, stir together the flour, 2 teaspoons granulated sugar, the baking powder, cream of tartar, and baking soda.

Favorite Berry Claflouti
Prep: 15 min. Bake: 30 min. Cool: 30 min.

Claflouti, a classic French dessert, is usually made with cherries. This Easy Summer Dessert winner from our June 1997 issue calls for berries and replaces the traditional heavy cream with yogurt.

- 4   eggs whites
- 2   eggs
- ⅓   cup granulated sugar
- 3   Tbsp. honey
- 2   Tbsp. fruit-flavored liqueur (such as orange or raspberry liqueur), or ½ tsp. rum extract plus 2 Tbsp. orange juice
- 1   tsp. vanilla
      Dash salt
- 1½ cups plain fat-free yogurt
- 1   cup all-purpose flour
- 3   cups fresh raspberries, blueberries, and/or sliced strawberries*
- 2   tsp. sifted powdered sugar

1. Preheat oven to 375°F. In a large mixing bowl, beat egg whites and eggs slightly; add granulated sugar, honey, liqueur, vanilla, and salt. Beat with a wire whisk or an electric mixer on low speed until light and frothy. Add yogurt; stir until smooth. Add flour; beat until smooth.

2. Grease a 10-inch quiche dish; arrange berries in the bottom of the dish. Pour batter over berries. Bake for 30 to 35 minutes or until center appears set when shaken. Cool on a wire rack for 30 minutes. Serve warm. Just before serving, sprinkle with powdered sugar. Makes 8 servings.

*Test Kitchen Tip: Do not use frozen berries.

Nutrition facts per serving: 196 cal., 2 g total fat (0 g sat. fat), 54 mg chol., 93 mg sodium, 36 g carbo., 2 g fiber, 8 g pro.

Strawberry Crown Trifle

Prep: 50 min. Bake: 20 min.
Chill: 4 to 24 hr. (for filling) + 8 to 24 hr. (for trifle)

In June 1974, we featured this stunning dessert on the cover of *Better Homes and Gardens*® magazine.

1	**recipe Fluffy Filling (right)**
1	**cup sifted cake flour or all-purpose flour**
1	**tsp. baking powder**
¼	**tsp. salt**
½	**cup milk**
2	**Tbsp. butter**
2	**eggs**
1	**cup granulated sugar**
1	**tsp. vanilla**
3	**pints fresh strawberries**
3	**Tbsp. granulated sugar**
⅓	**cup strawberry liqueur, orange liqueur, or orange juice**
	Powdered sugar
	Whipped cream

1. Prepare Fluffy Filling. Preheat oven to 350°F. Grease and flour two 8×1½-inch round cake pans. Set aside.

2. In a medium bowl, stir together flour, baking powder, and salt. In a small saucepan, heat milk and butter until butter melts; keep hot.

3. In a large mixing bowl, beat eggs with an electric mixer on high speed for 3 to 4 minutes or until thick and lemon colored. Gradually add the 1 cup granulated sugar, beating constantly on medium speed for 4 to 5 minutes. Add flour mixture to egg mixture; stir just until combined. Stir in hot milk mixture and the vanilla. Turn batter into prepared pans.

4. Bake about 20 minutes or until a wooden toothpick inserted near the centers of cakes comes out clean. Cool in pans on wire racks for 10 minutes. Remove from pans. Cool completely on wire racks.

5. Crush enough of the strawberries to measure 2 cups crushed strawberries. Stir the 3 tablespoons sugar into crushed strawberries. Set aside remaining whole strawberries for garnish.

6. To assemble, split cake layers in half horizontally to make four layers. Fit *one layer* into bottom of a 2-quart soufflé dish* (8 inches in diameter); spread *1 cup* of the sweetened crushed strawberries over the top. Top with second cake layer; sprinkle with *half* of the liqueur or orange juice. Spread with Fluffy Filling. Place third cake layer on top; spread remaining crushed strawberries over. Sprinkle cut side of fourth cake layer with remaining liqueur or orange juice; place, cut side down, over strawberries and cake layers in dish. Cover; chill for at least 8 hours or up to 24 hours. To serve, sift powdered sugar over trifle. Top with whipped cream and reserved whole strawberries. Makes 12 servings.

Fluffy Filling: In a small saucepan, combine ⅓ cup granulated sugar, 1 tablespoon cornstarch, and ⅛ teaspoon salt. Stir in 1 cup milk. Cook and stir over medium-high heat until bubbly. Slowly stir ½ *cup* of the hot mixture into 2 egg yolks, beaten. Add egg mixture to remaining hot milk mixture in saucepan. Cook and stir for 2 minutes more. Remove from heat. Stir in 1 tablespoon butter and 1 teaspoon vanilla. Cover surface with plastic wrap; chill for at least 4 hours or up to 24 hours. Just before assembling trifle, in a small bowl, beat ½ cup whipping cream until soft peaks form; fold into chilled mixture.

Make-ahead directions: Prepare as directed through step 4, except do not prepare Fluffy Filling. Place cake layers on a baking sheet. Freeze until firm. Place each layer in a freezer bag or wrap in freezer wrap. Seal, label, and freeze for up to 3 months. To serve, prepare Fluffy Filling. Remove cake layers from freezer bags or plastic wrap. Thaw at room temperature. Assemble and serve as directed in steps 5 and 6.

*Test Kitchen Tip: If you don't have a soufflé dish, substitute a straight-sided glass bowl.

Nutrition facts per serving: 270 cal., 9 g total fat (5 g sat. fat), 95 mg chol., 169 mg sodium, 41 g carbo., 2 g fiber, 4 g pro.

Peach-a-Berry Cobbler

Prep: 30 min. Bake: 40 min. Cool: 30 min.

Looking for a knockout summer dessert? Try this two-fruit cobbler recipe from 1960. The fluffy topper is ideal for soaking up the juices from the fruit.

- 1 **cup all-purpose flour**
- ½ **cup granulated sugar**
- 1½ **tsp. baking powder**
- ½ **cup milk**
- ¼ **cup butter, softened**
- ¼ **cup packed brown sugar**
- 4 **tsp. cornstarch**
- 3 **cups sliced fresh peaches (peeled if desired) or frozen unsweetened peach slices**
- 1 **cup fresh or frozen blueberries**
- 1 **Tbsp. butter**
- 1 **Tbsp. lemon juice**
- 2 **Tbsp. coarse sugar or granulated sugar**
- ¼ **tsp. ground nutmeg or cinnamon**
  Vanilla ice cream (optional)

1. Preheat oven to 350°F. For topping, in a medium bowl, stir together flour, the ½ cup granulated sugar, and the baking powder. Add milk and the ¼ cup butter. Stir until nearly smooth (small pieces of butter will remain).

2. For filling, in a medium saucepan, stir together brown sugar and cornstarch; stir in ⅓ cup *cold water*. Add peaches and blueberries. Cook and stir over medium heat until thickened and bubbly. Add the 1 tablespoon butter and the lemon juice; stir until butter melts. Pour into an ungreased 2-quart casserole. Spoon topping over hot filling; spread evenly over filling. In a small bowl, stir together the coarse sugar and nutmeg or cinnamon; sprinkle over topping.

3. Bake 40 to 45 minutes or until filling bubbles around edges and a wooden toothpick inserted into topper* comes out clean. Cool on a wire rack for 30 to 40 minutes. Serve warm. If desired, serve with ice cream. Makes 6 servings.

Nutrition facts per serving: 328 cal., 10 g total fat (6 g sat. fat), 27 mg chol., 203 mg sodium, 58 g carbo., 3 g fiber, 4 g pro.

All-Peach Cobbler: Prepare as directed, except substitute 1 cup sliced fresh or frozen peaches for the blueberries.

Nutrition facts per serving: 344 cal., 11 g total fat (7 g sat. fat), 29 mg chol., 218 mg sodium, 60 g carbo., 3 g fiber, 4 g pro.

*Test Kitchen Tip: To test topper for doneness, make a small hole in crisp top, then insert toothpick.

Peach-a-Berry Cobbler

Big Apple Dumplings

Prep: 45 min. Bake: 40 min.

A reader wrote in 1993 suggesting we once again publish this 1950 prizewinning dumpling recipe. When we taste-tested it, we agreed with her whole-heartedly—it truly was worth a repeat performance.

- 2 cups water
- 1¼ cups sugar
- ½ tsp. ground cinnamon
- ¼ cup butter
- 2 cups all-purpose flour
- ½ tsp. salt
- ⅔ cup shortening
- 6 to 8 Tbsp. half-and-half or milk
- 2 Tbsp. chopped raisins or golden raisins
- 2 Tbsp. chopped walnuts
- 1 Tbsp. honey
- 2 Tbsp. sugar
- ½ tsp. ground cinnamon
- 6 medium cooking apples (such as Granny Smith or Jonathan) (5 to 6 oz. each)
- 1 Tbsp. butter

1. For sauce, in a medium saucepan, combine the water, the 1¼ cups sugar, and ½ teaspoon cinnamon. Bring to boiling; reduce heat. Simmer, uncovered, for 5 minutes. Stir in the ¼ cup butter. Set aside.

2. Meanwhile, for pastry, in a medium bowl, combine flour and salt. Using a pastry blender, cut in shortening until pieces are pea-size. Sprinkle *1 tablespoon* of the half-and-half over part of the mixture; gently toss with a fork. Push moistened dough to the side of the bowl. Repeat moistening dough, using *1 tablespoon* of the half-and-half at a time, until all of the dough is moistened. Form dough into a ball. On a lightly floured surface, roll dough to an 18×12-inch rectangle.* Using a pastry wheel or sharp knife, cut into six 6-inch squares.

3. Preheat oven to 375°F. In a small bowl, combine raisins, walnuts, and honey. In another small bowl, stir together the 2 tablespoons sugar and ½ teaspoon cinnamon. Set aside.

4. Peel and core the apples. Place *an apple* on *each* pastry square. Fill centers of apples with raisin mixture. Sprinkle with sugar-cinnamon mixture; dot with the 1 tablespoon butter. Moisten edges of each pastry square with water; fold corners to center over apple. Pinch to seal edges, except for a small portion on top of each dumpling.

5. Place dumplings in a 3-quart rectangular baking dish. Pour sauce over dumplings. Bake for 40 to 45 minutes or until apples are tender and pastry is golden. Let cool slightly before serving. To serve, spoon sauce over dumplings. Makes 6 servings.

Big Apple Dumplings

*Test Kitchen Tip: If desired, roll pastry slightly larger, trim to 18×12-inch rectangle, and cut pastry trimmings into leaf shapes. Place pastry leaves on ungreased baking sheet. Bake in a 375°F oven about 10 minutes or until golden. Garnish apple dumplings with pastry leaves.

Nutrition facts per serving: 739 cal., 37 g total fat (18 g sat. fat), 33 mg chol., 307 mg sodium, 101 g carbo., 5 g fiber, 5 g pro.

Praline Baked Apples

Prep: 15 min. Bake: 30 min.

Brown sugar, cinnamon, and pecans turn ordinary baked apples into a standout dessert for two.

- ¼ cup apple juice or apple cider
  - Dash ground cinnamon
- 2 small red baking apples
- 2 Tbsp. pecans or walnuts, coarsely chopped
- 2 Tbsp. brown sugar
  - Dash ground cinnamon
  - Vanilla ice cream (optional)

1. Preheat oven to 350°F. In a small bowl, combine apple juice and dash cinnamon. Divide the mixture between two 6-ounce custard cups. Core apples; remove peel from the top of each apple. Place the apples in the custard cups.

2. Place the custard cups in a shallow baking pan. In another small bowl, combine nuts, brown sugar, and dash cinnamon. Sprinkle over the apples.

3. Cover and bake for 30 to 40 minutes or until apples are tender. Serve warm. If desired, serve with ice cream. Makes 2 servings.

Nutrition facts per serving: 195 cal., 5 g total fat (1 g sat. fat), 0 mg chol., 6 mg sodium, 39 g carbo., 4 g fiber, 1 g pro.

Pear and Blueberry Crisp

Pear and Blueberry Crisp

Prep: 25 min. Bake: 30 min. Cool: 40 min.

The topping for this blueberry and pear tempter whirls together in seconds in a food processor.

 8 **medium pears (about 2¾ lb.)**
 ¼ **cup granulated sugar**
 1 **Tbsp. cornstarch**
 2 **cups fresh or frozen blueberries, thawed**
 4 **tsp. lemon juice**
1¼ **cups all-purpose flour**
 ½ **cup granulated sugar**
 ½ **cup packed brown sugar**
 ½ **cup cold butter, cut up**
 2 **Tbsp. cognac or brandy (optional)**

1. Preheat oven to 400°F. Peel and core pears; cut into large chunks. In a very large bowl, stir together the ¼ cup granulated sugar and the cornstarch. Add pears, blueberries, and lemon juice, stirring gently to combine. Transfer to a 3-quart rectangular baking dish.

2. In a food processor, combine flour, the ½ cup granulated sugar, the brown sugar, and butter. Pulse with several on-off turns until mixture is crumbly. (Or in a large bowl, combine flour, the ½ cup granulated sugar, and the brown sugar. Using a pastry blender, cut in butter until mixture is crumbly.) Sprinkle over fruit.

3. Bake for 30 to 35 minutes or until top is lightly browned and syrup is bubbly. Remove from oven. If desired, drizzle with cognac. Cool in baking dish on wire rack for 40 minutes. Serve warm. Makes 10 servings.

Nutrition facts per serving: 338 cal., 11 g total fat (6 g sat. fat), 26 mg chol., 106 mg sodium, 62 g carbo., 4 g fiber, 2 g pro.

Rhubarb Surprise Crisp

Prep: 30 min. Bake: 30 min.

Fresh basil is the surprise that makes this top Summer Cobblers and Crisps prizewinner so delicious.

 ⅔ **cup granulated sugar**
 2 **or 3 tsp. cornstarch**
 ¼ **tsp. ground cinnamon**
 2 **cups sliced fresh rhubarb or frozen unsweetened sliced rhubarb, thawed**
 2 **cups coarsely chopped fresh strawberries**
 2 **Tbsp. snipped fresh basil**
 ½ **cup all-purpose flour**
 ½ **cup rolled oats**
 ⅓ **cup packed brown sugar**
 ¼ **tsp. salt**
 3 **Tbsp. butter, melted**
 Fresh basil sprigs (optional)

1. Preheat oven to 375°F. In a medium bowl, combine the ⅔ cup granulated sugar, the cornstarch (for fresh rhubarb, use 2 teaspoons cornstarch; for frozen, use 3 teaspoons cornstarch), and cinnamon. Stir in rhubarb, strawberries, and snipped basil. Spoon into a 2-quart square baking dish; set aside.

2. In another medium bowl, stir together flour, oats, brown sugar, and salt. Stir in melted butter. Sprinkle onto fruit. Bake for 30 to 35 minutes or until fruit is tender and topping is golden. Serve warm. If desired, garnish with basil sprigs. Makes 6 servings.

Nutrition facts per serving: 276 cal., 7 g total fat (5 g sat. fat), 31 mg chol., 167 mg sodium, 52 g carbo., 3 g fiber, 3 g pro.

Rhubarb Surprise Crisp

Hazelnut Pavlova With Coffee Cream

Prep: 45 min. Bake: 35 min. Stand: 1 hr.
Chill: 2 to 24 hr.

In March 1999, we were Going Nuts—with our Prize Tested Recipes® contest, that is. And this dazzling meringue torte captured our fancy for first place.

4	egg whites
1	tsp. vanilla
¼	tsp. cream of tartar
1⅓	cups sugar
1	cup ground hazelnuts (filberts)
2	oz. semisweet chocolate
3	Tbsp. butter, softened
1	3-oz. pkg. cream cheese, softened
⅓	cup sugar
1	cup whipping cream
3	Tbsp. coffee liqueur
¼	cup coarsely chopped hazelnuts (filberts)

1. For meringue shells, let egg whites stand at room temperature for 30 minutes. Meanwhile, draw two 8-inch circles on a foil-lined baking sheet; set aside.

2. Preheat oven to 300°F. In a large mixing bowl, combine egg whites, vanilla, and cream of tartar. Beat egg white mixture with an electric mixer on medium speed until soft peaks form (tips curl). Gradually add the 1⅓ cups sugar, *1 tablespoon* at a time, beating about 7 minutes on high speed or until stiff peaks form (tips stand straight) and sugar is almost dissolved. Gently fold in the 1 cup ground hazelnuts.

3. Spread *half* of the egg white mixture onto *each* circle on baking sheet. Bake for 35 minutes. Turn off oven. To dry meringues, let stand in oven, with door closed, for 1 hour.

4. Just before assembling, in a small saucepan, combine chocolate and *1 tablespoon* of the butter; cook over low heat until melted, stirring constantly. Set aside to cool. In a medium mixing bowl, beat cream cheese with the remaining 2 tablespoons butter until smooth; beat in the ⅓ cup sugar. Gradually add whipping cream, beating on low speed until combined; beat on medium speed just until soft peaks form (tips curl). Stir in coffee liqueur.

5. To assemble, carefully peel meringue shells from foil. Place a meringue shell on a platter. Drizzle with the chocolate mixture. Spread with *half* of the whipped cream mixture. Place second meringue shell on top. Spread with remaining whipped cream mixture. Sprinkle with the chopped nuts. Cover loosely and chill for at least 2 hours or up to 24 hours. Serves 12 to 16.

Nutrition facts per serving: 355 cal., 23 g total fat (11 g sat. fat), 58 mg chol., 77 mg sodium, 36 g carbo., 2 g fiber, 4 g pro.

Cherry-Nut Ice Cream (top scoop)
and Chocolate-Almond Ice Cream
(bottom scoop)

Cooked Vanilla Ice Cream

Prep: 30 min. Cool: 1 hr. Freeze: per manufacturer's
directions Ripen: 4 hr. (optional)

Enjoy this delightfully fluffy frozen custard plain or
with one of the flavor options listed opposite.

- 1½ **cups sugar**
- 2 **envelopes unflavored gelatin**
- ⅛ **tsp. salt**
- 8 **cups (2 quarts) half-and-half**
   or light cream
- 2 **eggs, beaten**
- 4 **tsp. vanilla**

1. In a large saucepan, combine sugar, gelatin, and
salt. Stir in *4 cups (1 quart)* of the half-and-half. Cook
and stir over medium heat until mixture almost boils and
sugar dissolves. Stir *about 1 cup* of the hot mixture into
beaten eggs. Return egg mixture to remaining hot
mixture in saucepan. Cook and stir for 2 minutes more.
Cool for 1 hour.

2. Stir in remaining 4 cups (1 quart) half-and-half and
the vanilla. Freeze in a 4- to 5-quart ice cream freezer
according to manufacturer's directions. If desired, ripen
for 4 hours. Makes about 3 quarts (24 servings).

Nutrition facts per ½-cup serving: 161 cal., 10 g total fat (6 g sat. fat),
47 mg chol., 51 mg sodium, 16 g carbo., 0 g fiber, 3 g pro.

Ripening Ice Cream

Letting homemade ice creams rest after freezing
is called ripening. Although it isn't absolutely
necessary, ripening improves the ice cream's
texture and helps keep it from melting too quickly.

• *To ripen in a traditional-style ice cream freezer,*
after churning, remove the lid and dasher and cover
the top of the freezer can with waxed paper or foil.
Plug the hole in the lid with a small piece of cloth;
replace the lid. Pack the outer freezer bucket with
enough ice and rock salt to cover the top of the
freezer can (use 1 cup salt for each 4 cups ice).
Ripen about 4 hours.

• *When using an ice cream freezer with an
insulated freezer bowl,* transfer the ice cream to a
covered freezer container and ripen by freezing in
your regular freezer about 4 hours (or check the
manufacturer's recommendations).

Yesterday

Although ice cream dates back to
the time of our founding fathers, it
wasn't until the 1930s that it became
more than a special-occasion delicacy.
Even then, almost all of our ice
cream recipes started with a cooked
egg custard that needed to be cooled
before freezing.

Easy Vanilla Ice Cream

Prep: 5 min. Freeze: per manufacturer's directions
Ripen: 4 hr. (optional)

4   cups half-and-half or light cream
1½ cups sugar
1   Tbsp. vanilla
2   cups whipping cream

1. In a large bowl, combine half-and-half, sugar, and vanilla. Stir until sugar dissolves. Stir in whipping cream. Freeze in a 4- or 5-quart ice cream freezer according to the manufacturer's directions. If desired, ripen for 4 hours. Makes 2 quarts (16 servings).

Nutrition facts per ½-cup serving: 253 cal., 18 g total fat (11 g sat. fat), 63 mg chol., 36 mg sodium, 22 g carbo., 0 g fiber, 2 g pro.

Add a Flavor Dress up the ice cream recipes on these two pages with any of these luscious flavor options.

Butter Pecan Ice Cream: Prepare desired ice cream as directed, except in a heavy, small skillet cook ½ cup chopped pecans, ¼ cup sugar, and 1 tablespoon butter over medium-high heat until sugar begins to melt, shaking skillet occasionally; do not stir. Reduce heat to low and cook until sugar turns golden, stirring frequently. Immediately spread on a baking sheet lined with greased foil. Cool; break into chunks. Stir nut mixture into ice cream mixture before freezing.

Cherry-Nut Ice Cream: Prepare desired ice cream as directed, except add 1 cup chopped maraschino cherries, 3 tablespoons maraschino cherry juice, and 1 cup chopped walnuts to the ice cream mixture before freezing.

Chocolate-Almond Ice Cream: Prepare desired ice cream as directed, except reduce sugar to 1 cup. Stir one 16-ounce can (1½ cups) chocolate-flavored syrup and ½ cup chopped almonds, toasted (tip, page 102), into ice cream mixture before freezing.

Coffee Ice Cream: Prepare desired ice cream as directed, except add 2 to 3 tablespoons instant coffee crystals to the sugar mixture. If desired, stir ½ cup miniature semisweet chocolate pieces into ice cream mixture before freezing.

Coffee Ice Cream (back left) and Butter Pecan Ice Cream (front)

Today

Over the years, we've published numerous ice cream recipes. This creamy stir-together version from the 2002 edition of the *New Cook Book* skips the step of cooking a custard.

277

Irresistible Chocolate

Chocolate—nothing brings an enthusiastic response from *Better Homes and Gardens*® readers faster than this indulgent confection. Our staff shares our readers' passion for the all-time favorite ingredient and has come up with countless ways to enjoy it. This delightful collection brings you more than 75 years' worth of our finest chocolate recipes. Cookies, cakes, pies, puddings, candy—you name it, and you'll find it in this chocolate-lovers' chapter.

283

290

281

293

300

297

Best-Ever Chocolate Cake

Stand: 30 min. Prep: 30 min. Bake: 30 min. Cool: 1 hr.

In 2002, our staff set out to find the richest, moistest, chocolatiest cake ever. After testing and retesting, this cake won the day.

¾	**cup butter**
3	**eggs**
2	**cups all-purpose flour**
¾	**cup unsweetened cocoa powder**
1	**tsp. baking soda**
¾	**tsp. baking powder**
2	**cups sugar**
2	**tsp. vanilla**
1½	**cups milk**
1	**recipe Chocolate Frosting (top right)**
	White and dark chocolate curls (optional)
1	**recipe Candied Nuts (right) (optional)**

1. Allow butter and eggs to stand at room temperature for 30 minutes. Lightly grease bottoms of three 8×1½-inch round cake pans or two 9×1½-inch round cake pans or two 8×8×2-inch baking pans. Line bottoms of pans with waxed paper. Grease and lightly flour waxed paper and sides of pans. Set pans aside.

2. Preheat oven to 350°F. In a medium bowl, stir together the flour, cocoa powder, baking soda, baking powder, and ½ teaspoon *salt;* set aside.

3. In a large mixing bowl, beat butter with an electric mixer on medium to high speed for 30 seconds. Gradually add sugar, about ¼ *cup* at a time, beating on medium speed for 3 to 4 minutes or until well mixed. Scrape side of bowl; continue beating on medium speed for 2 minutes. Add eggs, *one* at a time, beating after each addition (about 1 minute total). Beat in vanilla.

4. Alternately add flour mixture and milk to beaten mixture, beating on low speed just until combined after each addition. Beat on medium to high speed for 20 seconds more. Spread evenly into the prepared pans.

5. Bake for 30 to 35 minutes for round cake pans, 35 to 40 minutes for 8-inch square pans, or until a wooden toothpick inserted in the centers comes out clean. Cool cake layers in pans for 10 minutes. Remove from pans. Peel off waxed paper. Cool completely on wire racks.

6. Prepare Chocolate Frosting; fill and frost cake layers. If desired, top with chocolate curls and Candied Nuts. Store cake in the refrigerator. Makes 12 to 16 servings.

Chocolate Frosting: In a large saucepan, combine one 12-ounce package (2 cups) semisweet chocolate pieces and ½ cup butter; heat over low heat until melted, stirring often. Cool for 5 minutes. Stir in one 8-ounce carton dairy sour cream. Gradually add 4½ cups sifted powdered sugar (about 1 pound), beating on medium speed until mixture is smooth.

Nutrition facts per serving: 760 cal., 35 g total fat (20 g sat. fat), 118 mg chol., 475 mg sodium, 99 g carbo., 5 g fiber, 7 g pro.

Candied Nuts: Grease a baking sheet well; set aside. In a heavy, 10-inch skillet, cook 1½ cups nuts, ½ cup sugar, 2 tablespoons butter, and ½ teaspoon vanilla until sugar begins to melt, shaking occasionally (do not stir). Cook over low heat until sugar is golden, stirring often. Pour onto prepared baking sheet. Cool. Break up.

One-Bowl Chocolate Cake

Prep: 20 minutes   Bake: 30 minutes   Cool: 1 hour

1	**cup all-purpose flour**
1	**cup sugar**
½	**cup unsweetened cocoa powder**
½	**teaspoon baking soda**
¼	**teaspoon baking powder**
¼	**teaspoon salt**
¾	**cup milk**
⅓	**cup cooking oil**
1	**teaspoon vanilla**
1	**egg**
1	**recipe Chocolate Glaze (below)**

1. Preheat oven to 350°F. Grease and lightly flour a 9×1½-inch round or 8×8×2-inch baking pan; set aside.

2. In a large bowl, combine flour, sugar, cocoa powder, baking soda, baking powder, and salt. Add milk, oil, and vanilla. Beat with an electric mixer on low speed just until combined. Beat on medium speed for 2 minutes. Add egg; beat 2 minutes more. Pour batter into prepared pan.

3. Bake for 30 to 35 minutes or until a wooden toothpick inserted in center comes out clean. Cool cake in pan on a wire rack for 10 minutes. Remove from pan. Cool completely on a wire rack. Prepare Chocolate Glaze; spoon over cooled cake. Makes 8 servings.

Chocolate Glaze: In a saucepan, combine 4 ounces semisweet chocolate, chopped, and 3 tablespoons butter; cook and stir over low heat until melted. Remove from heat. Using a wooden spoon, beat in 1½ cups sifted powdered sugar and 3 tablespoons hot water until smooth. Stir in more hot water, if needed, for drizzling.

Nutrition facts per serving: 454 cal., 20 g total fat (7 g sat. fat), 41 mg chol., 230 mg sodium, 66 g carbo., 1 g fiber, 5 g pro.

Originally submitted to a Dallas newspaper by a homemaker in the late 1950s, German chocolate cake quickly made headlines across the country. In 1962, *Better Homes and Gardens*® magazine published the recipe and included it in that year's edition of the *New Cook Book*.

German Chocolate Cake

Stand: 30 min. Prep: 25 min. Bake: 20 min. Cool: 1 hr.

3	eggs
⅔	cup butter
1½	cups all-purpose flour
¾	tsp. baking soda
1	4-oz. pkg. sweet baking chocolate
1	cup sugar
1	tsp. vanilla
¾	cup buttermilk or sour milk*
1	recipe Coconut-Pecan Frosting (right)

1. Separate eggs. Allow egg yolks, egg whites, and butter to stand at room temperature for 30 minutes. Meanwhile, grease and lightly flour two 9×1½-inch or 8×1½-inch round cake pans; set pans aside. In a bowl, combine flour, baking soda, and ½ teaspoon *salt;* set aside.

2. Preheat oven to 350°F. In a small saucepan, combine chocolate and ⅓ cup *water*. Cook and stir over low heat until melted; cool.

3. In a large mixing bowl, beat butter with an electric mixer on medium to high speed for 30 seconds. Gradually add sugar, beating until well mixed. Scrape side of bowl; continue beating for 2 minutes more. Beat in egg yolks, *one* at a time, beating well after each addition (about 1 minute total). Beat in the cooled chocolate mixture and vanilla. Alternately add flour mixture and buttermilk to beaten mixture; beat on low speed until combined after each addition.

4. Thoroughly wash the beaters. In a medium mixing bowl, beat egg whites with an electric mixer on high speed until stiff peaks form (tips stand straight). Gently fold egg whites into batter; spread into prepared pans.

5. Bake for 20 to 25 minutes for 9-inch pans, 25 to 30 minutes for 8-inch pans, or until a wooden toothpick inserted in centers comes out clean. Cool layers in pans on wire racks for 10 minutes. Remove from pans. Cool completely on wire racks. Prepare Coconut-Pecan Frosting; frost tops of cake layers. Stack layers. Serves 12 to 16.

Coconut-Pecan Frosting: In a medium saucepan, beat 1 egg with a fork. Stir in one 5-ounce can (⅔ cup) evaporated milk, ⅔ cup sugar, and ¼ cup butter. Cook and stir over medium heat for 6 to 8 minutes or until thickened and bubbly. Remove from heat; stir in 1⅓ cups flaked coconut and ½ cup chopped pecans. Cover and cool completely.

*Test Kitchen Tip: To make ¾ cup sour milk, place 2 teaspoons lemon juice or vinegar in a glass measuring cup. Add enough milk to make ¾ cup total liquid; stir. Let stand for 5 minutes before using.

Nutrition facts per serving: 484 cal., 29 g total fat (15 g sat. fat), 115 mg chol., 371 mg sodium, 52 g carbo., 2 g fiber, 7 g pro.

Double-Chocolate Lava Baby Cakes

Prep: 20 min. Bake: 10 + 5 min. Cool: 3 min.

Cut into one of these minicakes and the exquisite Praline Sauce flows out like lava from a volcano. These double-chocolate delights are so rich, you may have to share one with a friend.

6	oz. semisweet chocolate pieces (1 cup)*
¾	cup butter
1	recipe Praline Sauce (opposite)
3	eggs
3	egg yolks
⅓	cup granulated sugar
1½	tsp. vanilla
⅓	cup all-purpose flour
3	Tbsp. unsweetened cocoa powder
⅓	cup pecan halves, toasted (tip, page 102)

1. Preheat oven to 400°F. Lightly grease and flour six 1- to 1¼-cup soufflé dishes or six 10-ounce custard cups. Place soufflé dishes or custard cups in a shallow baking pan and set pan aside. In a heavy, small saucepan, combine semisweet chocolate and butter; heat over low heat until melted, stirring constantly. Remove from heat; cool.

2. Meanwhile, prepare Praline Sauce; cover and keep warm until needed.

3. In a large mixing bowl, beat eggs, egg yolks, granulated sugar, and vanilla with an electric mixer on high speed about 5 minutes or until thick and lemon-colored. Beat in cooled chocolate mixture on medium speed. Sift flour and cocoa powder over chocolate mixture; beat on low speed just until combined. Divide batter evenly among prepared dishes or cups.

Double-Chocolate Lava Baby Cakes

4. Bake for 10 minutes. Remove cakes from oven. Using a small spatula or table knife, puncture top of each partially baked cake and gently enlarge to make a dime-size hole. Slowly spoon *about 1 tablespoon* Praline Sauce into center of each cake (it will sink into the center). Return to oven. Bake about 5 minutes more or until cakes feel firm along the edges.

5. Cool cakes in soufflé dishes or custard cups on wire racks for 3 minutes. Using a small spatula or knife, loosen cake edges from sides of dishes or cups and slip cakes out upright onto dessert plates. Serve immediately.

6. Meanwhile, stir the pecan halves into the remaining Praline Sauce. If necessary, stir 1 to 2 teaspoons *hot water* into remaining sauce to thin it. Serve warm Praline Sauce with cakes. Makes 6 servings.

Praline Sauce: In a heavy, medium saucepan, combine ½ cup granulated sugar, ⅓ cup packed brown sugar, and 2 tablespoons dark-colored corn syrup. Stir in ½ cup whipping cream. Cook over medium-high heat until mixture boils, stirring constantly to dissolve sugar. Reduce heat. Cook, uncovered, about 10 minutes or until thickened, stirring occasionally.

*Test Kitchen Tip: Be sure to use real semisweet chocolate pieces. Do not substitute products labeled imitation chocolate pieces or chocolate-flavored pieces.

Nutrition facts per serving: 700 cal., 48 g total fat (21 g sat. fat), 302 mg chol., 281 mg sodium, 67 g carbo., 1 g fiber, 8 g pro.

Truffle Cake with Raspberry Sauce

Prep: 25 min. Bake: 25 min. Cool: 30 min. + 1 hr.
Chill: 4 to 24 hr.

Just in time for Valentine's Day, this 1993 Best Chocolate Desserts winner from a Florida reader is enough to steal your heart.

  4 **egg whites**
 16 **oz. semisweet chocolate, cut up**
 ½ **cup butter**
  1 **Tbsp. granulated sugar**
1½ **tsp. all-purpose flour**
  4 **egg yolks**
  1 **12-oz. jar seedless raspberry jam**
  1 **Tbsp. raspberry liqueur or orange juice**
     Whipped cream or powdered sugar (optional)
     Fresh raspberries (optional)

1. Let egg whites stand at room temperature. Preheat oven to 350°F. Grease and flour an 8-inch springform pan; set aside. In a heavy, large saucepan, stir chocolate and butter over low heat just until chocolate is melted. Remove from heat; cool slightly (about 5 minutes). Stir in granulated sugar and flour. Using a wooden spoon, beat in egg yolks, *one* at a time, just until combined.

2. In a medium mixing bowl, beat egg whites with an electric mixer on high speed until stiff peaks form (tips stand straight). Fold into chocolate mixture. Pour into the prepared pan. Bake for 25 to 30 minutes or until edges puff (toothpick will not come out clean). Cool in pan on a wire rack for 30 minutes. Remove side of pan; cool 1 hour more. (Cake may seem soft; it firms up on chilling.) Cover; chill for at least 4 hours or up to 24 hours.

3. To serve, cut cake into wedges. In a small saucepan, heat and stir jam and liqueur over low heat just until jam is melted. Drizzle jam onto dessert plates; top each with a cake wedge.* If desired, top with whipped cream or dust with powdered sugar and garnish with fresh raspberries. Makes 12 servings.

*Test Kitchen Tip: If the cake sticks to the bottom of the pan when serving, place the pan bottom on a warm, moist dishcloth for 1 minute before cutting.

Nutrition facts per serving: 363 cal., 22 g total fat (12 g sat. fat), 93 mg chol., 115 mg sodium, 42 g carbo., 3 g fiber, 5 g pro.

Yesterday

This classic pie has changed very little in the seven-plus decades since we first published it—still made from scratch with simple off-the-shelf ingredients.

Dark Chocolate Cream Pie

Prep: 45 min. Bake: 30 min. Cool: 1 hr. Chill: 3 to 6 hr.

Unsweetened chocolate, sometimes called baking or bitter chocolate, has an intense flavor because it's pure chocolate without any added sugar.

1	recipe Baked Pastry Shell (page 262)
4	eggs
1	cup sugar
¼	cup cornstarch
2½	cups half-and-half, light cream, or milk
3	oz. unsweetened chocolate, chopped
1	Tbsp. butter or margarine
2½	tsp. vanilla
½	tsp. cream of tartar
½	cup sugar

1. Prepare Baked Pastry Shell. Preheat oven to 325°F. Separate eggs; set egg whites aside for meringue.

2. For filling, in a medium saucepan, combine the 1 cup sugar and the cornstarch. Gradually stir in half-and-half and unsweetened chocolate. Cook and stir over medium-high heat until thickened and bubbly; reduce heat. Cook and stir for 2 minutes more. Remove from heat. Slightly beat egg yolks with a rotary beater or fork. Gradually stir about *1 cup* of the hot filling into yolks. Add yolk mixture to hot filling in saucepan. Bring to a gentle boil; reduce heat. Cook and stir for 2 minutes more. Remove from heat. Stir in butter and *1½ teaspoons* of the vanilla. Keep warm.

3. For meringue, in a large mixing bowl, combine egg whites, cream of tartar, and the remaining 1 teaspoon vanilla. Beat with an electric mixer on medium speed about 1 minute or until soft peaks form (tips curl). Gradually add the ½ cup sugar, *1 tablespoon* at a time, beating on high speed about 5 minutes more or until mixture forms stiff, glossy peaks (tips stand straight) and sugar is dissolved.

4. Pour warm filling into baked shell. Immediately spread meringue on top, carefully sealing to edge of pastry to prevent shrinkage. Bake for 30 minutes. Cool on a wire rack for 1 hour. Chill for at least 3 hours or up to 6 hours; cover for longer storage. Makes 8 servings.

Nutrition facts per serving: 425 cal., 21 g total fat (9 g sat. fat), 138 mg chol., 151 mg sodium, 51 g carbo., 1 g fiber, 7 g pro.

Extreme Chocolate Pie

Prep: 35 min. Bake: 20 min.
Cool: 1 hr. Chill: 4 to 24 hr.

A brownie crust, both dark and unsweetened chocolates, and a whipped cream topper create the "extreme" chocolate flavor of this luscious pie.

1	8-oz. pkg. brownie mix
1	cup sugar
¾	cup butter
6	oz. unsweetened chocolate, melted and cooled
1	tsp. vanilla
¾	cup refrigerated or frozen egg product, thawed
1	1.45-oz. bar dark sweet chocolate, coarsely chopped
1	recipe Chocolate Whipped Cream (below) (optional)

1. Preheat oven to 350°F. Grease a 9-inch pie plate; set aside. For crust, prepare brownie mix according to package directions. Spread in the bottom of prepared pie plate. Bake for 20 to 25 minutes or until a wooden toothpick inserted in center comes out clean. Cool on a wire rack.

2. For filling, in a medium mixing bowl, beat sugar and butter with an electric mixer on medium speed about 4 minutes or until fluffy. Stir in the melted and cooled chocolate and the vanilla. Gradually add egg product, beating on low speed until combined. Beat on medium to high speed about 1 minute or until light and fluffy, scraping side of bowl.

3. Spoon filling over brownie crust. Cover and chill for at least 4 hours or up to 24 hours.

4. To serve, sprinkle with coarsely chopped chocolate bar. If desired, prepare Chocolate Whipped Cream to serve with pie. Makes 10 servings.

Chocolate Whipped Cream: In a chilled, small mixing bowl, combine ½ cup whipping cream, 1 tablespoon sugar, and 1½ teaspoons unsweetened cocoa powder. Beat with chilled beaters of an electric mixer on medium speed until soft peaks form (tips curl).

Nutrition facts per serving: 475 cal., 33 g total fat (19 g sat. fat), 77 mg chol., 289 mg sodium, 47 g carbo., 3 g fiber, 5 g pro.

Today

We did traditional chocolate pie one better by creating this rich dessert with a brownie crust, French silk-style filling, and a Chocolate Whipped Cream topper—a slice of paradise for any chocolate lover.

Chocolate Chip Scones

Chocolate Chip Scones
Prep: 20 min. Bake: 18 min.

No collection of chocolate recipes is complete without these flaky scones, which beat all the competition in our June 1997 Biscuits, Scones, and More contest.

  2 **cups all-purpose flour**
  ⅓ **cup unsweetened cocoa powder**
  ⅓ **cup packed brown sugar**
  2 **tsp. baking powder**
  ¾ **tsp. baking soda**
  ⅛ **tsp. salt**
  ½ **cup butter**
  1 **egg yolk**
  1 **8-oz. carton plain yogurt**
  ½ **cup miniature semisweet chocolate pieces**
  1 **recipe Powdered Sugar Glaze (above right)**
    Powdered sugar (optional)

1. Preheat oven to 375°F. In a large bowl, combine flour, cocoa powder, brown sugar, baking powder, baking soda, and salt. Using a pastry blender, cut in butter until mixture resembles coarse crumbs. Make a well in the center of the flour mixture.

2. In a small bowl, beat egg yolk with a whisk; whisk in yogurt. Add to flour mixture. Add chocolate pieces. Stir just until moistened (batter should be lumpy).

3. Turn out dough onto a lightly floured surface. Knead dough by folding and gently pressing dough for 10 to 12 strokes or until nearly smooth. Roll or pat dough into a 9-inch circle; cut into 10 wedges. Place wedges 1 inch apart on an ungreased baking sheet.

4. Bake about 18 minutes or until bottoms are lightly browned. Remove from baking sheet; cool slightly. Prepare Powdered Sugar Glaze; drizzle over scones. If desired, dust tops of scones with powdered sugar. Serve warm. Makes 10 scones.

Powdered Sugar Glaze: In a small bowl, stir together ½ cup sifted powdered sugar, 1 tablespoon melted butter or margarine, 1 teaspoon milk, and 1 teaspoon vanilla. Stir in enough additional milk, ¼ *teaspoon* at a time, to make a glaze of drizzling consistency.

Nutrition facts per scone: 289 cal., 14 g total fat (7 g sat. fat), 50 mg chol., 317 mg sodium, 37 g carbo., 1 g fiber, 5 g pro.

Chocolate Swirl Coffee Cake
Prep: 30 min. Rise: 1½ + 1 hr. Bake: 45 min. Cool: 1 hr.

We've published quite a parade of coffee cakes since our first issue in August 1924. This 1981 coffee cake is distinctive because it's leavened by yeast, giving it a fluffy, tender texture. But what really makes it a star is the velvety chocolate-cinnamon filling.

  4 **to 4½ cups all-purpose flour**
  2 **pkg. active dry yeast**
  ¾ **cup sugar**
  ⅔ **cup water**
  ½ **cup butter**
  ⅓ **cup evaporated milk**
  ½ **tsp. salt**
  4 **egg yolks**
  ¾ **cup semisweet chocolate pieces (tip, page 283)**
  ⅓ **cup evaporated milk**
  2 **Tbsp. sugar**
  ½ **tsp. ground cinnamon**
  1 **recipe Nut Topping (opposite)**

1. In a large mixing bowl, stir together *1½ cups* of the flour and the yeast; set aside. In a medium saucepan, heat and stir the ¾ cup sugar, the water, butter, ⅓ cup evaporated milk, and the salt just until warm (120°F to 130°F) and butter almost melts. Add milk mixture to flour mixture along with egg yolks. Beat with an electric mixer on low speed for 30 seconds, scraping side of bowl constantly. Beat on high speed for 3 minutes. Using a wooden spoon, stir in as much of the remaining flour as you can.

2. Turn out dough onto a lightly floured surface. Knead in enough of the remaining flour to make a moderately soft dough that is smooth and elastic (3 to 5 minutes total). Shape dough into a ball. Place in a lightly greased bowl, turning once to grease surface. Cover and let rise in a warm place until double in size (about 1½ hours).

3. Punch down dough. Turn out dough onto a lightly floured surface. Cover and let rest for 10 minutes.

4. Meanwhile, in a small saucepan, combine chocolate pieces, ⅓ cup evaporated milk, the 2 tablespoons sugar, and the cinnamon. Cook and stir over low heat until chocolate melts. Remove from heat; cool completely (mixture will thicken as it cools).

5. Grease a 10-inch tube pan; set aside. Roll dough into a 15×10-inch rectangle. Spread chocolate mixture to within 1 inch of the edges. Starting from a long side, roll up into a spiral. Pinch seam and ends to seal. Place, seam side down, in prepared tube pan; seal ends together.

6. Prepare Nut Topping; sprinkle over dough in pan (will seem generous, but will cover top of risen cake). Cover and let rise in a warm place until nearly double in size (about 1 hour).

7. Preheat oven to 350°F. Bake for 45 to 50 minutes or until cake sounds hollow when lightly tapped. Cool in pan on a wire rack for 15 minutes. Remove from pan. Cool on a wire rack. If desired, serve warm. Makes 16 servings.

Nut Topping: In a bowl, combine ¼ cup all-purpose flour, ¼ cup sugar, and 1 teaspoon ground cinnamon. Using a pastry blender, cut in ¼ cup butter until mixture resembles coarse crumbs. Stir in ¼ cup chopped walnuts or pecans.

Nutrition facts per serving: 322 cal., 15 g total fat (8 g sat. fat), 81 mg chol., 180 mg sodium, 44 g carbo., 2 g fiber, 6 g pro.

Chocolate Challah

Prep: 45 min. Rise: 1½ + 1 hr. Bake: 35 min. Cool: 1 hr.

Meals for Jewish holidays sometimes include a sweet version of challah (HAH-luh) as part of the celebration. This chocolaty version surprises with dates, nuts, and orange peel.

2¾	to 3¼ cups all-purpose flour
⅓	cup unsweetened cocoa powder
1	pkg. active dry yeast
¾	cup milk*
½	cup sugar
¼	cup butter or margarine*
½	tsp. salt
1	egg
½	cup chopped pecans
¼	cup chopped pitted dates
1	Tbsp. finely shredded orange peel
1	recipe Three Glazes (right)

1. In a large mixing bowl, stir together *1 cup* of the flour, the cocoa powder, and yeast; set aside.

2. In a medium saucepan, heat milk, sugar, butter, and salt just until warm (120°F to 130°F) and butter almost melts. Add milk mixture to flour mixture along with egg. Beat with an electric mixer on low to medium speed for 30 seconds, scraping side of the bowl constantly. Beat on high speed for 3 minutes. Using a wooden spoon, stir in pecans, dates, and orange peel. Stir in as much of the remaining flour as you can.

3. Turn out dough onto a lightly floured surface. Knead in enough of the remaining flour to make a moderately soft dough that is smooth and elastic (3 to 5 minutes total). Shape dough into ball. Place in a lightly greased bowl; turn once to grease surface. Cover and let rise in a warm place until double in size (about 1½ hours).

4. Punch down dough. Turn out dough onto a lightly floured surface. Divide dough into thirds. Cover and let rest for 10 minutes. Lightly grease a baking sheet. Shape each portion of dough into a 16-inch-long rope (3 ropes total). Place the ropes about 1 inch apart on prepared baking sheet.

5. Starting in the middle of the ropes, loosely braid by bringing the left rope under the center rope. Next bring right rope under the new center rope. Repeat to the end. On the other end, braid by bringing alternate ropes over center rope. Press ends together to seal; tuck under. Cover; let rise in a warm place until nearly double in size (about 1 hour).

6. Preheat oven to 325°F. Bake about 35 minutes or until bread sounds hollow when lightly tapped. If necessary to prevent overbrowning, cover loosely with foil for the last 10 to 15 minutes of baking. Remove from baking sheet. Cool on a wire rack. Prepare Three Glazes; drizzle over challah in a decorative pattern. Serves 24.

Three Glazes: In a medium bowl, stir together 1½ cups sifted powdered sugar and 4 teaspoons softened butter or margarine.* Add enough warm water (1 to 2 tablespoons) to make the icing a drizzling consistency. Divide icing evenly into 3 portions. To first portion, stir in 1 teaspoon unsweetened cocoa powder, adding more warm water a drop at a time, if necessary, until icing is of drizzling consistency. For second portion, combine ¼ teaspoon instant coffee crystals and a few drops hot water, stirring until coffee is dissolved. Add coffee mixture to powdered sugar mixture, adding more warm water a drop at a time, if necessary, until icing is of drizzling consistency. Leave the third portion white.

*Test Kitchen Tip: If you prefer a nondairy recipe, replace butter with pareve margarine and milk with soy milk.

Nutrition facts per serving: 144 cal., 5 g total fat (2 g sat. fat), 26 mg chol., 81 mg sodium, 23 g carbo., 1 g fiber, 3 g pro.

Cappuccino Chip Muffins

3. Bake about 18 minutes or until a wooden toothpick inserted in centers comes out clean. Cool in muffin cups on a wire rack for 5 minutes. Remove from muffin cups. Serve warm. Makes 18 muffins.

*Test Kitchen Tip: To make 1⅓ cups sour milk, place 4 teaspoons lemon juice or vinegar in a glass measuring cup. Add enough milk to make 1⅓ cups total liquid; stir. Let stand for 5 minutes before using.

Nutrition facts per muffin: 190 cal., 10 g total fat (2 g sat. fat), 12 mg chol., 90 mg sodium, 21 g carbo., 1 g fiber, 3 g pro.

Brownie Pudding Cake

Prep: 15 min. Bake: 40 min. Cool: 45 min.

The recipe for this warm, fudgy cake-topped pudding was sent in by a Des Moines, Iowa, reader in 1944.

1	cup all-purpose flour
¾	cup granulated sugar
2	Tbsp. unsweetened cocoa powder
2	tsp. baking powder
¼	tsp. salt
½	cup milk
2	Tbsp. cooking oil
1	tsp. vanilla
½	cup chopped walnuts
¾	cup packed brown sugar
¼	cup unsweetened cocoa powder
1½	cups boiling water
	Vanilla ice cream (optional)

1. Preheat oven to 350°F. Grease an 8×8×2-inch baking pan; set aside. In a medium bowl, stir together flour, granulated sugar, the 2 tablespoons cocoa powder, the baking powder, and salt. Stir in the milk, oil, and vanilla. Stir in walnuts.

2. Pour batter into prepared baking pan. In a small bowl, stir together brown sugar and the ¼ cup cocoa powder. Stir in the boiling water; slowly pour water mixture over batter.

3. Bake for 40 minutes. Cool on a wire rack for 45 minutes. Spoon warm cake into dessert bowls; spoon sauce over cake. If desired, serve with vanilla ice cream. Makes 6 to 8 servings.

Nutrition facts per serving: 412 cal., 13 g total fat (2 g sat. fat), 2 mg chol., 254 mg sodium, 71 g carbo., 1 g fiber, 6 g pro.

Cappuccino Chip Muffins

Prep: 15 min. Bake: 18 min. Cool: 5 min.

These chocolate and espresso-flavored muffins capitalized on our readers' fondness for cappuccino.

2	cups all-purpose flour
⅔	cup sugar
3	Tbsp. unsweetened cocoa powder
1½	tsp. baking powder
1½	tsp. instant espresso coffee powder or 2 tsp. instant coffee crystals
½	tsp. ground cinnamon
¼	tsp. baking soda
⅛	tsp. salt
1⅓	cups buttermilk or sour milk*
1	egg
½	cup cooking oil
¾	cup miniature semisweet chocolate pieces
¼	cup chopped hazelnuts (filberts) or pecans

1. Preheat oven to 400°F. Lightly grease eighteen 2½-inch muffin cups or line with paper bake cups. In a large bowl, stir together flour, sugar, cocoa powder, baking powder, espresso powder, cinnamon, baking soda, and salt. Make a well in center of flour mixture; set aside.

2. In a medium bowl, combine buttermilk, egg, and oil; add all at once to flour mixture. Stir just until moistened. Stir in chocolate pieces and nuts. Spoon batter into prepared muffin cups, filling each three-fourths full.

Trilevel Brownies

Prep: 30 min. Bake: 10 + 25 min.

In 1989, to celebrate the first 60 years of the *Better Homes and Gardens®* Test Kitchen, we featured our 30 best recipes. This 1963 brownie recipe with three sweet layers was among the chosen few.

1   cup rolled oats
½   cup all-purpose flour
½   cup packed brown sugar
¼   tsp. baking soda
½   cup butter, melted
1   egg
¾   cup granulated sugar
⅔   cup all-purpose flour
¼   cup milk
¼   cup butter, melted
1   oz. unsweetened chocolate, melted and cooled
1   tsp. vanilla
¼   tsp. baking powder
½   cup chopped walnuts
1   oz. unsweetened chocolate
2   Tbsp. butter
1½ cups sifted powdered sugar
½   tsp. vanilla
    Walnut halves (optional)

1. Preheat oven to 350°F. For the bottom layer, in a small bowl, stir together oats, the ½ cup flour, the brown sugar, and baking soda. Stir in the ½ cup melted butter. Pat the mixture onto the bottom of an ungreased 11×7×1½-inch baking pan. Bake for 10 minutes.

2. Meanwhile, for the middle layer, in a medium bowl, stir together egg, granulated sugar, the ⅔ cup flour, the milk, the ¼ cup melted butter, the 1 ounce melted chocolate, the 1 teaspoon vanilla, and the baking powder until smooth. Fold in chopped walnuts. Spread batter evenly over baked layer in pan. Bake about 25 minutes more or until a wooden toothpick inserted in center comes out clean. Place on a wire rack while preparing top layer.

3. For the top layer, in a medium saucepan, heat and stir the 1 ounce chocolate and the 2 tablespoons butter over low heat until melted. Stir in powdered sugar and the ½ teaspoon vanilla. Stir in enough *hot water* (1 to 2 tablespoons) to make a mixture that is almost pourable. Spread over brownies. If desired, garnish with walnut halves. Cool in pan on a wire rack. Cut into bars. Makes 32 brownies.

Nutrition facts per brownie: 141 cal., 7 g total fat (4 g sat. fat), 21 mg chol., 76 mg sodium, 18 g carbo., 1 g fiber, 2 g pro.

Fudge Ecstasies

Prep: 20 min. Bake: 8 min. per batch

These oh-so-chocolaty treats get their marvelous flavor from a whopping 14 ounces of chocolate!

1   12-oz. pkg. (2 cups) semisweet chocolate pieces (tip, page 283)
2   oz. unsweetened chocolate, chopped
2   Tbsp. butter
2   eggs
⅔   cup sugar
¼   cup all-purpose flour
1   tsp. vanilla
¼   tsp. baking powder
1   cup chopped nuts

1. Preheat oven to 350°F. Grease cookie sheets; set aside. In a heavy, medium saucepan, combine *1 cup* of the chocolate pieces, the unsweetened chocolate, and the butter; cook and stir over low heat until melted. Remove from heat; add the eggs, sugar, flour, vanilla, and baking powder. Using a wooden spoon, stir vigorously until combined, scraping side of saucepan. Stir in remaining 1 cup chocolate pieces and the nuts.

2. Drop dough by rounded teaspoons 2 inches apart onto the prepared cookie sheets. Bake for 8 to 10 minutes or until edges are firm and surfaces are dull and crackled. Transfer to a wire rack and let cool. Makes about 36 cookies.

Nutrition facts per cookie: 103 cal., 7 g total fat (3 g sat. fat), 14 mg chol., 15 mg sodium, 11 g carbo., 1 g fiber, 2 g pro.

When Spanish explorers arrived in Mexico in 1519, the Aztec Indians served them a bitter, syrupy beverage made from cocoa beans called "chocolatl." To make it less bitter, the Spanish added sugar and sometimes vanilla and cinnamon. And so the first chocolate recipes were created.

Buried Cherry Cookies

2. Shape dough into 1-inch balls; place on ungreased cookie sheets. Press down center of each ball with thumb. Place a cherry in the center of each cookie.

3. For frosting, in a small saucepan, combine chocolate pieces and sweetened condensed milk (do not use evaporated milk). Heat and stir over low heat until chocolate is melted. Stir in *4 teaspoons* of the reserved cherry juice. Spoon *about 1 teaspoon* frosting over *each* cherry, spreading to cover cherry. (If necessary, thin frosting with additional cherry juice.)

4. Bake about 10 minutes or until edges are firm. Transfer to wire racks and let cool. Makes 42 to 48 cookies.

Nutrition facts per cookie: 97 cal., 4 g total fat (2 g sat. fat), 13 mg chol., 56 mg sodium, 14 g carbo., 0 g fiber, 1 g pro.

Buried Cherry Cookies
Prep: 30 min. Bake: 10 min. per batch

A reader from Traverse City, Michigan nominated these cookies as her best-loved *Better Homes and Gardens*® recipe. What makes them unique is frosting the cookies before baking.

1	10-oz. jar maraschino cherries, undrained (42 to 48 cherries)
1½	cups all-purpose flour
½	cup unsweetened cocoa powder
½	cup butter, softened
1	cup sugar
¼	tsp. salt
¼	tsp. baking powder
¼	tsp. baking soda
1	egg
1½	tsp. vanilla
1	cup semisweet chocolate pieces (6 oz.) (tip, page 283)
½	cup regular or low-fat sweetened condensed milk

1. Preheat oven to 350°F. Drain cherries, reserving juice. Halve any large cherries. In a medium bowl, combine flour and cocoa powder; set aside. In a large mixing bowl, beat butter with an electric mixer on medium speed for 30 seconds. Add sugar, salt, baking powder, and baking soda. Beat until well mixed, scraping side of bowl. Add egg and vanilla; beat well. Gradually beat in as much of the flour mixture as you can with the mixer. Using a wooden spoon, stir in any remaining flour.

Melting Magic
Before the age of the microwave oven, the only way to melt chocolate was slowly heating and stirring on the range top, but now you have a choice.

• To use the range top, place chopped chocolate or chocolate pieces in a heavy saucepan over very low heat. Stir constantly until the chocolate begins to melt. Immediately remove from the heat and stir until the chocolate is smooth.

• To use the microwave oven, place up to 6 ounces of chopped chocolate or chocolate pieces in a microwave-safe bowl. Microwave, uncovered, on 100% (high) power for 1½ to 2 minutes or until the chocolate is soft enough to stir smooth. The chocolate will hold its shape after it starts to melt, so stir it once every minute during heating.

Triple-Chocolate Chunk Cookies

Prep: 25 min. Bake: 12 min. per batch
Cool: 1 min. per batch

From unsweetened to semisweet to white chocolate—you can enjoy them all in these two-fisted treats.

1	cup butter, softened
¾	cup granulated sugar
¾	cup packed brown sugar
1	tsp. baking soda
2	eggs
1	tsp. vanilla
3	oz. unsweetened chocolate, melted and cooled
2	cups all-purpose flour
1	8-oz. pkg. semisweet chocolate, cut into ½-inch pieces, or 1⅓ cups large semisweet chocolate pieces
1	6-oz. pkg. white chocolate baking squares, cut into ½-inch pieces, or 1 cup white baking pieces
1	cup chopped black walnuts, walnuts, or pecans (optional)

1. Preheat oven to 375°F. Lightly grease cookie sheets; set aside. In a large mixing bowl, beat butter with an electric mixer on medium to high speed for 30 seconds. Beat in granulated sugar, brown sugar, and baking soda until combined. Beat in eggs and vanilla until combined. Stir in melted chocolate. Beat in as much of the flour as you can with the mixer. Using a wooden spoon, stir in any remaining flour. Stir in semisweet chocolate and white chocolate pieces and, if desired, nuts.

2. Using a ¼-cup dry measure or scoop, drop mounds of dough about 4 inches apart on the prepared cookie sheets.

3. Bake for 12 to 14 minutes or until edges are firm. Cool on cookie sheets for 1 minute. Transfer cookies to a wire rack and let cool. Makes 22 cookies.

Nutrition facts per cookie: 280 cal., 17 g total fat (10 g sat. fat), 44 mg chol., 158 mg sodium, 33 g carbo., 1 g fiber, 3 g pro.

Chocolate Biscotti

Prep: 30 min. Bake: 20 + 8 + 7 min. Cool: 1 hr.

Double-baked Italian biscotti are popular at coffeehouses because their crispy texture makes them ideal for dipping into a steaming mug of java. This 1995 recipe should bring a smile of appreciation to the chocolate fans at your house.

½	cup butter, softened
⅔	cup sugar
¼	cup unsweetened cocoa powder
2	tsp. baking powder
2	eggs
1¾	cups all-purpose flour
¾	cup white baking pieces
½	cup large semisweet chocolate pieces or regular semisweet chocolate pieces

1. Preheat oven to 375°F. Lightly grease a cookie sheet; set aside. In a large mixing bowl, beat butter with an electric mixer on medium to high speed for 30 seconds. Add sugar, cocoa powder, and baking powder. Beat until combined, scraping side of bowl occasionally. Beat in eggs until combined. Beat in as much of the flour as you can with the mixer. Using a wooden spoon, stir in any remaining flour. Stir in white baking pieces and chocolate pieces.

2. Divide dough in half. Shape each half into a 9-inch-long roll. Place rolls on prepared cookie sheet; flatten slightly until each is about 2 inches wide.

3. Bake for 20 to 25 minutes or until a wooden toothpick inserted near centers comes out clean. Cool on cookie sheet for 1 hour. (If desired, wrap cooled rolls in plastic wrap and let stand overnight at room temperature.)

4. Preheat oven to 325°F. Using a serrated knife, cut each roll diagonally into ½-inch-thick slices. Place slices, cut sides down, on an ungreased cookie sheet. Bake in the 325°F oven for 8 minutes. Turn slices over and bake for 7 to 9 minutes more or until dry and crisp (do not overbake). Transfer to a wire rack; cool. Makes about 24.

Nutrition facts per cookie: 157 cal., 8 g total fat (5 g sat. fat), 29 mg chol., 91 mg sodium, 19 g carbo., 0 g fiber, 2 g pro.

Because chocolate was rationed during World War II, it was scarce in the forties. So, our staff made up for lost time in the fifites, publishing scores of chocolate recipes—from cakes to fudge.

Chocolaty Velvet Ice Cream
(recipe, page 294)

Yesterday

This recipe has been a perennial favorite because it creates a satiny smooth ice cream without an ice cream freezer. Sweetened condensed milk is the secret to its silky smoothness.

Today

Gelato caused delicious waves in the American frozen dessert scene during the 1990s. To reflect the popularity of the Italian-style ice cream, we included this rich recipe, based on stirred custard, in the 2002 version of our *New Cook Book*.

Chocolate Gelato (recipe, page 294)

293

Yesterday

Chocolaty Velvet Ice Cream

Prep: 10 min. Freeze: 8 hr.

(Photo on page 292.)

- 4   cups whipping cream
- 1   14-oz. can (1⅓ cups) sweetened condensed milk
- 1   16-oz. can (1½ cups) chocolate-flavored syrup
- ⅔   cup coarsely chopped walnuts, cashews, or almonds, toasted (tip, page 102)

1. In a large mixing bowl, combine whipping cream, sweetened condensed milk, and chocolate syrup. Beat with an electric mixer on medium to high speed until soft peaks form (tips curl). Fold in chopped nuts. Transfer the mixture to a 13×9×2-inch pan; freeze about 8 hours or until firm. Makes 2 quarts (16 servings).

Nutrition facts per serving: 372 cal., 28 g total fat (15 g sat. fat), 90 mg chol., 68 mg sodium, 31 g carbo., 0 g fiber, 4 g pro.

Today

Chocolate Gelato

Prep: 30 min. Chill: several hr. or overnight Freeze: per manufacturer's directions Ripen: 4 hr. (optional)

Try the berry version of this frozen delight, too. (Photo on page 293.)

- 4   cups whole milk
- 1⅓ cups sugar
- 12 egg yolks, beaten
- 12 oz. bittersweet or semisweet chocolate, melted
- 6   oz. semisweet chocolate, chopped (optional)
      Semisweet chocolate, chopped (optional)

1. In a large saucepan, combine milk, sugar, and egg yolks. Cook and stir over medium heat just until the mixture coats a metal spoon. Remove from heat. Add the melted chocolate, beating with a wire whisk or rotary beater until smooth. Cover surface with plastic wrap. Chill several hours or overnight until completely chilled. (Or to chill quickly, transfer to a large bowl. Place in a sink of ice water for 30 to 60 minutes; stir occasionally.)

2. Freeze egg mixture in a 4- or 5-quart ice cream freezer according to the manufacturer's directions. If desired, stir in the 6 ounces chopped chocolate. If desired, ripen for 4 hours (see information, page 276). If desired, garnish each serving with additional chopped chocolate. Makes about 2 quarts (16 servings).

Nutrition facts per serving: 250 cal., 13 g total fat (6 g sat. fat), 168 mg chol., 35 mg sodium, 31 g carbo., 2 g fiber, 6 g pro.

Berry Gelato: Prepare as directed, except omit chocolate. In a blender or food processor, place 3 cups fresh raspberries or cut-up strawberries. Cover and blend or process until smooth. You should have about 2 cups puree. (If desired, sieve berries and discard seeds; there should be about 1 cup sieved puree.) Stir raspberries or strawberries and, if desired, several drops of red food coloring into custard mixture. Chill completely; freeze in ice cream freezer and, if desired, ripen as directed.

Nutrition facts per serving: 155 cal., 6 g total fat (2 g sat. fat), 168 mg chol., 35 mg sodium, 22 g carbo., 1 g fiber, 4 g pro.

Chocolate Pots de Crème

Prep: 10 min. Cook: 10 min. Chill: 4 to 24 hr.

As the fitting finale to a memorable meal, bring out tiny cups of these chocolaty rich "pots of cream" along with a tray of elegant tea cookies.

- 2   cups whipping cream
- 6   oz. semisweet chocolate, coarsely chopped
- ⅓   cup sugar
- 4   egg yolks, beaten
- 1   tsp. vanilla
     White chocolate curls (optional)

1. In a heavy, medium saucepan, combine the whipping cream, chocolate, and sugar. Cook and stir over medium heat about 10 minutes or until mixture comes to a full boil and thickens. (If chocolate flecks remain, use a rotary beater or wire whisk to beat mixture until smooth.)

2. Gradually stir all of the hot mixture into egg yolks; stir in vanilla. Divide chocolate mixture evenly among 8 sake cups, small cups, pot de crème cups, or 3-ounce ramekins. Cover and chill for at least 4 hours or up to 24 hours before serving. If desired, garnish with white chocolate curls. Makes 8 servings.

Nutrition facts per serving: 375 cal., 32 g total fat (18 g sat. fat), 189 mg chol., 26 mg sodium, 22 g carbo., 2 g fiber, 4 g pro.

Mocha Pots de Crème: Prepare as directed, except add 1 tablespoon instant espresso coffee powder or 2 tablespoons instant coffee crystals to whipping cream mixture before heating.

Nutrition facts per serving: 375 cal., 32 g total fat (18 g sat. fat), 189 mg chol., 26 mg sodium, 22 g carbo., 2 g fiber, 4 g pro.

Choclava

Prep: 35 min. Bake: 45 min.

This chocolate version of the classic Greek pastry baklava was sent to us by a Tacoma, Washington, reader in 1985.

- 4 cups walnuts, finely chopped (1 lb.)
- 1 cup miniature semisweet chocolate pieces
- ¾ cup sugar
- 1½ tsp. ground cinnamon
- ¾ cup butter, melted
- ½ of a 16-oz. pkg. (20 sheets) frozen phyllo dough (14×9-inch rectangles), thawed
- ½ cup orange juice
- ⅓ cup sugar
- ⅓ cup water
- ⅓ cup honey
- 1 Tbsp. lemon juice

1. Preheat oven to 325°F. For filling, in a large bowl, stir together walnuts, chocolate pieces, the ¾ cup sugar, and the cinnamon; set aside.

2. Brush the bottom of a 13×9×2-inch baking pan with some of the melted butter. Unfold phyllo dough; cover with plastic wrap to prevent it from drying out. Layer *8* of the phyllo sheets in the pan, brushing each sheet with butter. Sprinkle *about 2 cups* of the nut mixture over phyllo in pan.

3. Top with *4* additional sheets of the phyllo, brushing each with more of the melted butter. Sprinkle with *2 more cups* of the nut mixture and top with *4 more* phyllo sheets, brushing each sheet with butter. Top with remaining nut mixture and remaining phyllo sheets, brushing each sheet with butter. Drizzle any remaining butter over top layer. Using a sharp knife, cut into diamond- or triangle-shape pieces, cutting to, but not through, the bottom layer.

Choclava

4. Bake for 45 to 50 minutes or until golden. Immediately finish cutting diamonds or triangles. Cool slightly in pan on a wire rack.

5. Meanwhile, in a small saucepan, combine orange juice, the ⅓ cup sugar, the water, the honey, and lemon juice. Bring to boiling; reduce heat. Simmer, uncovered, for 20 minutes. Pour over warm choclava in pan. Cool completely. Store leftovers in the refrigerator. Makes about 45 pieces.

Nutrition facts per piece: 156 cal., 11 g total fat (3 g sat. fat), 9 mg chol., 58 mg sodium, 14 g carbo., 1 g fiber, 2 g pro.

Chocolate Mousse

Prep: 15 min. Cool: 1 hr. Chill: 4 to 24 hr.

Although technically a mousse can be warm or chilled, main dish or dessert, it's the chilled sweet versions made with chocolate or pureed fruit that bring all the oohs and aahs. This 2002 semisweet chocolate recipe is a masterpiece.

- ½ cup whipping cream
- 6 oz. semisweet chocolate, cut up
- ⅓ cup sugar
- 2 Tbsp. butter
- ½ tsp. vanilla
  Dried egg whites equivalent to 3 fresh egg whites*
- ½ cup whipping cream
  Chocolate and caramel ice cream toppings

1. In a heavy, medium saucepan, combine ½ cup whipping cream, the chocolate, sugar, and butter. Cook over low heat, stirring constantly, until chocolate is melted (about 5 minutes). Remove from heat. Cool to room temperature (about 1 hour). Stir in the vanilla.

2. Meanwhile, in a medium mixing bowl, prepare and beat egg whites to soft peaks (tips curl) according to package directions. Set aside. Beat ½ cup whipping cream until soft peaks form (tips curl).

3. Gently fold *one-third* of the beaten egg whites into the melted chocolate mixture to lighten it. Fold in the remaining beaten egg whites. Fold in the whipped cream. Cover and chill for at least 4 hours or up to 24 hours.

4. Drizzle each dessert plate with some chocolate and caramel ice cream toppings. Top each with a scoop (about ⅓ cup) of the chocolate mixture. Makes 9 servings.

***Test Kitchen Tip:** Look in the baking section of the supermarket for dried egg whites.

Nutrition facts per serving: 359 cal., 19 g total fat (11 g sat. fat), 44 mg chol., 116 mg sodium, 46 g carbo., 2 g fiber, 5 g pro.

Choco Bread Pudding

Prep: 30 min. Bake: 40 min. Stand: 30 min.

Cooks of the 1920s and 1930s saw bread pudding as an economical way to use dried-out bread; cooks of today are more likely to view it as a cherished comfort food. This prizewinning 2001 rendition uses cubes of Jewish challah instead of regular bread.

12   oz. challah bread, cut into 1-inch cubes (about 9 cups)
1½ cups miniature semisweet chocolate pieces
4   eggs
3   cups half-and-half or light cream
1   cup packed brown sugar
¾ tsp. ground cinnamon
    Dash salt
1   cup chopped pecans
1   recipe Brown Sugar-Vanilla Sauce (below)

1. Preheat oven to 350°F. Lightly grease a 3-quart rectangular baking dish. In a large bowl, combine bread cubes and chocolate pieces. Transfer to prepared baking dish; set aside.

2. In a medium bowl, beat eggs with a whisk; stir in half-and-half, brown sugar, cinnamon, and salt. Slowly pour over bread. Press bread lightly with back of a spoon to moisten bread completely.

3. Sprinkle with pecans. Bake, uncovered, for 40 to 45 minutes or until a knife inserted near the center comes out clean. Prepare Brown Sugar-Vanilla Sauce; pour over the hot bread pudding. Let stand 30 minutes before serving. Makes 16 servings.

Brown Sugar-Vanilla Sauce: In a heavy, small saucepan, stir together ½ cup brown sugar and 1 tablespoon cornstarch. Stir in ⅓ cup half-and-half, ¼ cup water, and 2 tablespoons light-colored corn syrup. Cook and stir until thickened and bubbly (mixture may appear curdled at first). Cook and stir for 2 minutes more. Remove saucepan from heat; stir in 1 tablespoon butter and ½ teaspoon vanilla.

Make-ahead directions: Prepare as directed through step 2. Cover and chill for up to 24 hours. Continue as directed in step 3.

Nutrition facts per serving: 400 cal., 20 g total fat (9 g sat. fat), 86 mg chol., 90 mg sodium, 50 g carbo., 1 g fiber, 7 g pro.

Chocolate Soufflé

Prep: 25 min. Bake: 40 min.

The detailed directions in this classic chocolate soufflé recipe will help you turn out the showy dish without a hitch.

4   egg whites
    Butter
    Sugar
2   Tbsp. butter or margarine
3   Tbsp. all-purpose flour
¾ cup milk
½ cup semisweet chocolate pieces (tip, page 283)
4   egg yolks, beaten
½ tsp. vanilla
¼ cup sugar
    Whipped cream (optional)

1. Let egg whites stand at room temperature. Preheat oven to 350°F. Butter the sides of a 1½-quart soufflé dish. For a collar on the soufflé dish, measure enough foil to wrap around the top of the dish and add 3 inches. Fold the foil into thirds lengthwise. Lightly grease one side with butter; sprinkle with sugar. Place foil, sugar side in, around the outside of the dish so the foil extends about 2 inches above edge of the dish. Tape ends of foil together. Sprinkle inside of dish with sugar; set aside.

2. In a small saucepan, melt the 2 tablespoons butter. Stir in flour. Add milk all at once. Cook and stir until thickened and bubbly. Add chocolate; stir until melted. Remove from heat. Gradually stir chocolate mixture into beaten egg yolks. Set aside.

3. In a large mixing bowl, combine egg whites and vanilla; beat with an electric mixer on medium to high speed until soft peaks form (tips curl). Gradually add the ¼ cup sugar, beating until stiff peaks form (tips stand straight). Fold *about 1 cup* of the beaten egg whites into chocolate mixture. Fold chocolate mixture into remaining beaten whites. Transfer to prepared soufflé dish.

4. Bake for 40 to 45 minutes or until a knife inserted near the center comes out clean. Serve soufflé immediately. To serve, insert two forks back to back; gently pull soufflé apart into serving-size wedges. Use a large spoon to transfer to plates. If desired, top with whipped cream. Makes 6 servings.

Nutrition facts per serving: 216 cal., 12 g total fat (6 g sat. fat), 155 mg chol., 100 mg sodium, 22 g carbo., 1 g fiber, 6 g pro.

Chocolate Caramel Cheesecake

Prep: 35 min. Bake: 10 + 40 min.
Chill: 4 to 24 hr. Stand: 20 min.

2	cups crushed vanilla wafers (about 50 wafers)
6	Tbsp. butter, melted
1	14-oz. pkg. vanilla caramels (about 48 caramels)
1	5-oz. can (⅔ cup) evaporated milk
1	cup chopped pecans, toasted (tip, page 102)
2	8-oz. pkg. cream cheese, softened
½	cup sugar
1	tsp. vanilla
2	eggs
½	cup semisweet chocolate pieces, melted and slightly cooled (tip, page 283)
	Melted semisweet chocolate (optional)
	Caramel ice cream topping (optional)
	Whipped cream (optional)
	Chopped pecans, toasted (optional) (tip, page 102)
	Chocolate curls (optional)

1. Preheat oven to 350°F. For crust, combine crushed vanilla wafers and melted butter. Press onto the bottom and about 2 inches up the side of a 9-inch springform pan. Bake for 10 minutes. Cool and set aside.

2. In a saucepan, combine unwrapped caramels and evaporated milk. Cook and stir over low heat until smooth. Pour into prepared crust. Top with the 1 cup pecans. Chill.

3. For filling, in a medium bowl, combine cream cheese, sugar, and vanilla; beat with an electric mixer on medium speed until combined. Add eggs, beating on low speed just until combined (do not overbeat). Stir in melted chocolate. Pour over caramel-nut layer in pan.

4. Bake about 40 minutes or until a 2½-inch area around the outside edge appears set when gently shaken. Cool in pan on a wire rack for 15 minutes. Loosen from side of pan; cool completely on wire rack. Cover and chill for at least 4 hours or up to 24 hours.

5. To serve, let stand at room temperature for 20 minutes. If desired, garnish with melted chocolate, caramel topping, whipped cream, additional nuts, and chocolate curls. Makes 12 servings.

Nutrition facts per serving: 548 cal., 35 g total fat (15 g sat. fat), 106 mg chol., 322 mg sodium, 55 g carbo., 1 g fiber, 8 g pro.

Lower-Fat Chocolate Caramel Cheesecake: Prepare crust as directed in step 1, except use 1 cup crushed reduced-fat vanilla wafers and 3 tablespoons butter. Prepare caramel layer as directed in step 2, except substitute evaporated fat-free milk for the evaporated milk. Prepare filling as directed in step 3, except substitute reduced-fat cream cheese (Neufchâtel) for the cream cheese and ½ cup refrigerated or frozen egg substitute, thawed, for the eggs. Continue as directed in steps 4 and 5.

Nutrition facts per serving: 436 cal., 25 g total fat (10 g sat. fat), 37 mg chol., 320 mg sodium, 49 g carbo., 1 g fiber, and 8 g pro.

Hot Fudge Sauce

Prep: 10 min. Cook: 3 + 1 min.

Among the 1930s versions of chocolate sauce was a recipe that featured a mix of cocoa powder and evaporated milk. Over the years, our Test Kitchen has delighted in coming up with better and better sauces. This is the present front-runner.

- ½ **cup unsweetened cocoa powder**
- ⅓ **cup granulated sugar**
- ⅓ **cup packed dark brown sugar**
- ½ **cup whipping cream**
- 3 **Tbsp. butter or margarine**

1. In a small bowl, stir together cocoa powder, granulated sugar, and brown sugar; set aside.

2. In a heavy, small saucepan, combine whipping cream and butter; cook and stir over low heat until butter is melted. Cook and stir over medium heat about 3 minutes more or until mixture bubbles around edges.* Add sugar mixture. Cook, stirring constantly, for 1 to 2 minutes more or until sugar is dissolved and mixture is smooth and thickened. Serve immediately. Use sauce for sundaes, cakes, pastries, or other desserts. Makes 1 cup.

Make-ahead directions: Prepare as directed. Cover and store in the refrigerator for up to 1 week. To reheat on range top, in a heavy, small saucepan, heat sauce over low heat until heated through, stirring frequently. To reheat in microwave oven, place chilled sauce in a 2-cup microwave-safe measure. Microcook, uncovered, on 100% (high) power for 1 to 2 minutes or until heated through, stirring once or twice.

***Test Kitchen Tip:** Be sure not to rush cooking the sauce. Keeping the heat at medium and stirring constantly eliminates the danger of scorching the chocolate.

Nutrition facts per 1 tablespoon sauce: 89 cal., 5 g total fat (4 g sat. fat), 22 mg chol., 34 mg sodium, 10 g carbo., 0 g fiber, 1 g pro.

Chocolate Malt-Peppermint Cooler

Start to finish: 20 min.

During the summer months, *Better Homes and Gardens*® editors often ask readers for refreshing ideas to beat the heat. This sensational shake came from a Pennsylvania cook.

- 3 **cups chocolate milk**
- 1 **quart vanilla or chocolate ice cream**
- ¼ **cup malted milk powder**
- ½ **tsp. peppermint extract**
- ⅛ **tsp. ground cinnamon**
   Coarsely crushed hard peppermint candies
- 6 **peppermint sticks**

1. In a blender, place the chocolate milk, *half* of the ice cream, the malted milk powder, peppermint extract, and cinnamon. Cover and blend until mixture is smooth. Pour into 6 large, chilled glasses. Top each drink with a scoop of the remaining ice cream. Sprinkle with the crushed candy pieces. Place a peppermint stick in each glass. Makes 6 servings.

Nutrition facts per serving: 329 cal., 13 g total fat (8 g sat. fat), 49 mg chol., 199 mg sodium, 46 g carbo., 0 g fiber, 8 g pro.

Hot Minty Cocoa

Start to finish: 10 min.

The mint-chocolate chip ice cream in this prizewinning sipper makes it both festive and refreshing.

  4   cups milk
  ¾   cup sugar
  ½   cup unsweetened cocoa powder
  1   tsp. peppermint extract or ¼ to ½ cup peppermint schnapps
  1   pint mint-chocolate chip ice cream Chocolate-flavored syrup
  8   candy canes or peppermint sticks

1. In a large saucepan, combine milk, sugar, cocoa powder, and, if using, peppermint extract. Heat over medium heat until hot. *Do not boil.* If using, add schnapps; heat through. Pour into 8 large mugs. Float a scoop of ice cream in each mug. Drizzle with chocolate-flavored syrup. Serve with candy canes or peppermint sticks. Makes 8 servings.

Nutrition facts per serving: 263 cal., 8 g total fat (5 g sat. fat), 22 mg chol., 84 mg sodium, 42 g carbo., 0 g fiber, 7 g pro.

Exquisite Almond Truffles

Prep: 1 hr. Freeze: 2 hr. + 15 + 15 min.

Wrap up a box of these almond nuggets for an impressive birthday, Valentine's Day, or holiday gift. This 1989 prizewinning recipe helps you turn out professional-looking truffles time after time.

  20   oz. white baking pieces
  ¼   cup whipping cream
  ¼   cup cream of coconut*
  1   cup sliced almonds, toasted and chopped (tip, page 102)
  2   Tbsp. amaretto
  18   oz. semisweet chocolate pieces (3 cups) (tip, page 283)
  3   Tbsp. shortening
  2   Tbsp. shortening

1. For filling, in a medium saucepan, combine *16 ounces* of the white baking pieces, the whipping cream, and cream of coconut; heat and stir over low heat just until baking pieces are melted. Remove from heat. Stir in almonds and amaretto. Cover; freeze about 2 hours or until firm.

2. Divide filling into 48 portions; shape each portion into a ball. Place balls on baking sheet. Freeze for 15 minutes.

3. Meanwhile, in a 4-cup glass measure, combine the semisweet chocolate pieces and the 3 tablespoons shortening. In a large glass bowl, pour very warm tap water (100°F to 110°F) to a depth of 1 inch. Place measure with semisweet chocolate inside large bowl. (Water should cover bottom half of the glass measure.) Stir semisweet chocolate constantly with a rubber spatula until chocolate is completely melted and smooth. This takes about 20 minutes; be patient. If water cools, remove glass measure. Discard cool water; add warm water. Return glass measure to bowl with warm water.

4. Line a baking sheet with waxed paper. Using a fork, dip frozen balls, one at a time, into melted semisweet chocolate; place on baking sheet. Freeze for 15 minutes.

5. Meanwhile, in a 1-cup glass measure, combine the remaining 4 ounces white baking pieces and the 2 tablespoons shortening; melt over hot water. Drizzle over truffles.** Chill a few minutes until set. Makes 48.

***Test Kitchen Tip:** Look for cream of coconut in the liquor aisle of the supermarket.

****Test Kitchen Tip:** If you like, skip the white chocolate drizzle and roll the truffles in finely chopped toasted almonds.

Nutrition facts per truffle: 159 cal., 10 g total fat (5 g sat. fat), 6 mg chol., 13 mg sodium, 11 g carbo., 2 g fiber, 2 g pro.

Caring for Chocolate

To keep your precious chocolate supply at its best, remember a few storing hints.

• Store chocolate in a tightly covered container or a sealed plastic bag in a dry place that's between 60°F and 70°F. It will keep for up to a year.

• Keep cocoa powder in a tightly covered container in a cool, dry place. High temperatures and humidity will cause it to clump and lose its color.

• To keep white chocolate longer, freeze or refrigerate it for up to a year.

Yesterday

In the early days of *Better Homes and Gardens*® magazine, the only way to make smooth, creamy fudge was to beat it by hand, as in this recipe from 1930. Some of our readers and staff still prefer making fudge this way because of its velvety texture.

Old-Time Fudge

Prep: 20 min. Cook: 20 min. Cool: 50 min.

The kind of nuts you prefer in fudge often depends on what you knew as a child. Our staff members can't agree. Some prefer walnuts or black walnuts, some pecans, and still others, almonds.

　　Butter
　2　cups sugar
　¾　cup half-and-half or light cream
　2　oz. unsweetened chocolate, cut up
　1　tsp. light-colored corn syrup
　⅛　tsp. salt
　2　Tbsp. butter
　1　tsp. vanilla
　½　cup chopped nuts, toasted (optional) (tip, page 102)

1. Line a 9×5×3-inch loaf pan with foil, extending foil over edges of pan. Butter foil; set pan aside.

2. Butter the sides of a heavy 2-quart saucepan. In the saucepan, combine sugar, half-and-half, chocolate, corn syrup, and salt. Cook and stir over medium-high heat until mixture boils. Clip a candy thermometer to side of pan. Reduce heat to medium-low; continue boiling at a moderate, steady rate, stirring frequently, until thermometer registers 236°F, soft-ball stage (20 to 25 minutes). (Adjust heat as necessary to maintain a steady boil.)

3. Remove saucepan from heat. Add the 2 tablespoons butter and the vanilla, but *do not stir*. Cool, without stirring, until thermometer registers 110°F (50 to 60 minutes).

4. Remove thermometer from saucepan. Beat mixture vigorously with a clean wooden spoon just until fudge begins to thicken. If desired, add chopped nuts. Continue beating until the fudge becomes very thick and just starts to lose its gloss (6 to 8 minutes total).

5. Immediately spread fudge in the prepared pan. Score into squares while fudge is still warm.

6. When fudge is firm, use foil to lift it out of pan. Cut fudge into squares. Store tightly covered for up to 1 week. Makes about 1¼ pounds (32 pieces).

Make-ahead directions: Prepare as directed. Place fudge pieces in layers separated by waxed paper in a freezer container. Seal, label, and freeze for up to 2 months.

Nutrition facts per piece: 71 cal., 2 g total fat (1 g sat. fat), 4 mg chol., 20 mg sodium, 13 g carbo., 0 g fiber, 0 g pro.

Simple Fudge

Prep: 10 min. Cook: 10 + 6 min. Chill: 2 hr.

1½   cups sugar
1   5-oz. can (⅔ cup) evaporated milk
½   cup butter
2   cups tiny marshmallows
1   cup semisweet chocolate pieces (tip,
     page 283) or chopped bittersweet
     chocolate
½   cup chopped walnuts, toasted (tip,
     page 102)
½   tsp. vanilla

1. Line an 8×8×2-inch baking pan with foil, extending foil over edges of pan. Butter foil; set aside.

2. Butter sides of a 2-quart heavy saucepan. In saucepan, combine sugar, evaporated milk, and butter. Cook and stir over medium-high heat until mixture boils (about 10 minutes). Reduce heat to medium; continue cooking, stirring constantly, for 6 minutes. Remove saucepan from heat. Add marshmallows, chocolate, walnuts, and vanilla; stir until marshmallows and chocolate melt and mixture is combined. Beat by hand for 1 minute.

3. Spread fudge evenly in the prepared pan. Score into squares while warm. Cover and chill for 2 to 3 hours or until firm. When fudge is firm, use foil to lift it out of pan. Cut into squares. Store tightly covered in refrigerator for up to 1 month. Makes about 2 pounds (64 pieces).

Microwave Directions: Line an 8×8×2-inch baking pan with foil, extending foil over edges of pan. Butter foil; set aside. In a 2½-quart microwave-safe bowl, microwave butter, uncovered, on 100 percent powder (high) for 45 to 60 seconds (for 1,000- to 1,300-watt ovens) or 60 to 75 seconds (for 600- to 800-watt ovens) or until melted. Stir in the sugar and evaporated milk. Microwave, uncovered, on high 7 minutes (for 1,000- to 1,300-watt ovens) or 10 minutes (for 600- to 800-watt ovens), stirring every 3 minutes. Carefully remove bowl from microwave oven. Add marshmallows, chocolate, nuts, and vanilla; stir until marshmallows and chocolate are melted and mixture is combined. Beat by hand for 1 minute. Pour into prepared pan; continue with step 3 above.

Nutrition facts per piece: 59 cal., 3 g total fat (2 g sat. fat), 5 mg chol., 20 mg sodium, 8 g carbo., 0 g fiber, 0 g pro.

Peanut Butter-Chocolate Fudge: Prepare as directed, except substitute ½ cup peanut butter for the butter and, if desired, chopped peanuts for the walnuts.

Nutrition facts per piece: 58 cal., 3 g total fat (1 g sat. fat), 1 mg chol., 23 mg sodium, 9 g carbo., 0 g fiber, 1 g pro.

Today

Recipes using marshmallow creme revolutionized the way Americans made fudge in the 1950s—producing a smooth candy with minimal beating. Over the years, we kept tinkering with this remarkable recipe. This version uses easy-measuring tiny marshmallows and gives you a choice of semisweet or bittersweet chocolate.

Just like the perfect scarf accentuates a little black dress, the

perfect sauce or condiment enhances a meal. Sauces take plain

roasted meats from simple to sublime, pickles add intriguing

tart and sweet notes to sandwiches,

and jams or jellies bring out the best

All
The Little
Extras

in breads. On these pages, you'll our finest selection of little

extras. To liven up meals, take your pick of these sauces,

pickles, relishes, marinades, rubs, salsas, jellies, and jams.

311

306

307

304

310

308

Corn and Zucchini Relish
Peach and Pear Relish
Pickles with Sweet Peppers

Pickles with Sweet Peppers

Prep: 1 hr. Stand: 3 hr. Process: 10 min.

This tongue-tingling condiment for burgers, meats, and poultry was in the Cooks Round Table in the July 1942 issue of *Better Homes and Gardens*® magazine.

  4   quarts unpeeled medium cucumbers, cut into ⅛-inch-thick slices (16 cups)
  6   cups sliced white onion
1⅔ cups sliced green or red sweet peppers
 ⅓ cup pickling salt
  3   cloves garlic, halved
16 cups cracked ice
  5   cups sugar
  3   cups cider vinegar
  2   Tbsp. mustard seeds
1½ tsp. celery seeds
  1   tsp. ground turmeric

1. In a very large bowl, combine cucumbers, onion, sweet peppers, pickling salt, and garlic. Stir in cracked ice. Let stand for 3 hours; drain well. Remove garlic.

2. In an 8-quart Dutch oven or kettle, combine sugar, cider vinegar, mustard seeds, celery seeds, and turmeric; add drained cucumber mixture. Bring to boiling.

3. Pack cucumber mixture and liquid into hot, sterilized pint canning jars, leaving ½-inch headspace. Wipe jar rims; adjust lids. Process in a boiling-water canner for 10 minutes (start timing when water covering jars returns to boiling). Remove jars from canner; cool jars on wire racks. Makes 9 pints.

Nutrition facts per ¼-cup serving: 64 cal., 0 g total fat, 0 mg chol., 196 mg sodium, 16 g carbo., 1 g fiber, 0 g pro.

Corn and Zucchini Relish

Prep: 10 min. Chill: 4 to 24 hr.

Every year, our readers who've planted zucchini in their home gardens look for ways to use their supply. This colorful dill-accented corn relish is one of the easiest dishes we've created. Serve it with meat, fish, or poultry.

 1   cup frozen whole kernel corn*
 1   medium zucchini, chopped
 ¼ cup finely chopped red sweet pepper
 ¼ cup vinegar
 3   Tbsp. sugar
 ½ tsp. dried dill weed
 ¼ tsp. salt
 ¼ tsp. dry mustard

1. In a medium bowl, combine corn, zucchini, red sweet pepper, vinegar, sugar, dill weed, salt, and mustard. Cover and chill for at least 4 hours or up to 24 hours. Serve with a slotted spoon. Makes 2½ cups.

*Test Kitchen Tip: To use fresh corn, cook 1 cup kernels in a covered saucepan in a small amount of boiling water about 4 minutes or just until tender. Drain.

Nutrition facts per ¼-cup serving: 33 cal., 0 g total fat, 0 mg chol., 59 mg sodium, 8 g carbo., 1 g fiber, 1 g pro.

In July 1942, our magazine was scheduled to showcase the winners of a pickle recipe contest. To meet the press deadline, the recipes had to be tested in late winter—not prime cucumber season. So our Test Kitchen placed an order with a local company to have bushels of 4- to 6-inch cucumbers specially grown for delivery the first week of March.

Pear and Peach Relish

Prep: 45 min. Cook: 2 hr. Process: 15 min.

Cinnamon, cloves, nutmeg, and fiery serrano chile peppers punch up the feisty flavor of this knockout tomato relish recipe. Try it with frankfurters, bratwursts, or burgers.

4½	**lb. tomatoes**
4	**medium pears, peeled, cored, and cut into ½-inch chunks (4 cups)**
4	**medium peaches, peeled, pitted, and cut into ½-inch chunks (3½ cups)**
3	**medium green sweet peppers, seeded and chopped (2¼ cups)**
2	**cups chopped onion**
¾	**cup chopped red sweet pepper**
1	**to 2 red or green fresh serrano chile peppers, seeded and finely chopped (1 to 3 tsp.) (tip, page 32)**
3	**cups sugar**
1½	**cups cider vinegar**
4	**tsp. salt**
2	**tsp. ground nutmeg**
6	**inches stick cinnamon**
1	**tsp. whole cloves**

1. Wash tomatoes. Remove peels, stem ends, and cores.* Cut tomatoes into chunks (you should have about 6¾ cups). In a 6- or 8-quart stainless steel, enamel, or nonstick Dutch oven or kettle, combine tomatoes, pears, peaches, green sweet peppers, onion, red sweet pepper, and chile peppers. Stir in sugar, cider vinegar, salt, and nutmeg.

2. Tie cinnamon and cloves in a double thickness of 100%-cotton cheesecloth; stir into vegetable mixture. Bring to boiling; reduce heat to medium. Simmer, uncovered, about 2 hours or until thick; stir occasionally.

3. Discard spice bag. Immediately ladle hot mixture into hot, clean pint canning jars, leaving ½-inch headspace. (Refrigerate any extra relish; use within 3 days.) Wipe jar rims; adjust lids. Process in a boiling-water canner for 15 minutes (start timing when water covering jars returns to boiling). Remove jars from canner; cool jars on wire racks. Makes 4 pints.

*Test Kitchen Tip: To peel tomatoes, with a knife make a small "X" on the bottom of each tomato. Plunge into boiling water for 30 seconds. Rinse in cold water; remove the peel with a paring knife.

Nutrition facts per ¼-cup serving: 116 cal., 0 g total fat, 0 mg chol., 300 mg sodium, 29 g carbo., 2 g fiber, 1 g pro.

Check It Out

Although home canning techniques have been updated over the years, one thing remains the same—it's *essential* to review and follow the latest safety instructions. To find this important information, check with your state or local extension agent. Or call the Ball and Kerr Home Canners' hotline at 1-800-240-3340 or log on to www.homecanning.com on the Web.

Sherry Marinade

Start to finish: 5 min.

2	**Tbsp. cooking oil**
2	**Tbsp. dry sherry**
2	**Tbsp. stone-ground mustard**
1	**Tbsp. honey**
1½	**tsp. soy sauce**

1. In a small bowl, stir together all ingredients. Pour over meat, poultry, fish, or seafood; turn to coat. Marinate in the refrigerator for 30 minutes. Drain, discarding marinade. Grill or broil meat, poultry, fish, or seafood. Makes about ⅔ cup (enough to marinate 1 pound meat, poultry, fish, or seafood).

Nutrition facts per 1-tablespoon marinade: 35 cal., 3 g total fat (0 g sat. fat),, 0 mg chol., 86 mg sodium, 2 g carbo., 0 g fiber, 0 g pro.

Citrus-Honey Marinade

Start to finish: 5 min.

¼	**cup orange juice**
2	**Tbsp. lemon juice**
2	**Tbsp. Dijon-style mustard**
2	**Tbsp. honey**
1	**Tbsp. soy sauce**

1. In a small bowl, stir together all ingredients. Pour over meat, poultry, fish, or seafood; turn to coat. Marinate in the refrigerator for 1 hour, turning occasionally. Drain, reserving marinade. Grill or broil meat, poultry, fish, or seafood. Brush on reserved marinade once halfway through cooking. Discard any remaining marinade. Makes about ⅔ cup (enough to marinate 1 pound meat, poultry, fish, or seafood).

Nutrition facts per 1-tablespoon marinade: 19 cal., 0 g total fat, 0 mg chol., 99 mg sodium, 4 g carbo., 0 g fiber, 0 g pro.

Yesterday

Best Tomato Ketchup

Prep: 45 min. Cook: 1¼ hr. + 40 min. Process: 15 min.

For today's cooks who may have grown up with bottled ketchup, the texture of homemade will seem very different. It's more like salsa.

8	lb. tomatoes (24 medium)
½	cup chopped onion
¼	tsp. cayenne pepper
1	cup sugar
1	cup white vinegar
1½	inches stick cinnamon, broken
1½	tsp. whole cloves
1	tsp. celery seeds
¼	cup lemon juice
2	tsp. salt

1. Core and quarter tomatoes. In an 8- or 10-quart kettle, combine tomatoes, onion, and cayenne pepper. Bring to boiling; reduce heat. Boil gently, uncovered, for 15 minutes, stirring often. Press through a food mill.* Discard seeds and skins. (You should have about 10 cups pulp.)

2. Return tomato mixture to kettle; add sugar. Bring to boiling; reduce heat. Boil gently, uncovered, for 1¼ to 2 hours or until reduced by half, stirring occasionally. (Use a clean wooden or metal ruler to measure depth before and after cooking to determine when it is reduced by half.)

3. In a small saucepan, bring vinegar, cinnamon, cloves, and celery seeds to boiling. Remove from heat. Strain vinegar mixture into tomato mixture; discard spices. Stir in lemon juice and salt. Simmer about 40 minutes or until desired consistency, stirring often.

4. Ladle ketchup into hot, clean half-pint canning jars, leaving a ½-inch headspace. Wipe jar rims; adjust lids. Process in a boiling-water canner for 15 minutes (start timing when water covering jars returns to boiling). Remove jars from canner; cool on wire racks. Makes 3 half-pints.

***Test Kitchen Tip:** If you do not have a food mill, you can use a sturdy fine-mesh sieve, one that will allow the tomato pulp to pass through, but not the tomato seeds. Your yield may vary from the amount given.

Nutrition facts per 1-tablespoon serving: 37 cal., 0 g total fat, 0 mg chol., 118 mg sodium, 9 g carbo., 1 g fiber, 1 g pro.

By now, most of our readers are too busy to take on home canning, so it takes an extra special recipe to coax them into making ketchup from scratch. This gutsy version is worth the time and the effort, even with a jam-packed schedule.

Chipotle Ketchup

Prep: 45 min. Cook: 1 hr. + 30 min.
Chill: 2 hr. to 1 week

Fire up burgers, brats, or steak with this colorful condiment laced with chipotle peppers. Or use it as a dip for plantain or tortilla chips.

- **4 lb. tomatoes (12 medium)**
- **½ cup chopped onion**
- **1 or 2 dried chipotle chile peppers, crumbled (tip, page 32)**
- **½ cup sugar**
- **½ cup white vinegar**
- **1 tsp. dried marjoram, crushed**
- **1 tsp. salt**

1. Core and quarter tomatoes; drain. In a 4-quart Dutch oven, combine tomatoes, onion, and chipotle chile peppers. Bring to boiling, stirring often; reduce heat. Cover and simmer for 15 minutes. Press through food mill.* Discard seeds and skins.

2. Return tomato mixture to large saucepan; stir in sugar. Bring to boiling; reduce heat. Simmer, uncovered, for 1 to 1¼ hours or until reduced by half, stirring occasionally. (Use a clean wooden or metal ruler to measure depth of mixture before and after cooking to determine when it is reduced by half.)

3. Stir vinegar, marjoram, and salt into mixture. Simmer, uncovered, 30 to 45 minutes more or to desired consistency, stirring often. Transfer to a nonmetal bowl. Cover and chill for at least 2 hours or up to 1 week. Makes about 1¾ cups.

*Test Kitchen Tip: If you do not have a food mill, you can use a sturdy fine-mesh sieve, one that will allow the tomato pulp to pass through, but not the tomato seeds. Your yield may vary from the amount given.

Nutrition facts per 1-tablespoon serving: 29 cal., 0 g total fat, 0 mg chol., 89 mg sodium, 7 g carbo., 1 g fiber, 1 g pro.

Kansas City Barbecue Rub

Start to finish: 5 min.

Across the country, barbecue fans agree to disagree about which seasonings are best. Folks around Kansas City prefer their barbecue flavored with a spicy, yet sweet, rub. You will too.

- ¼ **cup sugar**
- 1 **Tbsp. seasoned salt**
- 1 **Tbsp. garlic salt**
- 1 **Tbsp. paprika**
- 1 **Tbsp. barbecue seasoning**
- 1½ **tsp. onion salt**
- 1½ **tsp. celery salt**
- 1½ **tsp. chili powder**
- 1½ **tsp. ground black pepper**
- ¾ **tsp. ground ginger**
- ¾ **tsp. lemon-pepper seasoning**
- ¼ **tsp. ground thyme**
- ⅛ **tsp. cayenne pepper**

1. In a small bowl, combine sugar, seasoned salt, garlic salt, paprika, barbecue seasoning, onion salt, celery salt, chili powder, black pepper, ginger, lemon-pepper seasoning, thyme, and cayenne pepper. Store in an airtight container for up to 3 months.

2. To use, sprinkle mixture evenly onto meat or poultry; rub in with your fingers. Grill or broil meat or poultry. Makes about ⅔ cup (enough for 6 to 8 pounds meat or poultry).

Nutrition facts per 1-teaspoon serving: 9 cal., 0 g total fat, 0 mg chol., 480 mg sodium, 2 g carbo., 0 g fiber, 0 g pro.

Sweet and Spunky Barbecue Sauce

Prep: 10 min. Cook: 25 min.

Slather this all-purpose sauce onto grilled meat or poultry—it's a lip-smackin' good blend of ketchup, molasses, mustard, and cayenne pepper.

- 1 **cup ketchup**
- ½ **cup water**
- 1 **small onion, chopped**
- ¼ **cup Worcestershire sauce**
- 3 **Tbsp. cider vinegar**
- 2 **Tbsp. packed brown sugar**
- 2 **Tbsp. molasses**
- 2 **tsp. dry mustard**
- 1 **tsp. garlic powder**
- 1 **tsp. chili powder**
- ¼ **tsp. cayenne pepper**

1. In a 2-quart saucepan, combine ketchup, the water, onion, Worcestershire sauce, cider vinegar, brown sugar, molasses, mustard, garlic powder, chili powder, and cayenne pepper. Bring to boiling; reduce heat. Simmer, uncovered, about 25 minutes or until desired consistency, stirring frequently. To store any leftover sauce, cover and chill for up to 3 days. Before using, reheat until bubbly, stirring occasionally. Makes about 1½ cups.

Nutrition facts per 1-tablespoon serving: 24 cal., 0 g total fat, 0 mg chol., 153 mg sodium, 6 g carbo., 0 g fiber, 0 g pro.

Kansas City Barbecue Rub (top left)
Mustard-Honey Sauce (right)
Sweet and Spunky Barbecue Sauce (bottom left)

In the 1960s and 1970s, a dish that went from kitchen to table in 30 minutes was considered fast. In the years since, prep times have been slashed. Cooks now prefer 15-minute dishes. Quick-fixing sauces and rubs are a natural solution.

Smoky Barbecue Sauce

Prep: 10 min. Cook: 30 min.

Sweet, yet tart, is the best way to describe this versatile sauce. The reader who submitted it serves it on chicken and ribs.

- 1 15-oz. can tomato sauce
- ½ cup cider vinegar
- ½ cup packed brown sugar
- 2 Tbsp. finely chopped onion
- 2 Tbsp. liquid smoke
- 1 Tbsp. Worcestershire sauce
- 1 clove garlic, minced
- 1 tsp. chili powder
- ¼ tsp. celery salt
- ⅛ to ¼ tsp. cayenne pepper
- ⅛ tsp. ground allspice
- 3 drops bottled hot pepper sauce

1. In a medium saucepan, stir together tomato sauce, cider vinegar, brown sugar, onion, liquid smoke, Worcestershire sauce, garlic, chili powder, celery salt, cayenne pepper, allspice, and hot pepper sauce. Bring just to boiling; reduce heat. Simmer, uncovered, for 30 minutes or until desired consistency. Makes about 3 cups.

Nutrition facts per 1-tablespoon serving: 12 cal., 0 g total fat , 0 mg chol., 54 mg sodium, 3 g carbo., 0 g fiber, 0 g pro.

Mustard-Honey Sauce

Prep: 10 min. Cook: 5 min. Stand: 15 min.

Mustard, honey, and brown sugar bring out the best in broiled or grilled meat, poultry, or fish.

- ¼ cup honey
- ¼ cup Dijon-style mustard
- 1 Tbsp. packed brown sugar
- 1 Tbsp. apple juice
- 1 Tbsp. chopped onion or ½ tsp. dried minced onion
  Dash salt
  Dash cayenne pepper

1. In a saucepan, stir together honey, mustard, brown sugar, apple juice, onion, salt, and cayenne pepper. Bring just to boiling; reduce heat. Simmer, uncovered, for 5 minutes. Let stand for 15 minutes to cool slightly. Makes ½ cup.

Nutrition facts per 1-tablespoon serving: 49 cal., 1 g total fat (0 g sat. fat), 0 mg chol., 61 mg sodium, 11 g carbo., 0 g fiber, 1 g pro.

Mushroom-Garlic Sauce

Start to finish: 25 min.

Ladle this versatile curry-flavored sauce over potatoes or polenta, as well as on meat and poultry.

- 2 Tbsp. olive oil
- 2 8-oz. pkg. fresh mushrooms, quartered
- ¼ cup finely chopped shallots
- 6 cloves garlic, minced
- ½ tsp. curry powder
- ⅛ to ¼ tsp. crushed red pepper
- ¾ cup chicken broth
- 2 tsp. soy sauce
- ¼ tsp. ground nutmeg
- ¼ cup dry white wine or chicken broth
- 1 Tbsp. cornstarch

1. In a large saucepan, heat oil over medium heat. Add mushrooms, shallots, garlic, curry powder, and crushed red pepper; cook until mushrooms are tender. Add the ¾ cup chicken broth, the soy sauce, and nutmeg; bring to boiling. In a small bowl, stir together wine or additional chicken broth and cornstarch; add to saucepan. Cook and stir until thickened and bubbly; cook and stir for 2 minutes more. Makes about 2½ cups.

Nutrition facts per ¼-cup serving: 53 cal., 4 g total fat (1 g sat. fat), 0 mg chol., 139 mg sodium, 3 g carbo., 0 g fiber, 2 g pro.

Raspberry Sauce

Start to finish: 10 min.

Preserves and chipotle peppers are a sensational match in this spoon-on for ham, pork, fish, or poultry.

- 1½ cups seedless raspberry preserves
- 2 Tbsp. white vinegar
- 2 or 3 canned chipotle chile peppers in adobo sauce, drained and chopped (tip, page 32)
- 3 cloves garlic, minced

1. In a saucepan, stir together raspberry preserves, vinegar, chipotle peppers, and garlic. Bring just to boiling; reduce heat. Simmer, uncovered, for 5 minutes. Serve with meat, fish, or poultry. To store any leftover sauce, cover and chill for up to 1 week. Before using, reheat until bubbly, stirring occasionally. Makes 1¾ cups.

Nutrition facts per 1-tablespoon serving: 49 cal., 0 g total fat, 0 mg chol., 11 mg sodium, 12 g carbo., 0 g fiber, 0 g pro.

Yesterday

In the 1970s as Mexican food mania swept across the U.S.A., cooks wanted to learn to make south-of-the-border specialties at home. We were happy to help out with Mexican-influenced recipes of all kinds, including this spunky salsa.

Sweet and Chunky Salsa

Prep: 45 min. Stand: 30 min. Cook: 45 min.
Process: 35 min.

Try this tri-pepper salsa with your favorite tortilla chips or Mexican entrées and you'll agree nothing is better than homemade.

7   lb. tomatoes (20 medium)*
4   red, yellow, or green sweet peppers
     (1½ lb.), chopped (3 cups)
2   cups coarsely chopped onion
1   cup vinegar
2   fresh Anaheim chile peppers or poblano
     chile peppers, seeded and chopped
     (about ¾ cup) (tip, page 32)
½   cup snipped fresh parsley
5   cloves garlic, minced
1   fresh jalapeño chile pepper, seeded and
     chopped (about 2 Tbsp.) (tip, page 32)
1   Tbsp. sugar
1   Tbsp. ground cumin
1   tsp. salt
½   tsp. ground black pepper

1. Peel (tip, page 305), core, seed, and coarsely chop tomatoes (you should have about 14 cups). Place tomatoes in a large colander. Let stand to drain about 30 minutes.

2. Place drained tomatoes in an 8-quart stainless steel, enamel, or nonstick heavy kettle. Bring to boiling; reduce heat. Boil gently, uncovered, for 45 to 50 minutes or until thickened and chunky; stir frequently. Add sweet peppers, onion, vinegar, Anaheim or poblano peppers, parsley, garlic, jalapeño pepper, sugar, cumin, salt, and black pepper. Return mixture to boiling. Remove from heat.

3. Ladle hot salsa into hot, clean pint canning jars, leaving a ½-inch headspace. Wipe jar rims; adjust lids. Process in a boiling-water canner for 35 minutes (start timing when water covering jars returns to boiling). Remove the jars from canner; cool on wire racks. Makes about 5 pints.

*Test Kitchen Tip: Use only vine-ripened tomatoes for this recipe—they provide the high acidity needed for safe boiling-water canning. Avoid using tomatoes from dead or frost-killed vines. If in doubt, store the salsa in the refrigerator.

Nutrition facts per ¼-cup serving: 26 cal., 0 g total fat, 0 mg chol., 66 mg sodium, 6 g carbo., 1 g fiber, 1 g pro.

Fiesta Salsa

Prep: 20 min. Chill: 4 to 24 hr.

Cranberry, apple, pear, and orange create a kaleidoscope of colors and flavors in this tantalizing relish. Serve it with pork, poultry, or fish.

- 8 **oz. fresh cranberries, chopped (2 cups)**
- 1 **small apple, peeled, cored, and finely chopped**
- 1 **small pear, peeled, cored, and finely chopped**
- 1 **orange, peeled, seeded, sectioned, and finely chopped**
- 1 **shallot, finely chopped**
- 1 **green onion, thinly sliced**
- 1 **to 2 fresh jalapeño chile peppers, seeded and finely chopped (tip, page 32)**
- ⅓ **cup sugar**
- 1 **Tbsp. lime juice**
- 1 **Tbsp. white wine vinegar**

1. In a medium nonmetal bowl,* combine cranberries, apple, pear, orange, shallot, green onion, and jalapeño peppers. Stir in the sugar, lime juice, and vinegar. Cover and chill for at least 4 hours or up to 24 hours. Stir before serving. Makes about 3 cups.

*Test Kitchen Tip: Use a stoneware, glass, enamelware, or a food-grade plastic bowl for this recipe. Do not use an aluminum, stainless-steel, brass, copper, zinc, or galvanized bowl.

Nutrition facts per ¼-cup serving: 49 cal., 0 g total fat, 0 mg chol., 1 mg sodium, 12 g carbo., 2 g fiber, 0 g pro.

Today

By the 1990s, our readers felt comfortable enough with Mexican food to improvise. The results were creative and delicious, as proven by this take-off on salsa that won a prize in our September 1998 Fall Fruit Favorites category.

Gingered Holiday Chutney

Prep: 35 min. Cook: 25 min. Process: 10 min.

This winner of the food gifts category of our 1985 Holiday Recipe Contest tastes terrific with roasted meat or poultry, or in a ham or turkey sandwich.

- 2 cups packed brown sugar
- ¾ cup vinegar
- ½ cup water
- ½ tsp. salt
- ¼ tsp. ground cinnamon
- ¼ tsp. cayenne pepper
- 1 large lemon
- 1 large lime
- 1 lb. pears (such as Anjou), peeled, cored, and coarsely chopped (about 3 cups)
- 1 cup chopped green sweet pepper
- 1 cup chopped red sweet pepper
- 1 cup chopped onion
- 1 cup golden raisins
- 1 Tbsp. finely chopped crystallized ginger

1. In a 4-quart Dutch oven or kettle, stir together brown sugar, vinegar, the water, salt, cinnamon, and cayenne pepper. Bring to boiling; reduce heat to medium-low. Simmer, uncovered, for 10 minutes. Meanwhile, finely shred peel from lemon and lime (about 2 tablespoons peel total); squeeze juice from lemon and lime (about ⅓ cup juice total).

2. Add peels, juices, pears, sweet peppers, onion, raisins, and crystallized ginger to hot mixture in Dutch oven or kettle. Return to boiling; reduce heat to medium-low. Simmer, uncovered, about 25 minutes or until thick, stirring occasionally (should have about 3¾ cups).

3. Immediately ladle hot chutney into hot, sterilized half-pint canning jars, leaving ¼-inch headspace. Wipe jar rims; adjust lids. Process in boiling-water canner for 10 minutes (start timing when water covering jars returns to boiling). Remove the jars from the canner; cool jars on wire racks. Makes 4 half-pints.

Nutrition facts per 1-tablespoon serving: 41 cal., 0 g total fat, 0 mg chol., 21 mg sodium, 11 g carbo., 0 g fiber, 0 g pro.

Pineapple-Cherry Chutney

Prep: 25 min. Cook: 30 min.

Perk up ham, pork, or poultry with this spunky relish.

- 2 cups chopped fresh pineapple or canned crushed pineapple (juice pack)
- ½ cup golden raisins
- ½ cup dried tart red cherries
- 3 Tbsp. finely chopped onion
- ½ cup granulated sugar
- ½ cup white wine vinegar
- 3 Tbsp. lemon juice
- 3 Tbsp. finely chopped crystallized ginger
- ¼ tsp. ground cinnamon

1. In a medium saucepan, combine pineapple, raisins, dried cherries, and onion. Stir in sugar, white wine vinegar, lemon juice, crystallized ginger, and cinnamon. Bring to boiling over medium heat; reduce heat. Boil gently, uncovered, about 30 minutes or until syrup is slightly thickened. Cool slightly. Store leftover chutney in the refrigerator up to 2 weeks. Makes about 3¼ cups.

Nutrition facts per 1-tablespoon serving: 21 cal., 0 g total fat, 0 mg chol., 1 mg sodium, 5 g carbo., 0 g fiber, 0 g pro.

Fruit Juice Jelly

Prep: 25 min. Process: 5 min.

Create any flavor you like by switching the juice you use. Just be sure the product is 100 percent fruit juice.

- 4 cups cranberry juice (not low-calorie) or unsweetened apple, grape, or orange juice
- ¼ cup lemon juice
- 1 1¾-oz. pkg. regular powdered fruit pectin
- 4½ cups sugar

1. In a heavy, 6-quart Dutch oven, combine desired fruit juice and lemon juice. Sprinkle with pectin. Let stand for 2 minutes; stir to dissolve. Cook over medium-high heat, stirring frequently, until a full rolling boil forms. Stir in sugar. Return to a full rolling boil, stirring frequently. Boil hard for 1 minute, stirring constantly. Remove from heat. With a metal spoon, quickly skim off foam.

2. Immediately ladle hot jelly into hot, sterilized half-pint canning jars, leaving ¼-inch headspace. Wipe jar rims; adjust lids. Process in a boiling-water canner for 5 minutes (start timing when water covering jars returns to boiling). Remove jars from canner; cool jars on wire racks until set. Makes 5 half-pints.

Nutrition facts per 1-tablespoon serving: 68 cal., 0 g total fat, 0 mg chol., 2 mg sodium, 18 g carbo., 0 g fiber, 0 g pro.

Apricot-Orange Marmalade

Stand: 30 min. Prep: 45 min. Cook: 20 min.
Process: 5 min.

Give jars of these golden preserves as gifts, but
save one for yourself to use as a toast topper or
cake filling.

- 2   cups water
- 1   lb. dried apricots (about 2⅔ cups)
- 2   medium grapefruit
- 3   medium oranges
- 1   medium lemon
- 5   cups sugar
- 4   tsp. finely shredded orange peel

1. In a small saucepan, bring water to boiling. Remove
from heat; add apricots. Let apricots stand about
30 minutes in hot water.

2. Transfer about *one-fourth* of the soaked apricots
with soaking liquid to a food processor; cover and process
until finely chopped. Transfer chopped apricot mixture to
an 8-quart heavy Dutch oven or kettle. Repeat with
remaining apricot mixture, *one-fourth* at a time. Set
apricots aside.

3. Peel grapefruit, removing and discarding pith (white
membrane). Section grapefruit, reserving juice; discard
seeds. Add grapefruit sections and juice to Dutch oven.

4. Cut up the unpeeled oranges and lemon; discard
seeds. Place *one-fourth* of the orange and lemon pieces
in food processor; cover and process until finely chopped.
Add chopped oranges and lemon to Dutch oven. Repeat
with remaining orange and lemon pieces, *one-fourth*
at a time.

5. Stir sugar and orange peel into mixture in Dutch
oven. Bring to boiling. Boil gently for 20 minutes or until
thick, stirring frequently to prevent scorching.

6. Immediately ladle hot marmalade into hot,
sterilized half-pint canning jars, leaving ¼-inch
headspace. Wipe jar rims; adjust lids. Process in a boiling-
water canner for 5 minutes (start timing when water
covering jars returns to boiling). Remove jars from
canner; cool jars on wire racks. Makes 9 half-pints.

Nutrition facts per 1-tablespoon serving: 36 cal., 0 g total fat, 0 mg chol.,
1 mg sodium, 9 g carbo., 0 g fiber, 0 g pro.

Apple-Pear Butter

Prep: 30 min. Cook: 30 min. + 1½ hr. Process: 5 min.

- 9   cups chopped unpeeled apples*
- 3   cups chopped unpeeled pears*
- 3   cups water
- 2   cups sugar
- 1   tsp. finely shredded lemon peel
- 1   tsp. ground cinnamon
- ½   tsp. ground cloves

1. In a heavy, 8- to 10-quart kettle, combine apples,
pears, and the water. Bring to boiling; reduce heat. Cover;
simmer for 30 minutes, stirring occasionally. Do not drain.

2. Press mixture through a fine-mesh sieve (you
should have about 6 cups sieved mixture). Discard
solids. Return sieved mixture to Dutch oven. Stir in sugar,
lemon peel, cinnamon, and cloves. Bring to boiling;
reduce heat. Simmer, uncovered, over low heat about
1½ hours or until very thick, stirring often.

3. Immediately ladle hot butter into hot, sterilized
half-pint canning jars, leaving ¼-inch headspace. Wipe
jar rims; adjust lids. Process in boiling-water canner for
5 minutes (start timing when water covering jars returns
to boiling). Remove jars from canner; cool jars on wire
racks. Makes about 4 half-pints.

***Test Kitchen Tip:** For good texture and flavor,
choose the fruit varieties best suited for canning: for
apples, pick Granny Smith, Golden Delicious, or Rome
Beauty; for pears, use Bartlett.

Nutrition facts per 1-tablespoon serving: 41 cal., 0 g total fat, 0 mg chol.,
0 mg sodium, 11 g carbo., 1 g fiber, 0 g pro.

Squeaky Clean We may
sound like your mom telling you to wash
up, but when you're canning, nothing is
too clean. You must sterilize any jars to
be used for food that will be processed
in a boiling-water canner for 10 minutes
or less. To sterilize, wash the jars in hot,
soapy water. Rinse thoroughly and place
in boiling water for 10 minutes. If you
live more than 1,000 feet above sea level,
add an extra minute for each additional
1,000 feet of elevation.

From a quick bite before soccer practice to a lavish spread to

celebrate a holiday or milestone, you can create terrific-tasting

meals for your family and guests with these menu suggestions.

Each one brings you   delicious, easy-to-fix

Family-Pleasing
Menus

recipe options that   work well together.

You'll find no-hassle suppers for every day, Sunday dinners and

holiday feasts, picnic and grill-out suggestions, a weekend

brunch, and more—all designed to fit your family's busy lifestyle.

Old-Fashioned Sunday Dinner

Take time this weekend to savor this homespun gather-the-family meal like Grandma used to make.

Cider-Braised Pork Roast, page 20

Green Bean and Sweet Onion Gratin, page 190

Baked potatoes

Cornmeal Yeast Rolls, page 207

Lemon Meringue Pie, page 265

Coffee or milk

Fuss-Free Weeknight Dinner

This no-hassle meal goes together in a flash if you keep a stash of chocolate chip cookies on hand in the freezer.

Zippy Beef, Mac, and Cheese, page 18

Tossed salad with Fresh Herb Vinaigrette, page 182

Seven-Grain Cereal Muffins, page 222

Chewy Chocolate Chip Cookies, page 228

Milk

South-of-the-Border Supper

Enjoy Mexican-restaurant cooking at home with this zesty menu. To speed things along, make the Spanish rice from a mix.

Sweet and Chunky Salsa, page 310, or purchased salsa with tortilla chips

Turkey Enchiladas, page 37

Spanish rice

One-Bowl Chocolate Cake, page 280

Margaritas or lemonade

Backyard Barbecue

When warm weather beckons you outdoors, fire up the grill and serve this belt-busting menu on the deck or patio.

Bistro Burgers, page 73

Hobo Potatoes, page 94

Three-Bean Salad, page 178

Rhubarb Surprise Crisp, page 274

Lemonade

Celebration Dinner

Whether it's to mark a birthday, toast a promotion, or merely rejoice over the coming of spring, pull out all the stops.

Pecan Salmon with Sweet Pepper Mayo, page 43

Lemon-Tarragon Asparagus Salad, page 180

Steamed cauliflower

Sunflower Seed Bread, page 198

Ginger Carrot Cake, page 254

Coffee, tea, or milk

Come-on-Over Brunch

Kick off the weekend or a holiday with this midmorning meal. You can bake the two breads ahead.

Herbed Egg and Cheese Casserole, page 52

Mixed fresh fruit bowl

Hot cooked bacon

Almond Twirl Bread, page 204

Island-Style Banana Bread, page 213

Coffee or Hot Minty Cocoa, page 299

Celebration Grill Out

From May Day through Indian summer, take advantage of great weather to entertain outside—an easy place to feed a crowd.

Marvelous Mustard Ribs, page 75
24-Hour Vegetable Salad, page 104
Baked Bean Quintet, page 108
Classic Corn Bread, page 216
Ice cream with Hot Fudge Sauce, page 298
Ranger Cookies, page 234
Iced tea and lemonade

Dessert Buffet

Cap off the evening with this assortment of sweets. You can make everything ahead, so the menu's perfect to serve after a concert or play.

White-Chocolate Cheesecake with
Triple-Raspberry Sauce, page 141
Best-Ever Chocolate Cake, page 280
Brandy Snaps, page 251
Paul's Pumpkin Bars, page 117
Peanut Butter-Chocolate Fudge, page 301
Flavored coffees and teas

Home-for-the-Holidays Dinner

Relive fond memories of holidays past with this merry menu.

Classic Roast Turkey with
Fruit-Chestnut Stuffing, page 120
Apple-Spiced Sweet Potatoes, page 109
Mashed potatoes and steamed green beans
Layered Cranberry-Apple Mold, page 133
Quaker Bonnet Biscuits, page 207
Toasted Pecan Pie, page 139
Paradise Pumpkin Pie, page 264

> **When a recipe has you puzzled, check this easy-to-use glossary for the answers to your questions about ingredients and cooking terms.**

Adobo sauce: A dark-red Mexican sauce made from ground chile peppers, herbs, and vinegar. Chipotle peppers often are available in cans of adobo sauce.

Almond paste: A smooth mixture made of ground, blanched almonds and sugar that's often used as a filling in pastries, cakes, and confections. For best baking results, use an almond paste without syrup or liquid glucose. Do not substitute marzipan candy.

Anchovy paste: A mixture of ground anchovies, vinegar, and seasonings. Anchovy paste is available in tubes in the canned fish or gourmet section of the supermarket.

Baking powder: A combination of dry acid, baking soda, and starch. Baking powder has the ability to release carbon dioxide in two stages: when liquid ingredients are added and when the mixture is heated.

Baking soda: A leavening agent that creates carbon dioxide. Baking soda must be used in conjunction with acidic ingredients—such as buttermilk, sour cream, brown sugar, or fruit juices—to create the bubbles that make the product rise.

Balsamic vinegar: Syrupy and slightly sweet, this dark-brown vinegar is made from the juice of the white Trebbiano grape. Its body, color, and sweetness come from being aged in wooden barrels.

Barbecue seasoning: This zesty combination blends spices that bring a smoke-flavored heat to foods. The spices may include salt, sugar, garlic, hot red pepper, hickory smoke flavor, onion, and others.

Basmati rice: An aromatic, long grain brown or white rice from India and California. Basmati rice is nutty and fluffy.

Bean sauce, bean paste: Popular in Asian cooking, both products are made from fermented soybeans and have a salty bean flavor. Japanese bean paste is called miso.

Bean threads: Thin, almost transparent noodles made from mung bean flour. They also are called bean noodles or cellophane noodles.

Bouillon: Dehydrated beef, chicken, fish, or vegetable stock. Bouillon can be found in compressed cubes or granular form (which is the same substance, but dissolves faster). Both can be reconstituted in hot liquid to substitute for stock or broth.

Bouquet garni: A French term for a bundle of herbs tied together or placed in a piece of cheesecloth, allowing it to be removed easily from a cooked dish. A bouquet garni is especially handy for blends that use bay leaves, which should always be removed from a dish before serving. A traditional French bouquet garni includes thyme, parsley, and bay leaf, but you can create one from just about any herbs you like.

Broth: The strained clear liquid in which meat, poultry, or fish has simmered with vegetables and herbs. Broth is similar to stock, but less intense, and can be substituted for it. Reconstituted bouillon also can be used when broth is specified.

Butter: For rich flavor, butter is usually the fat of choice. Butter also is recommended over margarine for consistent baking results (also see Margarine). Salted and unsalted butter can be used interchangeably; however, if you use unsalted butter, you may want to increase the amount of salt in the recipe.

Cajun seasoning: Though the blends available may differ, most are peppery hot. They can include onion, garlic, and salt with the classic Cajun trio of white, black, and red peppers.

Capers: The buds of a spiny shrub that grows from Spain to China. Capers have an assertive flavor best described as the marriage of citrus and olive, plus an added tang from a salt-and-vinegar brine. The smaller buds offer more flavor than the larger buds, but you can use either in recipes. You'll find them near the olives in the supermarket.

Chile peppers: Spicy pods of the *Capsicum* family of plants, these peppers also are known as chiles. They're available in many sizes and colors, with varying degrees of hotness (generally, the smaller the chile pepper, the hotter it is). Some of the more commonly called for chile peppers are:

Anaheim: A medium-hot chile pepper available in fresh and dried forms.

Ancho: The mild to medium-hot dried version of the poblano pepper.

Cascabel: A red chile pepper with medium heat; it's usually sold dried.

Chile de arbol: A long, slender, bright- to deep-red chile pepper that is extremely hot and comes in both dried and fresh forms.

Chipotle: The smoked version of the jalapeño. Chipotle is available either dried or canned in adobo, a spicy sauce.

Habañero: Native to the Caribbean, this chile pepper has searing heat and is sold fresh and dried.

Jalapeño: A hot to extremely hot short, oval chile pepper that ranges from green to reddish-green color.

Pasilla: A long, slender dried chile pepper with wrinkled skin and a rich flavor that's medium to very hot. In its fresh form, it's called chilaca.

Pequín: A tiny dried chile pepper loaded with blistering heat. It should be used sparingly.

Poblano: A mild to medium-hot chile pepper with deep, complex flavors.

Serrano: A hot, slender chile pepper that starts out as deep green and sometimes ripens to bright red.

Thai: A colorful little chile pepper with intense heat that's used to spice up Thai-inspired dishes.

Chili oil: A fiery oil, flavored with chile peppers, used as a seasoning.

Chili paste: A condiment, available in mild or hot versions, made from chile peppers, vinegar, and seasonings.

Chocolate: In general, six types of chocolate are available:

Milk chocolate is at least 10% pure chocolate with added cocoa butter, sugar, and milk solids.

Semisweet and bittersweet chocolates can be used interchangeably. They contain at least 35% pure chocolate plus cocoa butter and sugar.

Sweet chocolate is dark chocolate that contains at least 15% pure chocolate with extra cocoa butter and sugar.

Unsweetened chocolate is used for baking and cooking rather than eating by itself. This form contains pure chocolate and cocoa butter, but has no added sugar.

White chocolate, which has a milk flavor, contains cocoa butter, sugar, and milk solids. White baking bars, white baking pieces, white candy coating, and white confectionery bars are sometimes confused with white chocolate. Though they are often used interchangeably in recipes, they are not truly white chocolate because do not contain cocoa butter.

Chorizo: A spicy pork sausage used in Mexican and Spanish cuisine. Spanish chorizo is made with smoked pork, and Mexican chorizo is made with fresh pork.

Chutney: A spicy sweet-and-sour condiment often used in Indian cuisine. Chutney is made from chopped fruit (mango is a classic), vegetables, and spices enlivened by hot chile peppers, fresh ginger, or vinegar.

Clarified butter: Sometimes called drawn butter, clarified butter is butter from which the milk solids have been removed. Clarified butter is best known as a dipping sauce for seafood. Because clarified butter can be heated to high temperatures without burning, it's also used for quickly browning meats.

Coconut milk: A product made from water and coconut pulp and often used in Southeast Asian and Indian cooking. Coconut milk is not the clear liquid in the center of the coconut, nor should it be confused with cream of coconut, a sweetened coconut concoction often used to make mixed drinks such as piña coladas.

Cooking oil: Made from various vegetables, nuts, or seeds, this cooking product is a liquid at room temperature. Common types for general cooking include corn, soybean, canola, sunflower, safflower, peanut, and olive.

Couscous: A granular pasta popular in North Africa made from semolina. Look for couscous in the rice and pasta section of supermarkets.

Crème fraîche: A dairy product made from whipping cream and a bacterial culture. The bacteria causes the whipping cream to thicken and develop a sharp, tangy flavor.

Curry paste: A blend of herbs, spices, and fiery chile peppers often used in Indian and Thai cooking. Curry pastes are available in many varieties and are sometimes classified by color (green, red, or yellow), by heat (mild or hot), or by a particular style of curry (such as Panang or Masaman). Look for curry paste in Asian markets.

Demi-glace: A thick, intense meat-flavor gel often used as a foundation for soups and sauces. Demi-glace is available in gourmet shops or through mail-order catalogs.

Egg roll skins: Pastry wrappers used to encase a savory filling when making egg rolls. Egg roll skins are similar to, but larger than, wonton skins. Look for egg roll skin products in the produce aisle of the supermarket or at Asian markets.

Egg whites, dried: Pasteurized dried egg whites can be used where egg whites are needed; follow package directions for reconstituting them. Unlike raw egg whites, which must be thoroughly cooked before serving to kill harmful bacteria, pasteurized dried egg whites can be used in recipes that do not call for thoroughly cooking egg whites. Meringue powder may not be substituted, however, because of its added sugar and starch. You'll find dried egg whites in powdered form in the baking aisle of many supermarkets.

Extracts, oils: Products based on the aromatic essential oils of plant materials distilled by various means. In extracts, the highly concentrated oils usually are suspended in alcohol to make them easier to combine with other foods in cooking and baking. Almond, anise, lemon, mint, orange, peppermint, and vanilla are some commonly available extracts. Some undiluted oils also are available, usually at pharmacies. These include oil of anise, oil of cinnamon, oil of cloves, oil of peppermint, and oil of wintergreen.

Fines herbes: This French phrase describes an herb mix that usually contains chervil, parsley, chives, and tarragon.

Fish sauce: A pungent brown sauce made by fermenting fish, usually anchovies, in brine. It's often used in Southeast Asian cooking.

Five-spice powder: Combinations may vary, but this fragrant blend usually is made of cinnamon, anise seeds or star anise, fennel, black or Szechwan pepper, and cloves.

Flavoring: An imitation extract made of chemical compounds. Unlike a true extract or oil, a flavoring often does not contain any of the original food it resembles. Some common imitation flavorings available are banana, black walnut, brandy, cherry, chocolate, coconut, maple, pineapple, raspberry, rum, strawberry, and vanilla.

Flour: A milled food that can be made from many cereals, roots, and seeds, although wheat is the most popular. Here are the types of flour most commonly used in cooking:

All-purpose flour: This flour is made from a blend of soft and hard wheat flours and, as its name implies, can be used for many purposes, including baking, thickening, and coating. All-purpose flour usually is sold presifted and is available bleached or unbleached.

Bread flour: This flour contains more gluten than all-purpose flour, making it ideal for baking yeast breads, which rely on gluten for structure and height.

Cake flour: Made from a soft wheat, cake flour produces a tender, delicate crumb because the gluten is less elastic. It's too delicate for general baking, but can be used for cakes. Sift it before measuring and use 1 cup plus 2 tablespoons of cake flour for every 1 cup all-purpose flour.

Gluten flour: Because whole-grain flours are low in gluten, some whole-grain bread recipes often call for a little gluten flour to help the finished loaf attain the proper texture. Sometimes called wheat gluten, gluten flour is made by removing most of the starch from high-protein, hard wheat flour. If you can't find gluten flour at a supermarket, look for it at a health food store.

Pastry flour: A soft wheat blend with less starch than cake flour. As you would expect, it is used for making pastry.

Self-rising flour: An all-purpose flour with added salt and a leavening agent, such as baking powder. Self-rising flour generally is not used for making yeast products.

Food coloring: Liquid, paste, or powdered edible dyes used to tint foods.

Garlic: A strongly scented, pungent bulb of a plant related to an onion. A garlic clove is one of the several small segments that make up a garlic bulb. Elephant garlic is larger and milder, and more closely related to the leek.

Gelatin: A dry ingredient made from natural animal protein that can thicken or set a liquid. Gelatin is available in unflavored and flavored forms. Some recipes call for gelatin at various stages of gelling. "Partially set" means the mixture looks like unbeaten egg whites. At this point, solid ingredients may be added. "Almost firm" describes gelatin that is sticky to the touch. It can be layered at this stage. "Firm" gelatin holds a cut edge and is ready to serve.

Ginger: The root of a semitropical plant, this seasoning adds a spicy-sweet flavor to recipes (also called gingerroot).

Ginger, crystallized: A confection made from pieces of ginger (gingerroot) cooked in a sugar syrup, then coated with sugar. It's also known as candied ginger.

Herbes de Provence: This melange of herbs, common in the south of France, usually includes basil, fennel, lavender, marjoram, rosemary, sage, savory, and thyme.

Hoisin sauce: A sauce, popular in Asian cooking, that brings a multitude of sweet and spicy flavors to a dish. It's made from fermented soybeans, molasses, vinegar, mustard, sesame seeds, garlic, and chile peppers.

Honey: A sweetener produced by bees that feed on floral nectar. The flavor of honey depends upon the flowers the bees choose for feeding. Most honey is made from bees fed on clover, but other sources include thyme, lavender, orange blossom, apple, cherry, buckwheat, and tupelo. Generally, the lighter the color, the milder the flavor.

Italian seasoning: Common herbs found in this mix include basil, oregano, thyme, and rosemary. Sometimes garlic and red pepper are included.

Jamaican jerk seasoning: This zesty mixture can include salt, sugar, allspice, thyme, cloves, ginger, cinnamon, onion, and chile pepper.

Kosher salt: A coarse salt with no additives that many cooks prefer for its light, flaky texture and clean flavor. Kosher salt also has a lower sodium content than regular salt.

Lard: A product made from pork fat that sometimes is used for baking. Lard is especially noted for producing light, flaky piecrusts. Today, shortening is commonly used instead of lard.

Lemongrass: A highly aromatic, lemon-flavored herb often used in Asian cooking.

Lemon-pepper seasoning: This mixture, primarily salt with black pepper and grated lemon peel, adds a delicate lemon flavor to poultry and vegetables.

Margarine: A product generally made from vegetable oil that was developed as a substitute for butter. When baking, be sure to use a stick margarine that contains at least 80 percent fat. To be sure, check the nutrition information—margarine should have at least 100 calories per tablespoon.

Marinade: A seasoned liquid for soaking meat, poultry, fish, shellfish, or vegetables to flavor and sometimes tenderize them. Most marinades contain an acid, such as wine or vinegar.

Marsala: A fortified wine that can be either dry or sweet.

Meringue powder: A powder made from pasteurized dried egg whites, sugar, and edible gums. With additional sugar and water, the powder can be beaten to form a fluffy meringue. Added gums make the meringue more stable. Meringue powder is available in bakers' catalogs and specialty stores.

Mexican seasoning: This spicy blend often includes cumin, chile peppers, salt, onion, sweet peppers, garlic, oregano, and red pepper.

Milk and milk products: Varieties include:

Buttermilk: A low-fat or fat-free milk to which a bacterial culture has been added. It has a mildly acidic taste.

Evaporated milk: A product made by removing half of the water from whole milk. It lends a creamy richness to many recipes, including pumpkin pie. Evaporated milk also is available in low-fat and fat-free versions. Evaporated milk is not interchangeable with sweetened condensed milk.

Fat-free half-and-half: A product made mostly from skim milk with carrageenan for body. It adds a creamy flavor to recipes without adding fat.

Light cream and half-and-half: Light cream contains 18 to 30 percent milk fat; half-and-half is a mixture of milk and cream. They're interchangeable in most recipes; however, neither contains enough fat to be whipped.

Nonfat dry milk powder: A dried milk product that, when reconstituted, can be used in cooking.

Sour cream: A rich, smooth product made from light cream with a bacterial culture added. It's available in low-fat and fat-free varieties.

Sweetened condensed milk: A product made based on whole milk from which the water has been removed and sugar has been added. It's also available in low-fat and fat-free versions. Sweetened condensed milk is not interchangeable with evaporated milk or fresh milk.

Whipping cream: A cream that contains at least 30 percent milk fat. It can be beaten into soft peaks.

Whole, low-fat or light, reduced-fat, and fat-free milk: Because these milk types differ only in the amount of fat they contain and in the flavor they lend to foods, they may be used interchangeably in cooking.

Yogurt: A tangy, smooth product made from milk with a bacterial culture added. It's available in low-fat and fat-free varieties.

Mushroom: A plant in the fungus family that comes in many colors and shapes, with flavors ranging from mild and nutty to meaty, woodsy, and wild. Varieties to look for include:

Beech: A small mushroom with an all-white or light-brown cap. It has a crunchy texture and a mild, sweet, nutty flavor that works well in stir-fries and in sauces.

321

Chanterelle: A trumpet-shape mushroom with a bright yellow to orange color and a buttery flavor. It's best in simple recipes.

Crimini: Tan to rich brown in color, this mushroom can be used in most recipes that call for white mushrooms. It's similar in taste to the white mushroom, but has an earthier flavor.

Enoki: A delicately flavored white mushroom with a long, thin stem and tiny cap. It works well in salads and on soups.

Morel: A tan, black, or yellow spongy-looking mushroom with an intense rich and nutty flavor and aroma. Great for sauces, morels generally have a high price tag. They're also available dried.

Oyster: Available in a variety of sizes and colors, from cream to gray, oyster mushrooms have a velvety texture and mild flavor that melds well with poultry, veal, and seafood.

Porcini: Also known as cèpe, this pale-brown wild mushroom usually is available dried and is prized for a woodsy flavor that tastes terrific in soups and pasta sauces.

Portobello: Often used to bring heartiness to vegetarian entrées, this velvety brown mushroom boasts a deep flavor and comes in large, medium, and small sizes.

Shiitake: A brown mushroom prized for its meaty flavor and the texture it adds to pasta dishes and soups.

White: An umbrella-shape creamy white to light brown mushroom with a mild, woodsy flavor. It's a good all-purpose mushroom. Small white mushrooms sometimes are referred to as button mushrooms.

Wood ear: A variety favored for its yielding, yet crunchy, texture.

Nuts: Dried seeds or fruits with edible kernels that are surrounded by a hard shell or rind. With and without skins, shelled nuts are available in many forms—whole, halved, pieces, chopped, slivered, and ground.

Olive oil: This versatile oil is made from pressed olives. Extra-virgin olive oil, made from the first pressing, is considered the finest. With the most robust olive flavor and aroma, it has a rich golden-to-green hue. It's also the most expensive. Products labeled "olive oil" (once called pure olive oil) are usually lighter in color and have a more delicate flavor.

Olives: This fruit of the olive tree is available in more than 75 varieties. Among them are:

Alphonso: A huge, deep-purple olive from Chile with soft, meaty flesh and a slightly bitter, sour taste.

Arbequina: A green to pink, brine-cured olive with a slightly bitter taste.

Black or Mission: One of the most commonly available ripe olives with a smooth, mellow taste. It is sold unpitted, pitted, and sliced.

Cerignola: A huge, green or jet-black, brine-cured olive with lemon-apple flavor. This variety is difficult to pit.

Gaeta: A small, reddish-brown olive with a slightly earthy flavor.

Kalamata: A greenish-black-purple, brine-cured olive with a pungent, lingering flavor.

La Catalan: A brine-cured Spanish olive that's marinated with curry, celery, and pepper. It has a crisp, dense flesh and an assertive curry flavor.

Niçoise: A small, brownish-purple, brine-cured olive that's fruity and juicy, but not oily.

Nyon: A black, dry-roasted, tender olive that has a slightly bitter flavor.

Spanish-style or green: One of the most commonly available green olives with a salty, tart taste. It's sold unpitted, pitted, and stuffed.

Pancetta: Italian-style bacon made from the belly (or pancia) of a hog. Unlike bacon, pancetta is not smoked, but instead is seasoned with pepper and other spices, then cured with salt.

Pectin: A natural substance found in some fruits that helps to set up fruit-and-sugar mixtures used in jelly- or jam-making. Commercial pectin also is available.

Pesto: Traditionally an uncooked sauce made from crushed garlic, basil, and nuts blended with Parmesan cheese and olive oil. Today's pestos may be made with other herbs or greens and can be purchased. Tomato pesto also is available.

Phyllo dough: Prominent in Greek, Turkish, and Middle Eastern dishes, phyllo (or filo) consists of tissue-thin sheets of dough. When buttered, layered, and baked, the sheets form a delicate, flaky pastry.

Pine nut: A high-fat nut that comes from certain varieties of pine trees. Its flavor ranges from mild and sweet to pungent.

Prosciutto: To Italians, prosciutto means "ham." Cooks in America use the term to refer to a type of ham that has been seasoned, salt cured, and air-dried (rather than smoked).

Puff pastry: A butter-rich, multilayered pastry. When baked, the butter produces steam between the layers, causing the dough to puff up into many flaky layers.

Rice: An ancient grain available in thousands of varieties. Among them are:

Arborio rice: A short grain white rice used for risotto because it adds creaminess to the dish.

Aromatic rices: Varieties of fragrant rices, such as basmati, Texmati, wild pecan, or jasmine, that have flavors ranging from toasted nuts to popped corn.

Brown rice: Unpolished rice that has the bran layer intact. It has a chewy and nutty flavor.

Converted rice: Also called parboiled rice, this product is steamed and pressure-cooked before packaging. This process helps to retain nutrients and keeps the grains from sticking together when cooked.

Instant and quick-cooking rice: Rice that's partially or fully cooked before packaging, so it takes less time to cook before serving.

White rice: A commonly used form of rice available in long, medium, and short grain varieties. The shorter the grain, the more starch it contains. Because the starch causes rice to stick together when cooked, long grain rice cooks up lighter and fluffier than short grain rice.

Wild rice: Not a rice at all, but a marsh grass. It takes three times as long to cook as white rice, but the nutlike flavor and chewy texture are worth the wait.

Rice noodles, rice sticks: Thin noodles, popular in Asian cooking, made from finely ground rice and water. When fried, they puff into light, crisp strands. They also can be soaked to use in stir-fries and soups. Thicker varieties are called rice sticks. All are available in Asian markets. If you can't find these products, in recipes you can substitute vermicelli or capellini for rice noodles, linguine or fettuccine for rice sticks.

Rice vinegar: A mild-flavored vinegar made from fermented rice. Rice vinegar is interchangeable with rice wine vinegar, which is made from fermented rice wine. Seasoned rice vinegar, with added sugar and salt, can be used in recipes calling for rice vinegar, though you may wish to adjust the seasonings.

Roux: A French term that refers to a mixture of flour and a fat cooked to a golden- or rich-brown color and used for a thickening in sauces, soups, and gumbos.

Salad oil or vegetable oil: The most common varieties are made from soybeans, sunflowers, corn, peanuts, canola, and safflower. All are light yellow and have a neutral flavor.

Salsa: A sauce usually made from finely chopped tomatoes, onions, chile peppers, and cilantro.

Sea salt: A variety of salt derived from the evaporation of sea water. Some cooks prefer it over table salt for its clean flavor.

Sesame oil: This pale yellow oil is made from untoasted sesame seeds and has a mild sesame flavor. Toasted sesame oil, also called Oriental sesame oil, is made from toasted sesame seeds. It is a rich brown in color and has a concentrated flavor.

Sherry: A fortified wine that ranges from dry to sweet and light to dark.

Shortening: A vegetable oil that has been processed into solid form. Shortening commonly is used for baking or frying. Plain and butter-flavor types can be used interchangeably.

Shrimp paste: A pungent seasoning made from dried, salted shrimp that's been pounded into a paste. Shrimp paste gives Southeast Asian dishes an authentic, rich flavor.

Soba noodles: A Japanese noodle made from wheat and buckwheat flours. Narrow whole wheat ribbon pasta, such as linguine, makes a good substitute.

Somen noodles: Made from wheat flour, these dried Japanese noodles are very fine and most often white. In a pinch, substitute angel hair pasta.

Stock: The strained clear liquid in which meat, poultry, or fish has been simmered with vegetables or herbs. Stock is similar to broth but is richer and more concentrated. Stock and broth can be use interchangeably. Reconstituted bouillon also can be substituted for stock.

Sugar: A sweetener primarily made from sugar beets or sugarcane. Sugar comes in a variety of forms:

Brown sugar: A mix of granulated sugar and molasses. Dark brown sugar contains more molasses and, hence, has more molasses flavor, than light brown sugar (also known as golden brown sugar). In general, use either in recipes calling for brown sugar, unless one or the other is specified.

Coarse sugar: Often use for decorating baked goods, coarse sugar is in much larger grains than regular granulated sugar. Look for it where cake-decorating supplies are sold.

Granulated sugar: This white, granular, crystalline sugar is the one to use when a recipe calls for sugar without specifying a particular type. White sugar is most commonly available in a fine granulation, though superfine (also called ultrafine or castor sugar), a finer grind, also is available.

Powdered sugar: Also known as confectioner's sugar, this is granulated sugar that has been milled to a fine powder, then mixed with cornstarch to prevent lumping. Sift powdered sugar before using in frostings and icings.

Raw sugar: In the U.S., true raw sugar is not sold to consumers. Products labeled as raw sugar, such as Demerara sugar or turbinado sugar, have been refined. Cleaned by a steaming process, turbinado sugar is a coarse sugar with a mild molasses flavor. It is sold in many health food stores.

Vanilla sugar: A sugar infused with flavor from a dried vanilla bean.

Tahini: A flavoring agent, used in Middle Eastern cooking, made from ground sesame seeds. Look for it in Asian markets.

Tamari: A dark, thin sauce made from soybeans. Tamari is a slightly thicker, mellower cousin of soy sauce and is used to flavor Asian dishes. In a pinch, substitute soy sauce.

Tamarind paste: A thick, tart, brown Asian flavoring that comes from the fruit of a tamarind tree.

Tofu: Tofu, also referred to as bean curd, is made by curdling soy milk in a process similar to cheese-making. Although it's almost tasteless by itself, tofu acts like a sponge, easily absorbing other flavors. Types of tofu include:

Extra-firm or firm tofu: This type is dense and keeps its shape. Slice or cube it for stir-fries and pasta dishes.

Soft tofu: Ideal for whipping, blending, or crumbling, use soft tofu for dressings, dips, and desserts.

Tomatoes, dried: Sometimes referred to as sundried tomatoes, these shriveled-looking tomato pieces boast an intense flavor and chewy texture. They're available packed in olive oil or dried.

Tortilla: A small, thin, flat bread, that is popular in Mexican cooking. Tortillas can be made from corn or wheat flour and usually are served wrapped around a filling.

Vanilla: A liquid extract made from the seed of an orchid. A vanilla bean is the long, thin pod of the orchid. The pod itself, which has been dried and cured, should not be eaten. Instead the tiny seeds inside the pod are used. They bring an intense vanilla flavor and dark brown confetti-like flecks to dishes. Imitation vanilla, an artificial flavoring, makes an inexpensive substitute for vanilla.

Vinegar: A sour liquid that is a by-product of fermentation. Through fermentation, the alcohol from grapes, grains, apples, and other sources is changed to acetic acid to create vinegar.

Wasabi: A Japanese horseradish condiment with a distinctive, pale lime-green color and a head-clearing heat. Wasabi is available as a paste or as a fine powder. It's often used to flavor fish or as a condiment for sushi.

Wontons, wonton wrappers: Stuffed savory Asian pastries. The wrappers, paper-thin skins used to make wontons, can be found in the produce aisle of supermarkets or in Asian markets. Wonton wrappers are similar to, but smaller than, egg roll skins.

Yeast: A tiny, single-celled organism that feeds on the sugar in dough, creating carbon dioxide gas that makes dough rise. Three common forms of yeast are:

Active dry yeast: This is the most popular form. These tiny, dehydrated granules are mixed with flour or dissolved in warm water before they're used.

Bread-machine yeast: This highly active yeast was developed especially for use in dough processed in bread machines.

Quick-rising active dry yeast (sometimes called fast-rising or instant yeast): This is a more active strain of yeast than active dry yeast, and it substantially cuts down on the time dough takes to rise. This yeast usually is mixed with dry ingredients before warm liquids are added.

Zest: The colored outer portion of citrus fruit peel. It's rich in fruit oil and often is used as a seasoning.

Tips

Photographers
Kim Cornelison
Mike Dieter
Colleen Duffley
Tony Glaser
Bob Greenspan
Richard Jung
Jim Krantz
Pete Krumhardt
Scott Little
Andy Lyons
Jens Mortensen
Bill Stites
Steve Stitgen
Mark Thomas
Joan Vanderschuit
Food Stylists
Susan Draudt
Jill Lust
Dianna Nolin
Janet Pittman
Charles Worthington
Prop Stylist
Susan Mitchell

333

Nutrition information

With each recipe, we give you a useful nutrition analysis you easily can apply to your own needs. First, read "What you need" (below) to determine your dietary requirements. Then refer to the numbers listed after each recipe. You'll find the calorie count and the amount of fat, saturated fat, cholesterol, sodium, carbohydrates, fiber, and protein for each serving. To stay in line with the nutrition breakdown of each recipe, follow the suggested number of servings.

How we analyze

The Better Homes and Gardens® Test Kitchen computer analyzes each recipe for the nutritional value of a single serving.
- The analysis does not include optional ingredients.
- We use the first serving size listed when a range is given. For example: If we say a recipe "Makes 4 to 6 servings," the nutrition information is based on 4 servings.
- When ingredient choices (such as butter or margarine) appear in a recipe, we use the first one mentioned for analysis.
- When milk and eggs are recipe ingredients, the analysis is calculated using 2-percent (reduced-fat) milk and large eggs.

What you need

The dietary guidelines below suggest nutrient levels that moderately active adults should strive to eat each day. As your calorie levels change, adjust your fat intake too. Try to keep the percentage of calories from fat to no more than 30 percent. There's no harm in occasionally going over or under these guidelines, but the key to good health is maintaining a balanced diet most of the time.

Calories: About 2,000
Total fat: Less than 65 grams
Saturated fat: Less than 20 grams
Cholesterol: Less than 300 milligrams

Carbohydrates: About 300 grams
Sodium: Less than 2,400 milligrams
Dietary fiber: 20 to 30 grams

Lower-fat recipes

For recipes that are labeled lower-fat, each serving is significantly lower in fat and calories than those of the original recipe.

If you don't have: # Substitute:

If you don't have:	Substitute:
Bacon, 1 slice, crisp-cooked, crumbled	1 tablespoon purchased cooked bacon pieces
Baking powder, 1 teaspoon	½ teaspoon cream of tartar plus ¼ teaspoon baking soda
Balsamic vinegar, 1 tablespoon	1 tablespoon cider vinegar or red wine vinegar plus ½ teaspoon sugar
Bread crumbs, fine dry, ¼ cup	¾ cup soft bread crumbs, or ¼ cup cracker crumbs, or ¼ cup cornflake crumbs
Broth, beef or chicken, 1 cup	1 teaspoon or 1 cube instant beef or chicken bouillon plus 1 cup hot water
Butter, 1 cup	1 cup shortening plus, if desired, ¼ teaspoon salt
Buttermilk, 1 cup	1 tablespoon lemon juice or vinegar plus enough milk to make 1 cup (stir and let stand 5 minutes before using), or 1 cup plain yogurt
Chocolate, semisweet, 1 ounce	3 tablespoons semisweet chocolate pieces, or 1 ounce unsweetened chocolate plus 1 tablespoon granulated sugar, or 1 tablespoon unsweetened cocoa powder plus 2 teaspoons sugar and 2 teaspoons shortening
Chocolate, sweet baking, 4 ounces	¼ cup unsweetened cocoa powder plus ⅓ cup granulated sugar and 3 tablespoons shortening
Chocolate, unsweetened, 1 ounce	3 tablespoons unsweetened cocoa powder plus 1 tablespoon cooking oil or shortening, melted
Cornstarch, 1 tablespoon (for thickening)	2 tablespoons all-purpose flour
Corn syrup (light), 1 cup	1 cup granulated sugar plus ¼ cup water
Egg, 1 whole	2 egg whites, or 2 egg yolks, or ¼ cup refrigerated or frozen egg product, thawed
Flour, cake, 1 cup	1 cup minus 2 tablespoons all-purpose flour
Flour, self-rising, 1 cup	1 cup all-purpose flour plus 1 teaspoon baking powder, ½ teaspoon salt, and ¼ teaspoon baking soda
Garlic, 1 clove	½ teaspoon bottled minced garlic or ⅛ teaspoon garlic powder
Ginger, grated fresh, 1 teaspoon	¼ teaspoon ground ginger
Half-and-half or light cream, 1 cup	1 tablespoon melted butter or margarine plus enough whole milk to make 1 cup
Molasses, 1 cup	1 cup honey
Mustard, dry, 1 teaspoon	1 tablespoon prepared (in cooked mixtures)
Mustard, prepared, 1 tablespoon	½ teaspoon dry mustard plus 2 teaspoons vinegar
Onion, chopped, ½ cup	2 tablespoons dried minced onion or ½ teaspoon onion powder
Sour cream, dairy, 1 cup	1 cup plain yogurt
Sugar, granulated, 1 cup	1 cup packed brown sugar or 2 cups sifted powdered sugar
Sugar, brown, 1 cup packed	1 cup granulated sugar plus 2 tablespoons molasses
Tomato juice, 1 cup	½ cup tomato sauce plus ½ cup water
Tomato sauce, 2 cups	¾ cup tomato paste plus 1 cup water
Vanilla bean, 1 whole	2 teaspoons vanilla extract
Wine, red, 1 cup	1 cup beef or chicken broth in savory recipes; cranberry juice in desserts
Wine, white, 1 cup	1 cup chicken broth in savory recipes; apple juice or white grape juice in desserts
Yeast, active dry, 1 package	about 2¼ teaspoons active dry yeast

Seasonings

Apple pie spice, 1 teaspoon	½ teaspoon ground cinnamon plus ¼ teaspoon ground nutmeg, ⅛ teaspoon ground allspice, and dash ground cloves or ginger
Cajun seasoning, 1 tablespoon	½ teaspoon white pepper, ½ teaspoon garlic powder, ½ teaspoon onion powder, ½ teaspoon ground red pepper, ½ teaspoon paprika, and ½ teaspoon black pepper
Herbs, snipped fresh, 1 tablespoon	½ to 1 teaspoon dried herb, crushed, or ½ teaspoon ground herb
Poultry seasoning, 1 teaspoon	¾ teaspoon dried sage, crushed, plus ¼ teaspoon dried thyme or marjoram, crushed
Pumpkin pie spice, 1 teaspoon	½ teaspoon ground cinnamon plus ¼ teaspoon ground ginger, ¼ teaspoon ground allspice, and ⅛ teaspoon ground nutmeg

The *Better Homes and Gardens*® Test Kitchen dates back to 1928. That was where home economists prepared all the recipes planned for publication and food editors evaluated them at taste panels. When needed, the recipes were retested to clear up any hitches. Now, more than 75 years later, our current staff continues the same rigorous testing, tasting, and evaluating.